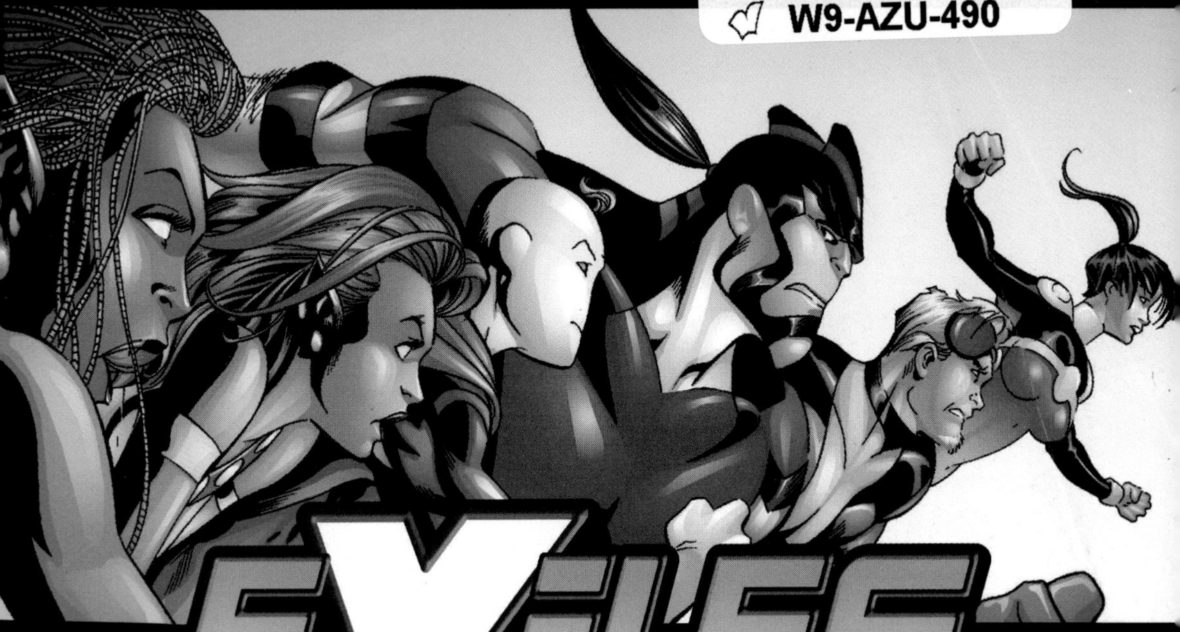

EXILES

WRITER
Judd Winick

PENCILERS
Mike McKone & Jim Calafiore

INKERS
Mark McKenna w/Eric Cannon, Walden Wong & Jon Holdredge

COLORS **Transparency Digital**
LETTERER **Paul Tutrone**
ASSISTANT EDITOR **Mike Raicht**
EDITOR **Mike Marts**

COLLECTIONS EDITOR **Jeff Youngquist**
ASSISTANT EDITOR **Jennifer Grünwald**
BOOK DESIGNER **Patrick McGrath**

EDITOR IN CHIEF **Joe Quesada**
PRESIDENT **Bill Jemas**

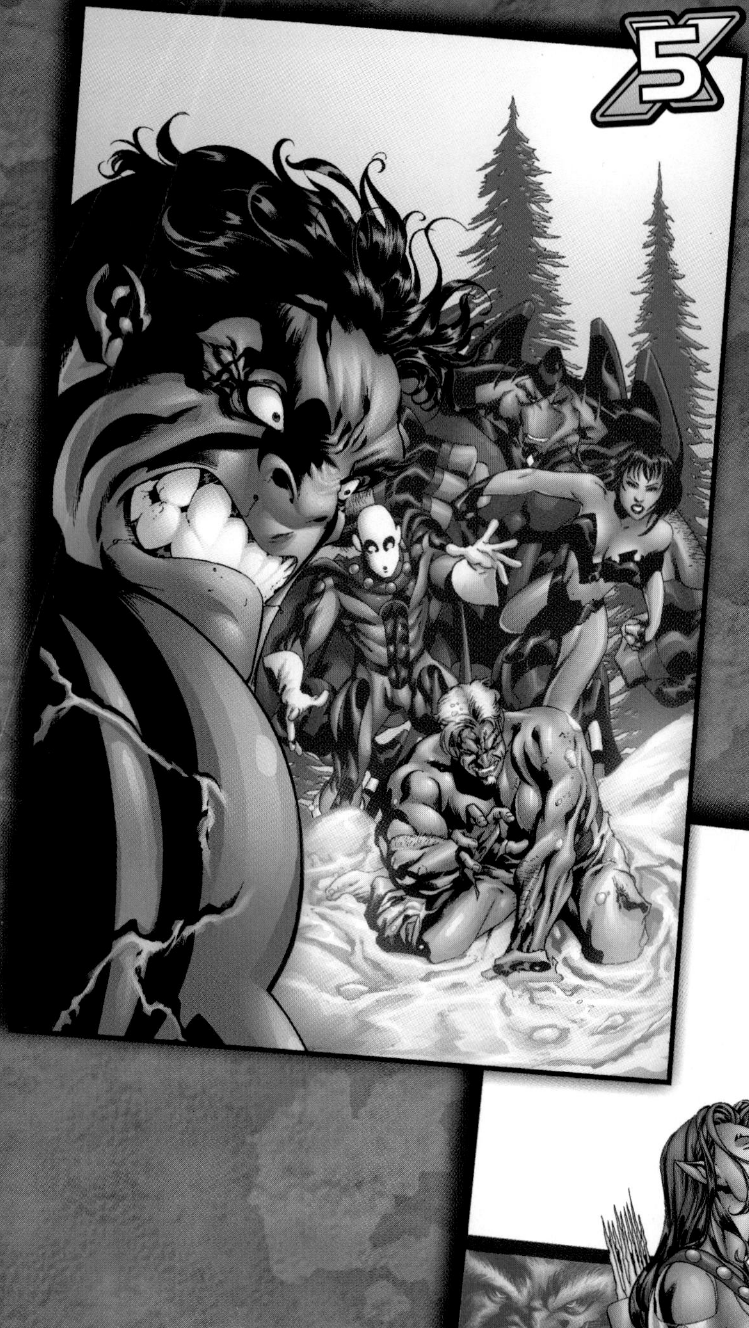
5

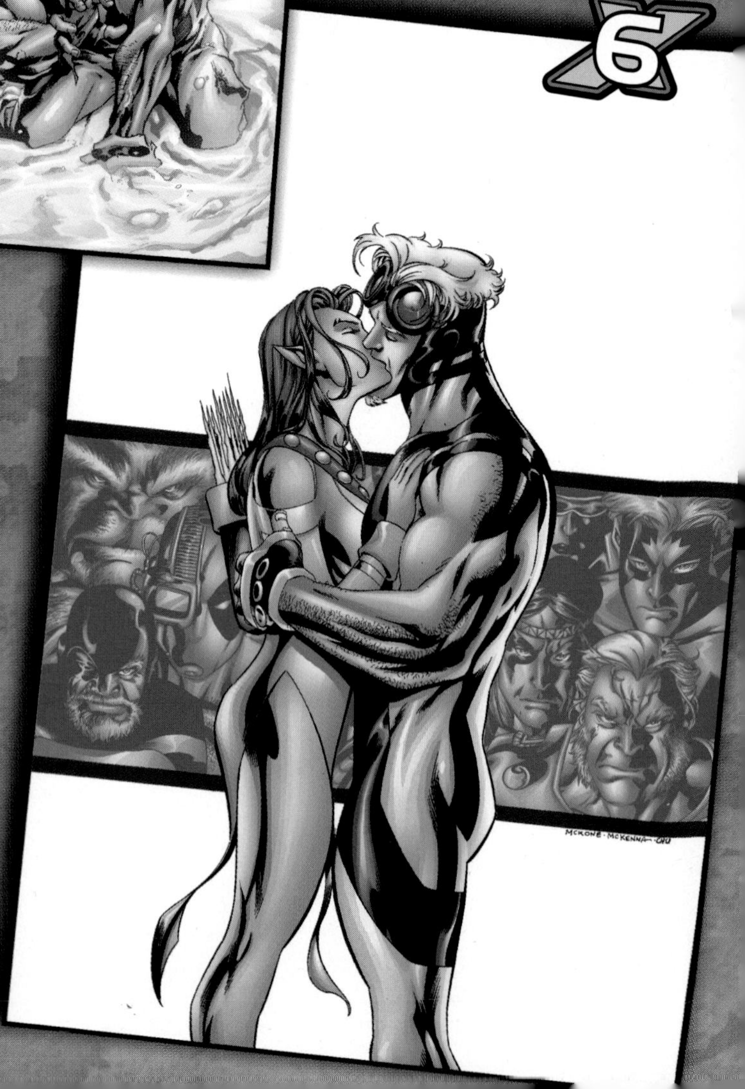
6
MCKONE·MCKENNA·CHU

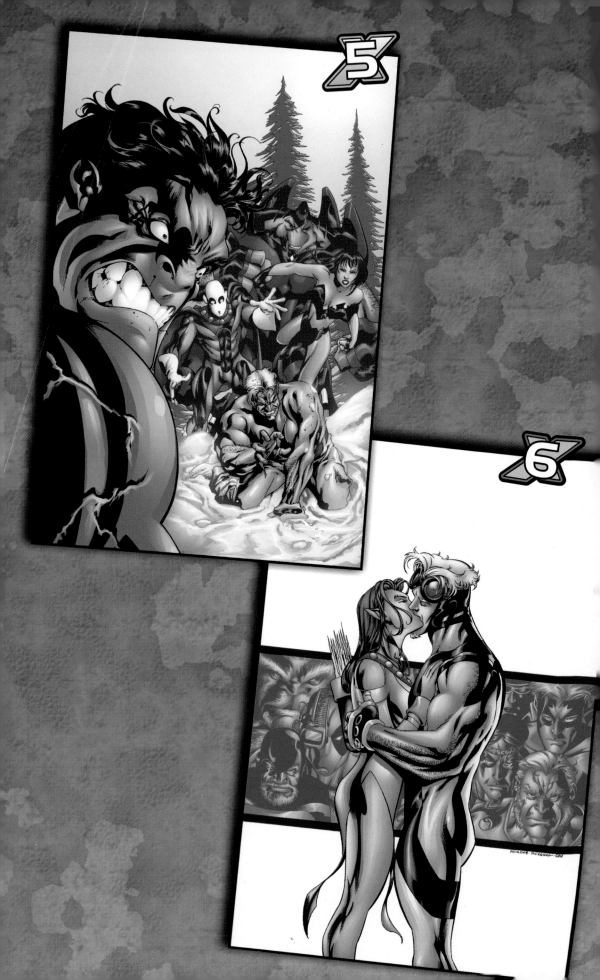

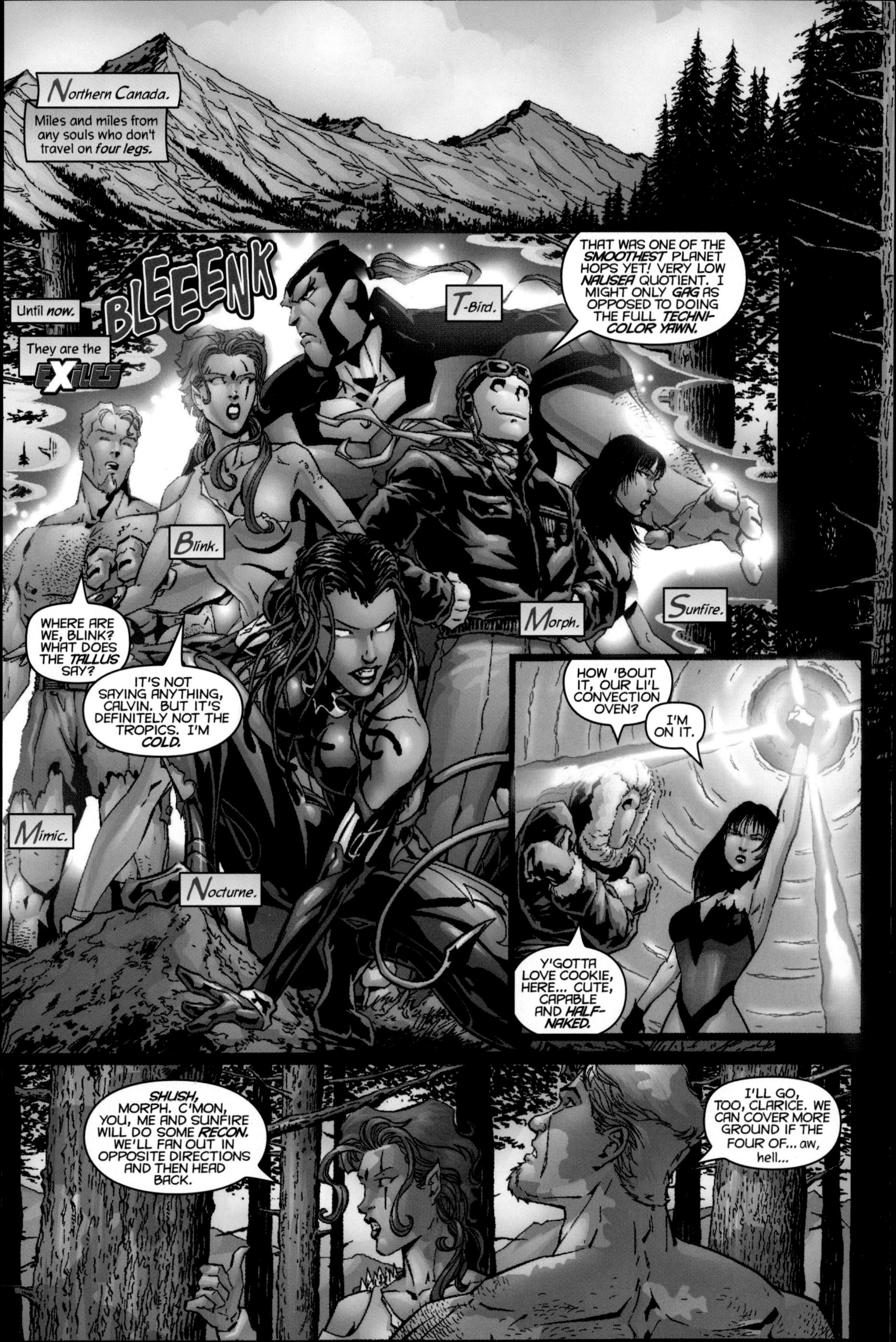
Northern Canada.
Miles and miles from any souls who don't travel on four legs.
Until now.
BLEEENK
They are the EXILES
T-Bird.
THAT WAS ONE OF THE SMOOTHEST PLANET HOPS YET! VERY LOW NAUSEA QUOTIENT. I MIGHT ONLY GAG AS OPPOSED TO DOING THE FULL TECHNI-COLOR YAWN.
Blink.
Morph.
Sunfire.
WHERE ARE WE, BLINK? WHAT DOES THE TALLUS SAY?
IT'S NOT SAYING ANYTHING, CALVIN. BUT IT'S DEFINITELY NOT THE TROPICS. I'M COLD.
Mimic.
Nocturne.
HOW 'BOUT IT, OUR LI'L CONVECTION OVEN?
I'M ON IT.
Y'GOTTA LOVE COOKIE, HERE... CUTE, CAPABLE AND HALF-NAKED.
SHUSH, MORPH. C'MON, YOU, ME AND SUNFIRE WILL DO SOME RECON. WE'LL FAN OUT IN OPPOSITE DIRECTIONS AND THEN HEAD BACK.
I'LL GO, TOO, CLARICE. WE CAN COVER MORE GROUND IF THE FOUR OF... aw, hell...

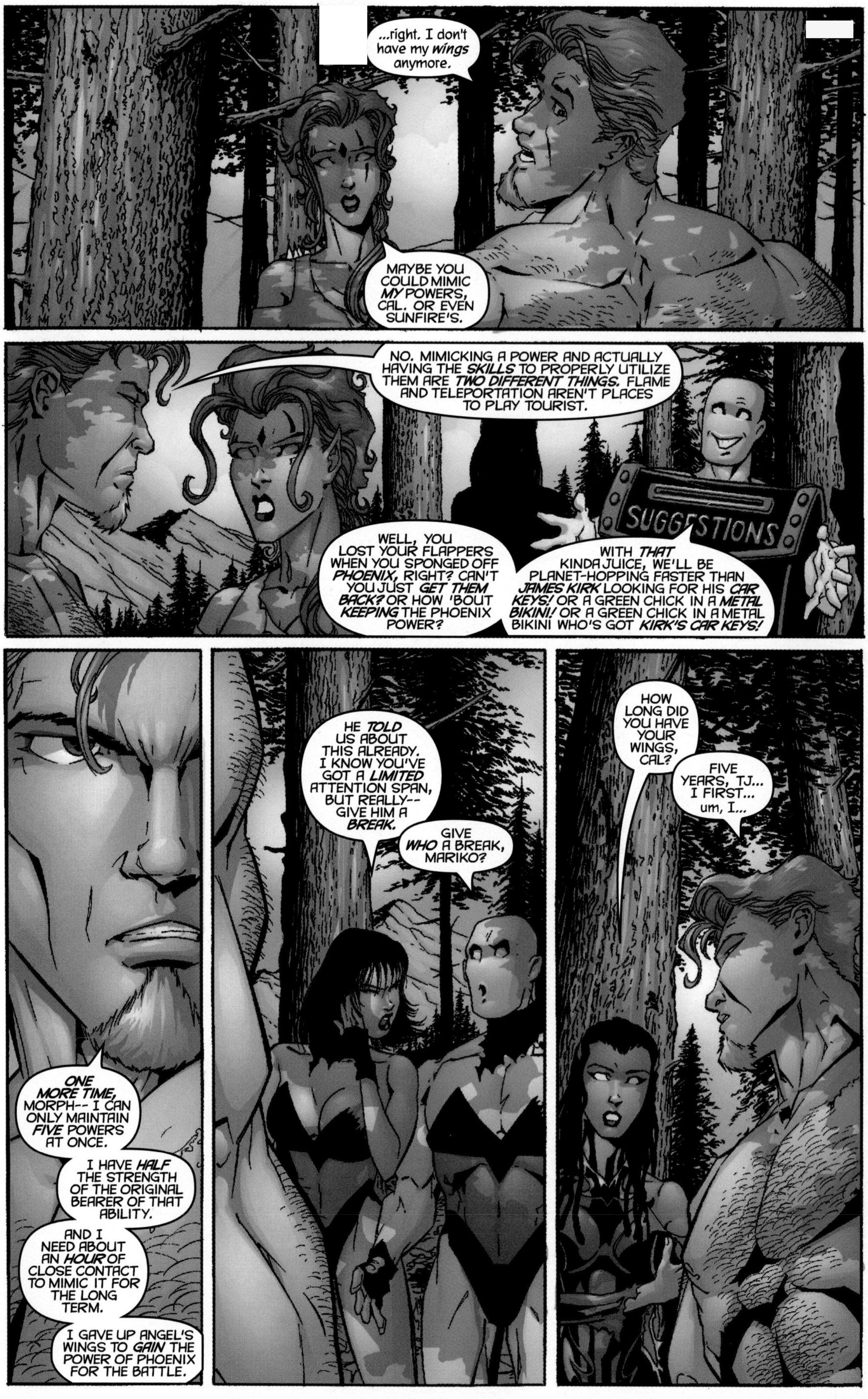
...right. I don't have my *wings* anymore.
MAYBE YOU COULD MIMIC *MY* POWERS, CAL. OR EVEN SUNFIRE'S.
NO. MIMICKING A POWER AND ACTUALLY HAVING THE *SKILLS* TO PROPERLY UTILIZE THEM ARE *TWO DIFFERENT THINGS.* FLAME AND TELEPORTATION AREN'T PLACES TO PLAY TOURIST.
SUGGESTIONS
WELL, YOU LOST YOUR FLAPPERS WHEN YOU SPONGED OFF *PHOENIX,* RIGHT? CAN'T YOU JUST *GET THEM BACK?* OR HOW 'BOUT *KEEPING* THE PHOENIX POWER?
WITH *THAT* KINDA JUICE, WE'LL BE PLANET-HOPPING FASTER THAN *JAMES KIRK* LOOKING FOR HIS *CAR KEYS!* OR A GREEN CHICK IN A *METAL BIKINI!* OR A GREEN CHICK IN A METAL BIKINI WHO'S GOT *KIRK'S CAR KEYS!*
ONE MORE TIME, MORPH-- I CAN ONLY MAINTAIN *FIVE* POWERS AT ONCE.
I HAVE *HALF* THE STRENGTH OF THE ORIGINAL BEARER OF THAT ABILITY.
AND I NEED ABOUT AN *HOUR* OF CLOSE CONTACT TO MIMIC IT FOR THE LONG TERM.
I GAVE UP ANGEL'S WINGS TO *GAIN* THE POWER OF PHOENIX FOR THE BATTLE.
HE *TOLD* US ABOUT THIS ALREADY. I KNOW YOU'VE GOT A *LIMITED* ATTENTION SPAN, BUT REALLY-- GIVE HIM A *BREAK.*
GIVE *WHO* A BREAK, MARIKO?
HOW LONG DID YOU HAVE YOUR WINGS, CAL?
FIVE YEARS, TJ... I FIRST... um, I...

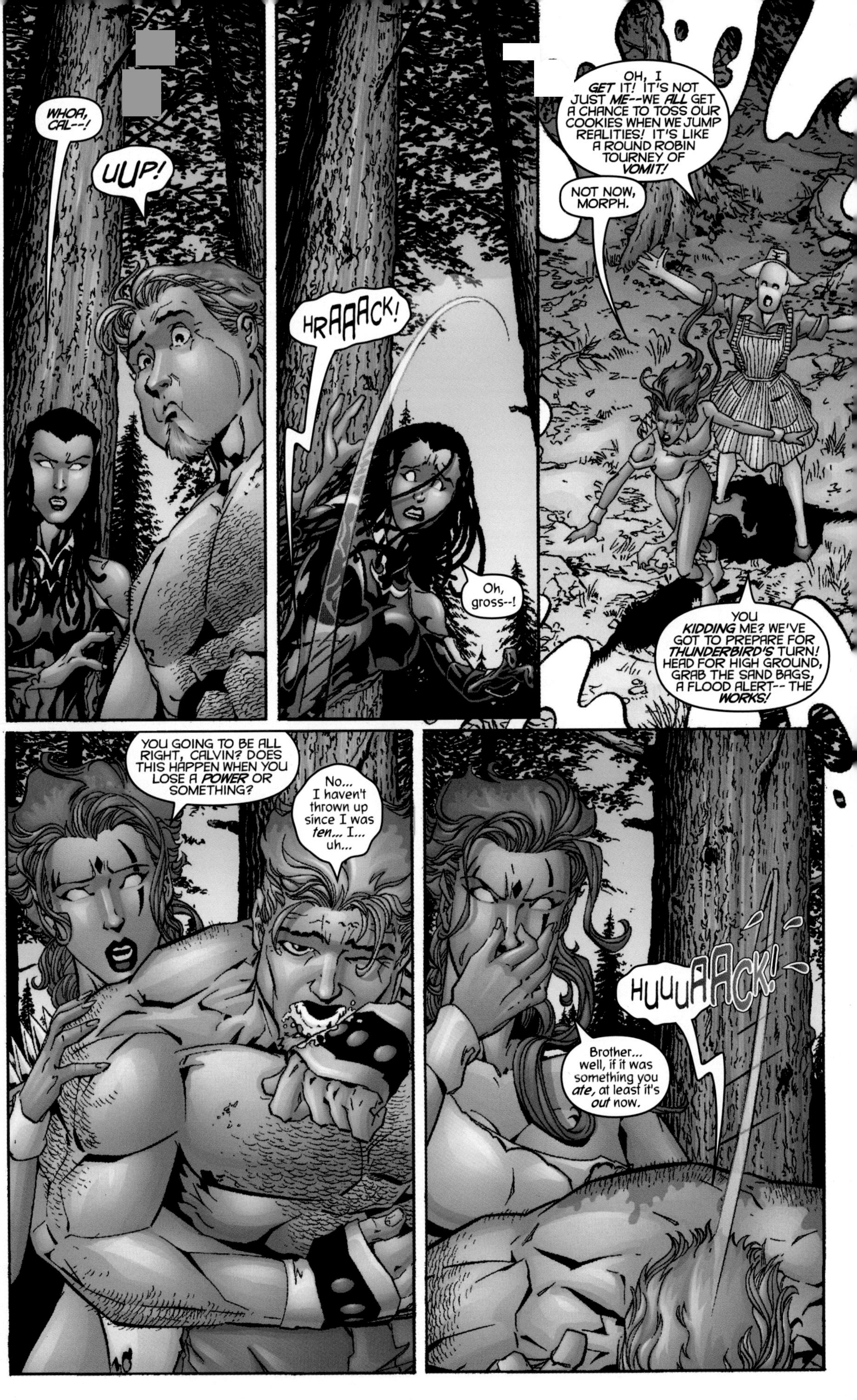
WHOA, CAL--!
UUP!
HRAAACK!
Oh, gross--!
OH, I GET IT! IT'S NOT JUST ME--WE ALL GET A CHANCE TO TOSS OUR COOKIES WHEN WE JUMP REALITIES! IT'S LIKE A ROUND ROBIN TOURNEY OF VOMIT!
NOT NOW, MORPH.
YOU KIDDING ME? WE'VE GOT TO PREPARE FOR THUNDERBIRD'S TURN! HEAD FOR HIGH GROUND, GRAB THE SAND BAGS, A FLOOD ALERT-- THE WORKS!
YOU GOING TO BE ALL RIGHT, CALVIN? DOES THIS HAPPEN WHEN YOU LOSE A POWER OR SOMETHING?
No... I haven't thrown up since I was ten... I... uh...
HUUUAACK!
Brother... well, if it was something you ate, at least it's out now.

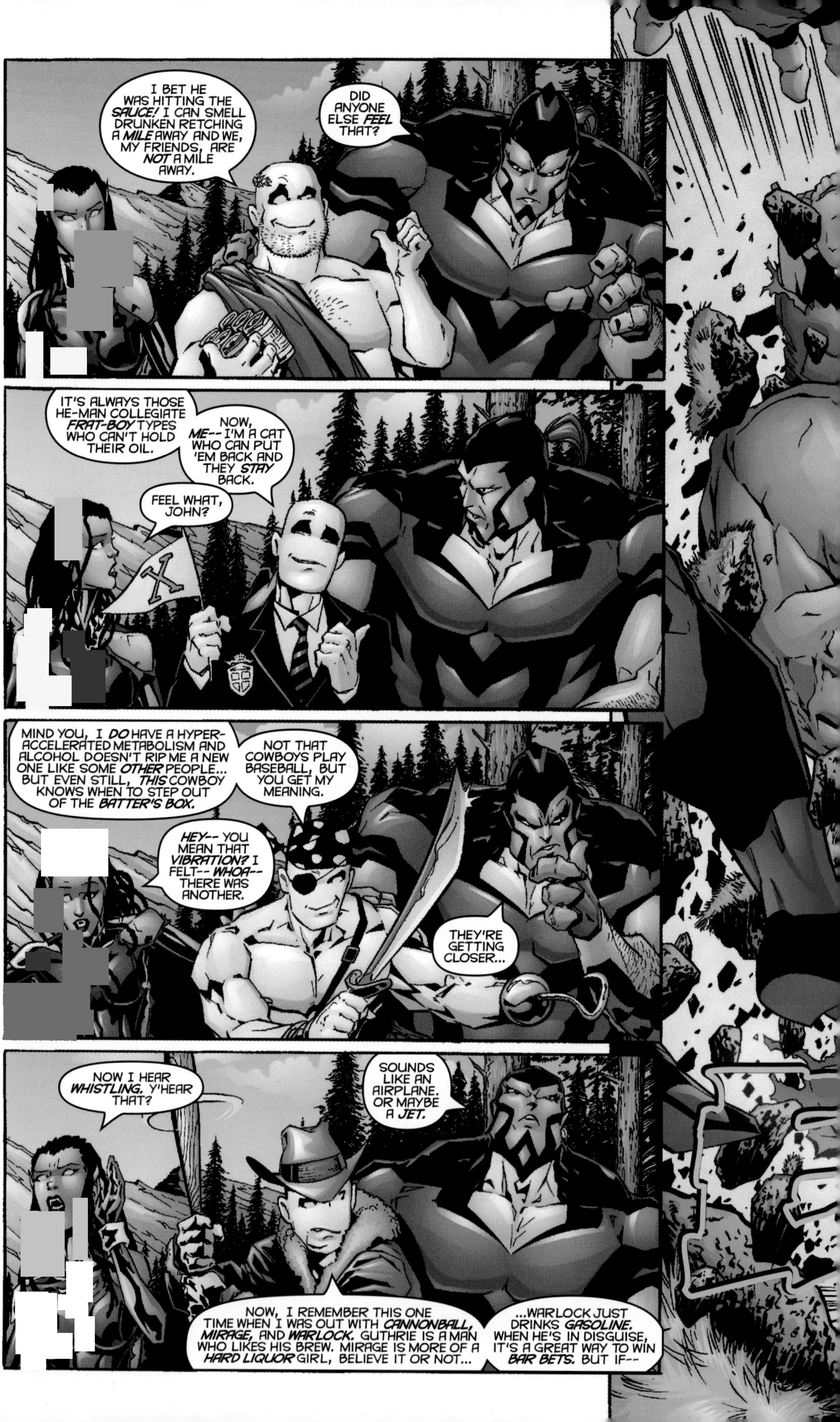
I BET HE WAS HITTING THE SAUCE! I CAN SMELL DRUNKEN RETCHING A MILE AWAY AND WE, MY FRIENDS, ARE NOT A MILE AWAY.
DID ANYONE ELSE FEEL THAT?
IT'S ALWAYS THOSE HE-MAN COLLEGIATE FRAT-BOY TYPES WHO CAN'T HOLD THEIR OIL.
NOW, ME-- I'M A CAT WHO CAN PUT 'EM BACK AND THEY STAY BACK.
FEEL WHAT, JOHN?
MIND YOU, I DO HAVE A HYPER-ACCELERATED METABOLISM AND ALCOHOL DOESN'T RIP ME A NEW ONE LIKE SOME OTHER PEOPLE... BUT EVEN STILL, THIS COWBOY KNOWS WHEN TO STEP OUT OF THE BATTER'S BOX.
NOT THAT COWBOYS PLAY BASEBALL, BUT YOU GET MY MEANING.
HEY-- YOU MEAN THAT VIBRATION? I FELT-- WHOA-- THERE WAS ANOTHER.
THEY'RE GETTING CLOSER...
NOW I HEAR WHISTLING. Y'HEAR THAT?
SOUNDS LIKE AN AIRPLANE. OR MAYBE A JET.
NOW, I REMEMBER THIS ONE TIME WHEN I WAS OUT WITH CANNONBALL, MIRAGE, AND WARLOCK. GUTHRIE IS A MAN WHO LIKES HIS BREW. MIRAGE IS MORE OF A HARD LIQUOR GIRL, BELIEVE IT OR NOT...
...WARLOCK JUST DRINKS GASOLINE. WHEN HE'S IN DISGUISE, IT'S A GREAT WAY TO WIN BAR BETS. BUT IF--

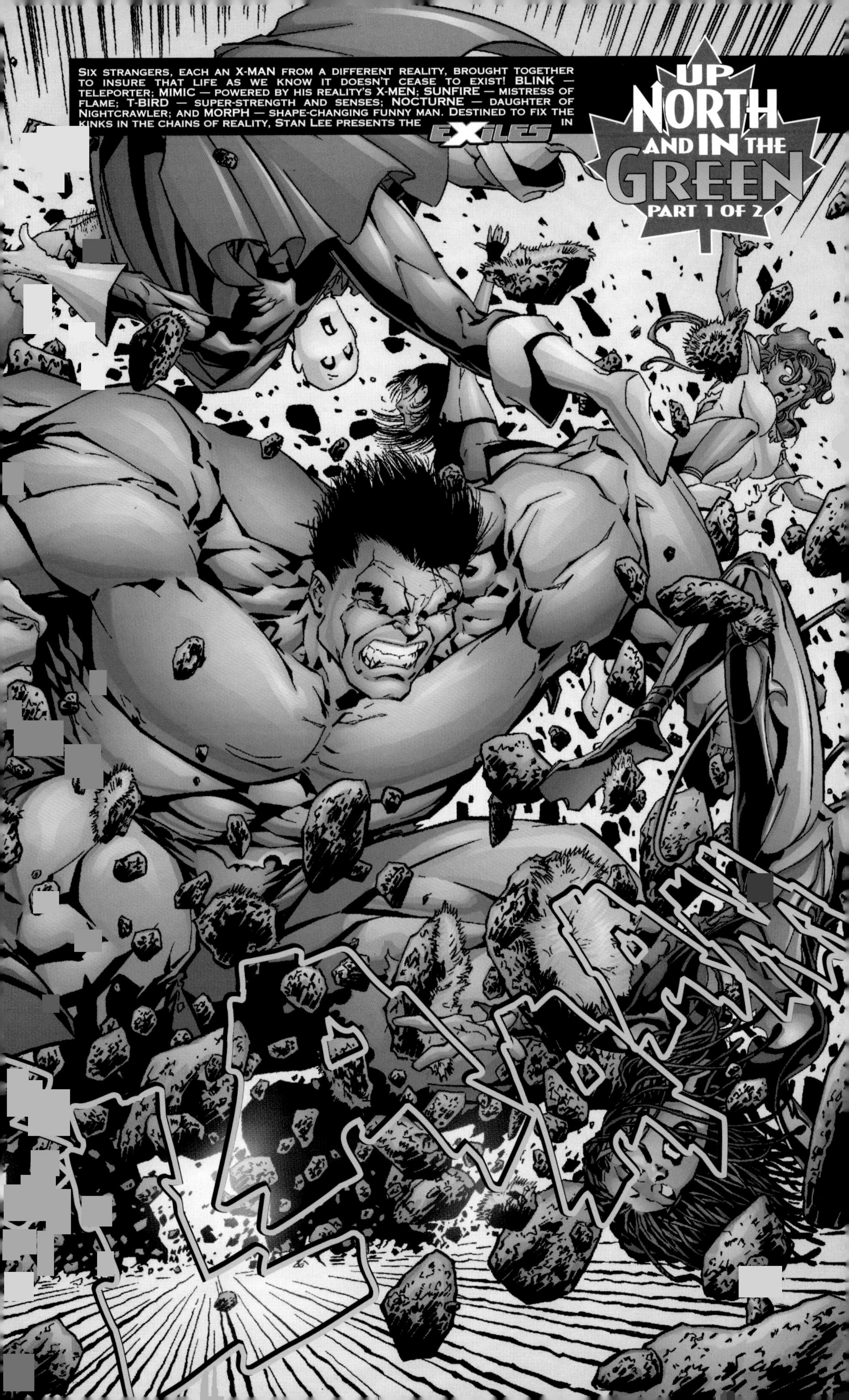
SIX STRANGERS, EACH AN X-MAN FROM A DIFFERENT REALITY, BROUGHT TOGETHER TO INSURE THAT LIFE AS WE KNOW IT DOESN'T CEASE TO EXIST! BLINK — TELEPORTER; MIMIC — POWERED BY HIS REALITY'S X-MEN; SUNFIRE — MISTRESS OF FLAME; T-BIRD — SUPER-STRENGTH AND SENSES; NOCTURNE — DAUGHTER OF NIGHTCRAWLER; AND MORPH — SHAPE-CHANGING FUNNY MAN. DESTINED TO FIX THE KINKS IN THE CHAINS OF REALITY, STAN LEE PRESENTS THE EXILES IN
UP NORTH AND IN THE GREEN
PART 1 OF 2

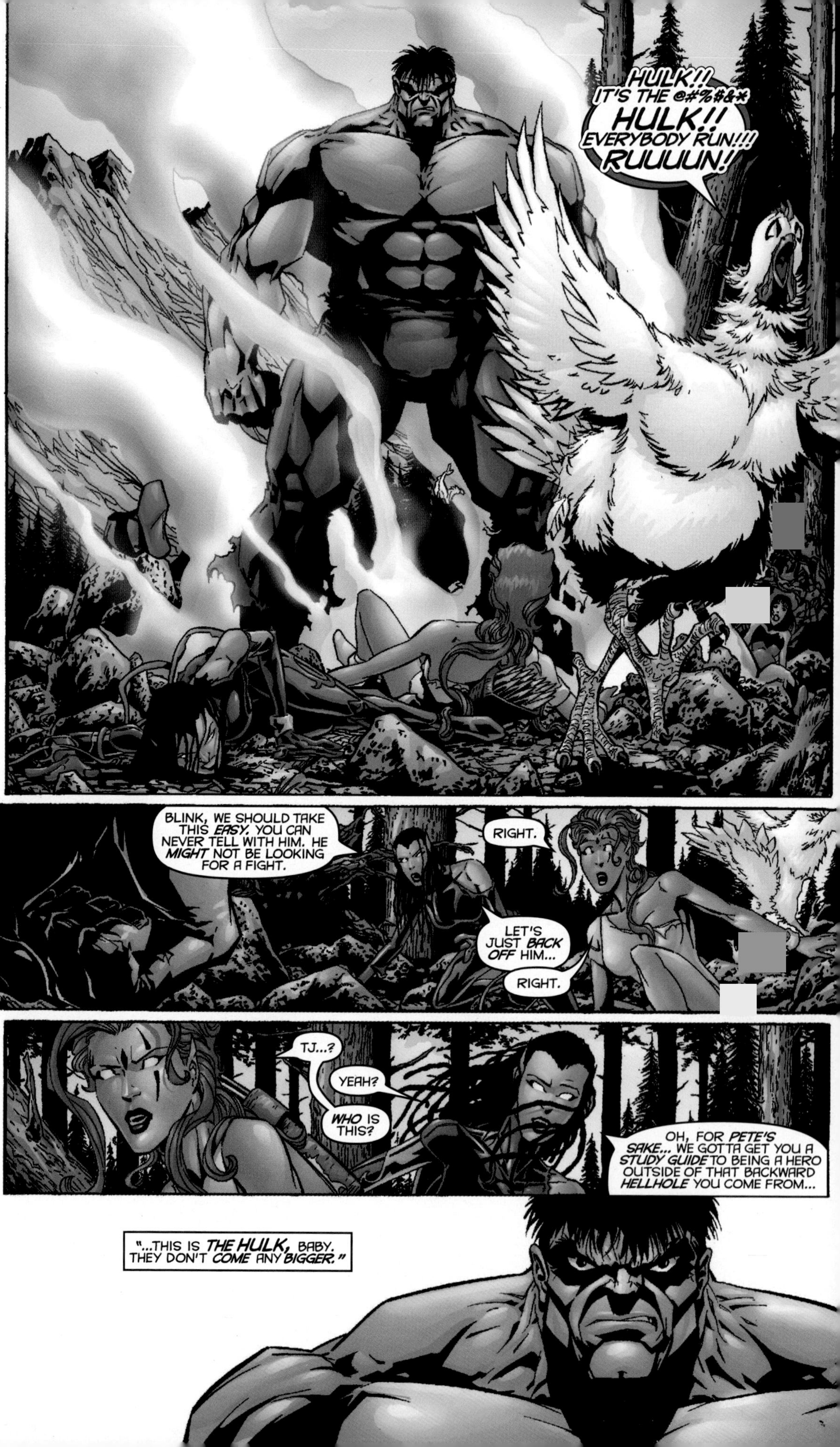
HULK!! IT'S THE @#%$&* HULK!! EVERYBODY RUN!!! RUUUUN!
BLINK, WE SHOULD TAKE THIS EASY. YOU CAN NEVER TELL WITH HIM. HE MIGHT NOT BE LOOKING FOR A FIGHT.
RIGHT.
LET'S JUST BACK OFF HIM...
RIGHT.
TJ...?
YEAH?
WHO IS THIS?
OH, FOR PETE'S SAKE... WE GOTTA GET YOU A STUDY GUIDE TO BEING A HERO OUTSIDE OF THAT BACKWARD HELLHOLE YOU COME FROM...
"...THIS IS THE HULK, BABY. THEY DON'T COME ANY BIGGER."

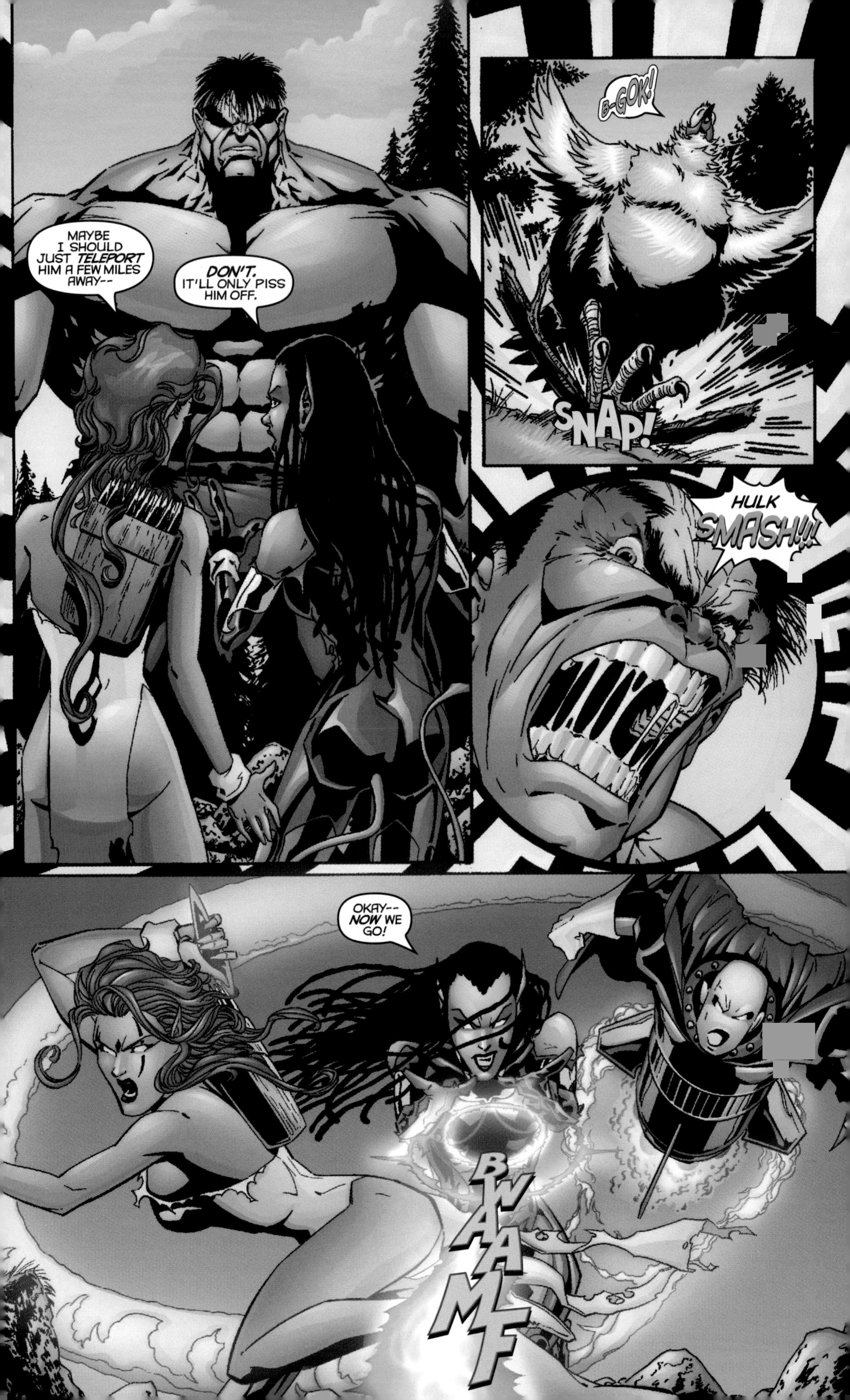
MAYBE I SHOULD JUST *TELEPORT* HIM A FEW MILES AWAY--
DON'T. IT'LL ONLY PISS HIM OFF.
B-GOK!
SNAP!
HULK SMASH!!!
OKAY-- *NOW* WE GO!
BWAAAMF

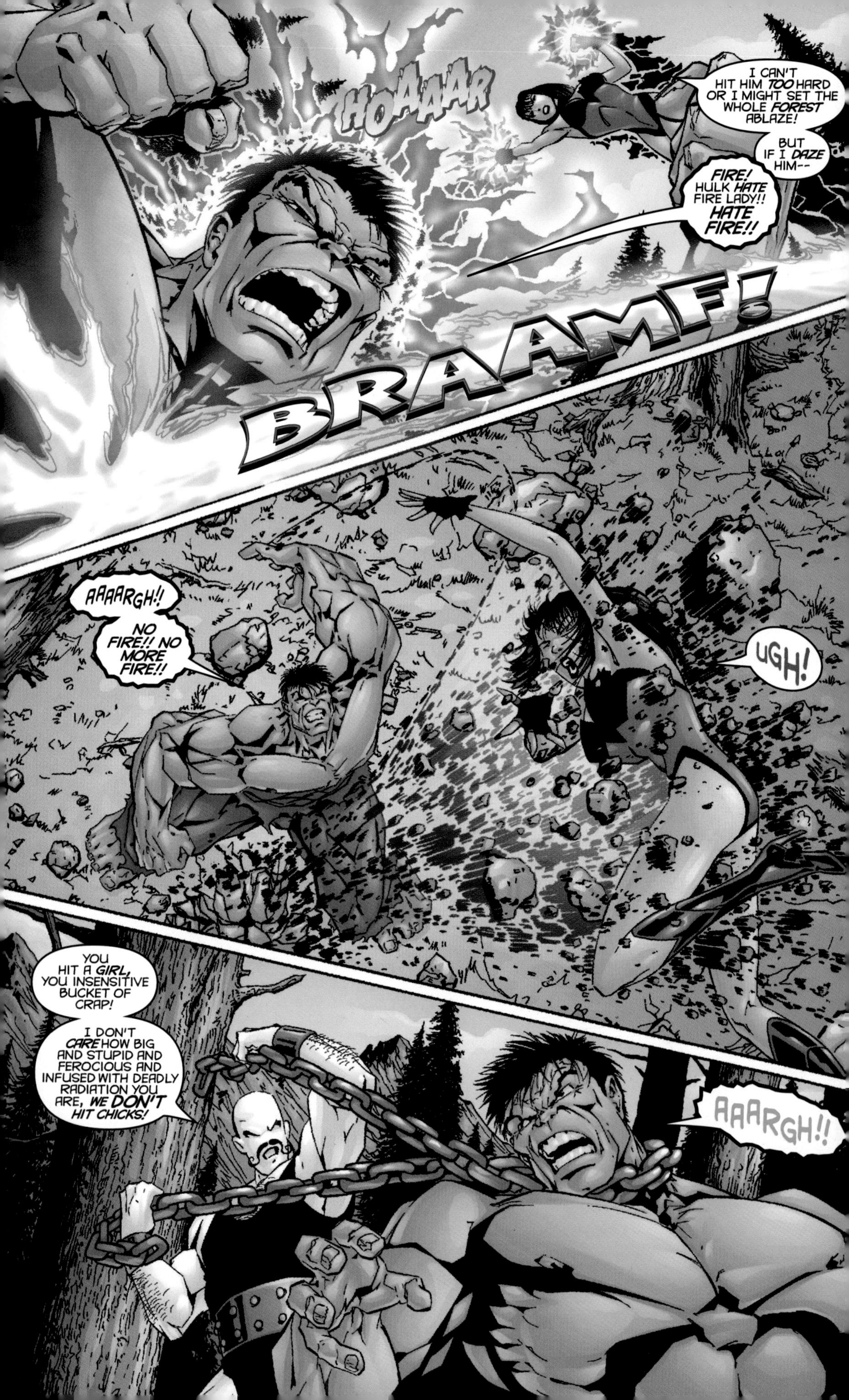
HOAAAR
I CAN'T HIT HIM TOO HARD OR I MIGHT SET THE WHOLE FOREST ABLAZE!
BUT IF I DAZE HIM--
FIRE! HULK HATE FIRE LADY!! HATE FIRE!!
BRAAMF!
AAAARGH!!
NO FIRE!! NO MORE FIRE!!
UGH!
YOU HIT A GIRL, YOU INSENSITIVE BUCKET OF CRAP!
I DON'T CARE HOW BIG AND STUPID AND FEROCIOUS AND INFUSED WITH DEADLY RADIATION YOU ARE, WE DON'T HIT CHICKS!
AAARGH!!

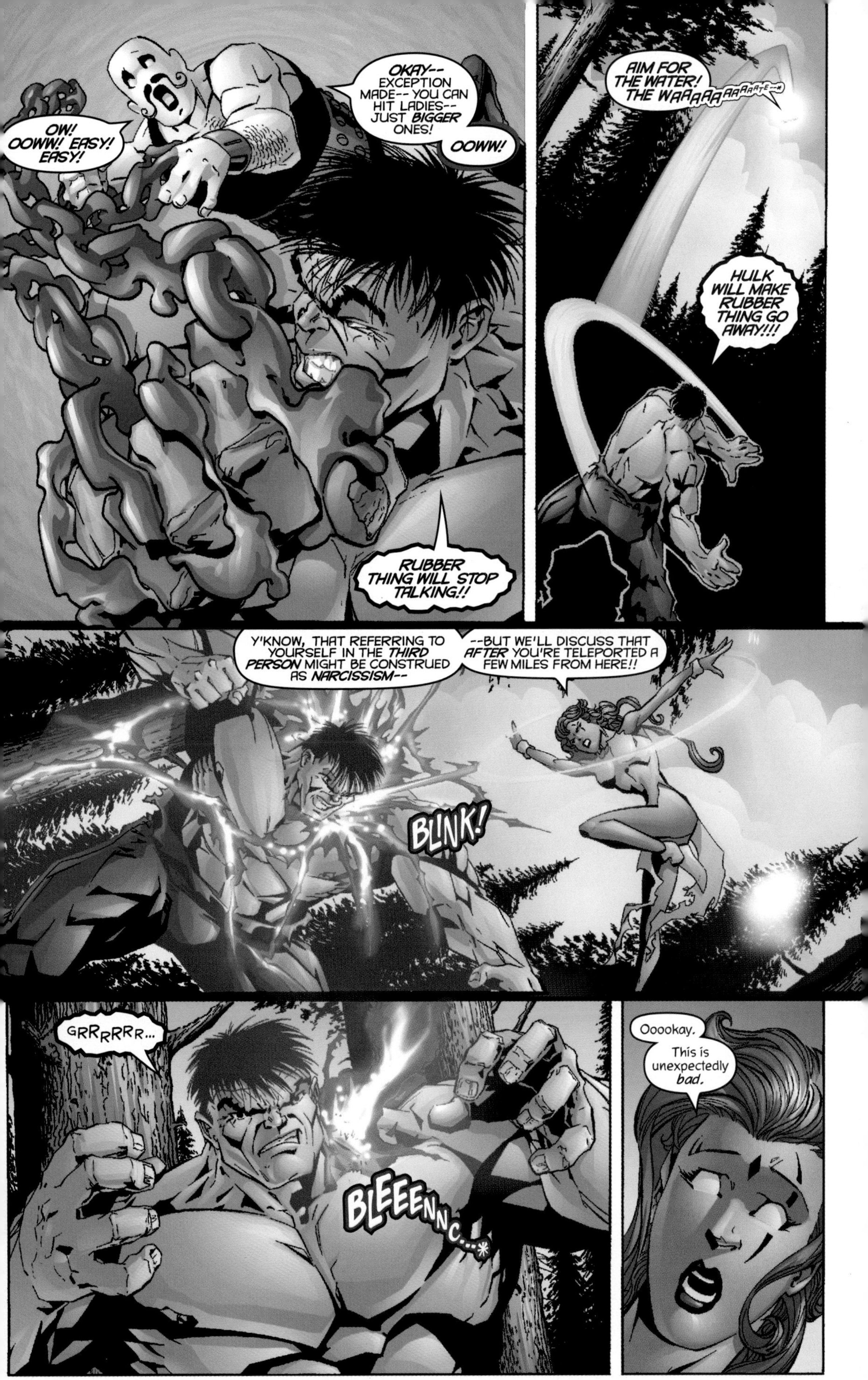
OKAY-- EXCEPTION MADE-- YOU CAN HIT LADIES-- JUST BIGGER ONES!
OW! OOWW! EASY! EASY!
OOWW!
RUBBER THING WILL STOP TALKING!!
AIM FOR THE WATER! THE WAAAAAAAAAAATE--*
HULK WILL MAKE RUBBER THING GO AWAY!!!
Y'KNOW, THAT REFERRING TO YOURSELF IN THE THIRD PERSON MIGHT BE CONSTRUED AS NARCISSISM--
--BUT WE'LL DISCUSS THAT AFTER YOU'RE TELEPORTED A FEW MILES FROM HERE!!
BLINK!
GRRRRRR...
BLEEENNC...*
Ooookay.
This is unexpectedly bad.

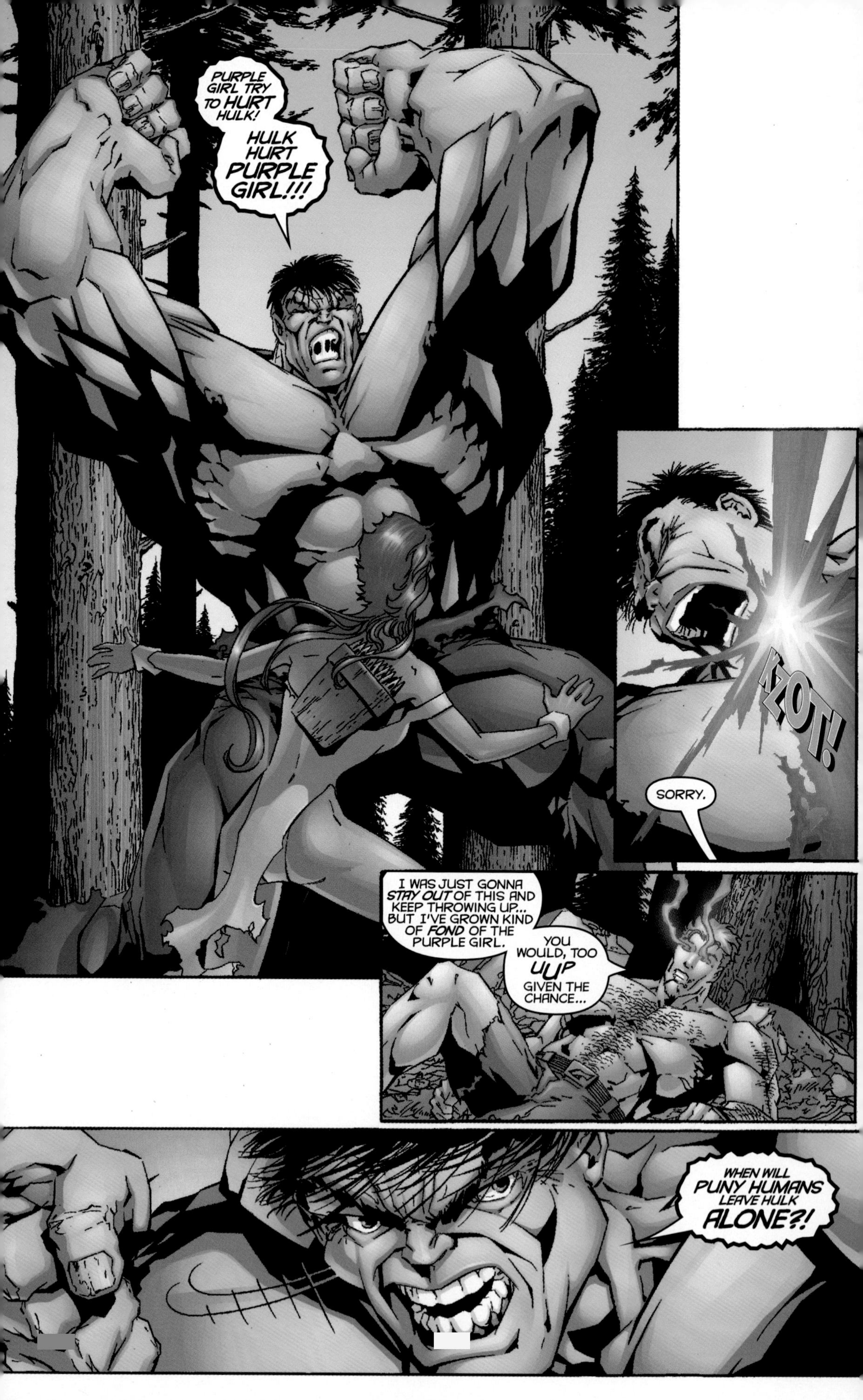
PURPLE GIRL TRY TO HURT HULK!
HULK HURT PURPLE GIRL!!!
KZOT!
SORRY.
I WAS JUST GONNA STAY OUT OF THIS AND KEEP THROWING UP... BUT I'VE GROWN KIND OF FOND OF THE PURPLE GIRL.
YOU WOULD, TOO UUP GIVEN THE CHANCE...
WHEN WILL PUNY HUMANS LEAVE HULK ALONE?!

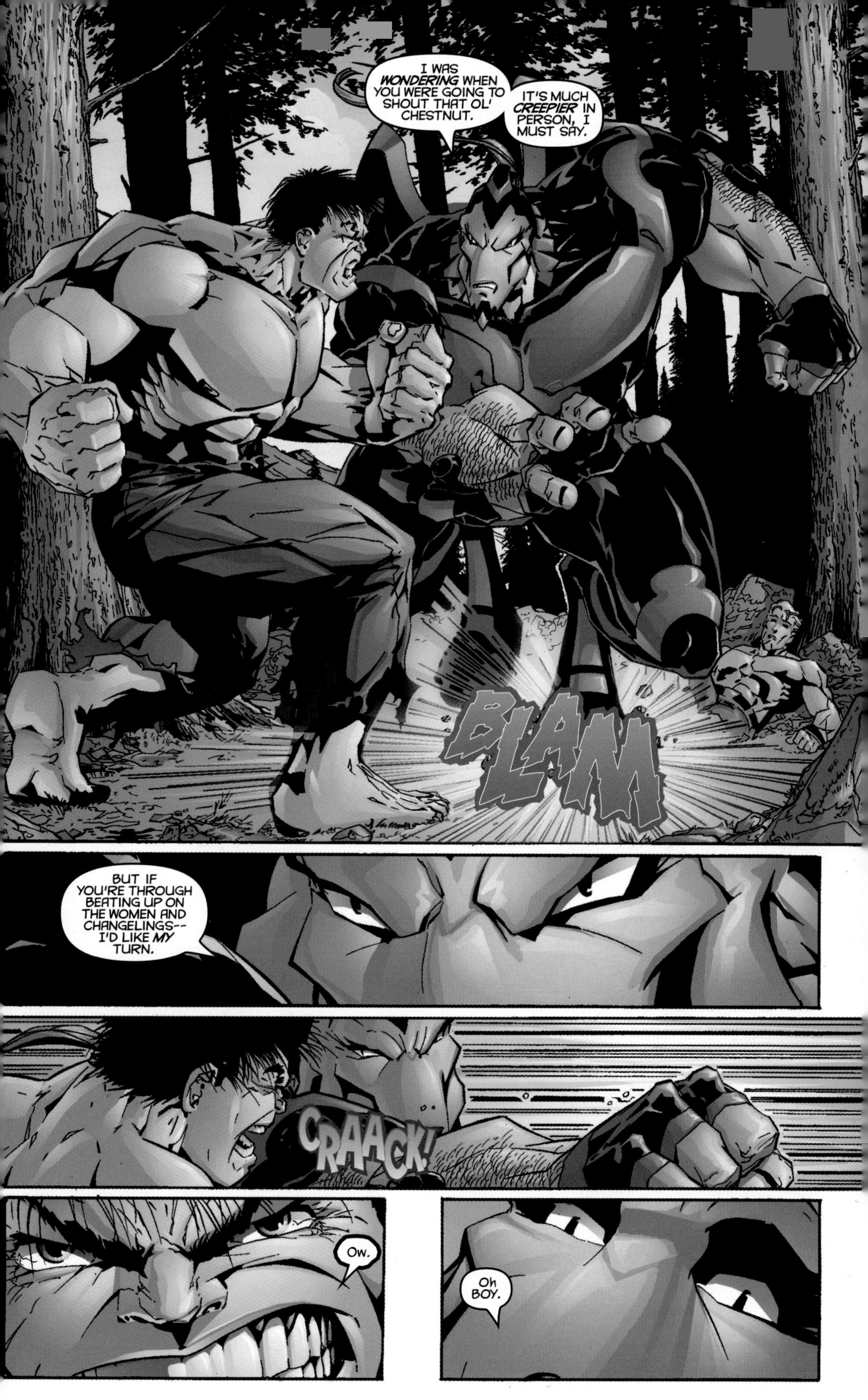
I WAS WONDERING WHEN YOU WERE GOING TO SHOUT THAT OL' CHESTNUT.
IT'S MUCH CREEPIER IN PERSON, I MUST SAY.
BLAM
BUT IF YOU'RE THROUGH BEATING UP ON THE WOMEN AND CHANGELINGS-- I'D LIKE MY TURN.
CRAACK!
OW.
Oh BOY.

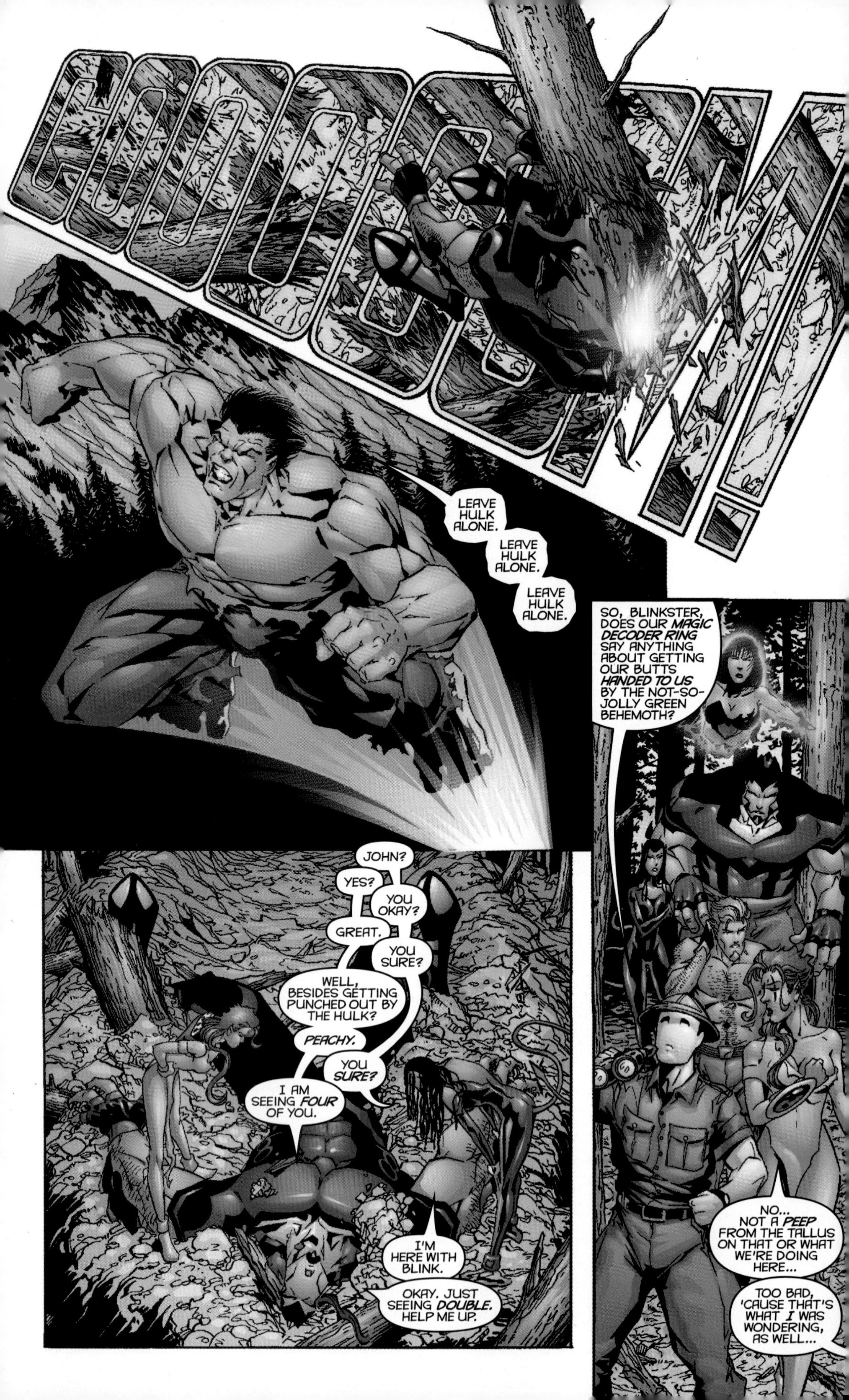

COOOOOOM!!
LEAVE HULK ALONE.
LEAVE HULK ALONE.
LEAVE HULK ALONE.
SO, BLINKSTER, DOES OUR MAGIC DECODER RING SAY ANYTHING ABOUT GETTING OUR BUTTS HANDED TO US BY THE NOT-SO-JOLLY GREEN BEHEMOTH?
JOHN?
YES?
YOU OKAY?
GREAT.
YOU SURE?
WELL, BESIDES GETTING PUNCHED OUT BY THE HULK?
PEACHY.
YOU SURE?
I AM SEEING FOUR OF YOU.
I'M HERE WITH BLINK.
OKAY. JUST SEEING DOUBLE. HELP ME UP.
NO... NOT A PEEP FROM THE TALLUS ON THAT OR WHAT WE'RE DOING HERE...
TOO BAD, 'CAUSE THAT'S WHAT I WAS WONDERING, AS WELL...

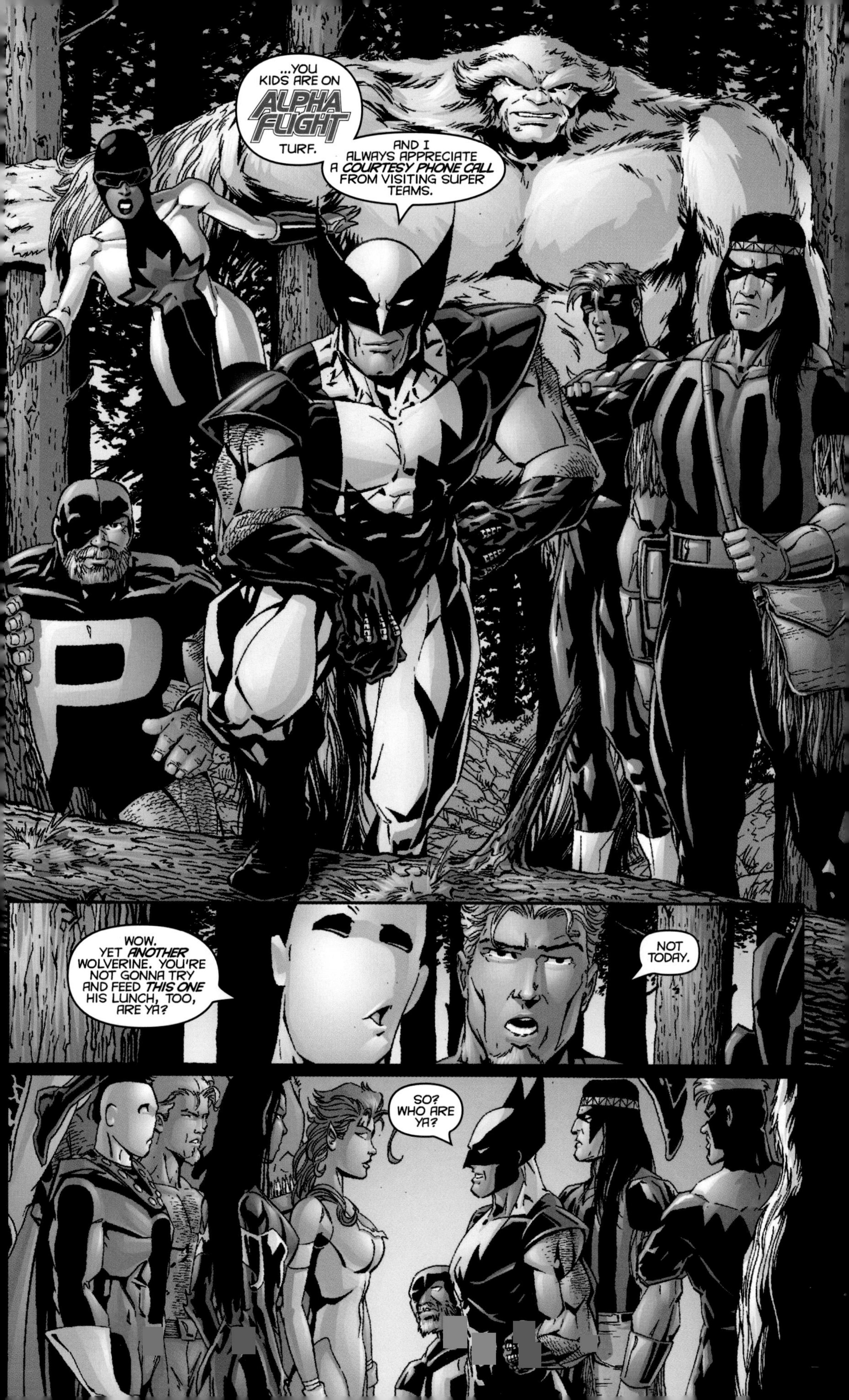
...YOU KIDS ARE ON ALPHA FLIGHT TURF.
AND I ALWAYS APPRECIATE A *COURTESY PHONE CALL* FROM VISITING SUPER TEAMS.
WOW. YET *ANOTHER* WOLVERINE. YOU'RE NOT GONNA TRY AND FEED *THIS ONE* HIS LUNCH, TOO, ARE YA?
NOT TODAY.
SO? WHO ARE YA?

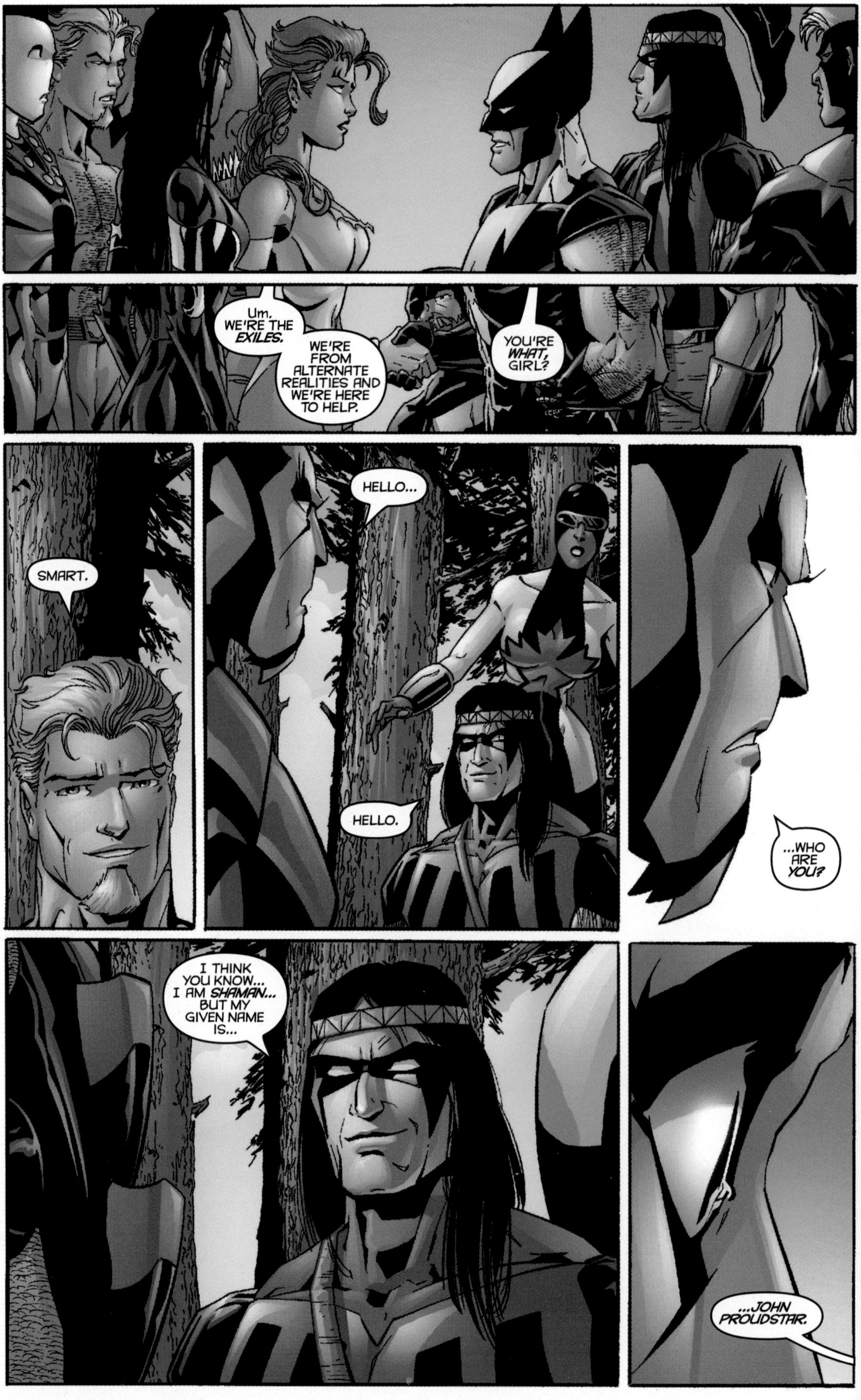
Um. WE'RE THE *EXILES.*
WE'RE FROM ALTERNATE REALITIES AND WE'RE HERE TO HELP.
YOU'RE *WHAT,* GIRL?
SMART.
HELLO...
HELLO.
...WHO ARE *YOU?*
I THINK YOU KNOW... I AM *SHAMAN*... BUT MY GIVEN NAME IS...
...JOHN PROUDSTAR.

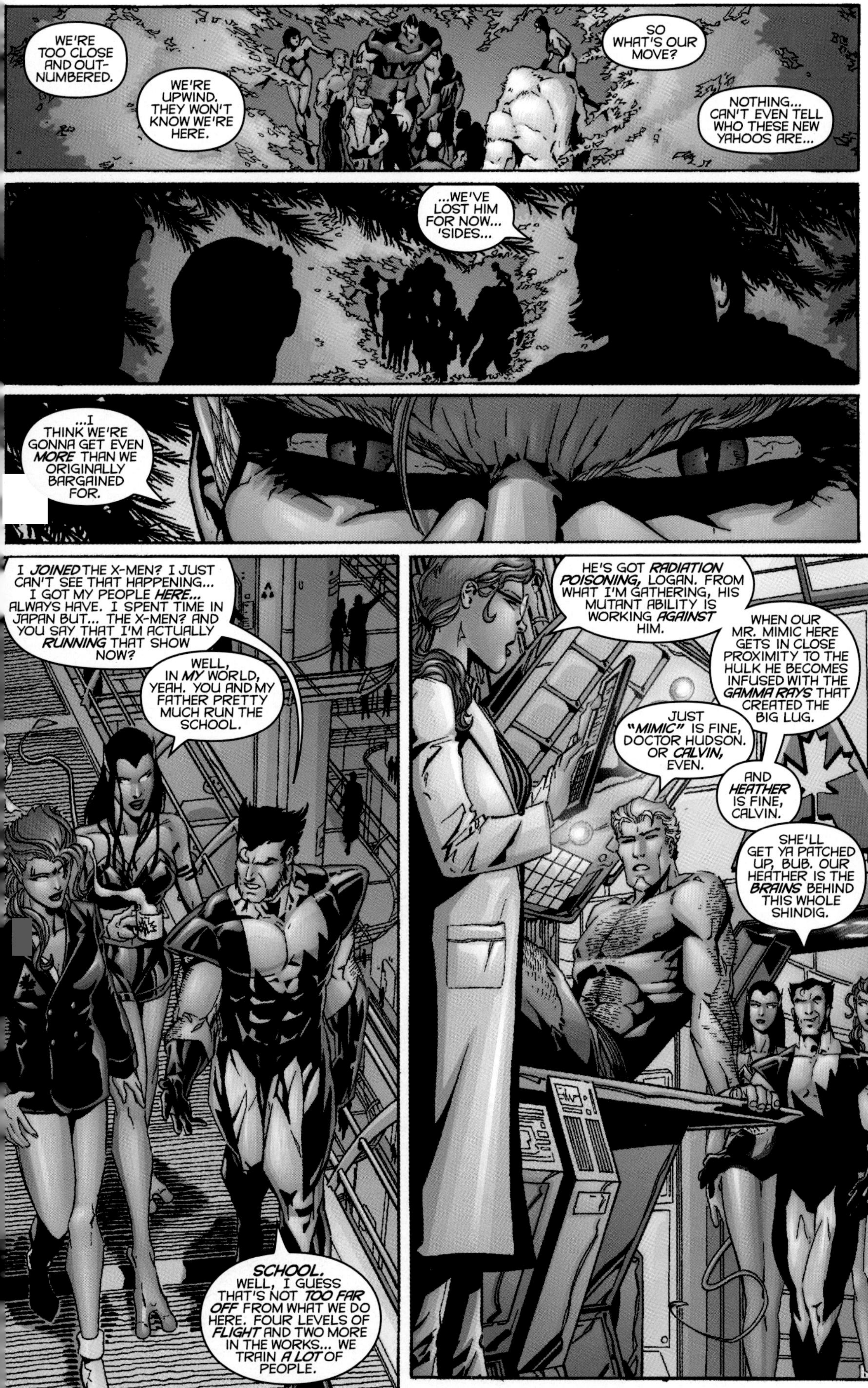
WE'RE TOO CLOSE AND OUT-NUMBERED.
WE'RE UPWIND. THEY WON'T KNOW WE'RE HERE.
SO WHAT'S OUR MOVE?
NOTHING... CAN'T EVEN TELL WHO THESE NEW YAHOOS ARE...
...WE'VE LOST HIM FOR NOW... 'SIDES...
...I THINK WE'RE GONNA GET EVEN MORE THAN WE ORIGINALLY BARGAINED FOR.
I JOINED THE X-MEN? I JUST CAN'T SEE THAT HAPPENING... I GOT MY PEOPLE HERE... ALWAYS HAVE. I SPENT TIME IN JAPAN BUT... THE X-MEN? AND YOU SAY THAT I'M ACTUALLY RUNNING THAT SHOW NOW?
WELL, IN MY WORLD, YEAH. YOU AND MY FATHER PRETTY MUCH RUN THE SCHOOL.
SCHOOL. WELL, I GUESS THAT'S NOT TOO FAR OFF FROM WHAT WE DO HERE. FOUR LEVELS OF FLIGHT AND TWO MORE IN THE WORKS... WE TRAIN A LOT OF PEOPLE.
HE'S GOT RADIATION POISONING, LOGAN. FROM WHAT I'M GATHERING, HIS MUTANT ABILITY IS WORKING AGAINST HIM.
WHEN OUR MR. MIMIC HERE GETS IN CLOSE PROXIMITY TO THE HULK HE BECOMES INFUSED WITH THE GAMMA RAYS THAT CREATED THE BIG LUG.
JUST "MIMIC" IS FINE, DOCTOR HUDSON. OR CALVIN, EVEN.
AND HEATHER IS FINE, CALVIN.
SHE'LL GET YA PATCHED UP, BUB. OUR HEATHER IS THE BRAINS BEHIND THIS WHOLE SHINDIG.

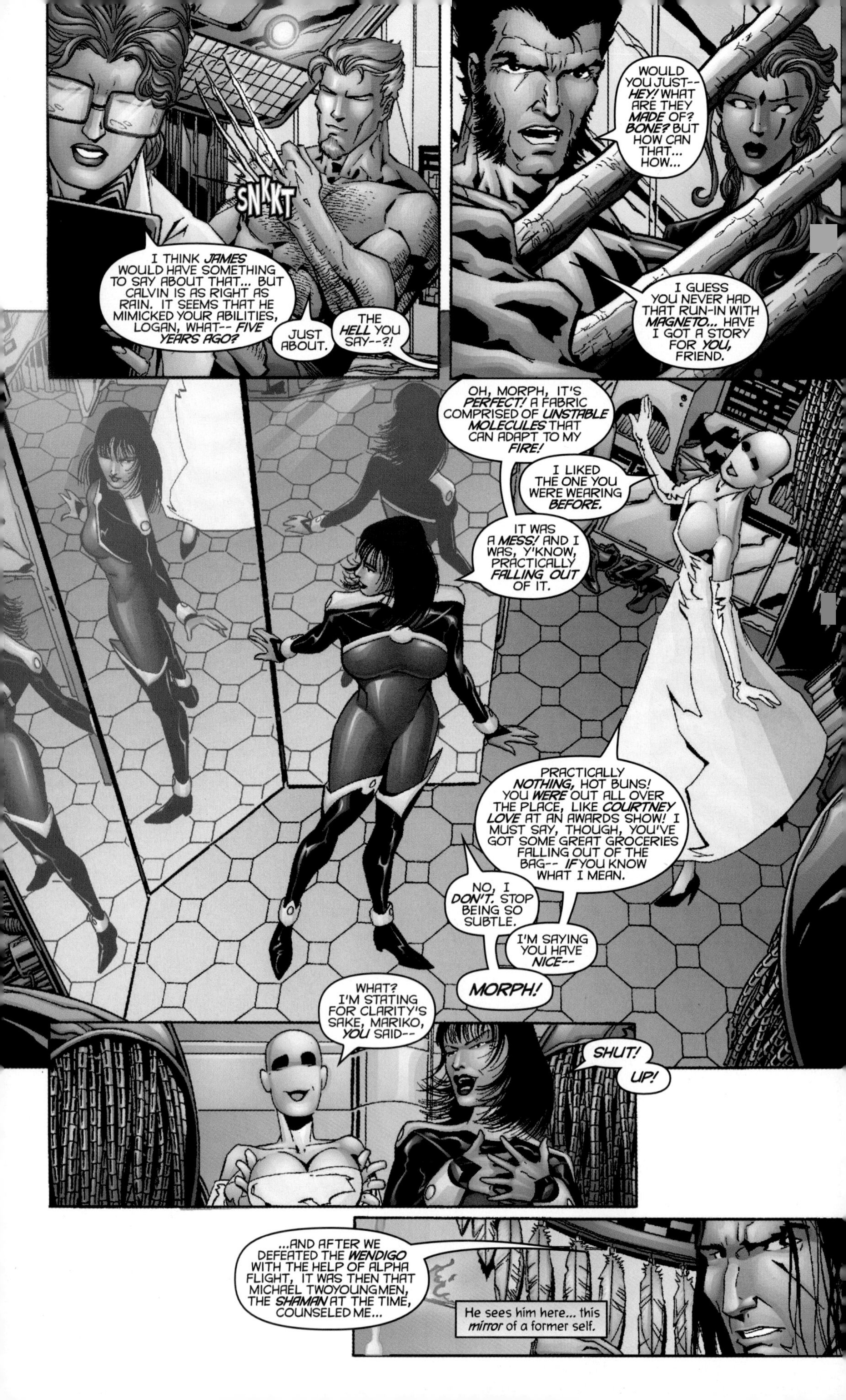
SNKKT
I THINK JAMES WOULD HAVE SOMETHING TO SAY ABOUT THAT... BUT CALVIN IS AS RIGHT AS RAIN. IT SEEMS THAT HE MIMICKED YOUR ABILITIES, LOGAN, WHAT-- FIVE YEARS AGO?
JUST ABOUT.
THE HELL YOU SAY--?!
WOULD YOU JUST-- HEY! WHAT ARE THEY MADE OF? BONE? BUT HOW CAN THAT... HOW...
I GUESS YOU NEVER HAD THAT RUN-IN WITH MAGNETO... HAVE I GOT A STORY FOR YOU, FRIEND.
OH, MORPH, IT'S PERFECT! A FABRIC COMPRISED OF UNSTABLE MOLECULES THAT CAN ADAPT TO MY FIRE!
I LIKED THE ONE YOU WERE WEARING BEFORE.
IT WAS A MESS! AND I WAS, Y'KNOW, PRACTICALLY FALLING OUT OF IT.
PRACTICALLY NOTHING, HOT BUNS! YOU WERE OUT ALL OVER THE PLACE, LIKE COURTNEY LOVE AT AN AWARDS SHOW! I MUST SAY, THOUGH, YOU'VE GOT SOME GREAT GROCERIES FALLING OUT OF THE BAG-- IF YOU KNOW WHAT I MEAN.
NO, I DON'T. STOP BEING SO SUBTLE.
I'M SAYING YOU HAVE NICE--
MORPH!
WHAT? I'M STATING FOR CLARITY'S SAKE, MARIKO, YOU SAID--
SHUT!
UP!
...AND AFTER WE DEFEATED THE WENDIGO WITH THE HELP OF ALPHA FLIGHT, IT WAS THEN THAT MICHAEL TWOYOUNGMEN, THE SHAMAN AT THE TIME, COUNSELED ME...
He sees him here... this mirror of a former self.

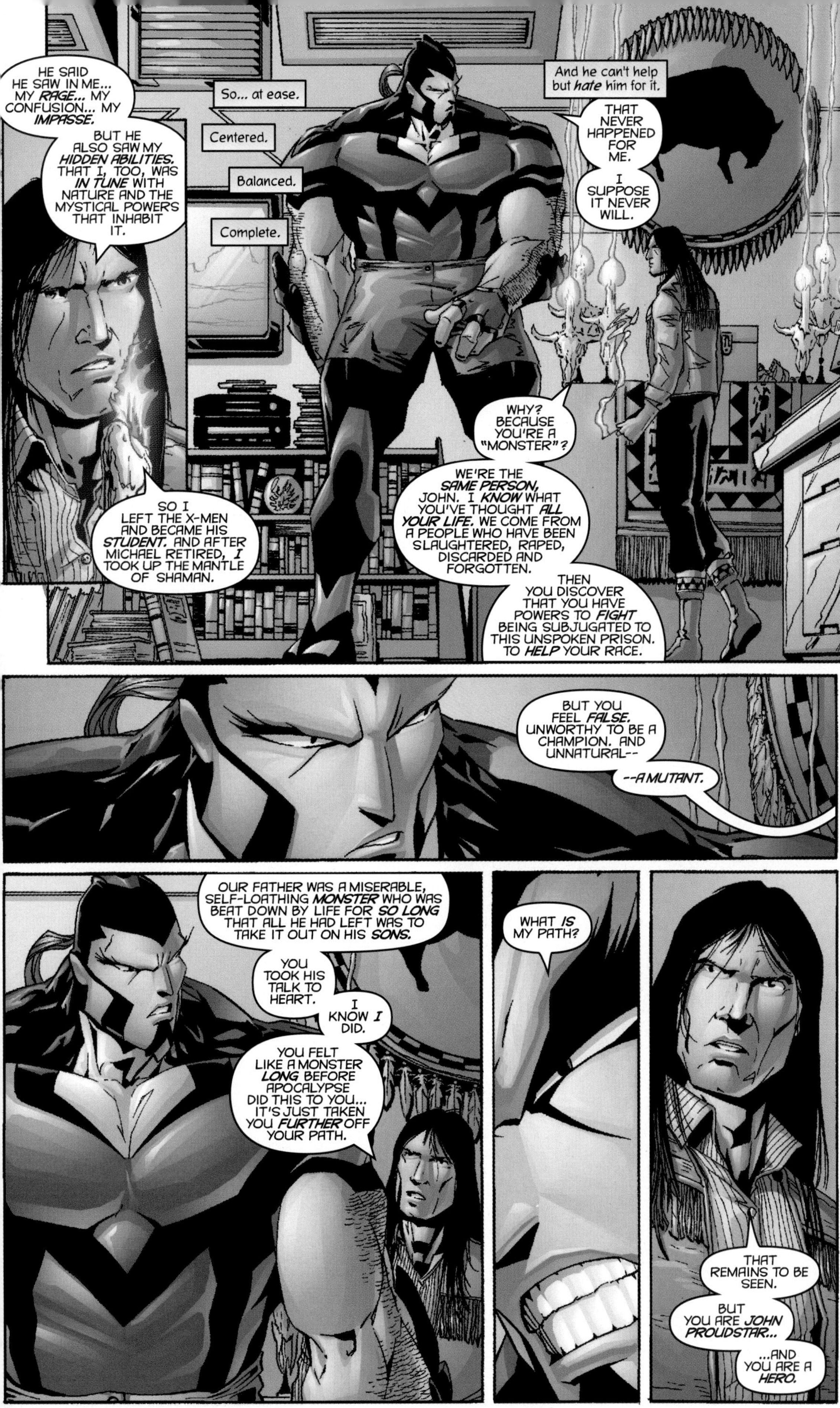
HE SAID HE SAW IN ME... MY RAGE... MY CONFUSION... MY IMPASSE.
BUT HE ALSO SAW MY HIDDEN ABILITIES. THAT I, TOO, WAS IN TUNE WITH NATURE AND THE MYSTICAL POWERS THAT INHABIT IT.
So... at ease.
Centered.
Balanced.
Complete.
And he can't help but hate him for it.
THAT NEVER HAPPENED FOR ME.
I SUPPOSE IT NEVER WILL.
SO I LEFT THE X-MEN AND BECAME HIS STUDENT. AND AFTER MICHAEL RETIRED, I TOOK UP THE MANTLE OF SHAMAN.
WHY? BECAUSE YOU'RE A "MONSTER"?
WE'RE THE SAME PERSON, JOHN. I KNOW WHAT YOU'VE THOUGHT ALL YOUR LIFE. WE COME FROM A PEOPLE WHO HAVE BEEN SLAUGHTERED, RAPED, DISCARDED AND FORGOTTEN.
THEN YOU DISCOVER THAT YOU HAVE POWERS TO FIGHT BEING SUBJUGATED TO THIS UNSPOKEN PRISON. TO HELP YOUR RACE.
BUT YOU FEEL FALSE. UNWORTHY TO BE A CHAMPION. AND UNNATURAL--
--A MUTANT.
OUR FATHER WAS A MISERABLE, SELF-LOATHING MONSTER WHO WAS BEAT DOWN BY LIFE FOR SO LONG THAT ALL HE HAD LEFT WAS TO TAKE IT OUT ON HIS SONS.
YOU TOOK HIS TALK TO HEART.
I KNOW I DID.
YOU FELT LIKE A MONSTER LONG BEFORE APOCALYPSE DID THIS TO YOU... IT'S JUST TAKEN YOU FURTHER OFF YOUR PATH.
WHAT IS MY PATH?
THAT REMAINS TO BE SEEN.
BUT YOU ARE JOHN PROUDSTAR...
...AND YOU ARE A HERO.

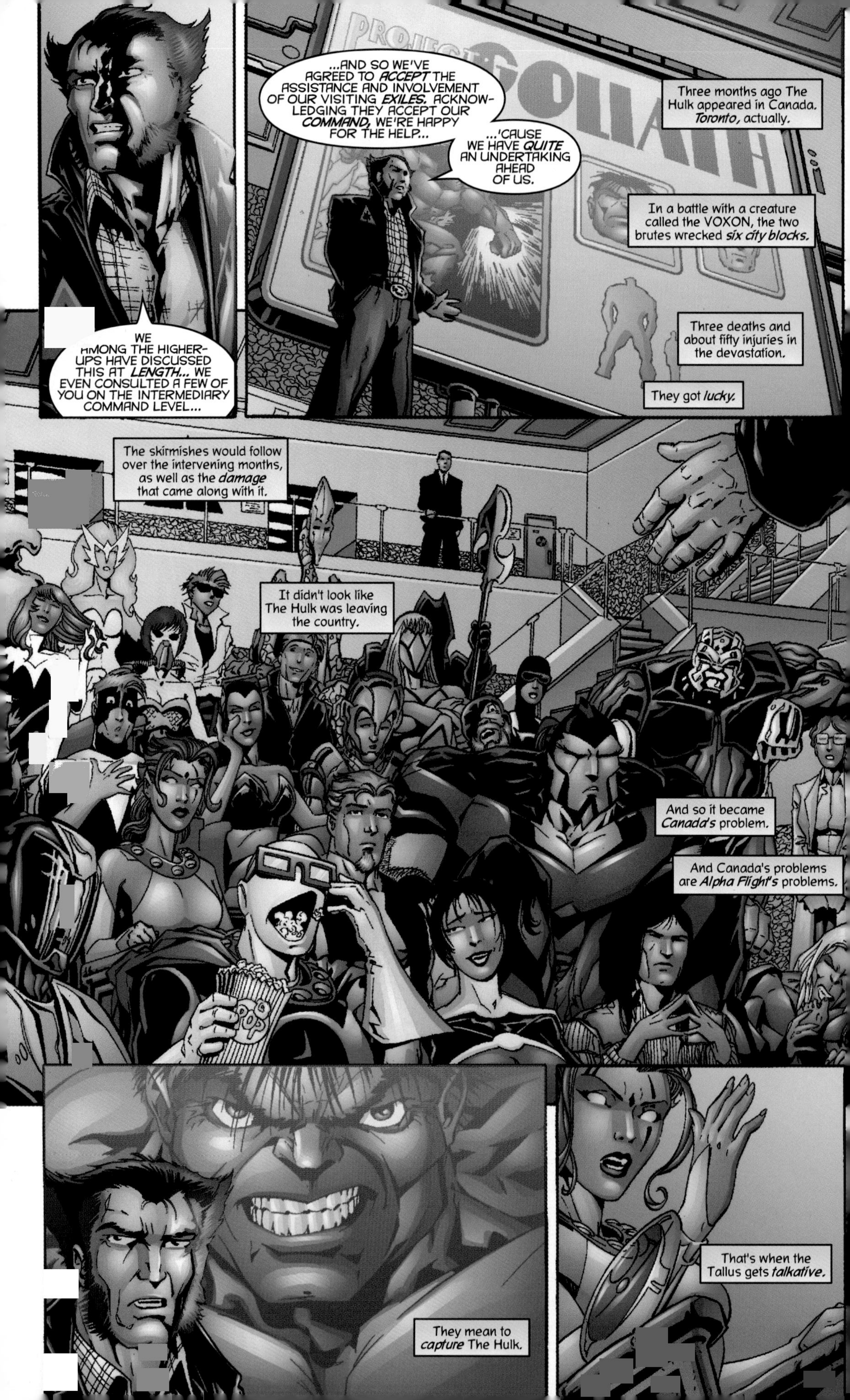

WE AMONG THE HIGHER-UPS HAVE DISCUSSED THIS AT LENGTH... WE EVEN CONSULTED A FEW OF YOU ON THE INTERMEDIARY COMMAND LEVEL...
...AND SO WE'VE AGREED TO ACCEPT THE ASSISTANCE AND INVOLVEMENT OF OUR VISITING EXILES. ACKNOWLEDGING THEY ACCEPT OUR COMMAND, WE'RE HAPPY FOR THE HELP...
...'CAUSE WE HAVE QUITE AN UNDERTAKING AHEAD OF US.
PROJECT GOLIATH
Three months ago The Hulk appeared in Canada. Toronto, actually.
In a battle with a creature called the VOXON, the two brutes wrecked six city blocks.
Three deaths and about fifty injuries in the devastation.
They got lucky.
The skirmishes would follow over the intervening months, as well as the damage that came along with it.
It didn't look like The Hulk was leaving the country.
And so it became Canada's problem.
And Canada's problems are Alpha Flight's problems.
POP
They mean to capture The Hulk.
That's when the Tallus gets talkative.

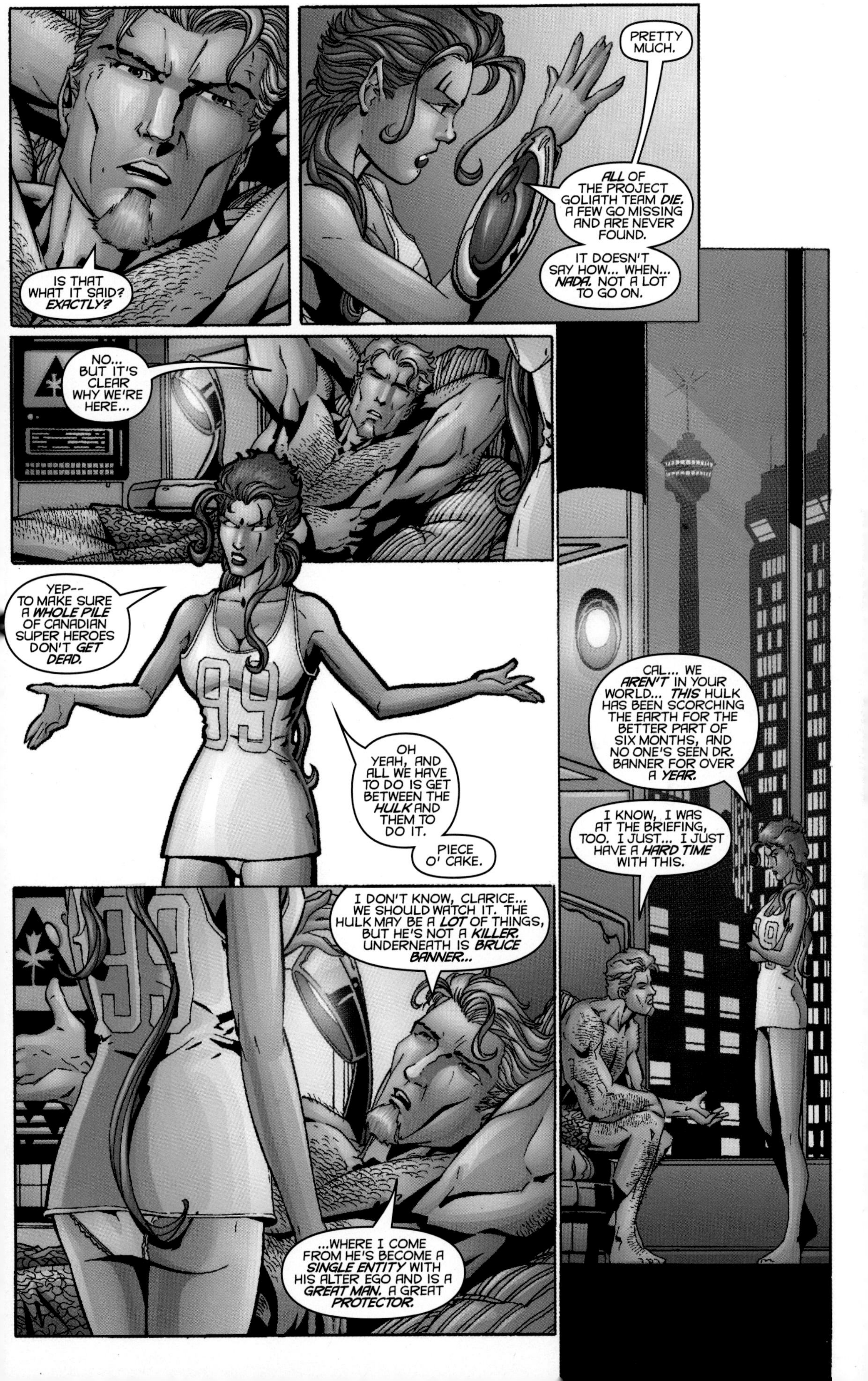

IS THAT WHAT IT SAID? EXACTLY?
PRETTY MUCH.
ALL OF THE PROJECT GOLIATH TEAM DIE. A FEW GO MISSING AND ARE NEVER FOUND.
IT DOESN'T SAY HOW... WHEN... NADA. NOT A LOT TO GO ON.
NO... BUT IT'S CLEAR WHY WE'RE HERE...
YEP-- TO MAKE SURE A WHOLE PILE OF CANADIAN SUPER HEROES DON'T GET DEAD.
OH YEAH, AND ALL WE HAVE TO DO IS GET BETWEEN THE HULK AND THEM TO DO IT.
PIECE O' CAKE.
I DON'T KNOW, CLARICE... WE SHOULD WATCH IT. THE HULK MAY BE A LOT OF THINGS, BUT HE'S NOT A KILLER. UNDERNEATH IS BRUCE BANNER...
...WHERE I COME FROM HE'S BECOME A SINGLE ENTITY WITH HIS ALTER EGO AND IS A GREAT MAN. A GREAT PROTECTOR.
CAL... WE AREN'T IN YOUR WORLD... THIS HULK HAS BEEN SCORCHING THE EARTH FOR THE BETTER PART OF SIX MONTHS, AND NO ONE'S SEEN DR. BANNER FOR OVER A YEAR.
I KNOW, I WAS AT THE BRIEFING, TOO. I JUST... I JUST HAVE A HARD TIME WITH THIS.

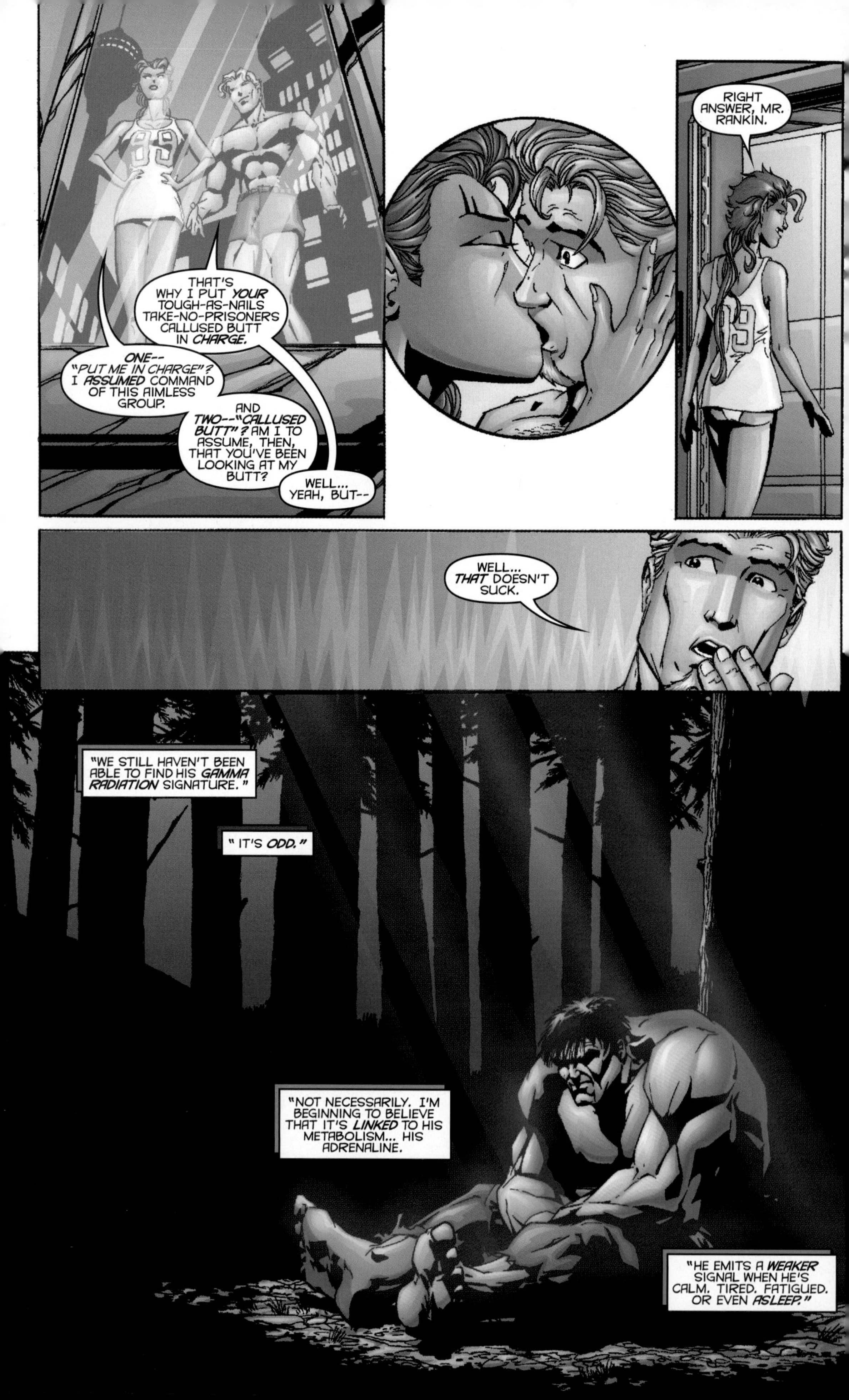
THAT'S WHY I PUT YOUR TOUGH-AS-NAILS TAKE-NO-PRISONERS CALLUSED BUTT IN CHARGE.
ONE-- "PUT ME IN CHARGE"? I ASSUMED COMMAND OF THIS AIMLESS GROUP.
AND TWO--"CALLUSED BUTT"? AM I TO ASSUME, THEN, THAT YOU'VE BEEN LOOKING AT MY BUTT?
WELL... YEAH, BUT--
RIGHT ANSWER, MR. RANKIN.
WELL... THAT DOESN'T SUCK.
"WE STILL HAVEN'T BEEN ABLE TO FIND HIS GAMMA RADIATION SIGNATURE."
"IT'S ODD."
"NOT NECESSARILY. I'M BEGINNING TO BELIEVE THAT IT'S LINKED TO HIS METABOLISM... HIS ADRENALINE.
"HE EMITS A WEAKER SIGNAL WHEN HE'S CALM. TIRED. FATIGUED. OR EVEN ASLEEP."

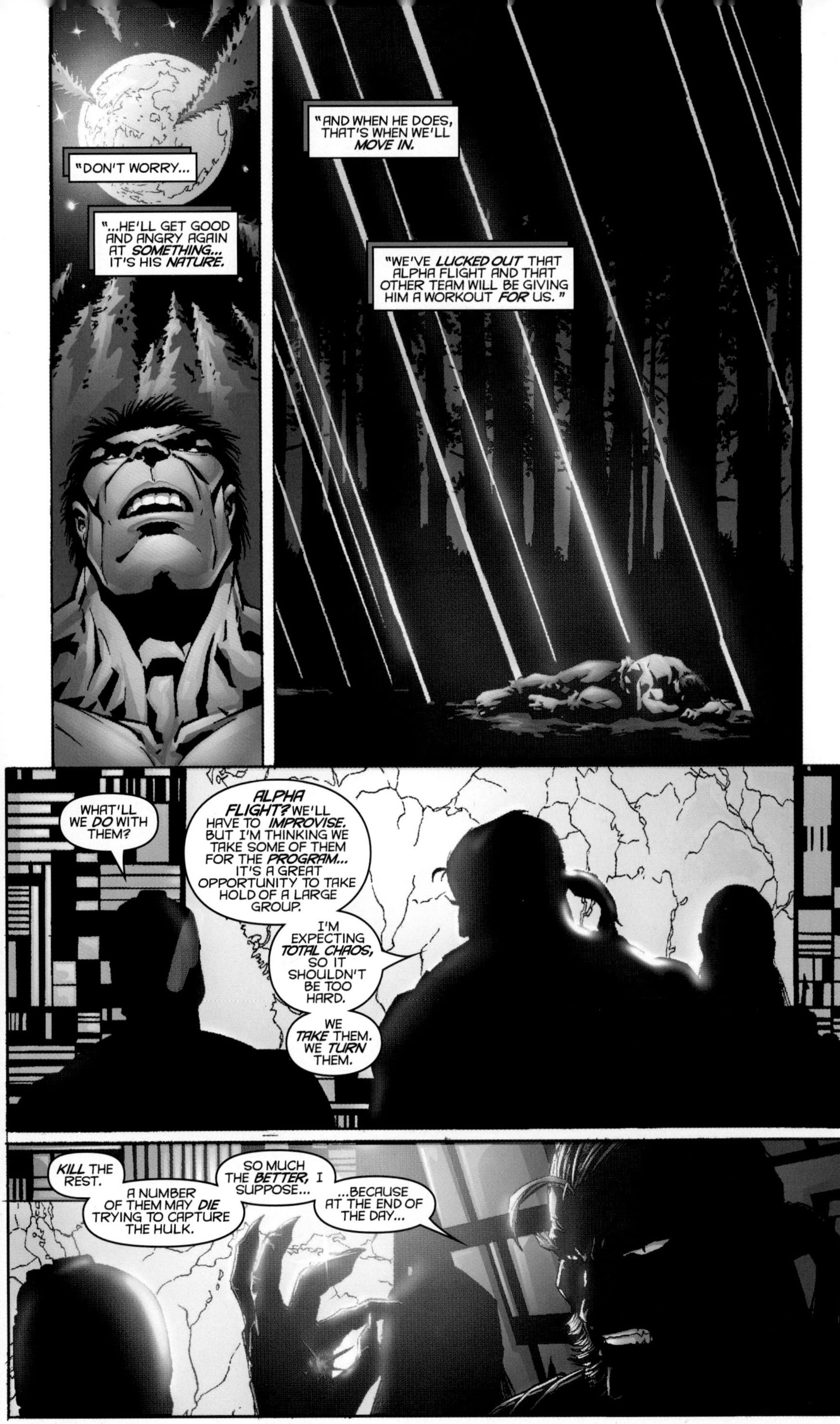
"DON'T WORRY...
"...HE'LL GET GOOD AND ANGRY AGAIN AT SOMETHING... IT'S HIS NATURE.
"AND WHEN HE DOES, THAT'S WHEN WE'LL MOVE IN.
"WE'VE LUCKED OUT THAT ALPHA FLIGHT AND THAT OTHER TEAM WILL BE GIVING HIM A WORKOUT FOR US."
WHAT'LL WE DO WITH THEM?
ALPHA FLIGHT? WE'LL HAVE TO IMPROVISE. BUT I'M THINKING WE TAKE SOME OF THEM FOR THE PROGRAM... IT'S A GREAT OPPORTUNITY TO TAKE HOLD OF A LARGE GROUP.
I'M EXPECTING TOTAL CHAOS, SO IT SHOULDN'T BE TOO HARD.
WE TAKE THEM. WE TURN THEM.
KILL THE REST.
A NUMBER OF THEM MAY DIE TRYING TO CAPTURE THE HULK.
SO MUCH THE BETTER, I SUPPOSE...
...BECAUSE AT THE END OF THE DAY...

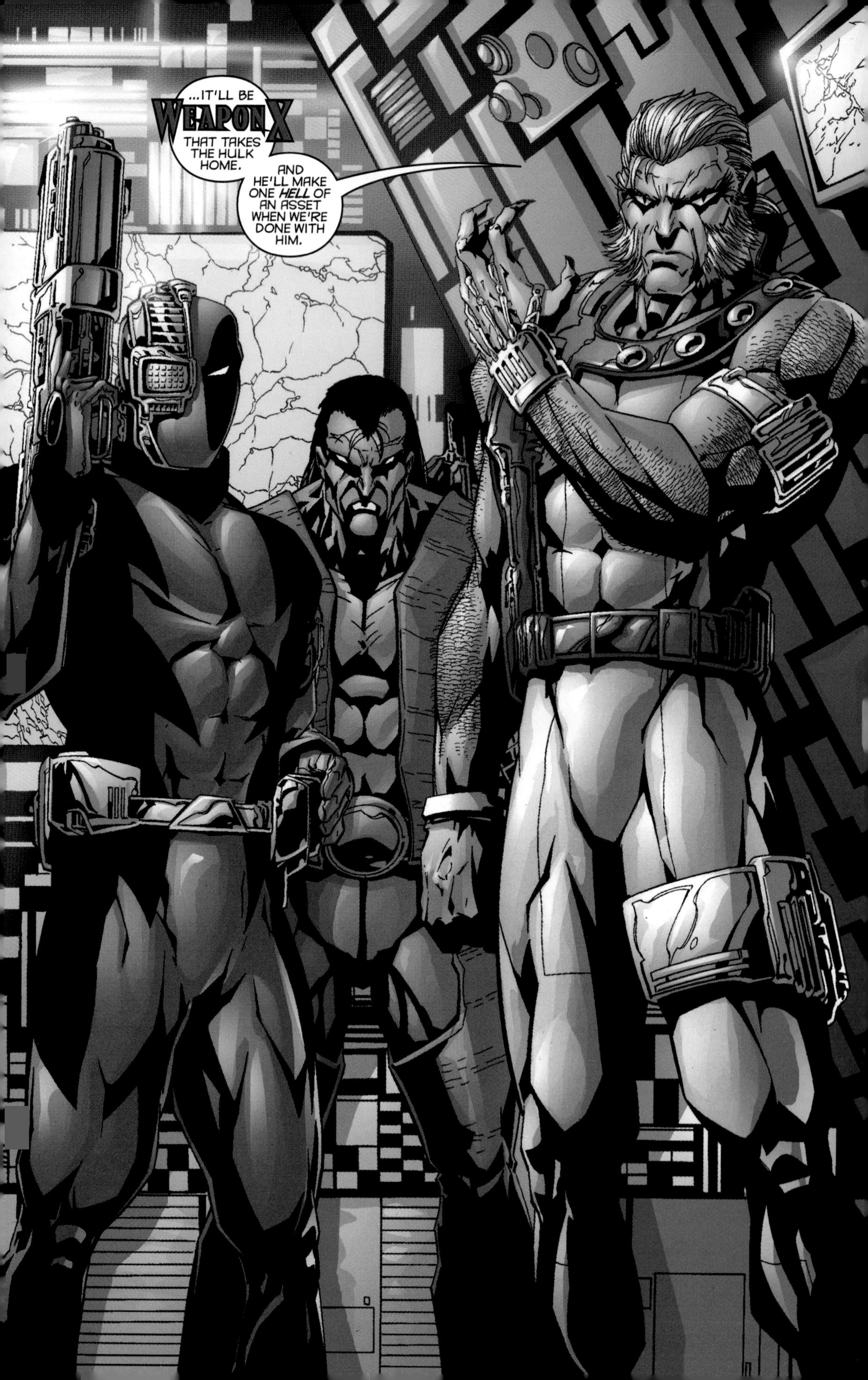
...IT'LL BE WEAPON X THAT TAKES THE HULK HOME.
AND HE'LL MAKE ONE HELL OF AN ASSET WHEN WE'RE DONE WITH HIM.

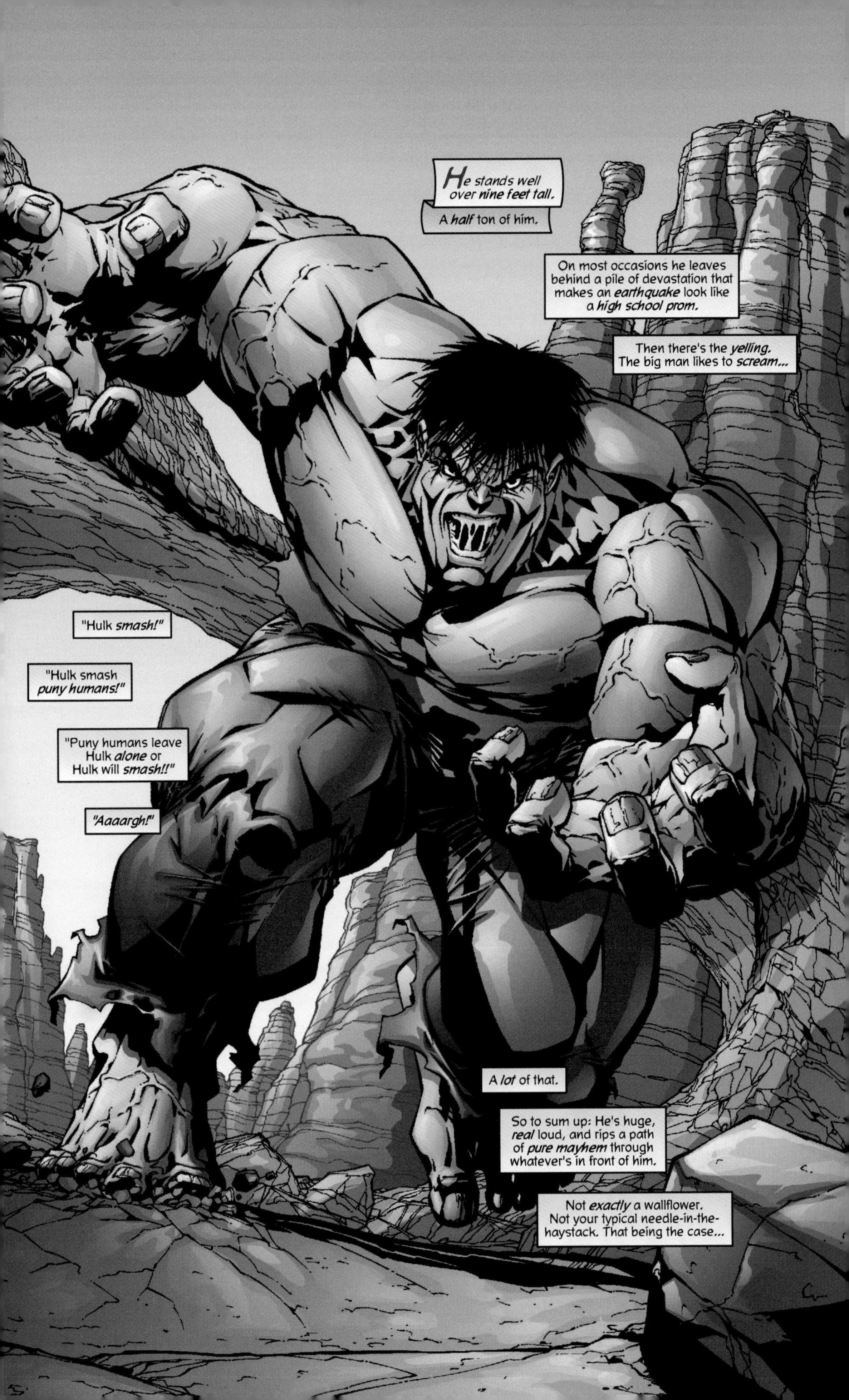

He stands well over nine feet tall.
A half ton of him.
On most occasions he leaves behind a pile of devastation that makes an earthquake look like a high school prom.
Then there's the yelling. The big man likes to scream...
"Hulk smash!"
"Hulk smash puny humans!"
"Puny humans leave Hulk alone or Hulk will smash!!"
"Aaaargh!"
A lot of that.
So to sum up: He's huge, real loud, and rips a path of pure mayhem through whatever's in front of him.
Not exactly a wallflower. Not your typical needle-in-the-haystack. That being the case...

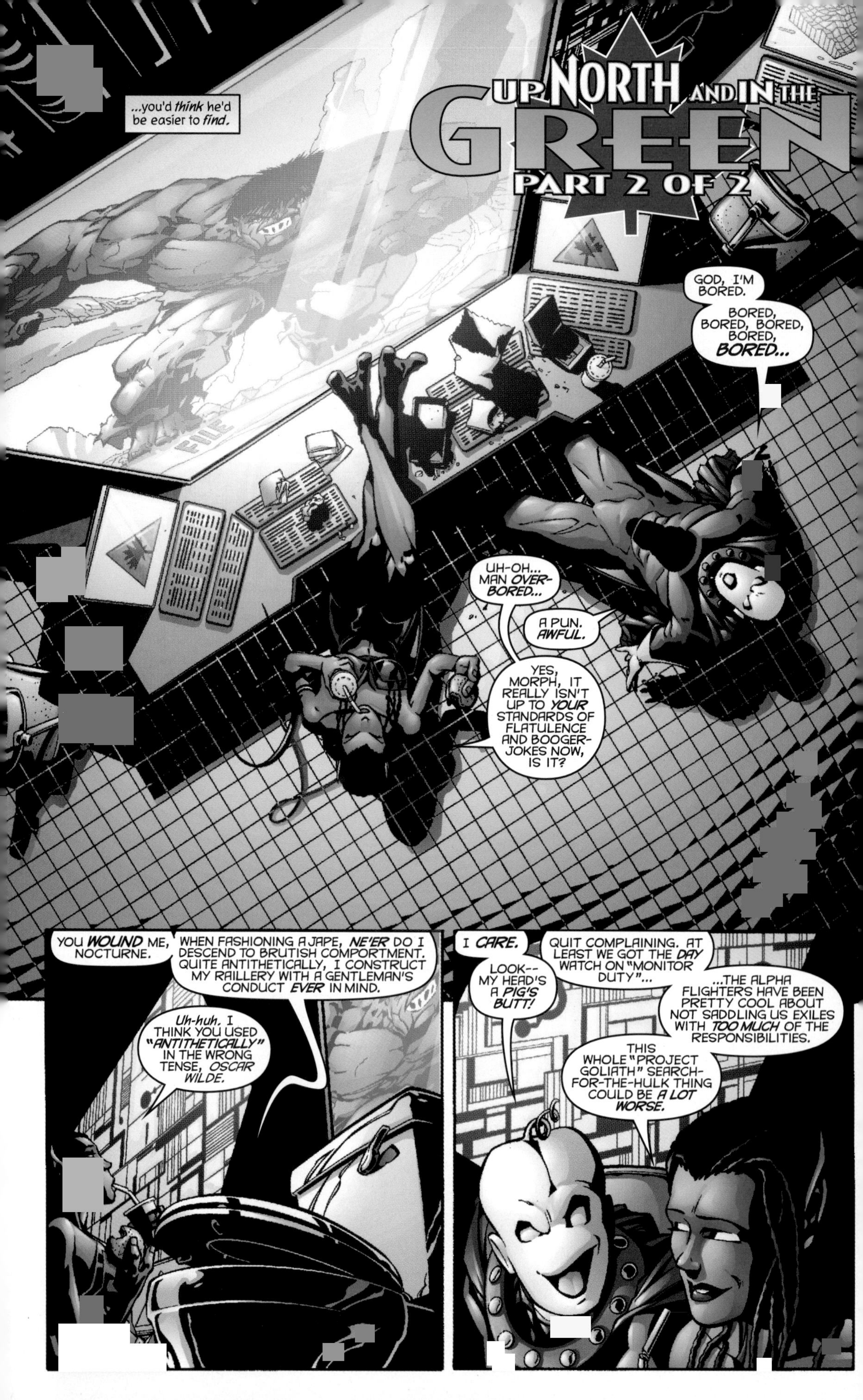

...you'd *think* he'd be easier to *find.*
UP NORTH AND IN THE GREEN
PART 2 OF 2
GOD, I'M BORED.
BORED, BORED, BORED, BORED, **BORED...**
UH-OH... MAN *OVER-BORED...*
A PUN. *AWFUL.*
YES, MORPH, IT REALLY ISN'T UP TO *YOUR* STANDARDS OF FLATULENCE AND BOOGER-JOKES NOW, IS IT?
YOU **WOUND** ME, NOCTURNE.
WHEN FASHIONING A JAPE, *NE'ER* DO I DESCEND TO BRUTISH COMPORTMENT. QUITE ANTITHETICALLY, I CONSTRUCT MY RAILLERY WITH A GENTLEMAN'S CONDUCT *EVER* IN MIND.
Uh-huh. I THINK YOU USED ***"ANTITHETICALLY"*** IN THE WRONG TENSE, *OSCAR WILDE.*
I *CARE.*
LOOK-- MY HEAD'S A *PIG'S BUTT!*
QUIT COMPLAINING. AT LEAST WE GOT THE *DAY* WATCH ON "MONITOR DUTY"...
...THE ALPHA FLIGHTERS HAVE BEEN PRETTY COOL ABOUT NOT SADDLING US EXILES WITH *TOO MUCH* OF THE RESPONSIBILITIES.
THIS WHOLE "PROJECT GOLIATH" SEARCH-FOR-THE-HULK THING COULD BE *A LOT WORSE.*

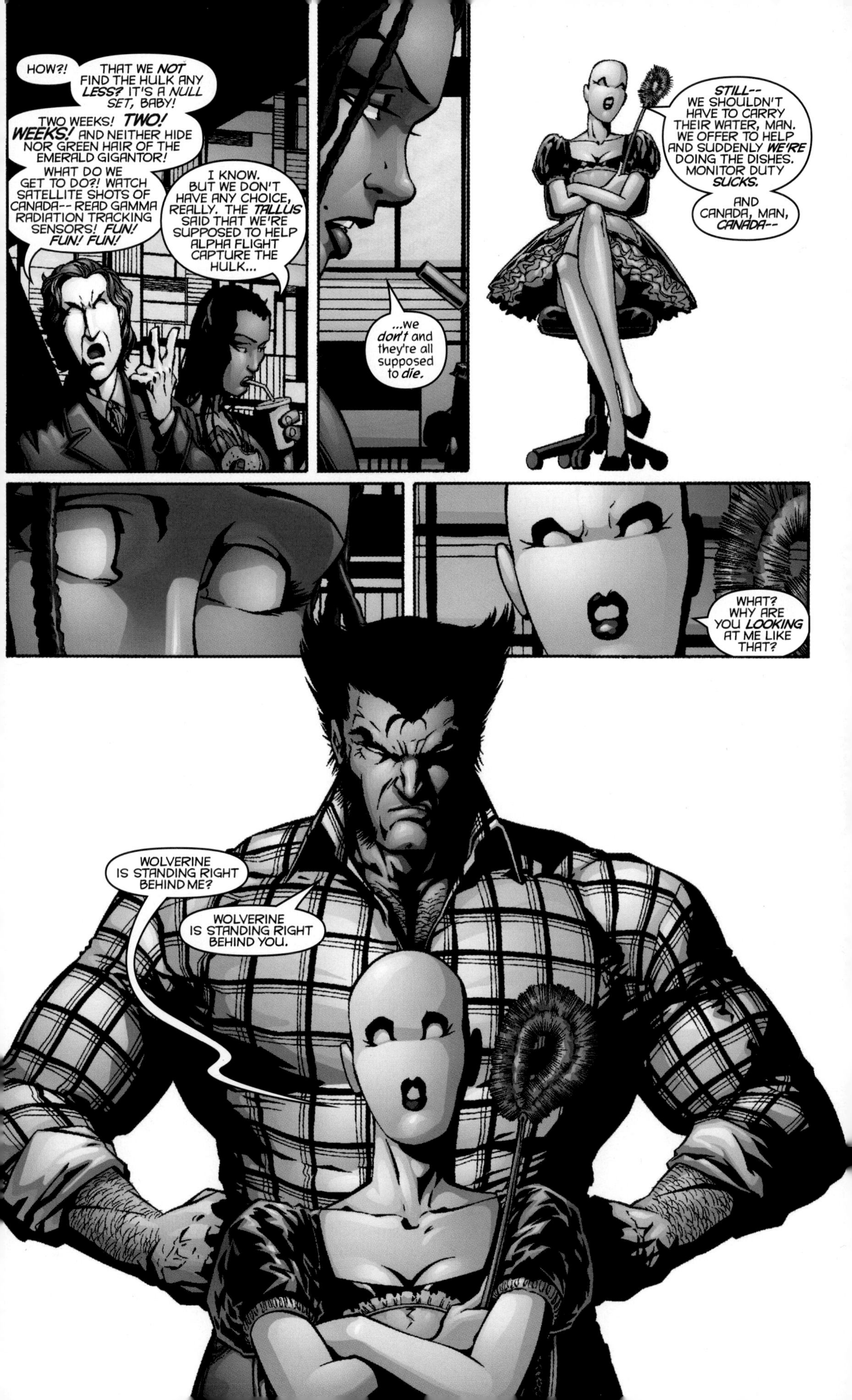
HOW?!
THAT WE NOT FIND THE HULK ANY LESS? IT'S A NULL SET, BABY!
TWO WEEKS! TWO! WEEKS! AND NEITHER HIDE NOR GREEN HAIR OF THE EMERALD GIGANTOR!
WHAT DO WE GET TO DO?! WATCH SATELLITE SHOTS OF CANADA-- READ GAMMA RADIATION TRACKING SENSORS! FUN! FUN! FUN!
I KNOW. BUT WE DON'T HAVE ANY CHOICE, REALLY. THE TALLUS SAID THAT WE'RE SUPPOSED TO HELP ALPHA FLIGHT CAPTURE THE HULK...
...we don't and they're all supposed to die.
STILL-- WE SHOULDN'T HAVE TO CARRY THEIR WATER, MAN. WE OFFER TO HELP AND SUDDENLY WE'RE DOING THE DISHES. MONITOR DUTY SUCKS.
AND CANADA, MAN, CANADA--
WHAT? WHY ARE YOU LOOKING AT ME LIKE THAT?
WOLVERINE IS STANDING RIGHT BEHIND ME?
WOLVERINE IS STANDING RIGHT BEHIND YOU.

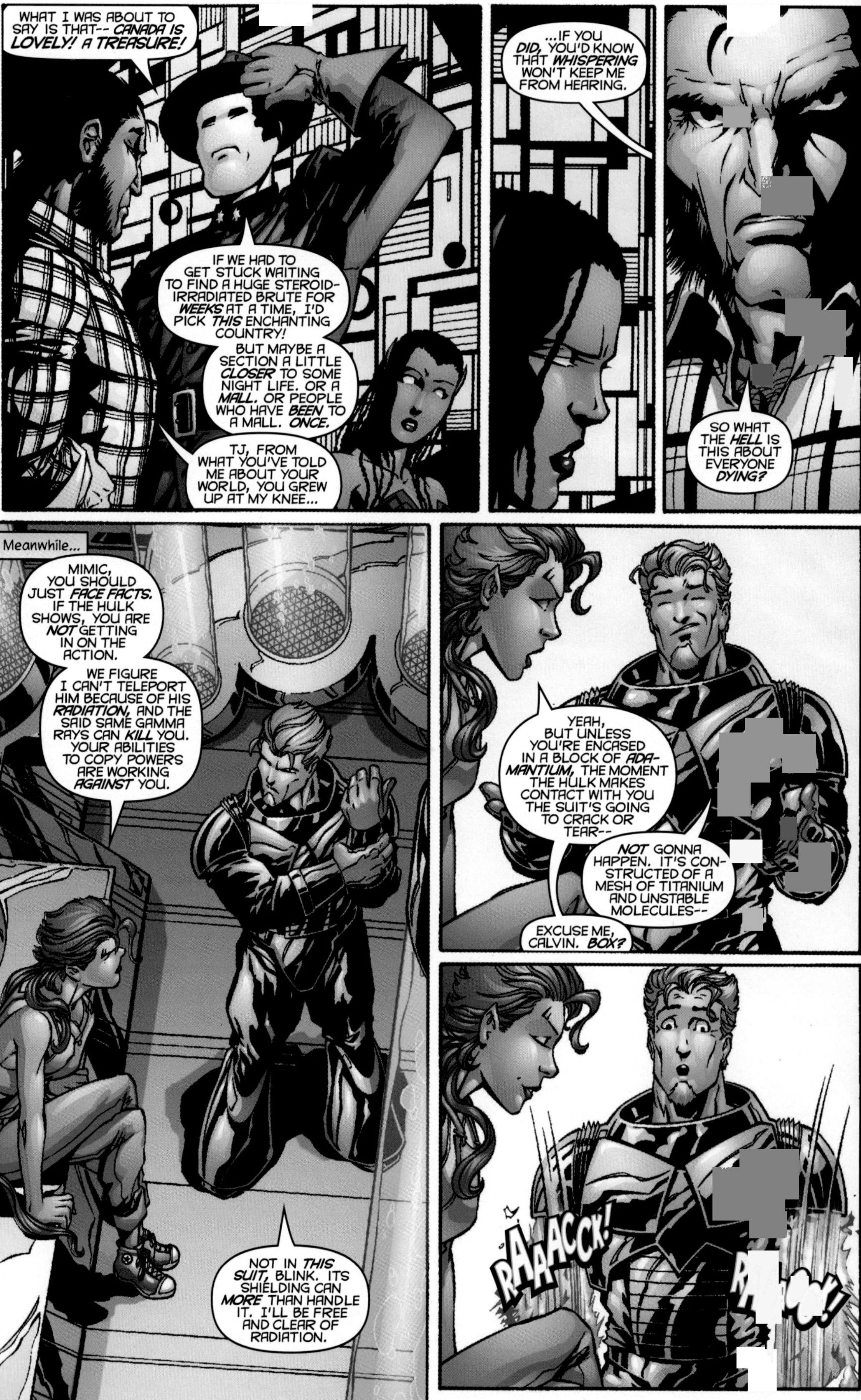
WHAT I WAS ABOUT TO SAY IS THAT-- CANADA IS LOVELY! A TREASURE!
IF WE HAD TO GET STUCK WAITING TO FIND A HUGE STEROID-IRRADIATED BRUTE FOR WEEKS AT A TIME, I'D PICK THIS ENCHANTING COUNTRY!
BUT MAYBE A SECTION A LITTLE CLOSER TO SOME NIGHT LIFE. OR A MALL. OR PEOPLE WHO HAVE BEEN TO A MALL. ONCE.
TJ, FROM WHAT YOU'VE TOLD ME ABOUT YOUR WORLD, YOU GREW UP AT MY KNEE...
...IF YOU DID, YOU'D KNOW THAT WHISPERING WON'T KEEP ME FROM HEARING.
SO WHAT THE HELL IS THIS ABOUT EVERYONE DYING?
Meanwhile...
MIMIC, YOU SHOULD JUST FACE FACTS. IF THE HULK SHOWS, YOU ARE NOT GETTING IN ON THE ACTION.
WE FIGURE I CAN'T TELEPORT HIM BECAUSE OF HIS RADIATION, AND THE SAID SAME GAMMA RAYS CAN KILL YOU. YOUR ABILITIES TO COPY POWERS ARE WORKING AGAINST YOU.
NOT IN THIS SUIT, BLINK. ITS SHIELDING CAN MORE THAN HANDLE IT. I'LL BE FREE AND CLEAR OF RADIATION.
YEAH, BUT UNLESS YOU'RE ENCASED IN A BLOCK OF ADAMANTIUM, THE MOMENT THE HULK MAKES CONTACT WITH YOU THE SUIT'S GOING TO CRACK OR TEAR--
NOT GONNA HAPPEN. IT'S CONSTRUCTED OF A MESH OF TITANIUM AND UNSTABLE MOLECULES--
EXCUSE ME, CALVIN. BOX?
RAAACCK!

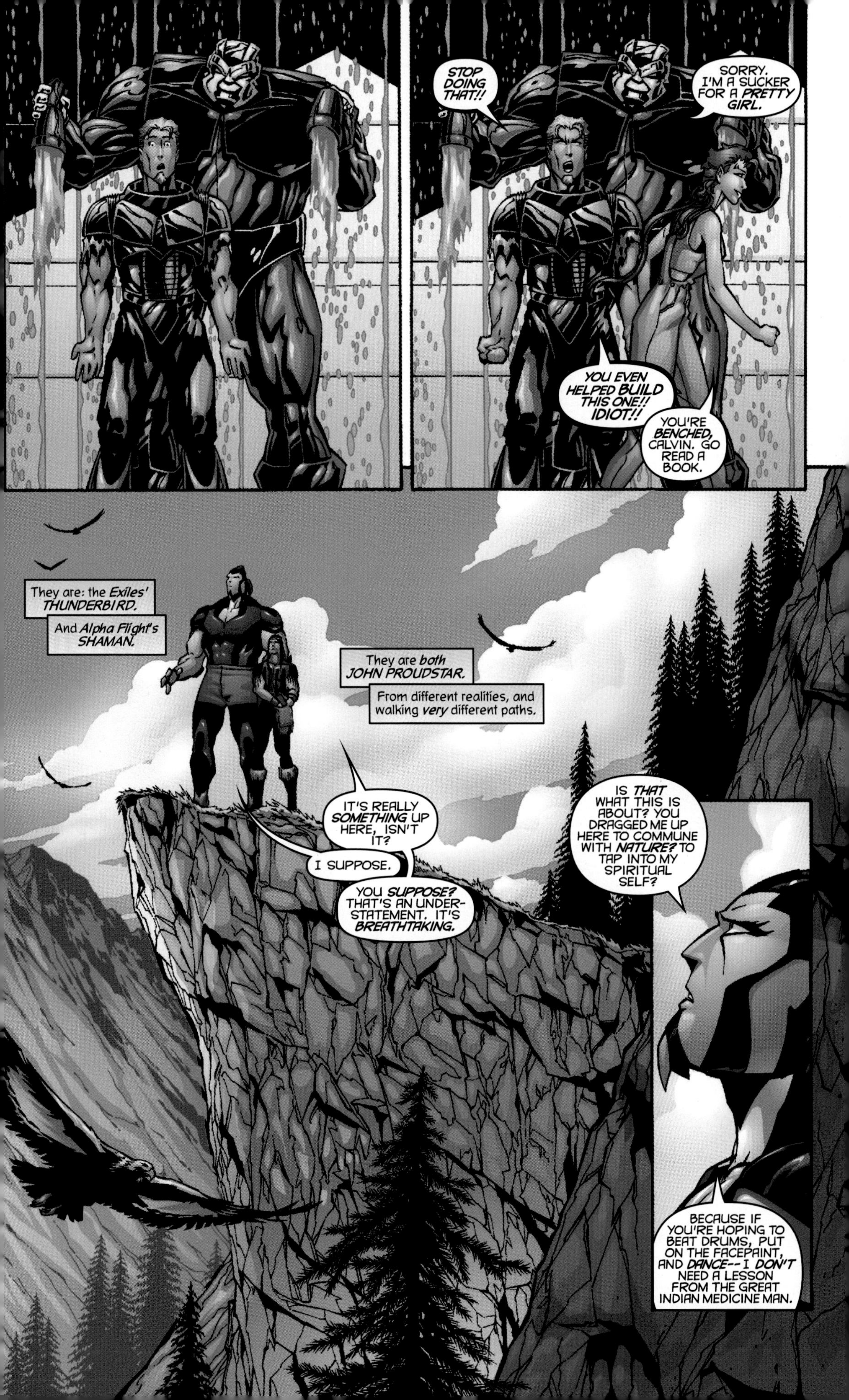
STOP DOING THAT!!
SORRY. I'M A SUCKER FOR A PRETTY GIRL.
YOU EVEN HELPED BUILD THIS ONE!! IDIOT!!
YOU'RE BENCHED, CALVIN. GO READ A BOOK.
They are: the Exiles' THUNDERBIRD.
And Alpha Flight's SHAMAN.
They are both JOHN PROUDSTAR.
From different realities, and walking very different paths.
IT'S REALLY SOMETHING UP HERE, ISN'T IT?
I SUPPOSE.
YOU SUPPOSE? THAT'S AN UNDER-STATEMENT. IT'S BREATHTAKING.
IS THAT WHAT THIS IS ABOUT? YOU DRAGGED ME UP HERE TO COMMUNE WITH NATURE? TO TAP INTO MY SPIRITUAL SELF?
BECAUSE IF YOU'RE HOPING TO BEAT DRUMS, PUT ON THE FACEPAINT, AND DANCE-- I DON'T NEED A LESSON FROM THE GREAT INDIAN MEDICINE MAN.

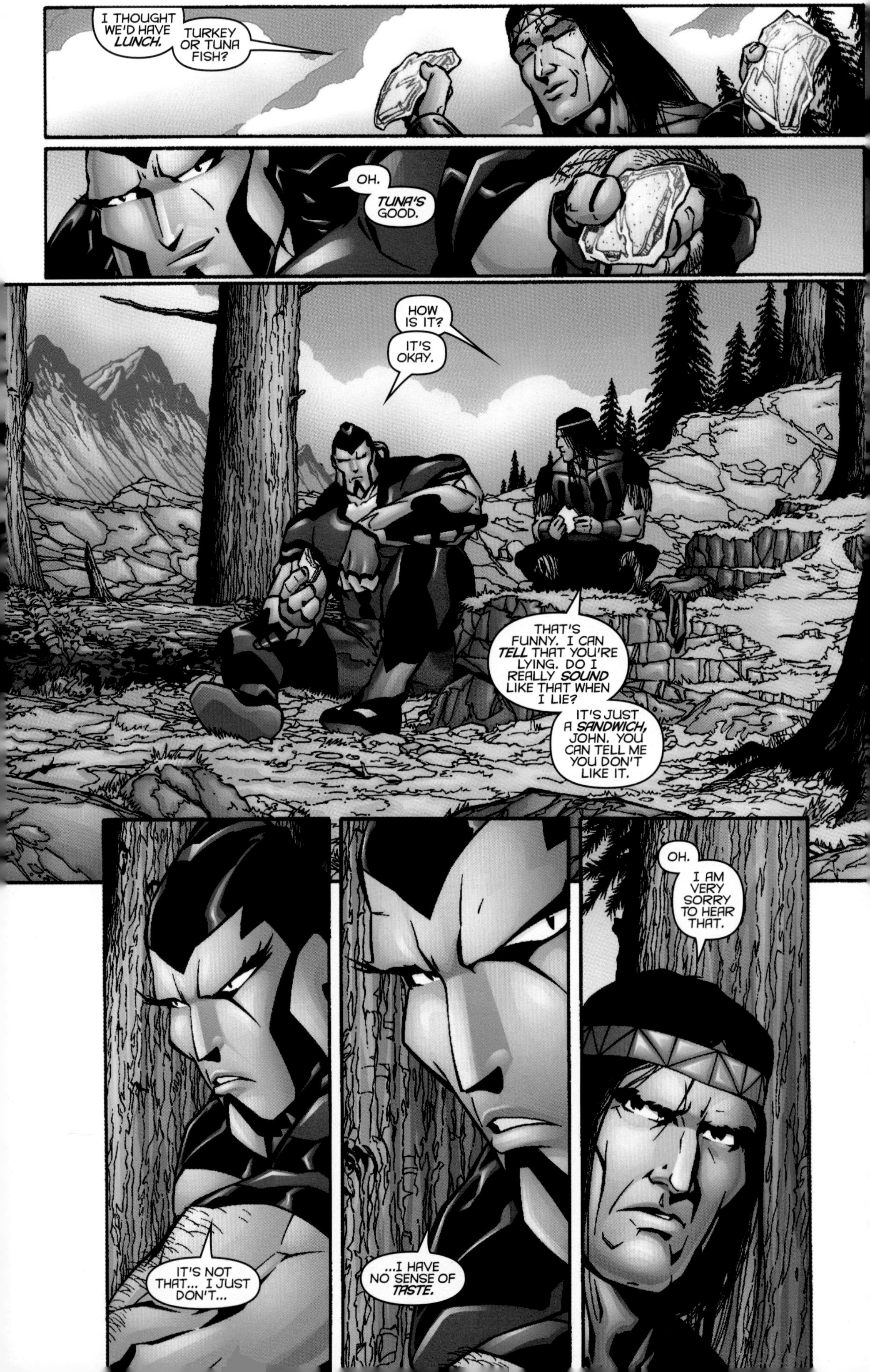
I THOUGHT WE'D HAVE LUNCH.
TURKEY OR TUNA FISH?
OH. TUNA'S GOOD.
HOW IS IT?
IT'S OKAY.
THAT'S FUNNY. I CAN TELL THAT YOU'RE LYING. DO I REALLY SOUND LIKE THAT WHEN I LIE?
IT'S JUST A SANDWICH, JOHN. YOU CAN TELL ME YOU DON'T LIKE IT.
IT'S NOT THAT... I JUST DON'T...
...I HAVE NO SENSE OF TASTE.
OH.
I AM VERY SORRY TO HEAR THAT.

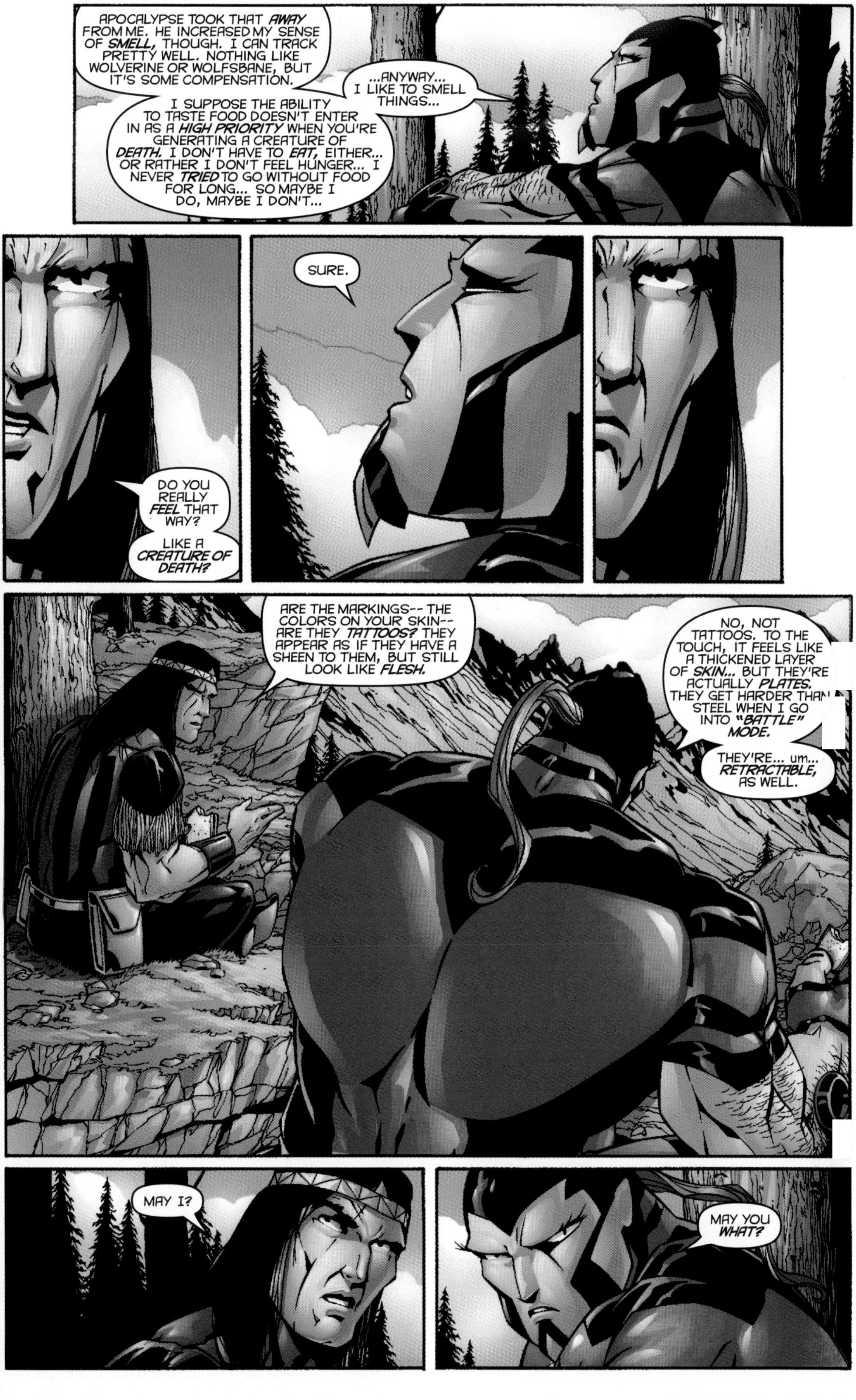
APOCALYPSE TOOK THAT AWAY FROM ME. HE INCREASED MY SENSE OF SMELL, THOUGH. I CAN TRACK PRETTY WELL. NOTHING LIKE WOLVERINE OR WOLFSBANE, BUT IT'S SOME COMPENSATION.
I SUPPOSE THE ABILITY TO TASTE FOOD DOESN'T ENTER IN AS A HIGH PRIORITY WHEN YOU'RE GENERATING A CREATURE OF DEATH. I DON'T HAVE TO EAT, EITHER... OR RATHER I DON'T FEEL HUNGER... I NEVER TRIED TO GO WITHOUT FOOD FOR LONG... SO MAYBE I DO, MAYBE I DON'T...
...ANYWAY... I LIKE TO SMELL THINGS...
DO YOU REALLY FEEL THAT WAY?
LIKE A CREATURE OF DEATH?
SURE.
ARE THE MARKINGS-- THE COLORS ON YOUR SKIN-- ARE THEY TATTOOS? THEY APPEAR AS IF THEY HAVE A SHEEN TO THEM, BUT STILL LOOK LIKE FLESH.
NO, NOT TATTOOS. TO THE TOUCH, IT FEELS LIKE A THICKENED LAYER OF SKIN... BUT THEY'RE ACTUALLY PLATES. THEY GET HARDER THAN STEEL WHEN I GO INTO "BATTLE" MODE.
THEY'RE... um... RETRACTABLE, AS WELL.
MAY I?
MAY YOU WHAT?

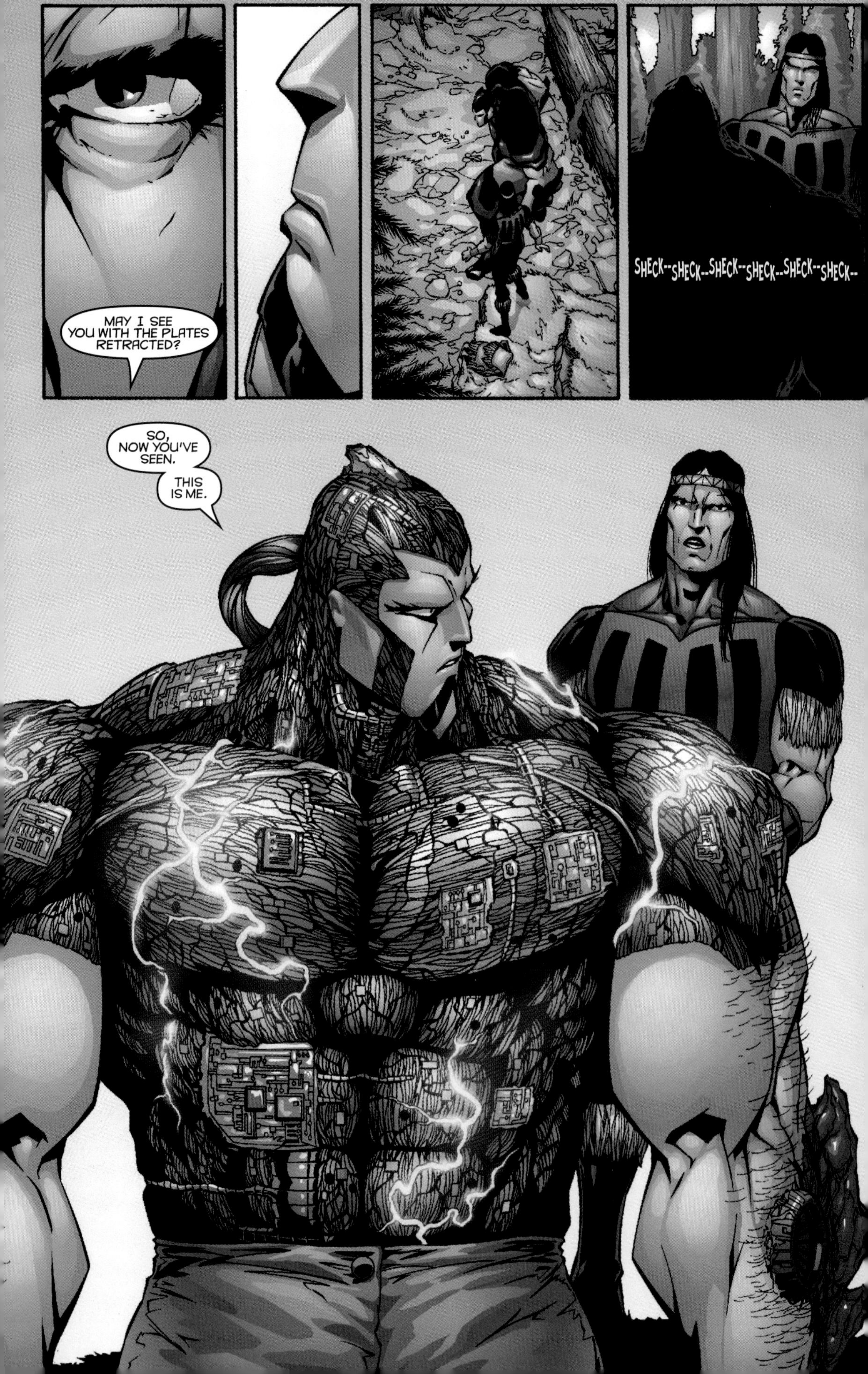
MAY I SEE YOU WITH THE PLATES RETRACTED?
SHECK--SHECK--SHECK--SHECK--SHECK--SHECK--
SO, NOW YOU'VE SEEN.
THIS IS ME.

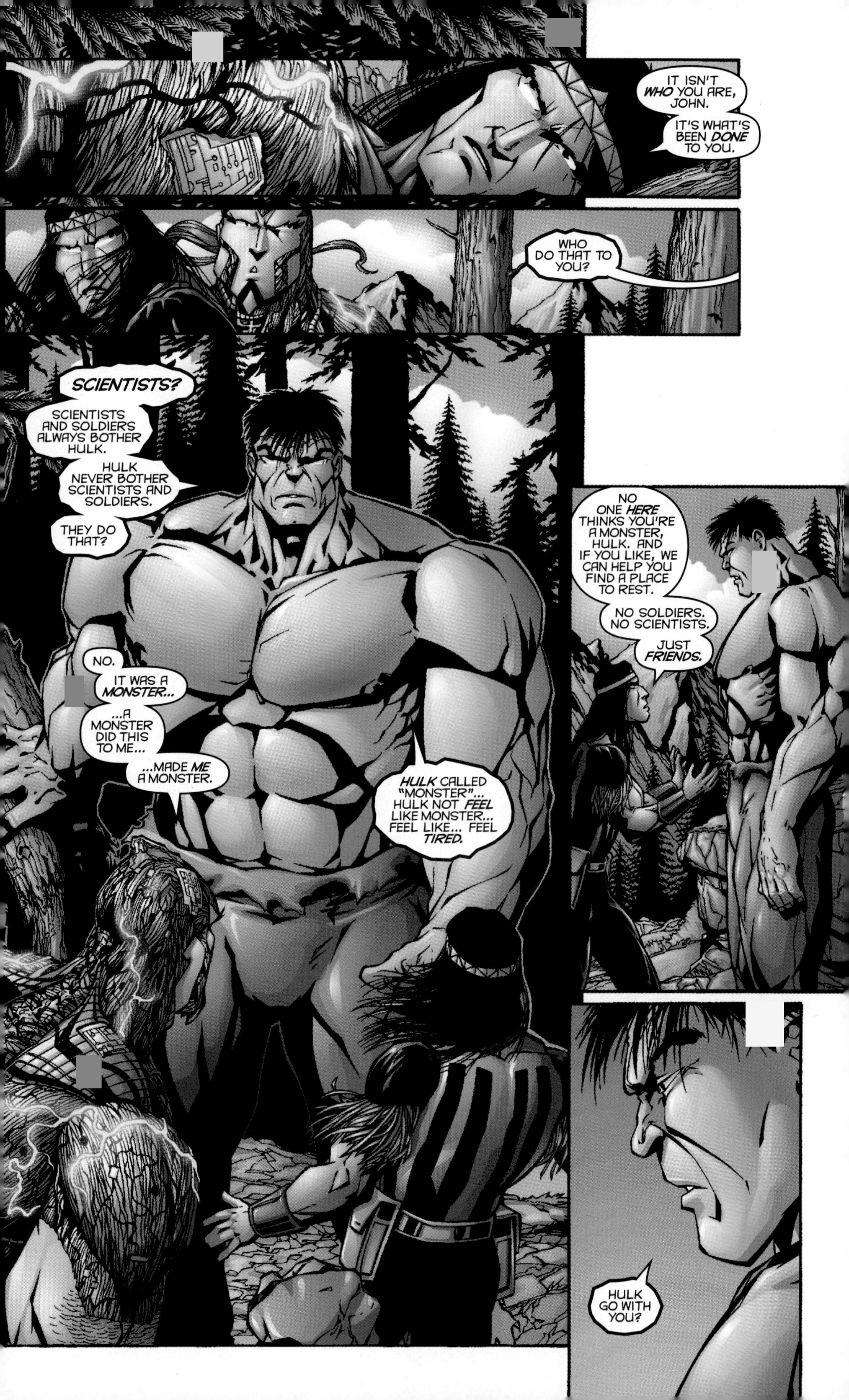
IT ISN'T WHO YOU ARE, JOHN.
IT'S WHAT'S BEEN DONE TO YOU.
WHO DO THAT TO YOU?
SCIENTISTS?
SCIENTISTS AND SOLDIERS ALWAYS BOTHER HULK.
HULK NEVER BOTHER SCIENTISTS AND SOLDIERS.
THEY DO THAT?
NO.
IT WAS A MONSTER...
...A MONSTER DID THIS TO ME...
...MADE ME A MONSTER.
HULK CALLED "MONSTER"... HULK NOT FEEL LIKE MONSTER... FEEL LIKE... FEEL TIRED.
NO ONE HERE THINKS YOU'RE A MONSTER, HULK. AND IF YOU LIKE, WE CAN HELP YOU FIND A PLACE TO REST.
NO SOLDIERS. NO SCIENTISTS.
JUST FRIENDS.
HULK GO WITH YOU?

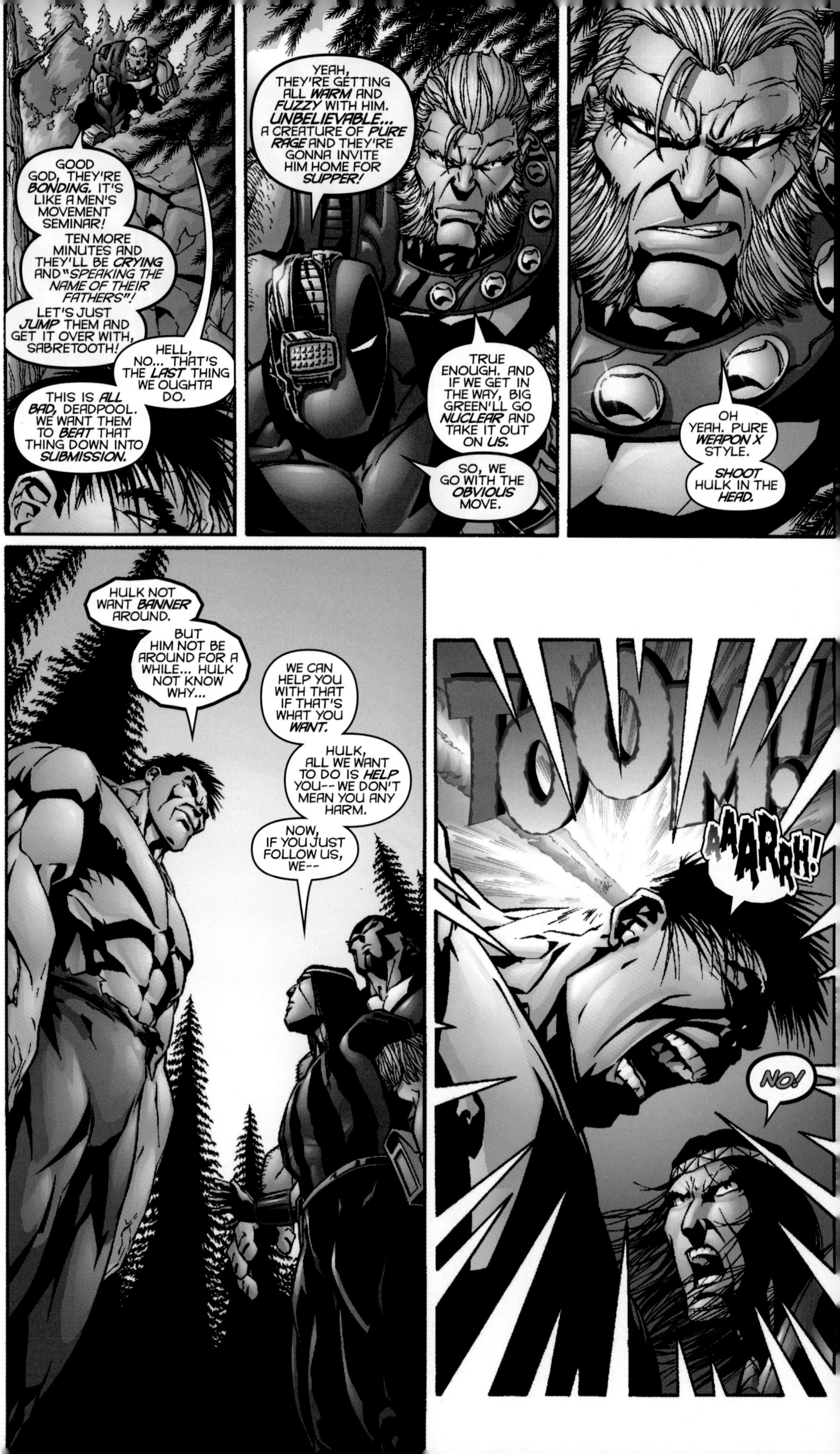
GOOD GOD, THEY'RE BONDING. IT'S LIKE A MEN'S MOVEMENT SEMINAR!
TEN MORE MINUTES AND THEY'LL BE CRYING AND "SPEAKING THE NAME OF THEIR FATHERS"!
LET'S JUST JUMP THEM AND GET IT OVER WITH, SABRETOOTH!
HELL, NO... THAT'S THE LAST THING WE OUGHTA DO.
THIS IS ALL BAD, DEADPOOL. WE WANT THEM TO BEAT THAT THING DOWN INTO SUBMISSION.
YEAH, THEY'RE GETTING ALL WARM AND FUZZY WITH HIM. UNBELIEVABLE... A CREATURE OF PURE RAGE AND THEY'RE GONNA INVITE HIM HOME FOR SUPPER!
TRUE ENOUGH. AND IF WE GET IN THE WAY, BIG GREEN'LL GO NUCLEAR AND TAKE IT OUT ON US.
SO, WE GO WITH THE OBVIOUS MOVE.
OH YEAH. PURE WEAPON X STYLE.
SHOOT HULK IN THE HEAD.
HULK NOT WANT BANNER AROUND.
BUT HIM NOT BE AROUND FOR A WHILE... HULK NOT KNOW WHY...
WE CAN HELP YOU WITH THAT IF THAT'S WHAT YOU WANT.
HULK, ALL WE WANT TO DO IS HELP YOU-- WE DON'T MEAN YOU ANY HARM.
NOW, IF YOU JUST FOLLOW US, WE--
TOOM!
AAARRH!
NO!

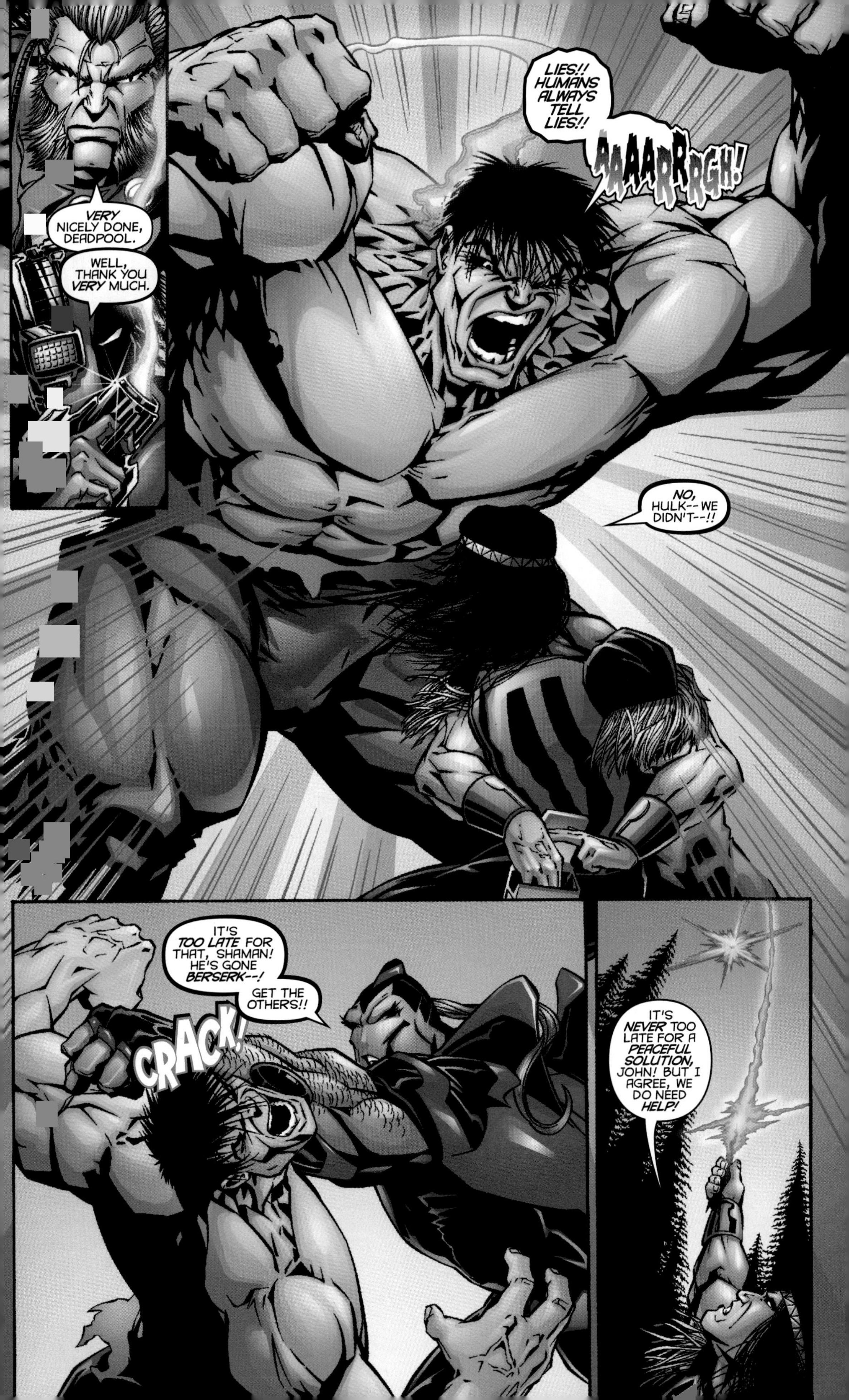
VERY NICELY DONE, DEADPOOL.
WELL, THANK YOU VERY MUCH.
LIES!! HUMANS ALWAYS TELL LIES!!
AAAARRRGH!
NO, HULK-- WE DIDN'T--!!
IT'S TOO LATE FOR THAT, SHAMAN! HE'S GONE BERSERK--!
GET THE OTHERS!!
CRACK!
IT'S NEVER TOO LATE FOR A PEACEFUL SOLUTION, JOHN! BUT I AGREE, WE DO NEED HELP!

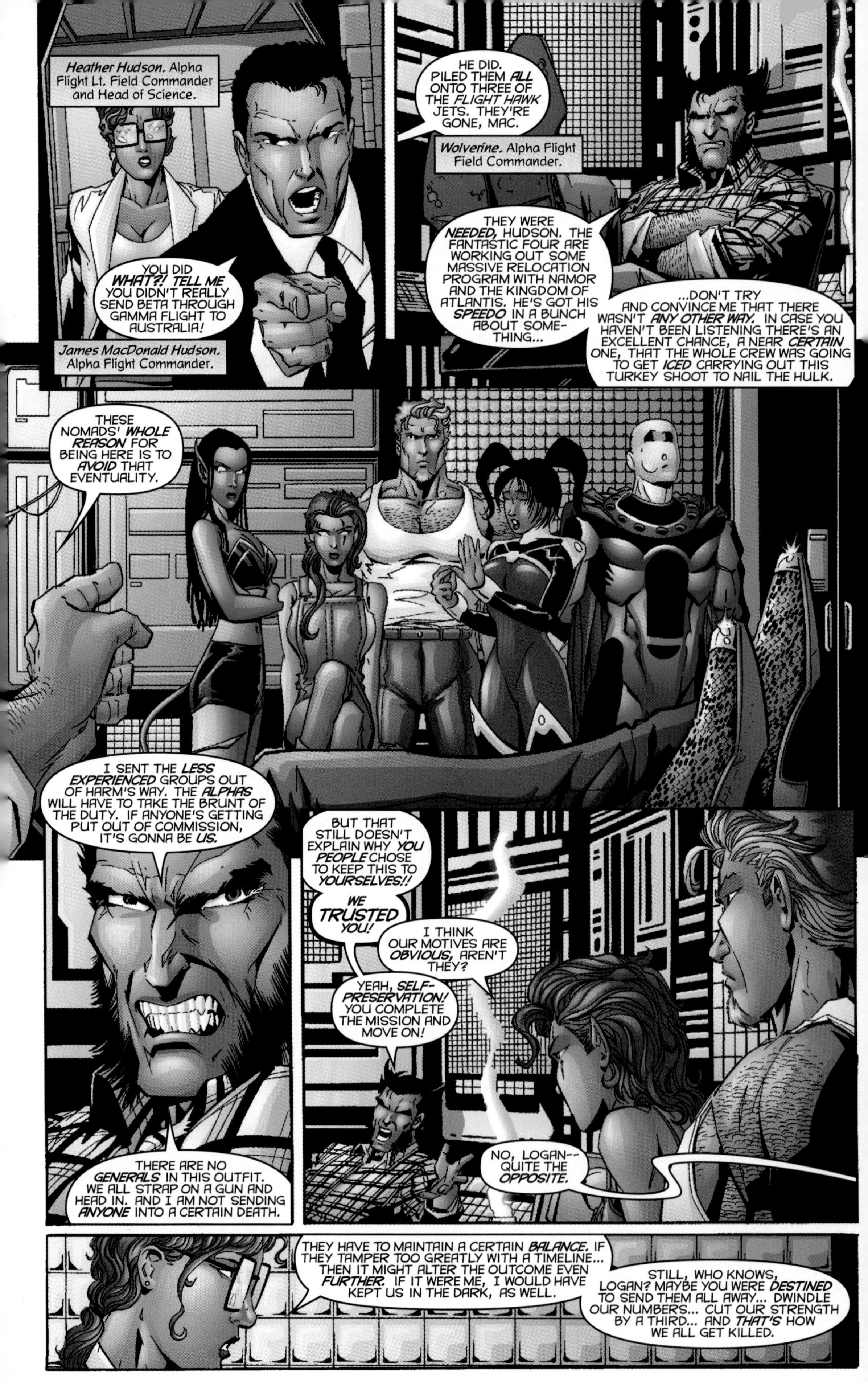
Heather Hudson. Alpha Flight Lt. Field Commander and Head of Science.
YOU DID WHAT?! TELL ME YOU DIDN'T REALLY SEND BETA THROUGH GAMMA FLIGHT TO AUSTRALIA!
James MacDonald Hudson. Alpha Flight Commander.
HE DID. PILED THEM ALL ONTO THREE OF THE FLIGHT HAWK JETS. THEY'RE GONE, MAC.
Wolverine. Alpha Flight Field Commander.
THEY WERE NEEDED, HUDSON. THE FANTASTIC FOUR ARE WORKING OUT SOME MASSIVE RELOCATION PROGRAM WITH NAMOR AND THE KINGDOM OF ATLANTIS. HE'S GOT HIS SPEEDO IN A BUNCH ABOUT SOME-THING...
...DON'T TRY AND CONVINCE ME THAT THERE WASN'T ANY OTHER WAY. IN CASE YOU HAVEN'T BEEN LISTENING THERE'S AN EXCELLENT CHANCE, A NEAR CERTAIN ONE, THAT THE WHOLE CREW WAS GOING TO GET ICED CARRYING OUT THIS TURKEY SHOOT TO NAIL THE HULK.
THESE NOMADS' WHOLE REASON FOR BEING HERE IS TO AVOID THAT EVENTUALITY.
I SENT THE LESS EXPERIENCED GROUPS OUT OF HARM'S WAY. THE ALPHAS WILL HAVE TO TAKE THE BRUNT OF THE DUTY. IF ANYONE'S GETTING PUT OUT OF COMMISSION, IT'S GONNA BE US.
THERE ARE NO GENERALS IN THIS OUTFIT. WE ALL STRAP ON A GUN AND HEAD IN. AND I AM NOT SENDING ANYONE INTO A CERTAIN DEATH.
BUT THAT STILL DOESN'T EXPLAIN WHY YOU PEOPLE CHOSE TO KEEP THIS TO YOURSELVES!!
WE TRUSTED YOU!
I THINK OUR MOTIVES ARE OBVIOUS, AREN'T THEY?
YEAH, SELF-PRESERVATION! YOU COMPLETE THE MISSION AND MOVE ON!
NO, LOGAN-- QUITE THE OPPOSITE.
THEY HAVE TO MAINTAIN A CERTAIN BALANCE. IF THEY TAMPER TOO GREATLY WITH A TIMELINE... THEN IT MIGHT ALTER THE OUTCOME EVEN FURTHER. IF IT WERE ME, I WOULD HAVE KEPT US IN THE DARK, AS WELL.
STILL, WHO KNOWS, LOGAN? MAYBE YOU WERE DESTINED TO SEND THEM ALL AWAY... DWINDLE OUR NUMBERS... CUT OUR STRENGTH BY A THIRD... AND THAT'S HOW WE ALL GET KILLED.

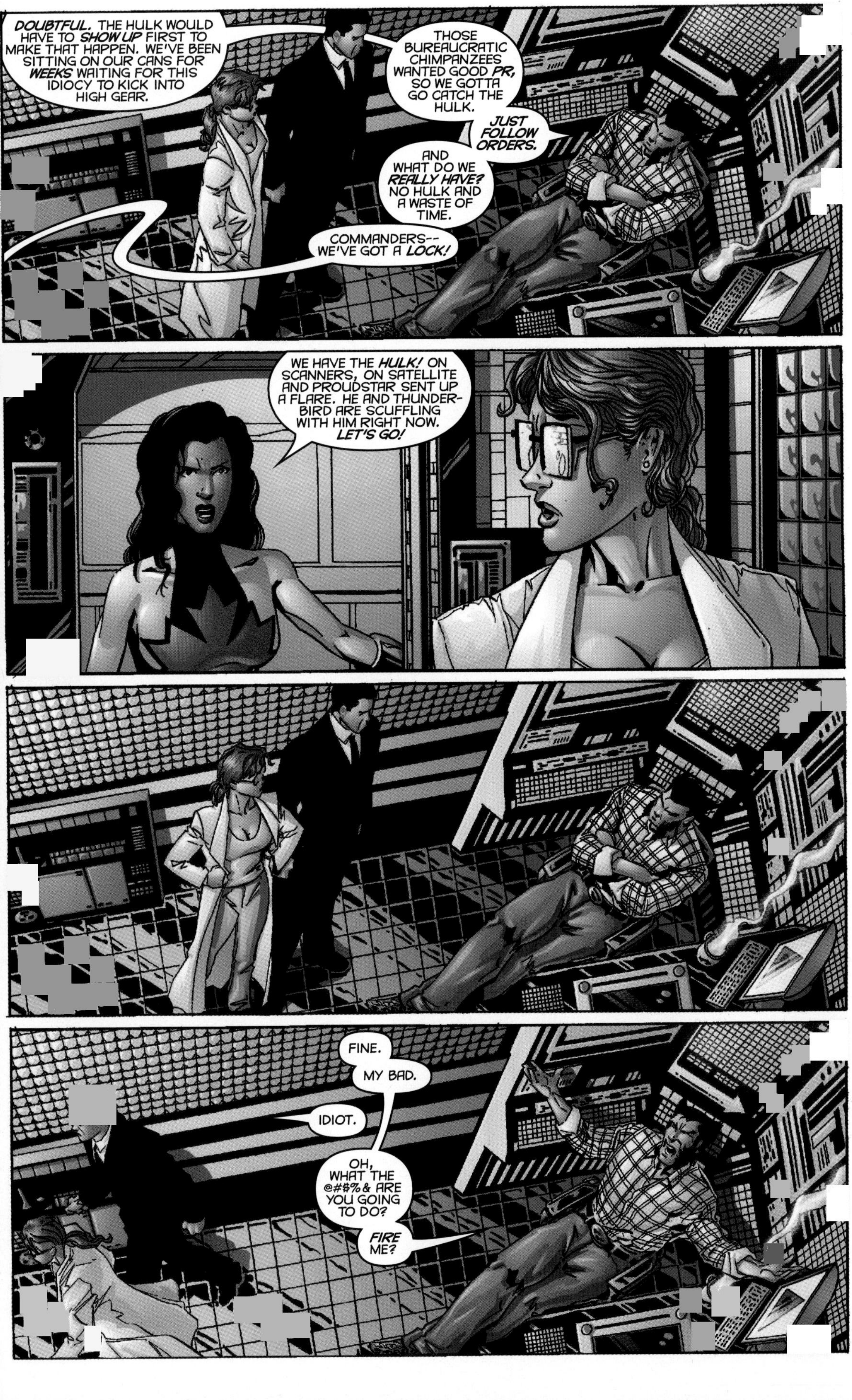
DOUBTFUL. THE HULK WOULD HAVE TO SHOW UP FIRST TO MAKE THAT HAPPEN. WE'VE BEEN SITTING ON OUR CANS FOR WEEKS WAITING FOR THIS IDIOCY TO KICK INTO HIGH GEAR.
THOSE BUREAUCRATIC CHIMPANZEES WANTED GOOD PR, SO WE GOTTA GO CATCH THE HULK.
JUST FOLLOW ORDERS.
AND WHAT DO WE REALLY HAVE? NO HULK AND A WASTE OF TIME.
COMMANDERS-- WE'VE GOT A LOCK!
WE HAVE THE HULK! ON SCANNERS, ON SATELLITE AND PROUDSTAR SENT UP A FLARE. HE AND THUNDER-BIRD ARE SCUFFLING WITH HIM RIGHT NOW. LET'S GO!
FINE.
MY BAD.
IDIOT.
OH, WHAT THE @#$%& ARE YOU GOING TO DO?
FIRE ME?

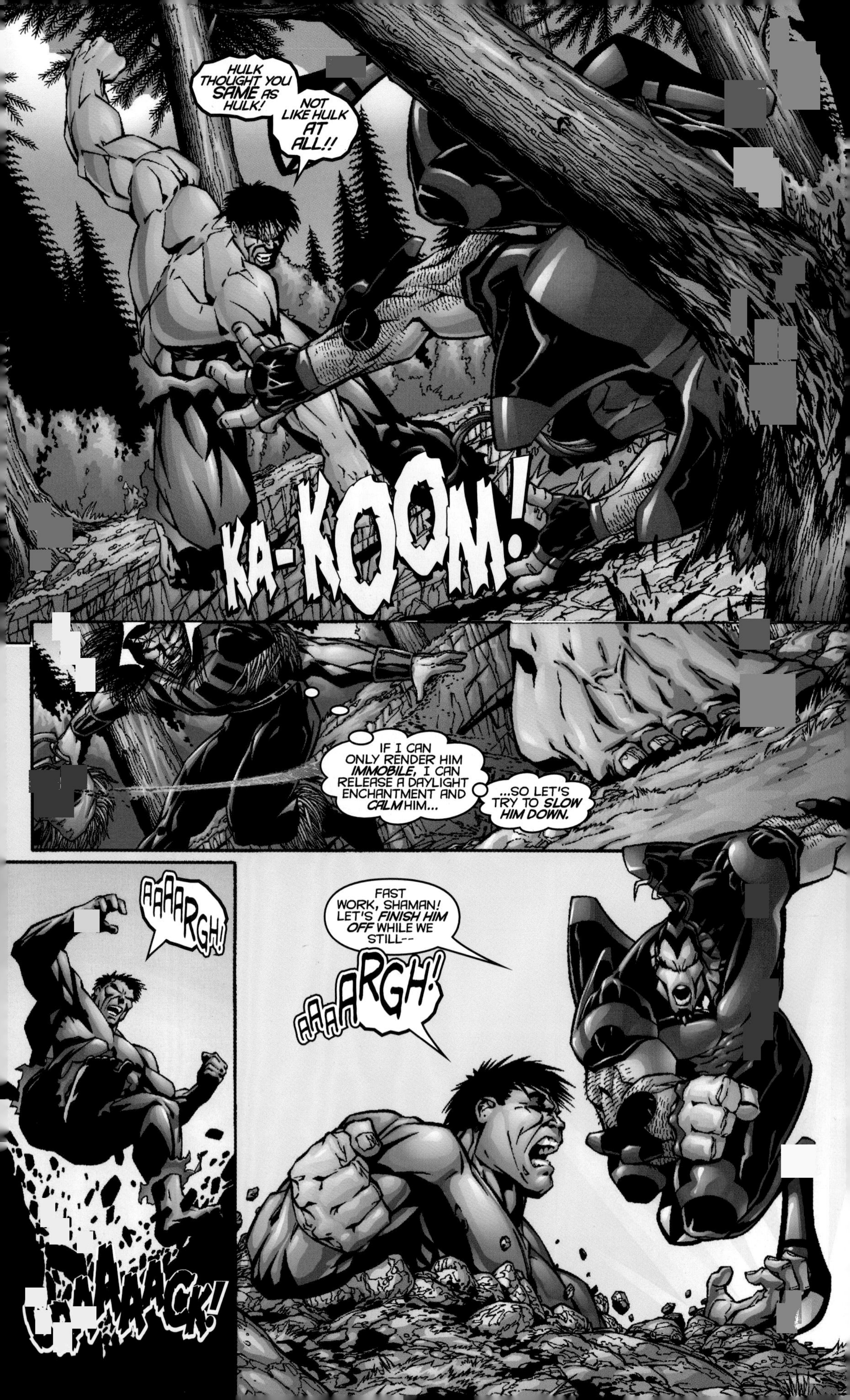
HULK THOUGHT YOU SAME AS HULK!
NOT LIKE HULK AT ALL!!
KA-KOOM!
IF I CAN ONLY RENDER HIM IMMOBILE, I CAN RELEASE A DAYLIGHT ENCHANTMENT AND CALM HIM...
...SO LET'S TRY TO SLOW HIM DOWN.
AAAARGH!
FAST WORK, SHAMAN! LET'S FINISH HIM OFF WHILE WE STILL--
AAAARGH!

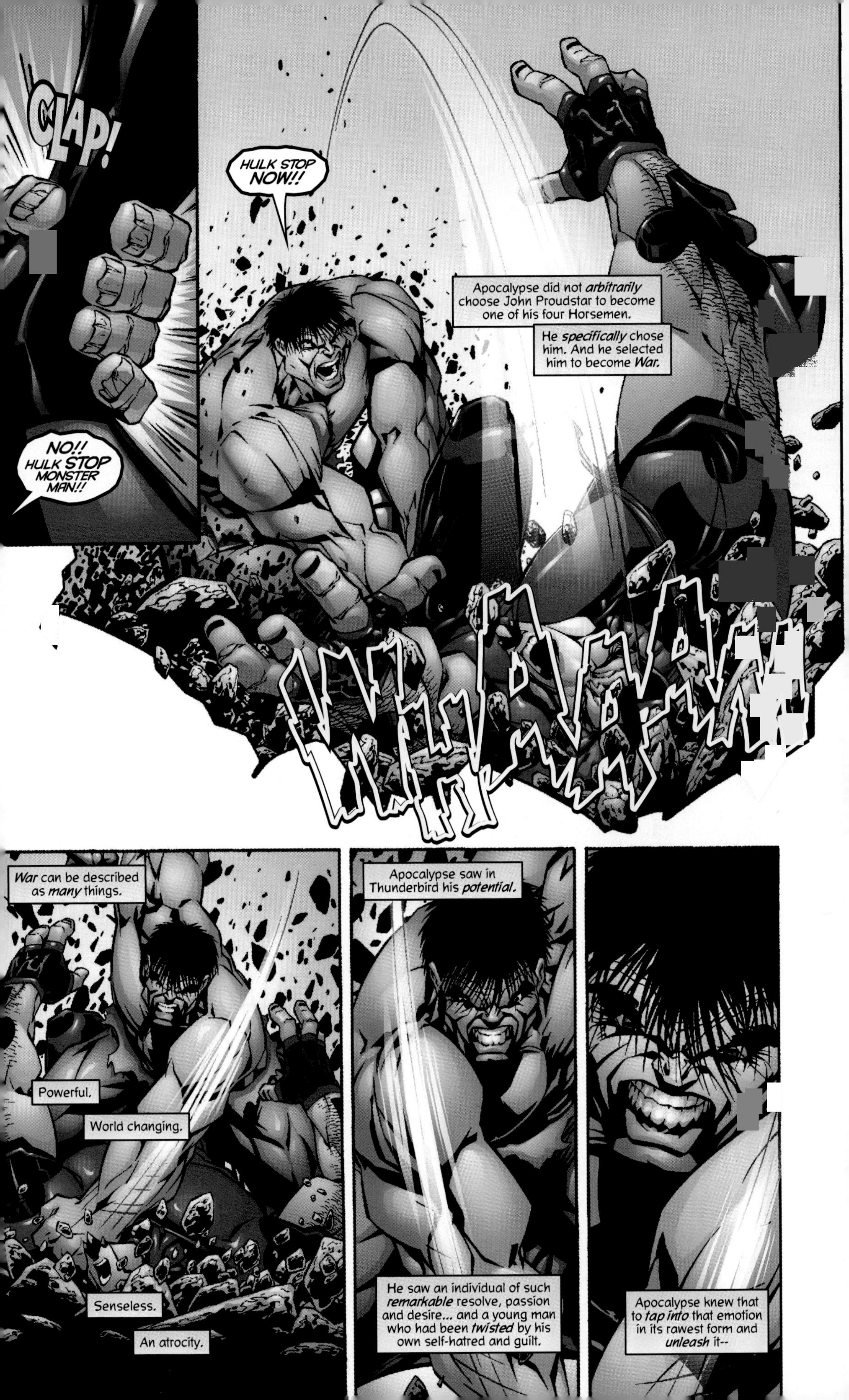
CLAP!
NO!! HULK STOP MONSTER MAN!!
HULK STOP NOW!!
Apocalypse did not arbitrarily choose John Proudstar to become one of his four Horsemen.
He specifically chose him. And he selected him to become War.
War can be described as many things.
Powerful.
World changing.
Senseless.
An atrocity.
Apocalypse saw in Thunderbird his potential.
He saw an individual of such remarkable resolve, passion and desire... and a young man who had been twisted by his own self-hatred and guilt.
Apocalypse knew that to tap into that emotion in its rawest form and unleash it--

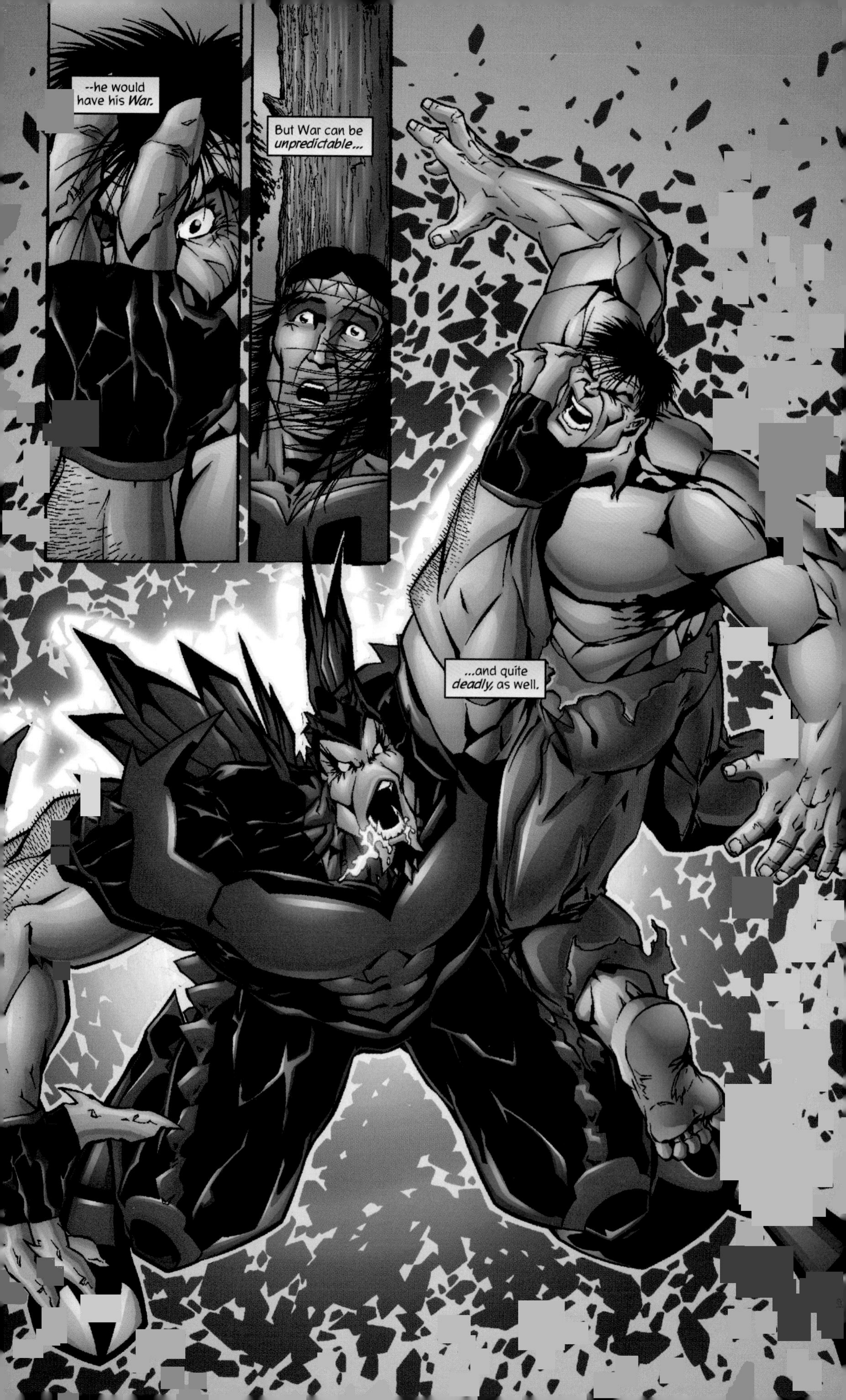
--he would have his *War.*
But War can be *unpredictable...*
...and quite *deadly,* as well.

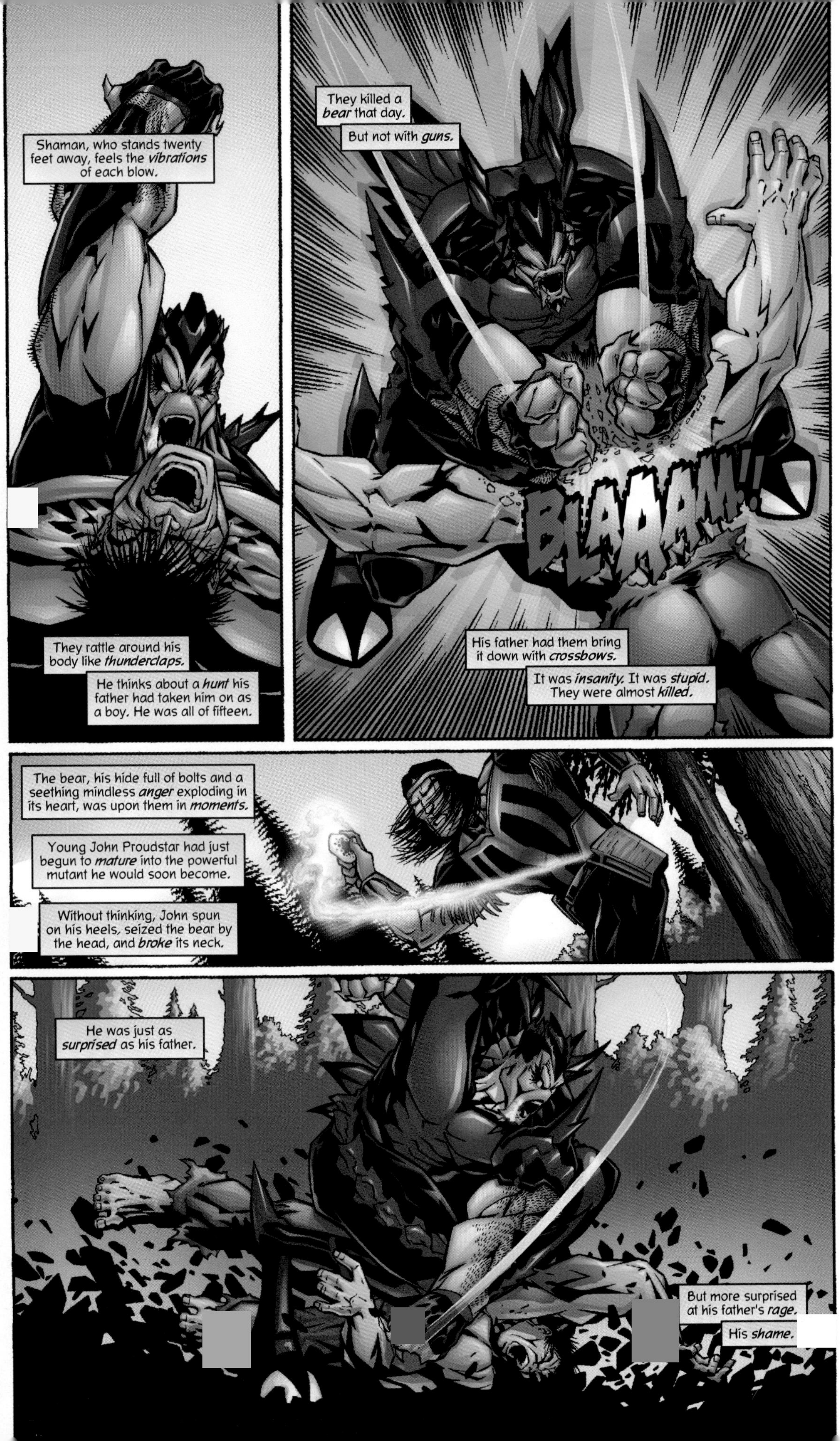
Shaman, who stands twenty feet away, feels the *vibrations* of each blow.
They rattle around his body like *thunderclaps.*
He thinks about a *hunt* his father had taken him on as a boy. He was all of fifteen.
They killed a *bear* that day.
But not with *guns.*
BLAAAM!!
His father had them bring it down with *crossbows.*
It was *insanity.* It was *stupid.* They were almost *killed.*
The bear, his hide full of bolts and a seething mindless *anger* exploding in its heart, was upon them in *moments.*
Young John Proudstar had just begun to *mature* into the powerful mutant he would soon become.
Without thinking, John spun on his heels, seized the bear by the head, and *broke* its neck.
He was just as *surprised* as his father.
But more surprised at his father's *rage.*
His *shame.*

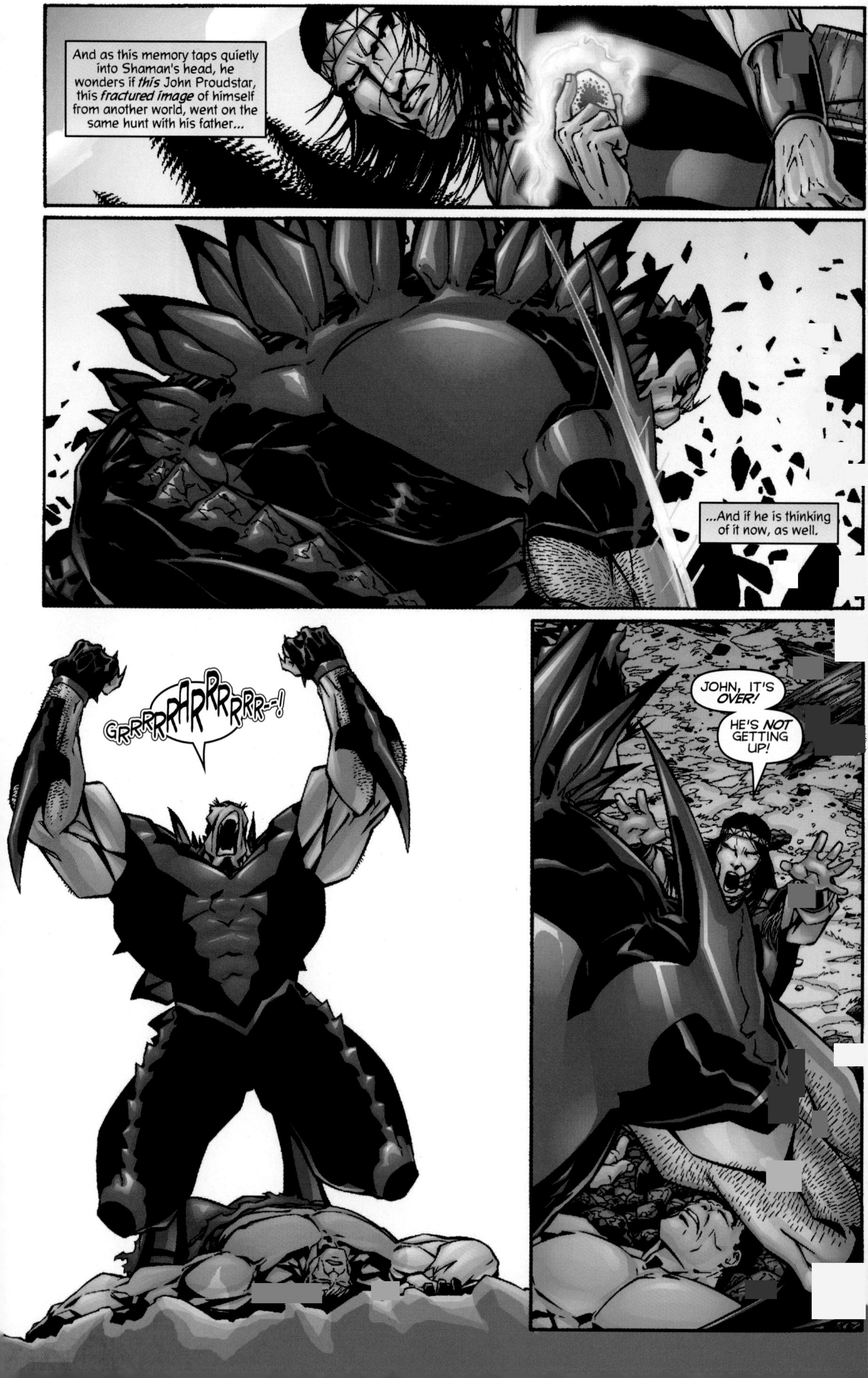
And as this memory taps quietly into Shaman's head, he wonders if *this* John Proudstar, this *fractured image* of himself from another world, went on the same hunt with his father...
...And if he is thinking of it now, as well.
GRRRRRARRRRRR--!
JOHN, IT'S *OVER!*
HE'S *NOT* GETTING UP!

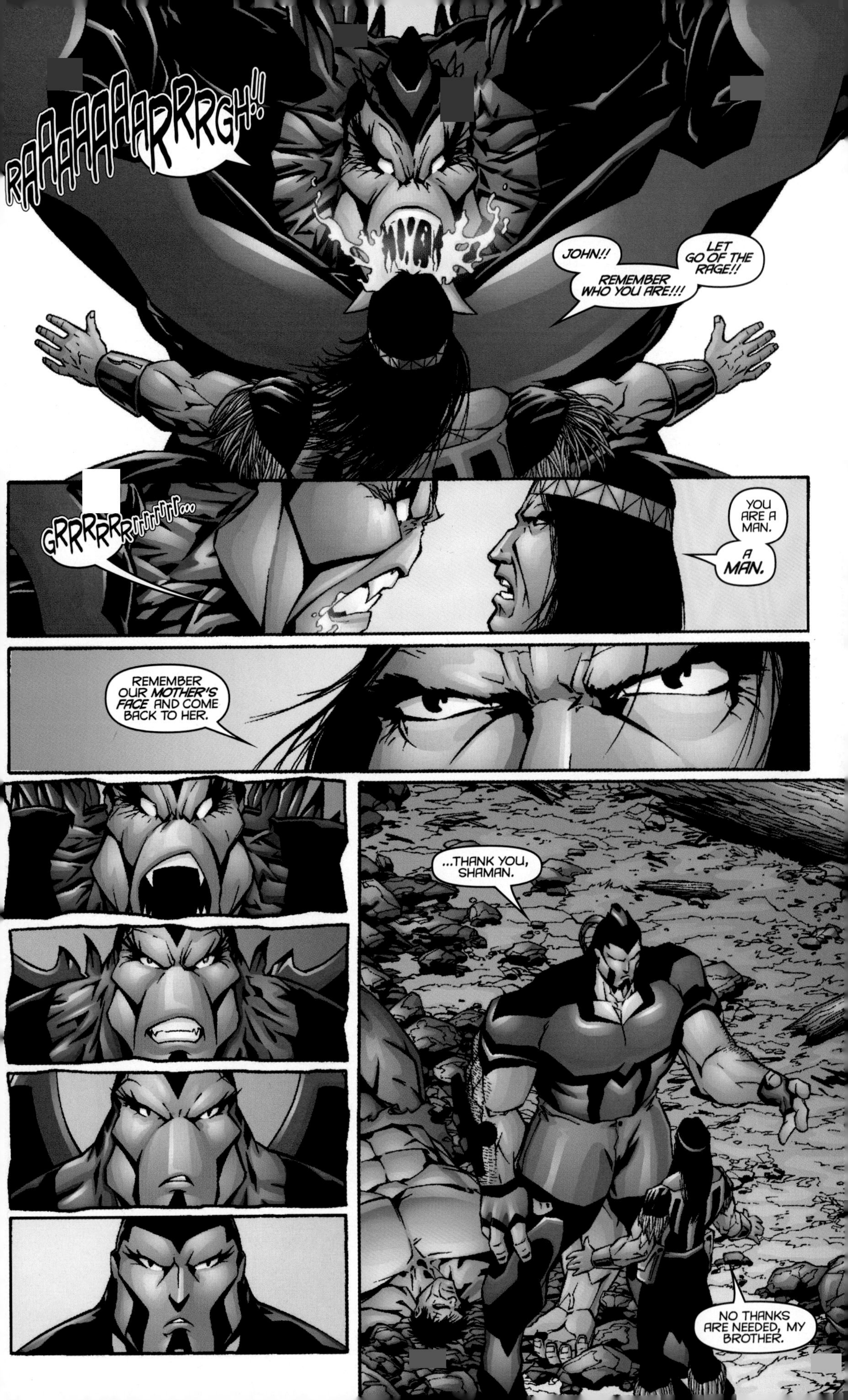

RAAAAAAARRRGH!!
JOHN!!
REMEMBER WHO YOU ARE!!!
LET GO OF THE RAGE!!
GRRRRRRrrrrrr...
YOU ARE A MAN.
A MAN.
REMEMBER OUR MOTHER'S FACE AND COME BACK TO HER.
...THANK YOU, SHAMAN.
NO THANKS ARE NEEDED, MY BROTHER.

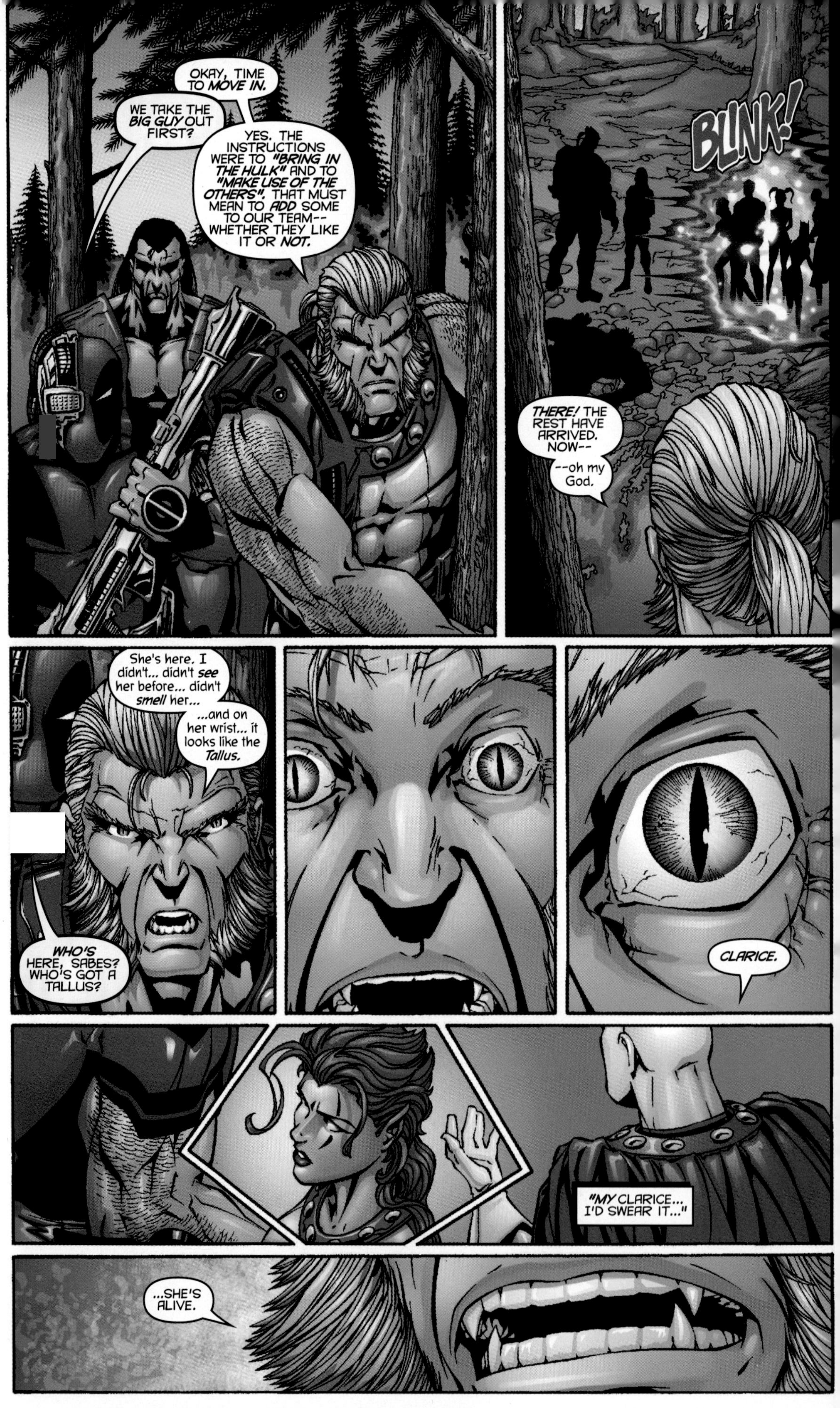
OKAY, TIME TO MOVE IN.
WE TAKE THE BIG GUY OUT FIRST?
YES. THE INSTRUCTIONS WERE TO "BRING IN THE HULK" AND TO "MAKE USE OF THE OTHERS". THAT MUST MEAN TO ADD SOME TO OUR TEAM-- WHETHER THEY LIKE IT OR NOT.
BLINK!
THERE! THE REST HAVE ARRIVED. NOW--
--oh my God.
She's here. I didn't... didn't see her before... didn't smell her...
...and on her wrist... it looks like the Tallus.
WHO'S HERE, SABES? WHO'S GOT A TALLUS?
CLARICE.
"MY CLARICE... I'D SWEAR IT..."
...SHE'S ALIVE.

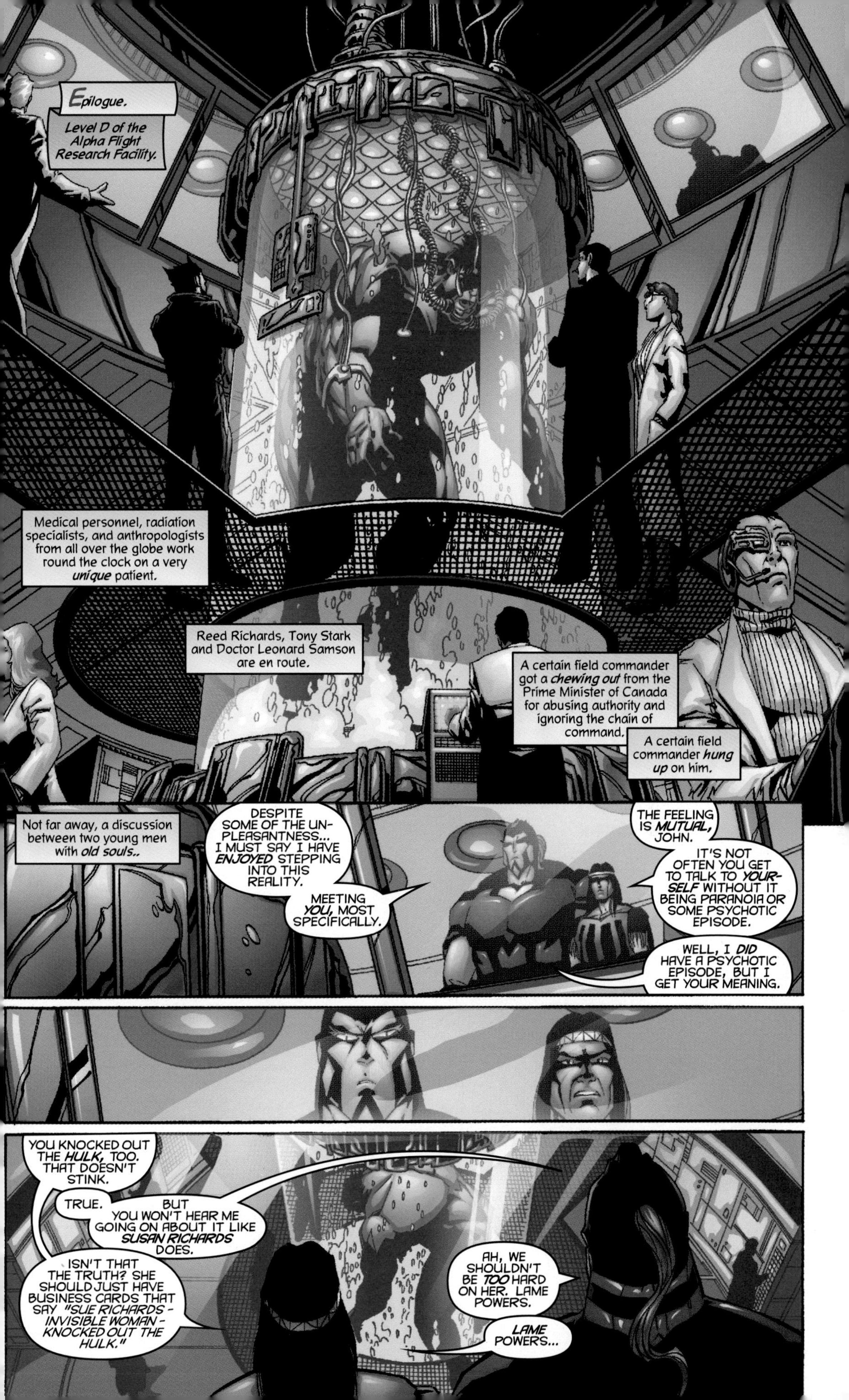
Epilogue.
Level D of the Alpha Flight Research Facility.
Medical personnel, radiation specialists, and anthropologists from all over the globe work round the clock on a very *unique* patient.
Reed Richards, Tony Stark and Doctor Leonard Samson are en route.
A certain field commander got a *chewing out* from the Prime Minister of Canada for abusing authority and ignoring the chain of command.
A certain field commander *hung up* on him.
Not far away, a discussion between two young men with *old souls..*
DESPITE SOME OF THE UNPLEASANTNESS... I MUST SAY I HAVE *ENJOYED* STEPPING INTO THIS REALITY.
MEETING *YOU,* MOST SPECIFICALLY.
THE FEELING IS *MUTUAL,* JOHN.
IT'S NOT OFTEN YOU GET TO TALK TO *YOURSELF* WITHOUT IT BEING PARANOIA OR SOME PSYCHOTIC EPISODE.
WELL, I *DID* HAVE A PSYCHOTIC EPISODE, BUT I GET YOUR MEANING.
YOU KNOCKED OUT THE *HULK,* TOO. THAT DOESN'T STINK.
TRUE.
BUT YOU WON'T HEAR ME GOING ON ABOUT IT LIKE *SUSAN RICHARDS* DOES.
ISN'T THAT THE TRUTH? SHE SHOULD JUST HAVE BUSINESS CARDS THAT SAY *"SUE RICHARDS - INVISIBLE WOMAN - KNOCKED OUT THE HULK."*
AH, WE SHOULDN'T BE *TOO* HARD ON HER. LAME POWERS.
LAME POWERS...

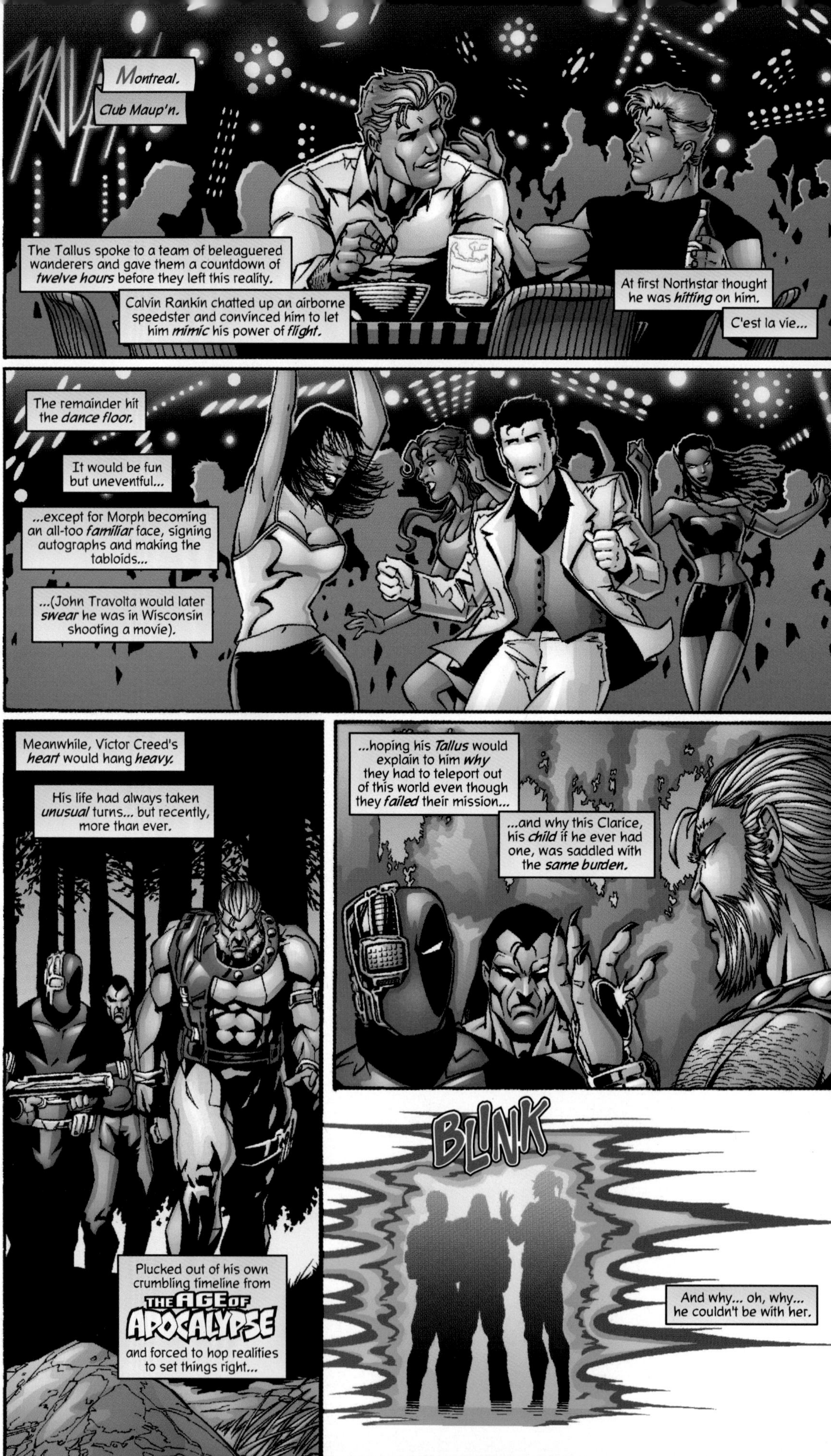
Montreal.
Club Maup'n.
The Tallus spoke to a team of beleaguered wanderers and gave them a countdown of *twelve hours* before they left this reality.
Calvin Rankin chatted up an airborne speedster and convinced him to let him *mimic* his power of *flight.*
At first Northstar thought he was *hitting* on him.
C'est la vie...
The remainder hit the *dance floor.*
It would be fun but uneventful...
...except for Morph becoming an all-too *familiar* face, signing autographs and making the tabloids...
...(John Travolta would later *swear* he was in Wisconsin shooting a movie).
Meanwhile, Victor Creed's *heart* would hang *heavy.*
His life had always taken *unusual* turns... but recently, more than ever.
Plucked out of his own crumbling timeline from
THE AGE OF APOCALYPSE
and forced to hop realities to set things right...
...hoping his *Tallus* would explain to him *why* they had to teleport out of this world even though they *failed* their mission...
...and why this Clarice, his *child* if he ever had one, was saddled with the *same burden.*
BLINK
And why... oh, why... he couldn't be with her.

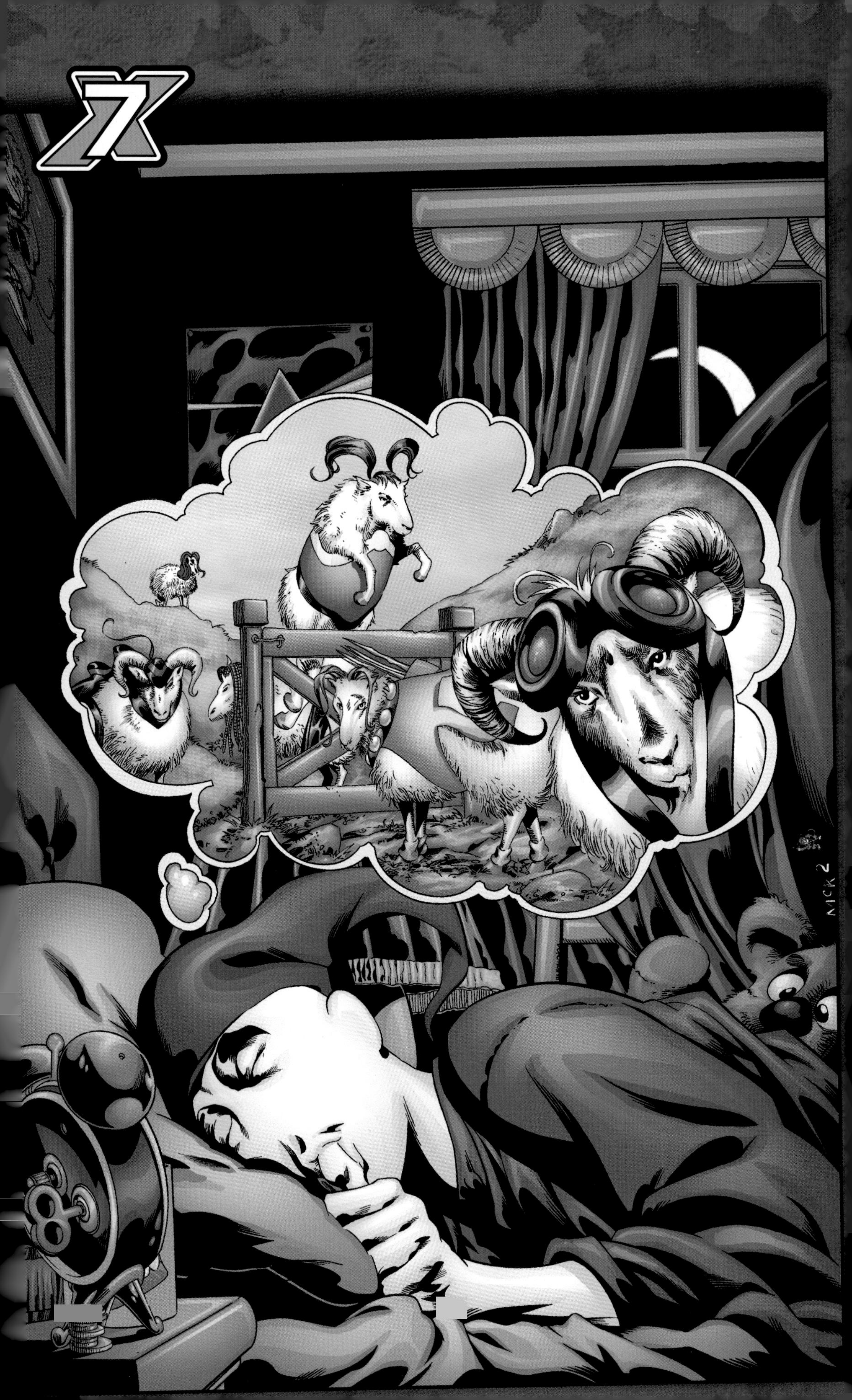

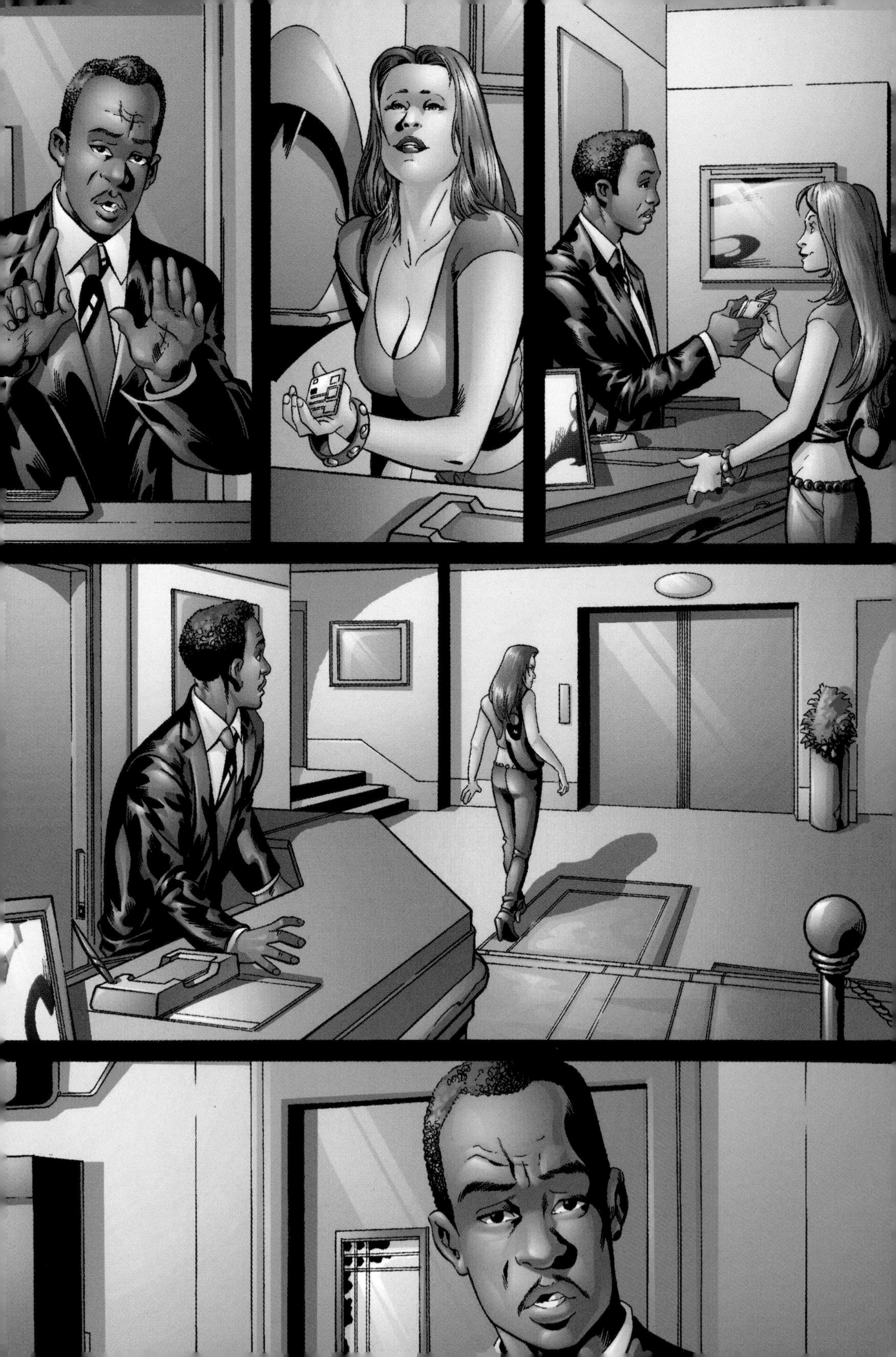

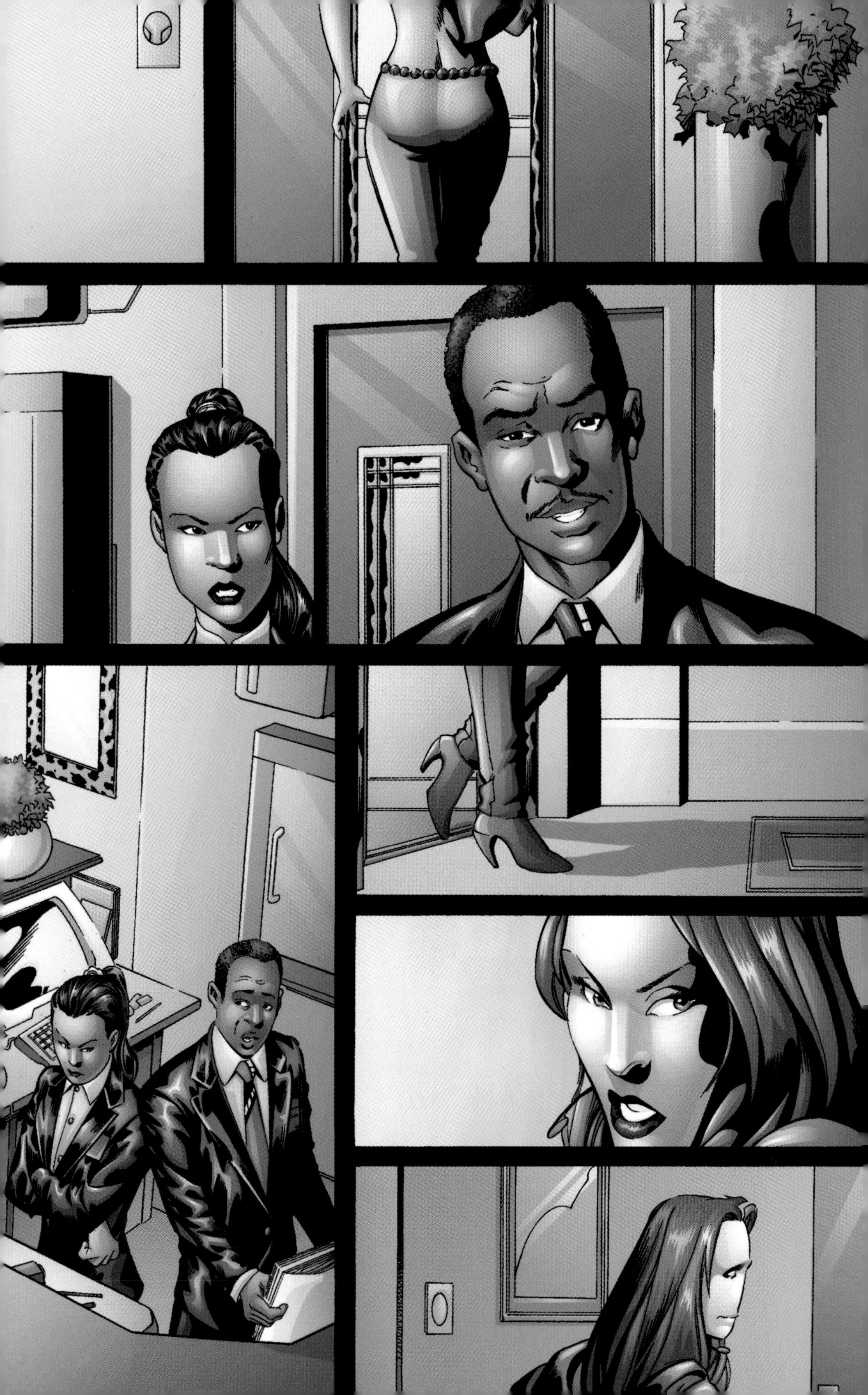

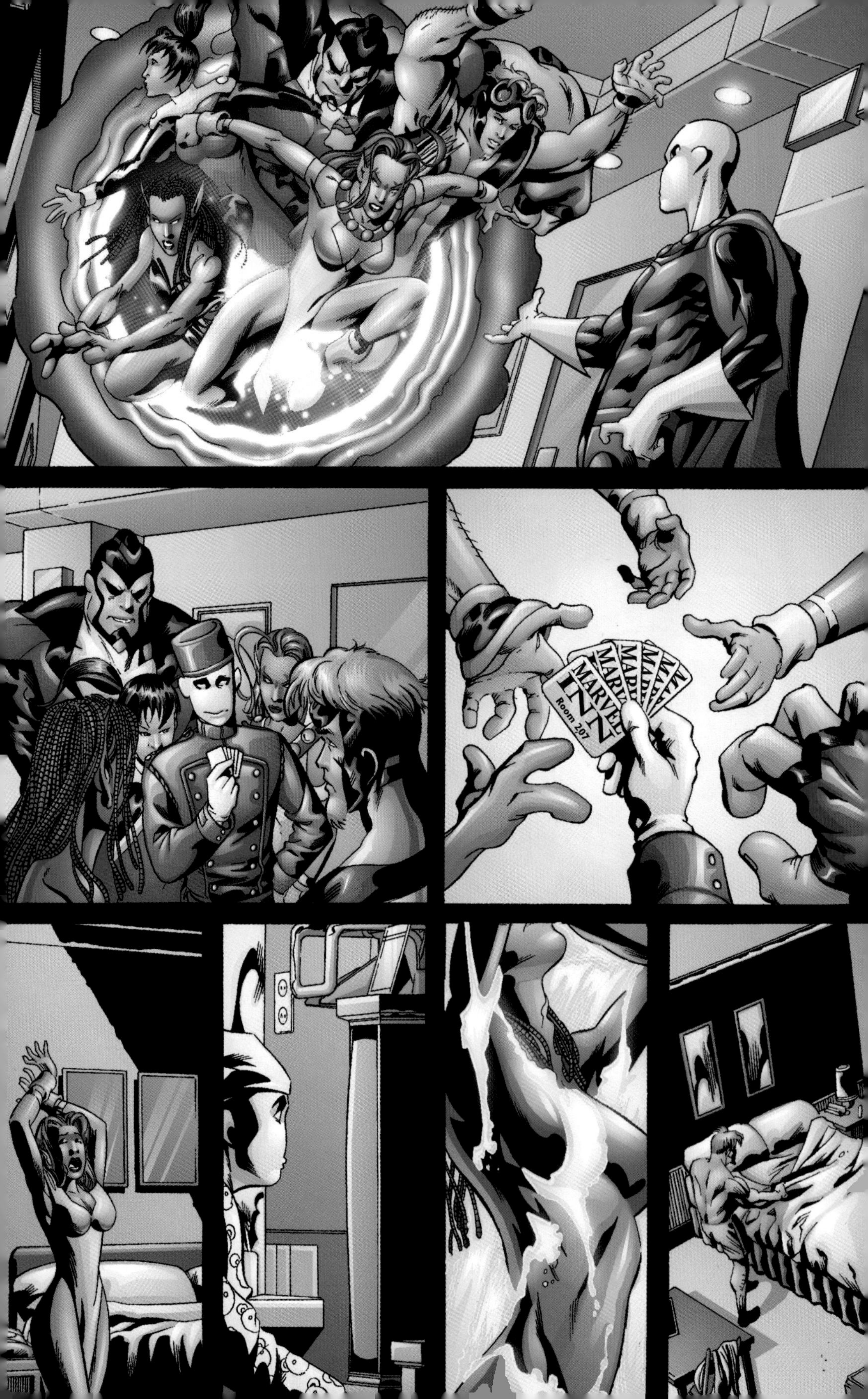

MARVEL INN
Room 207

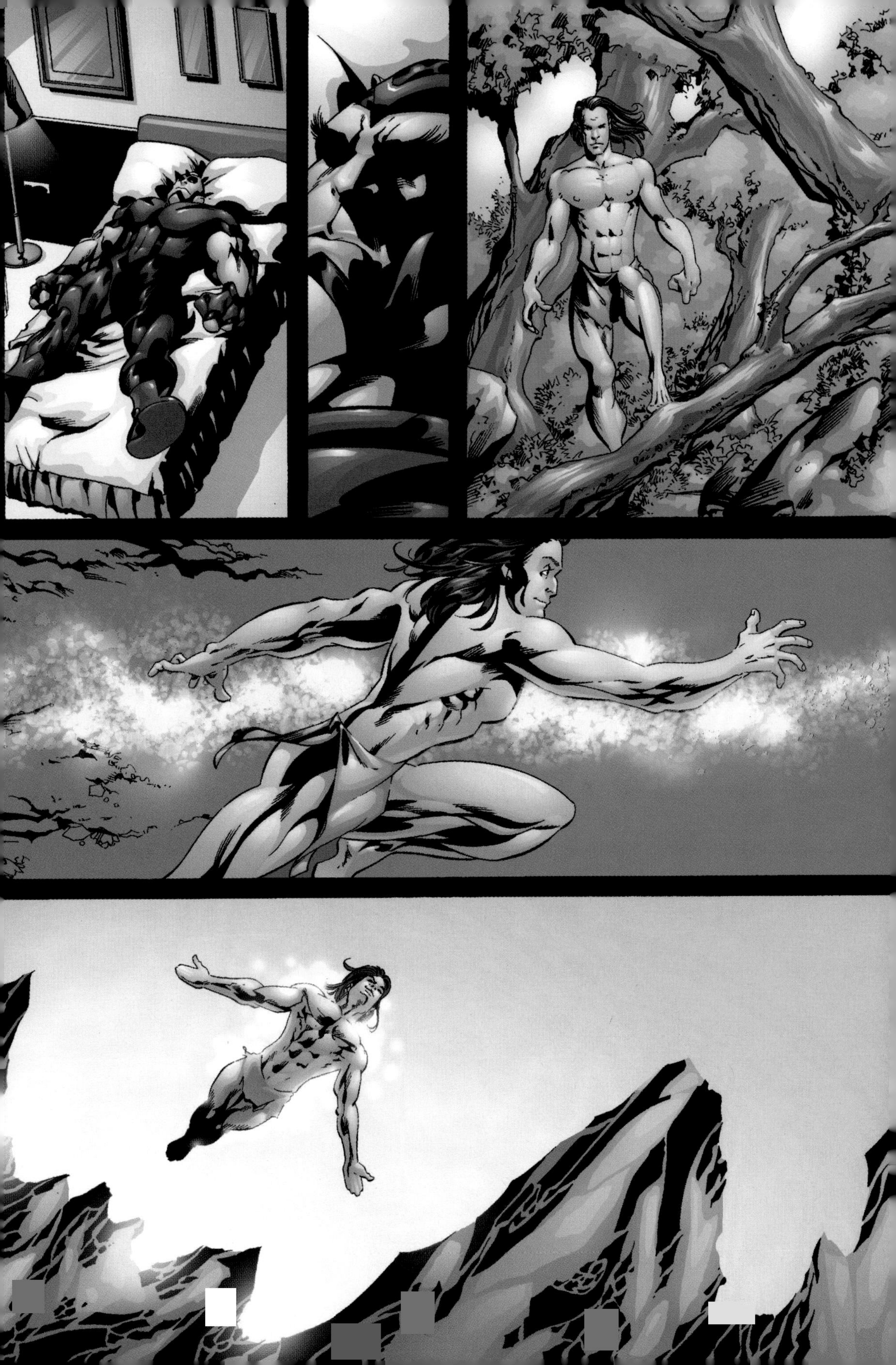

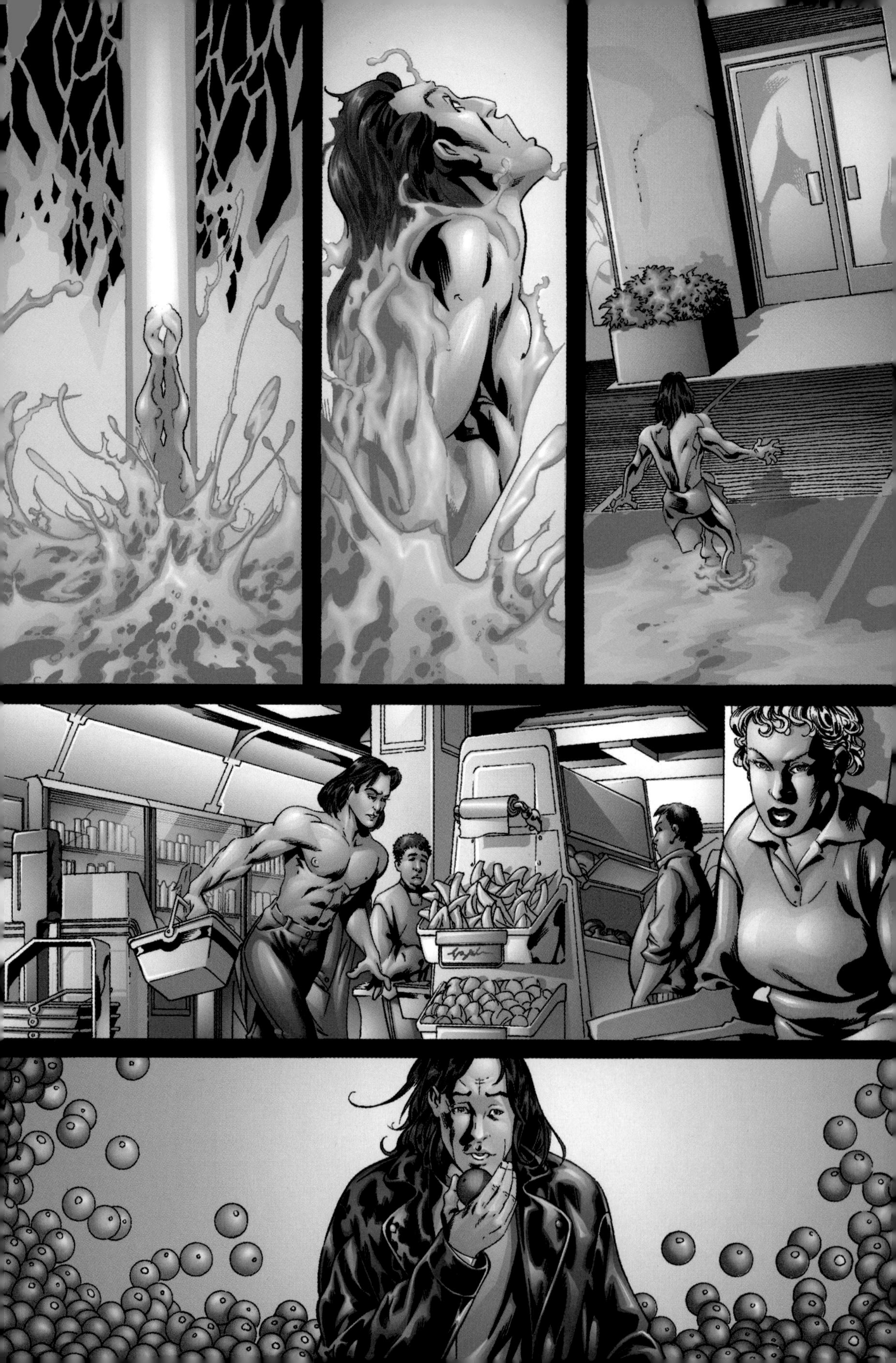

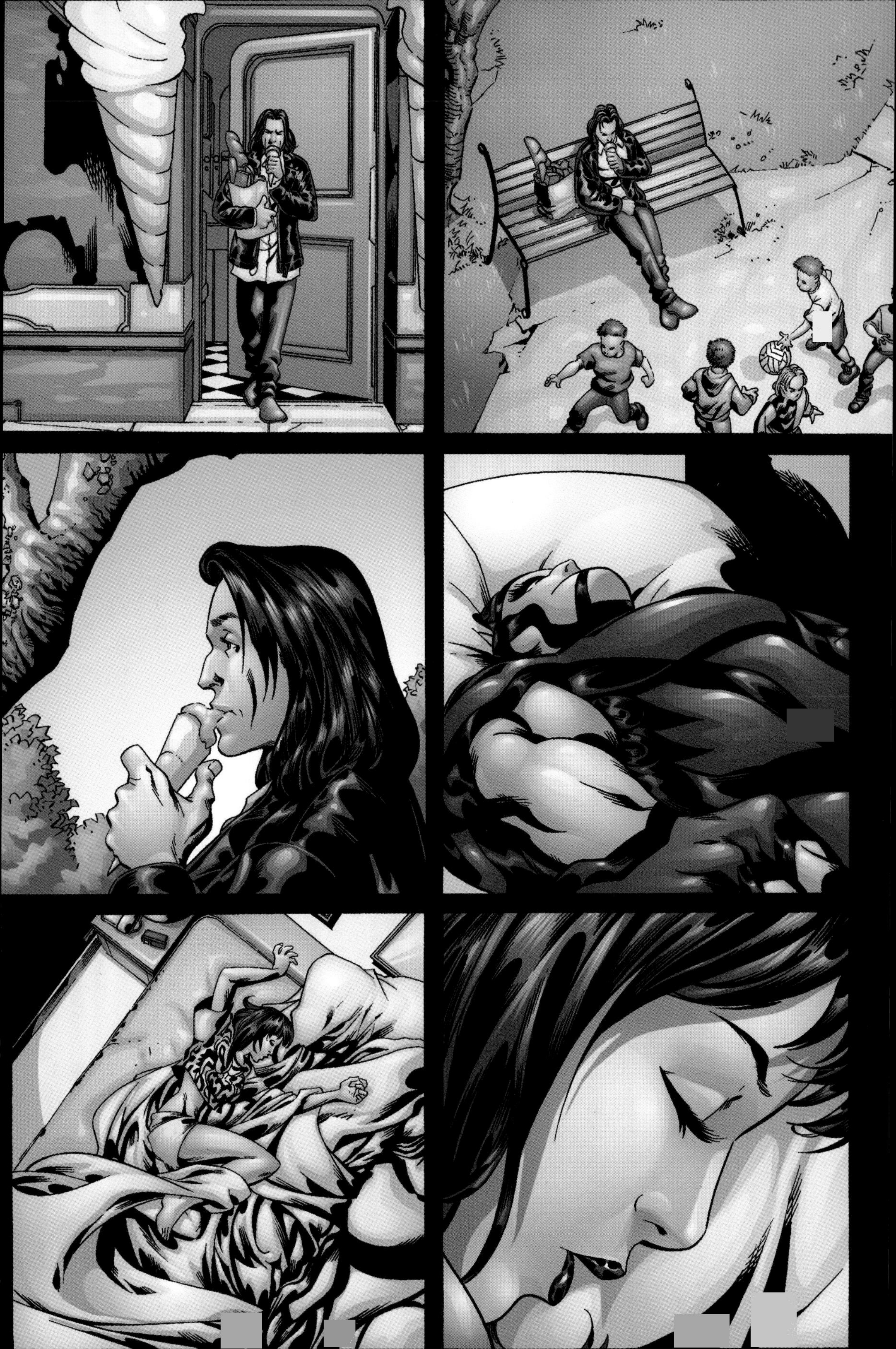

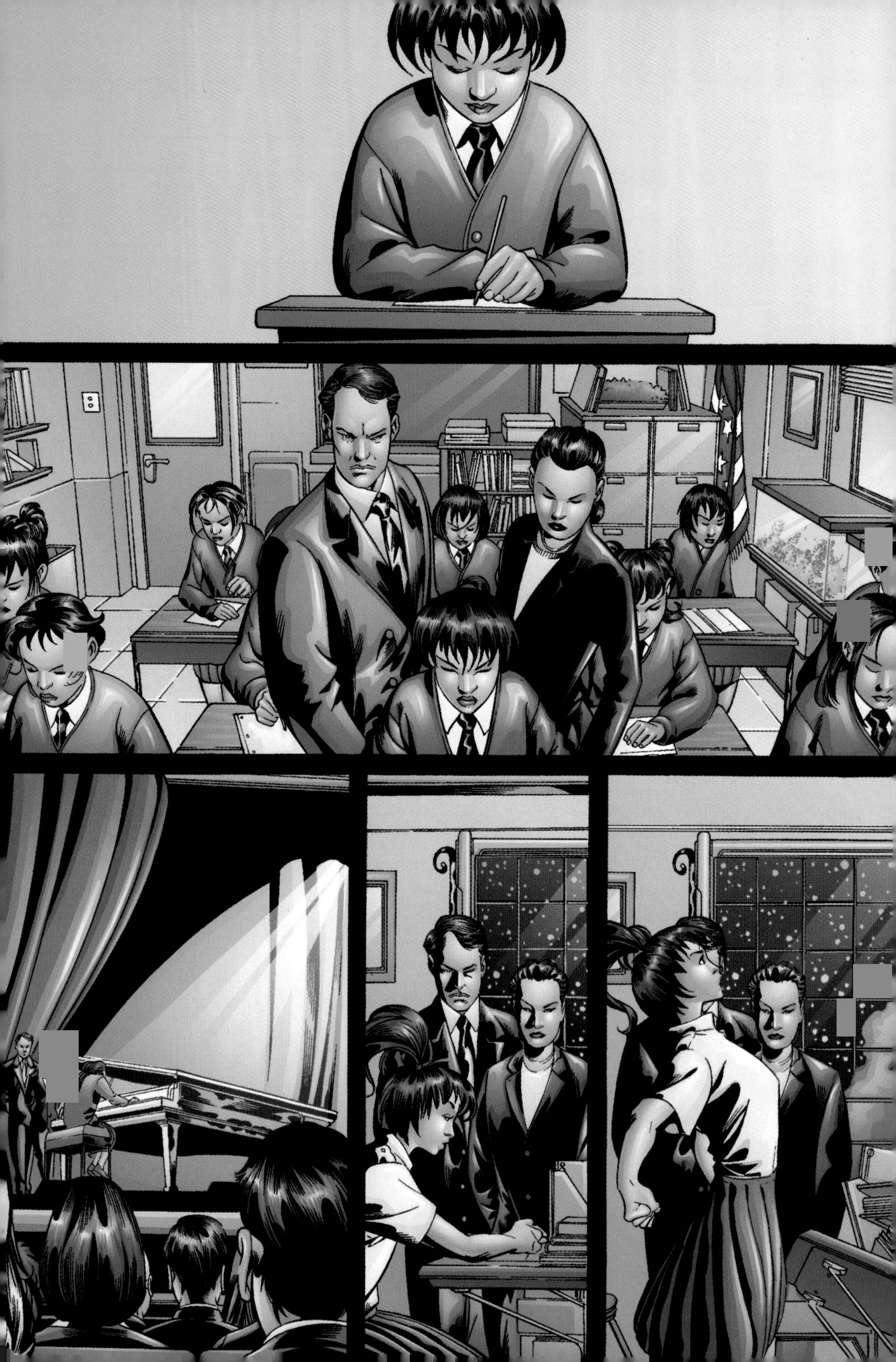

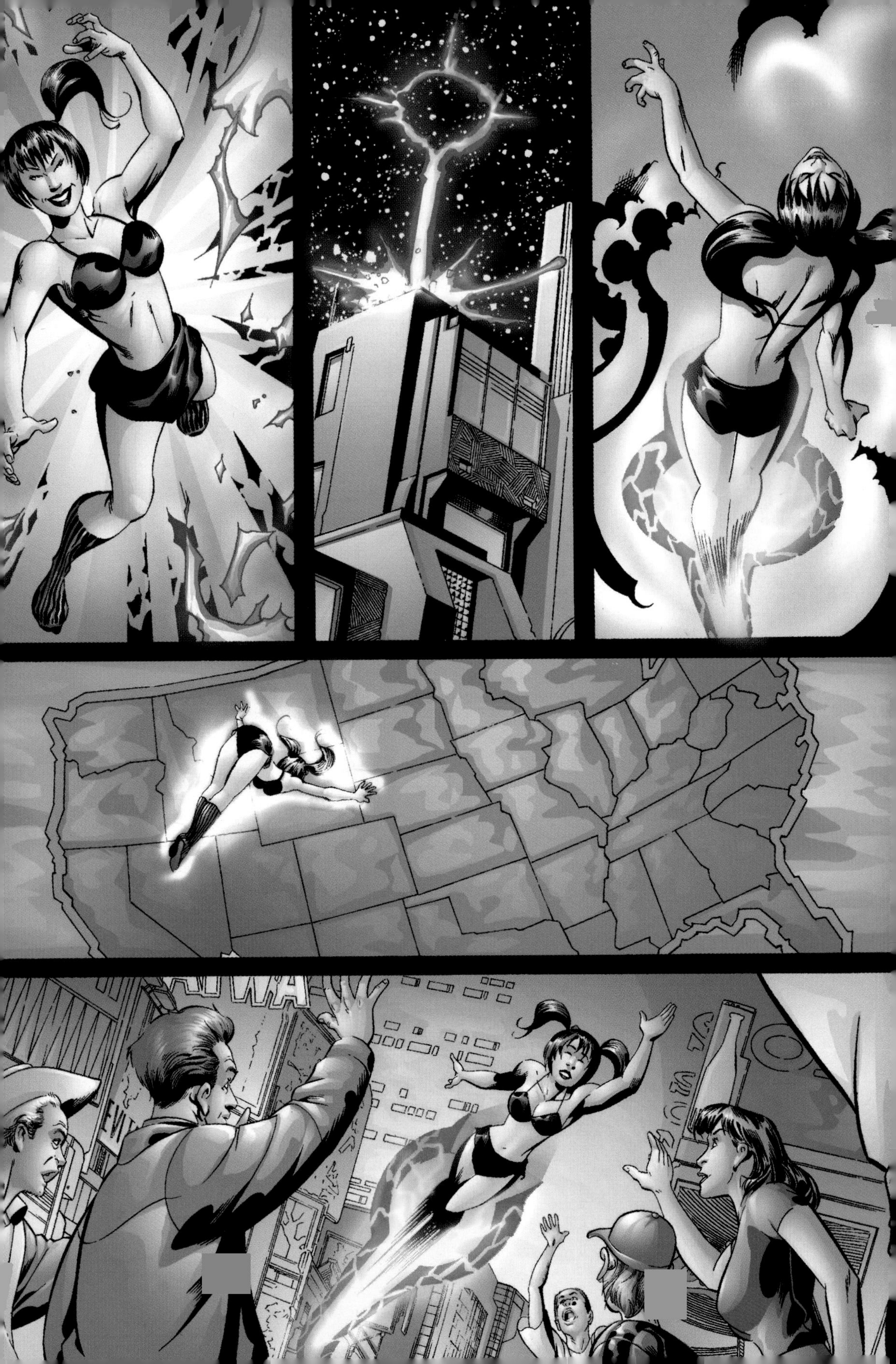

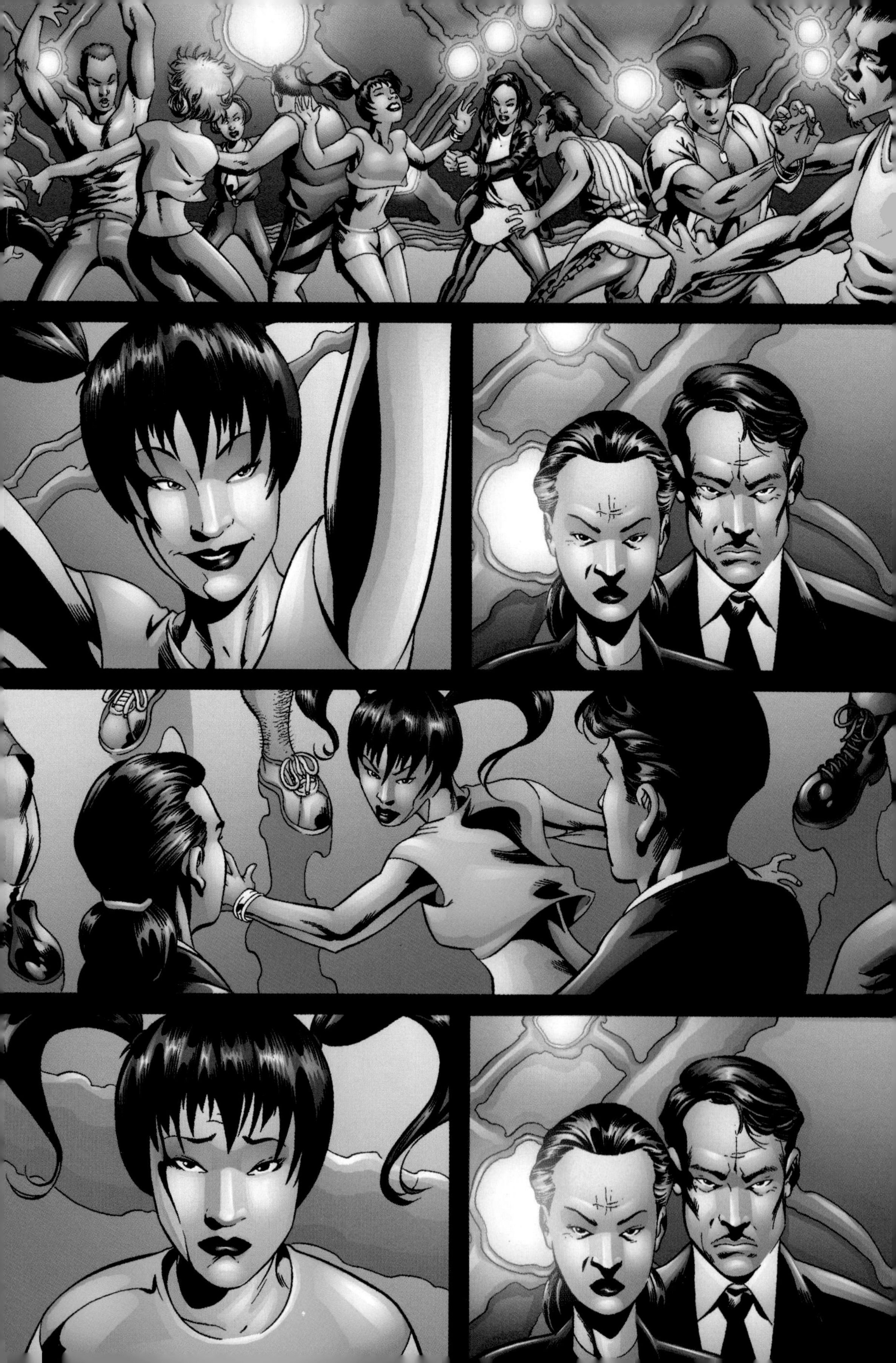

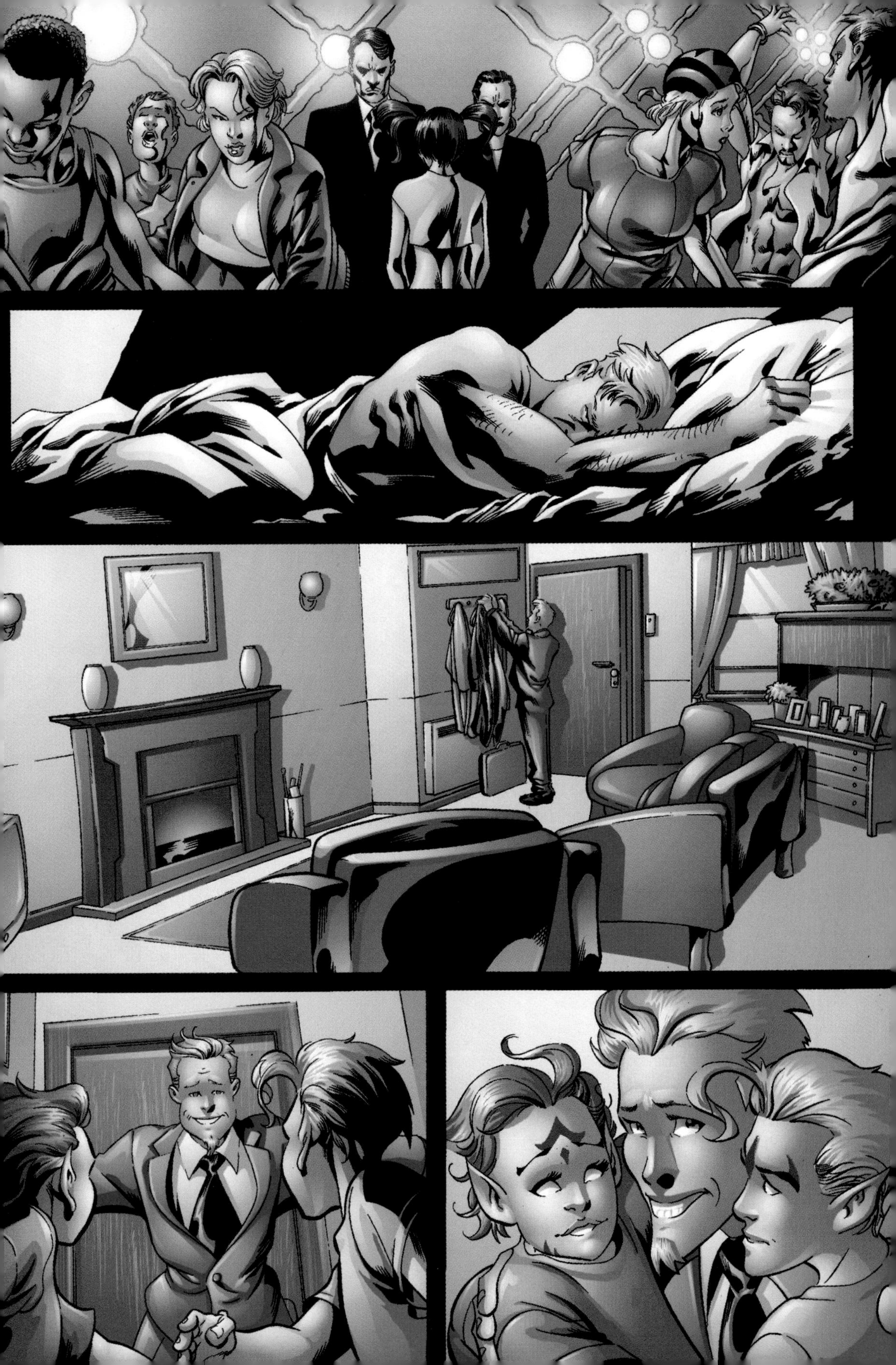

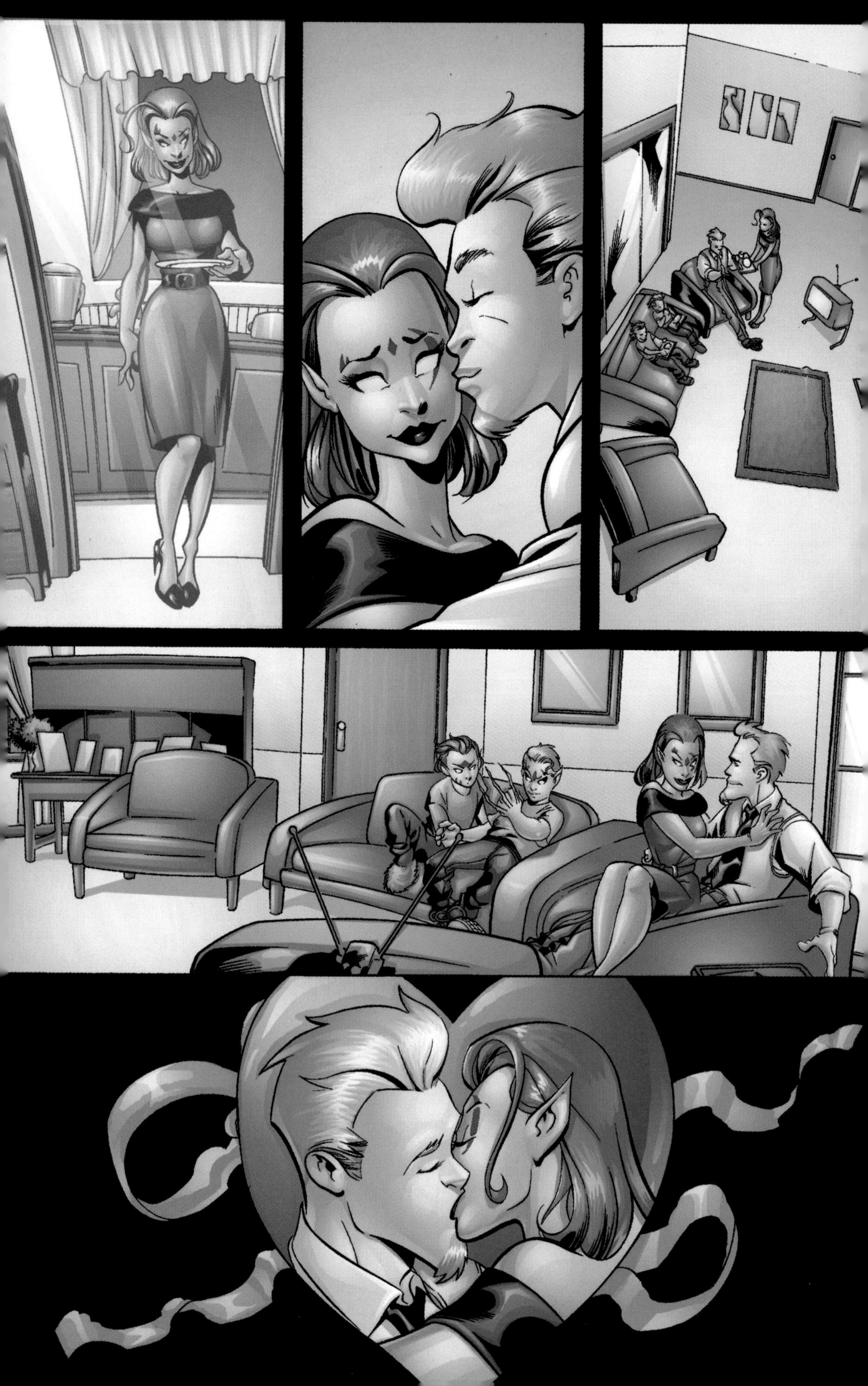

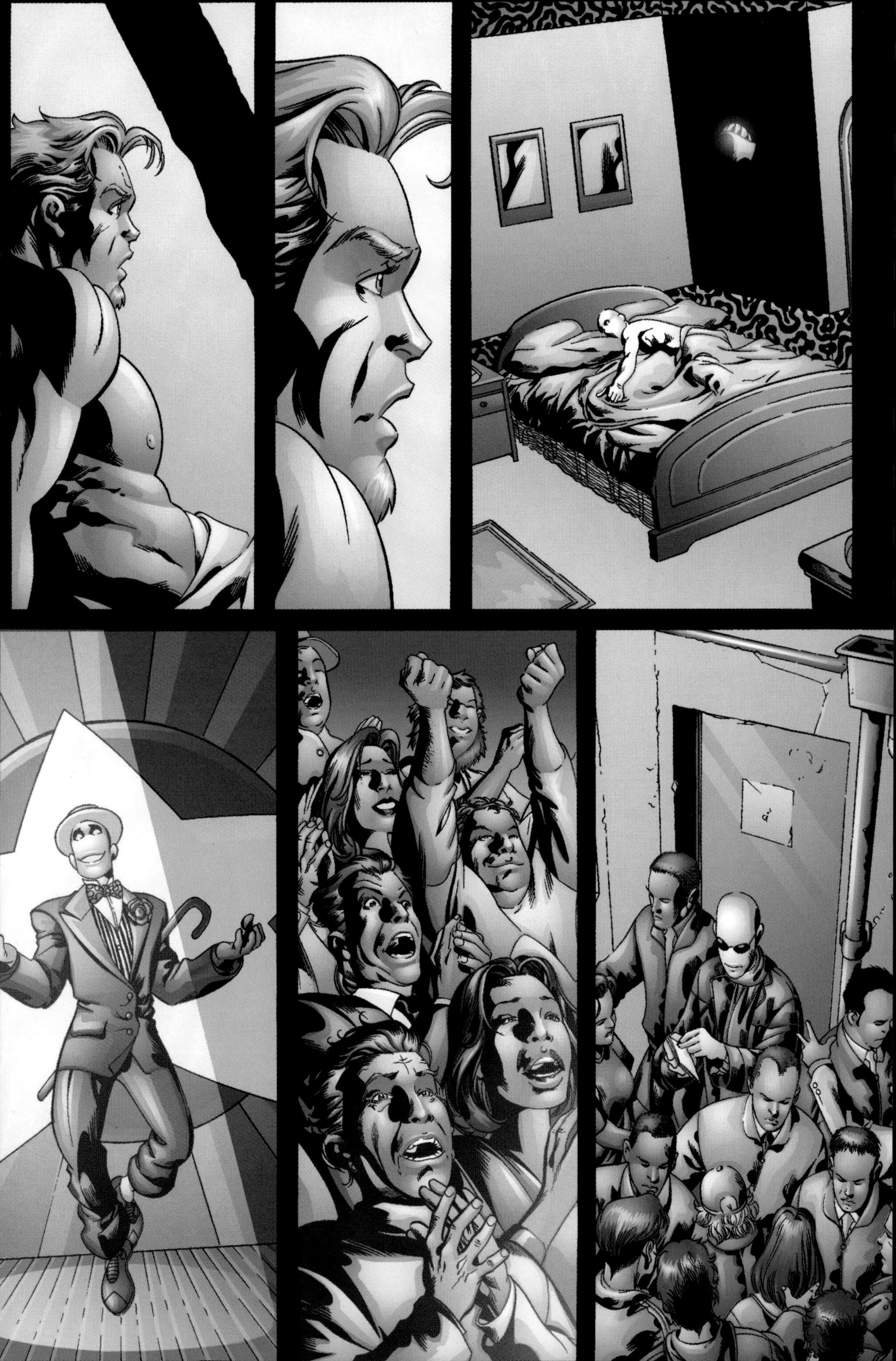

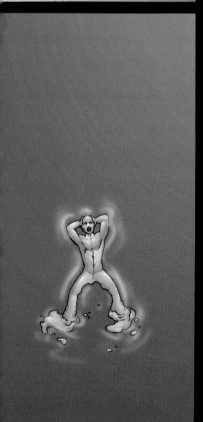

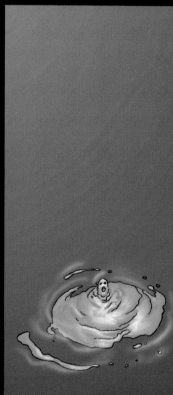

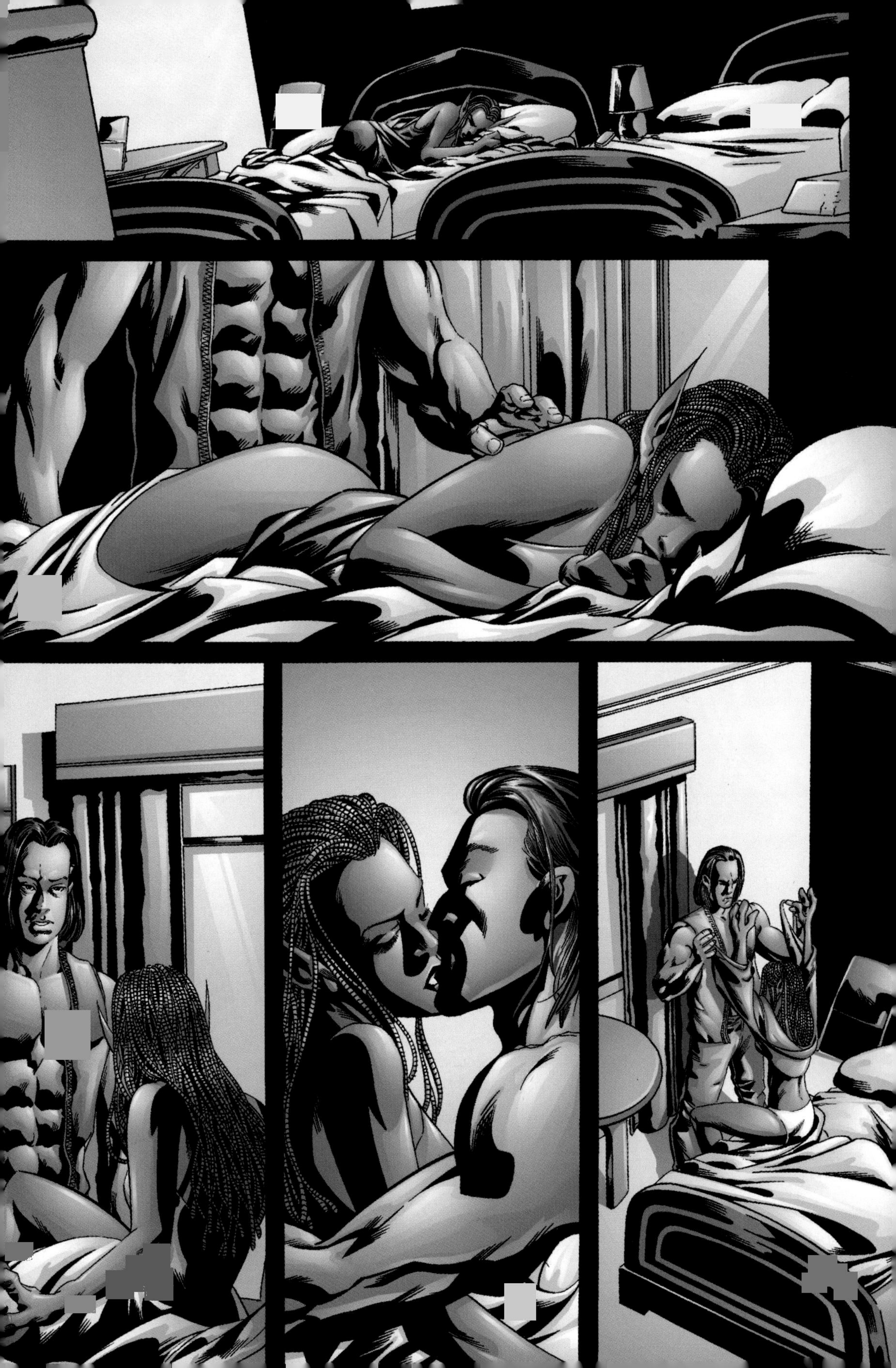

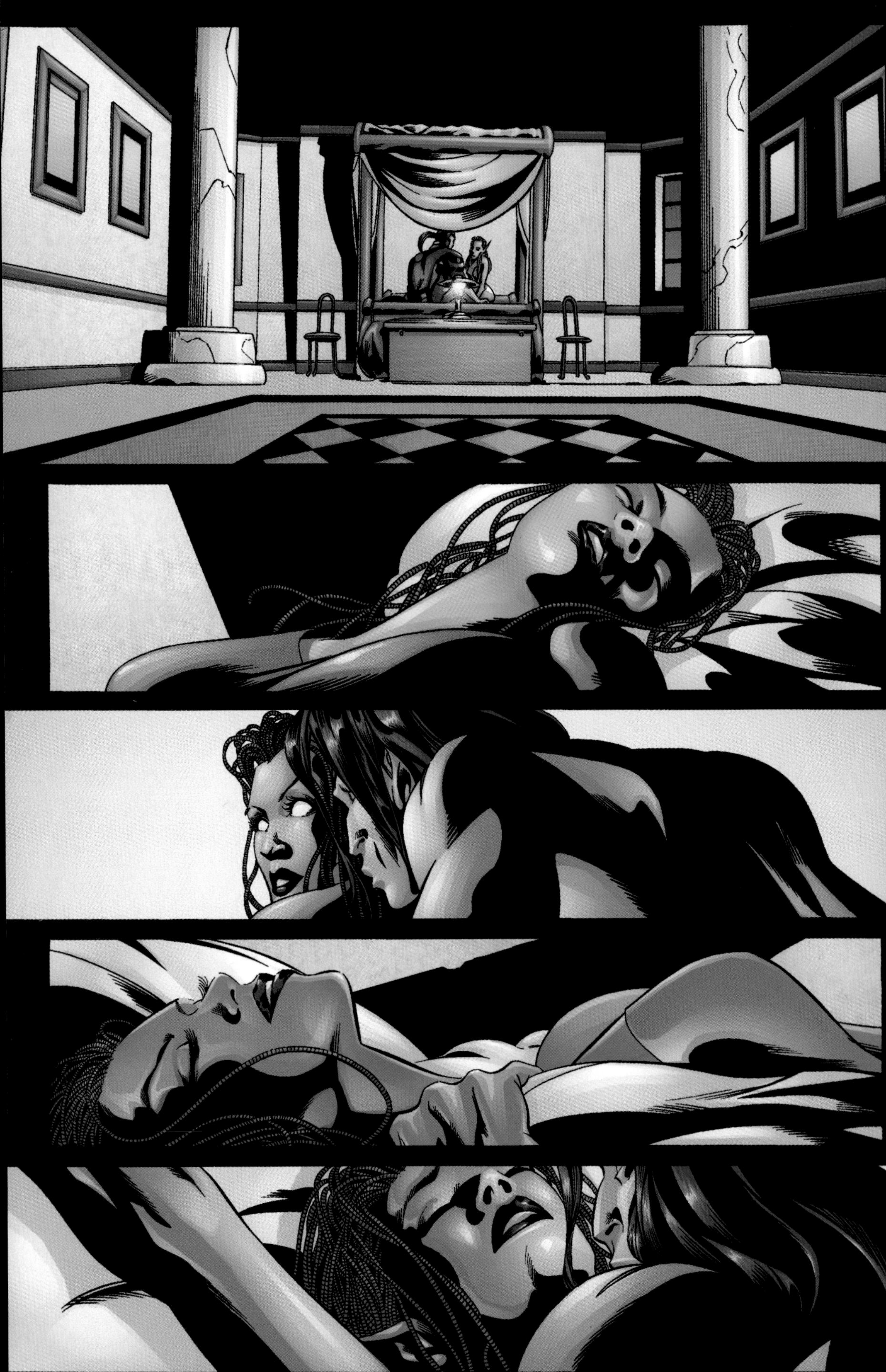

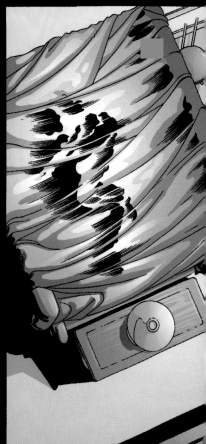

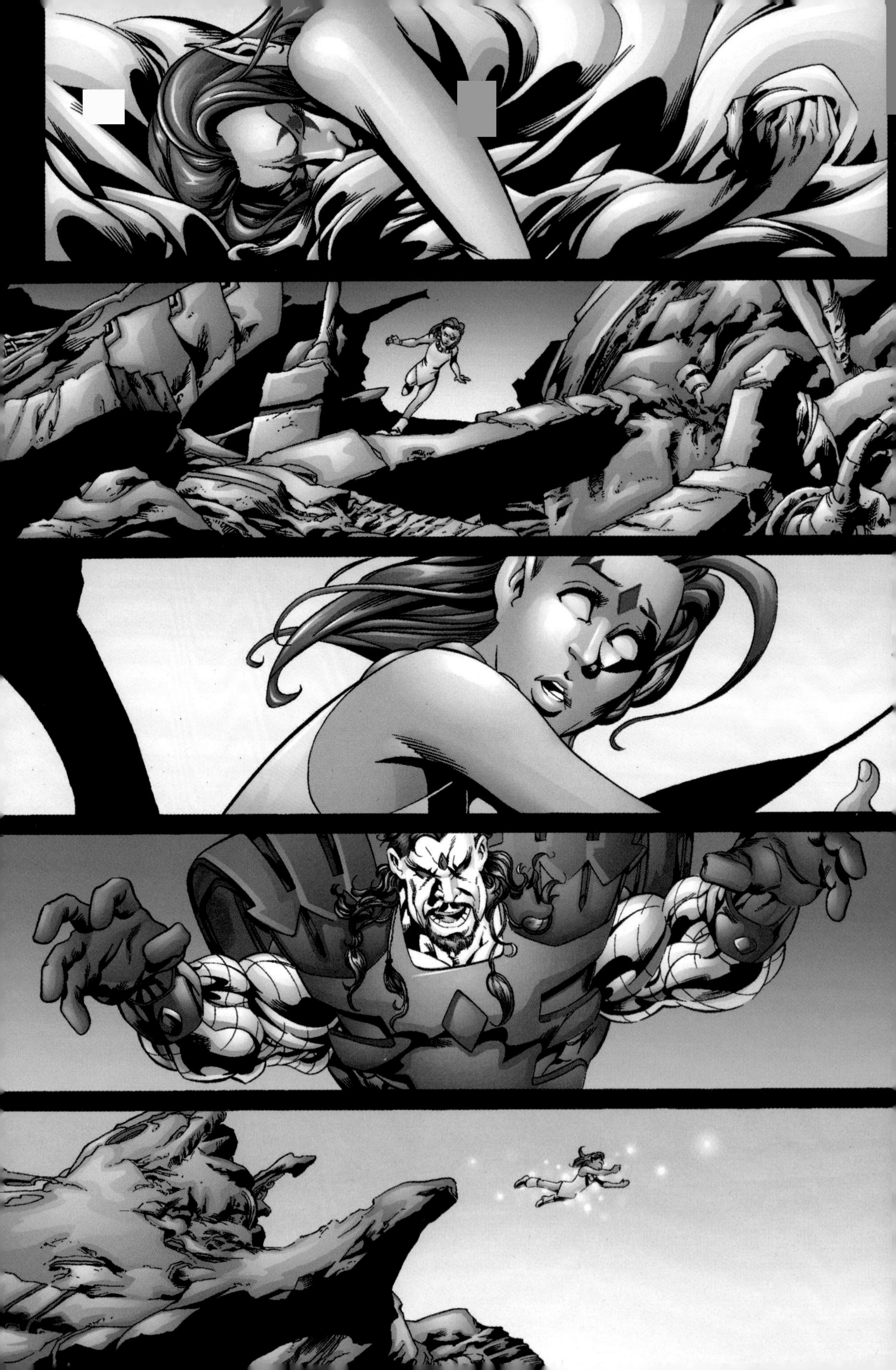

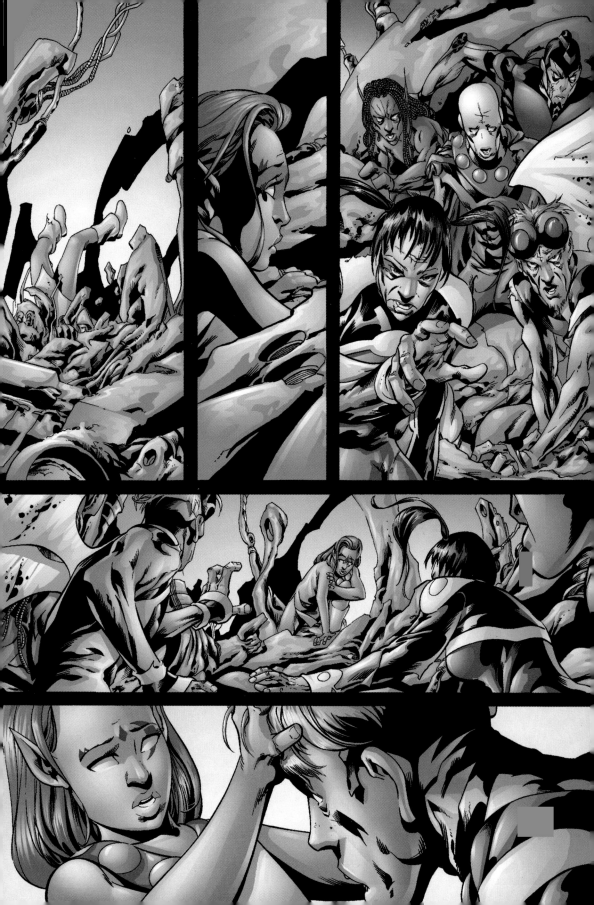

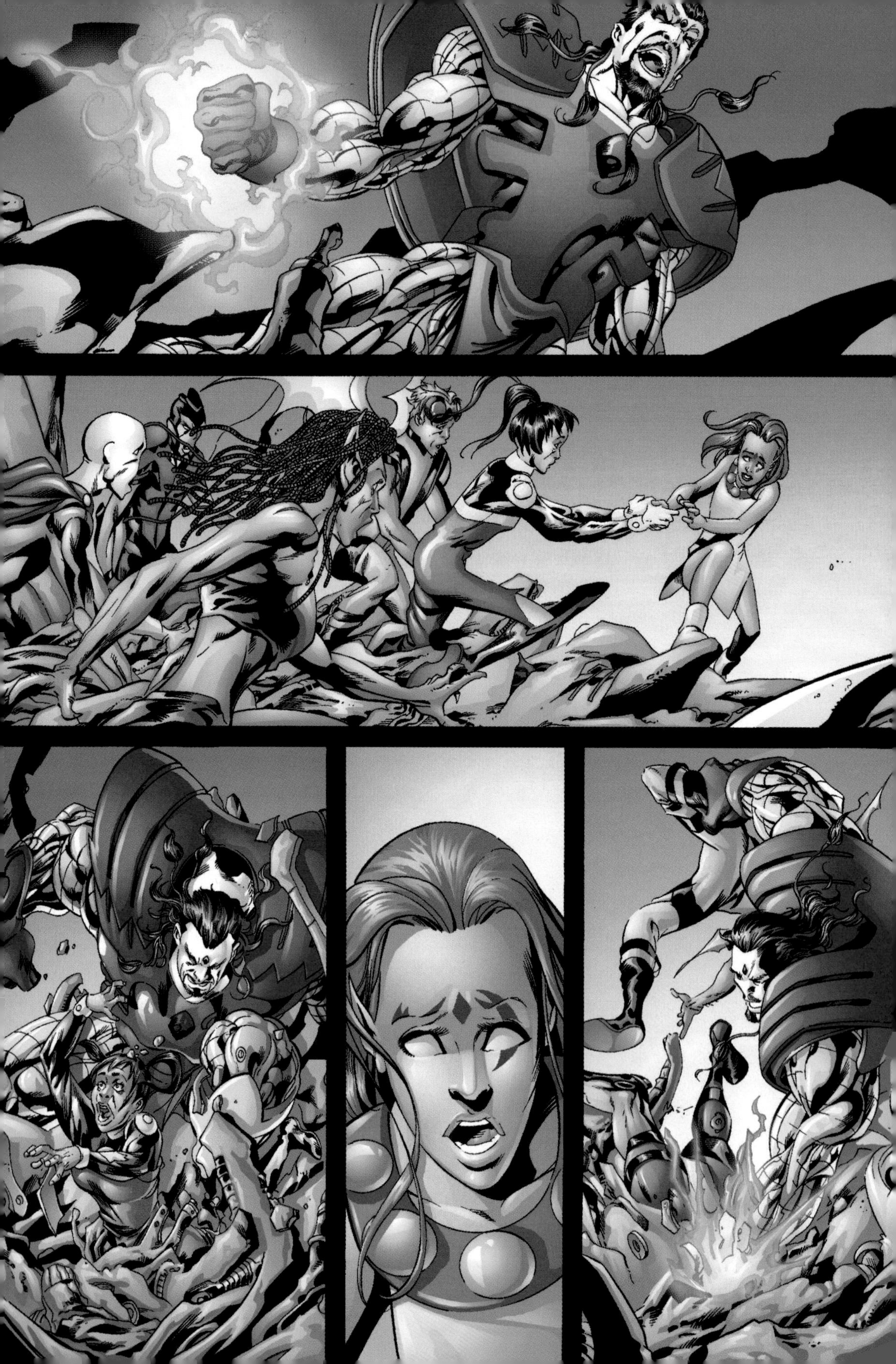

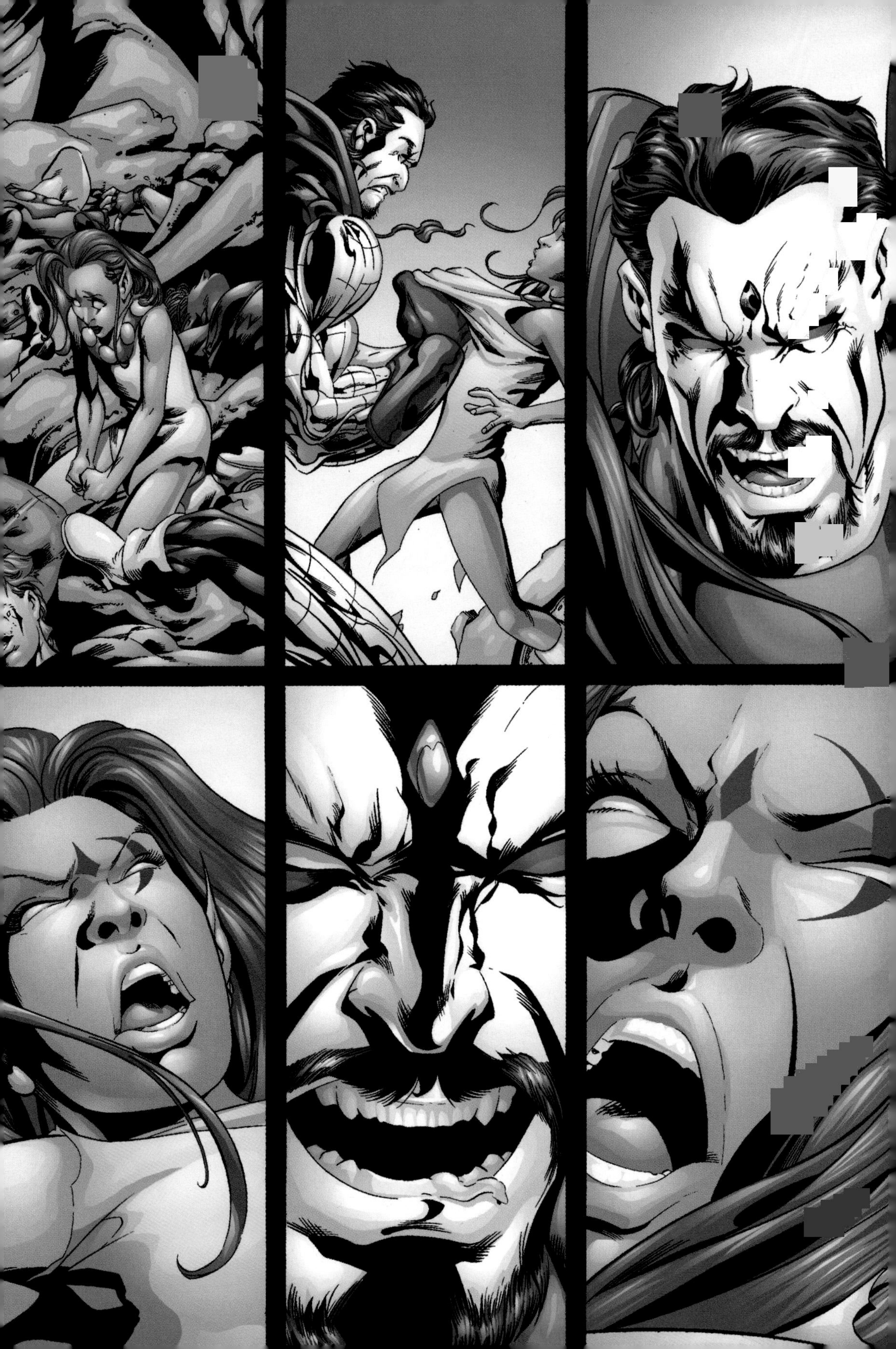

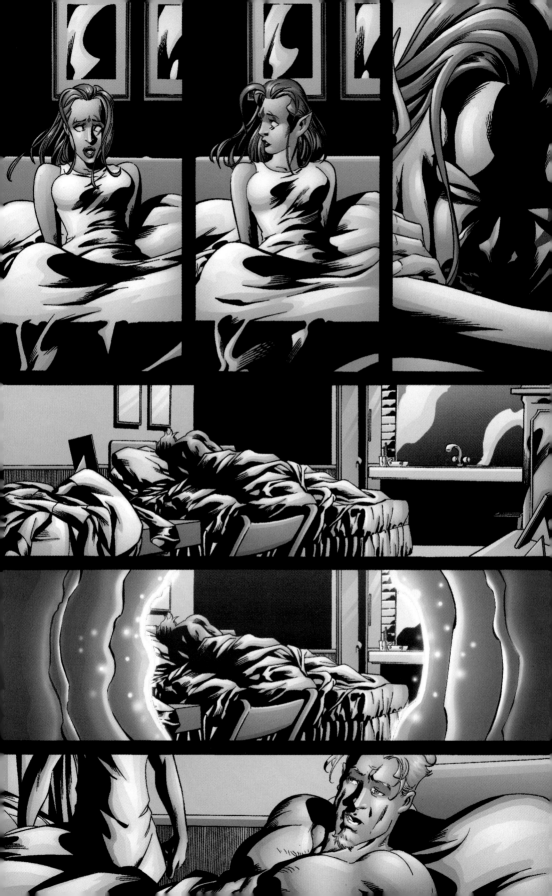

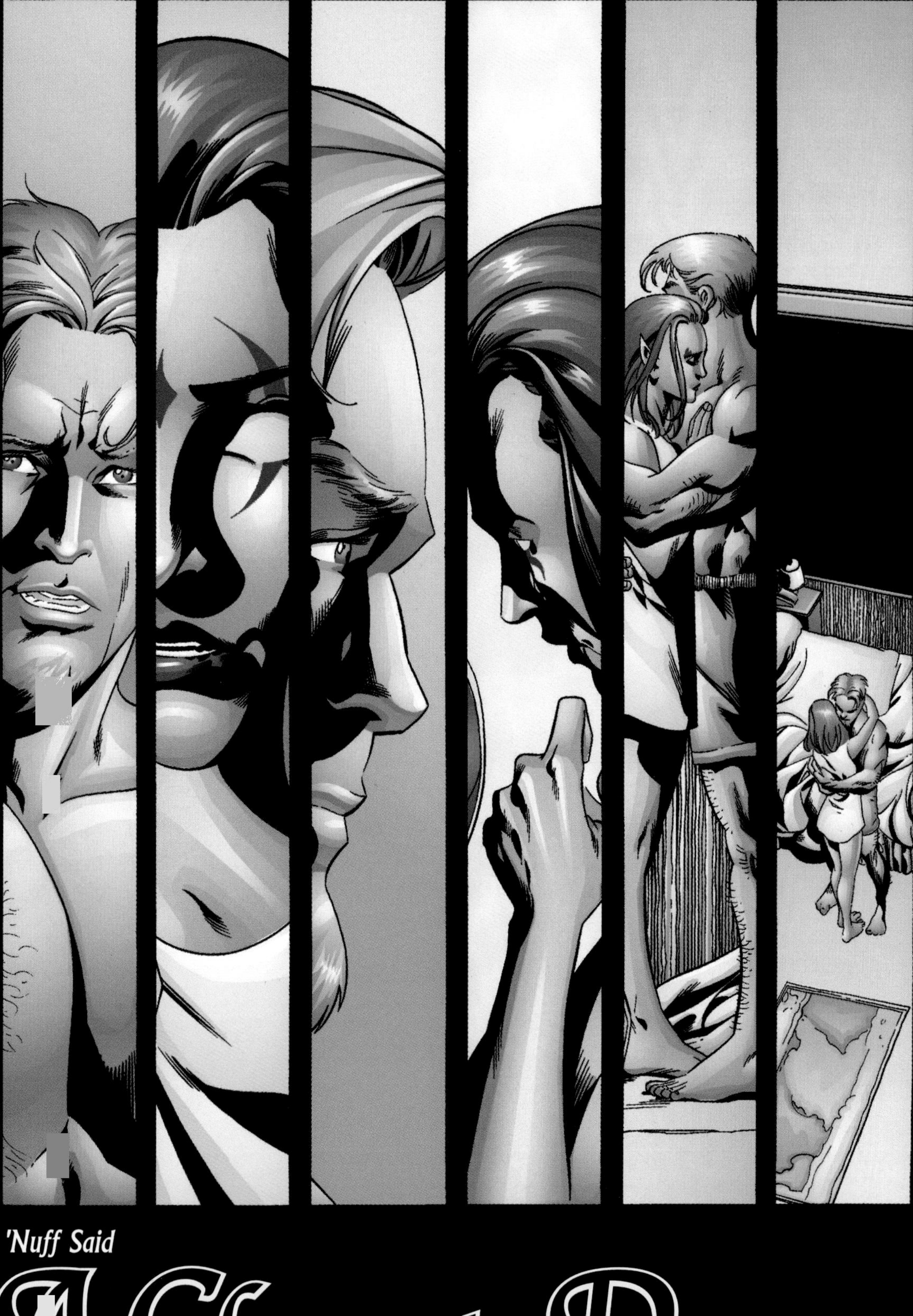

'Nuff Said

A Chance to Dream...

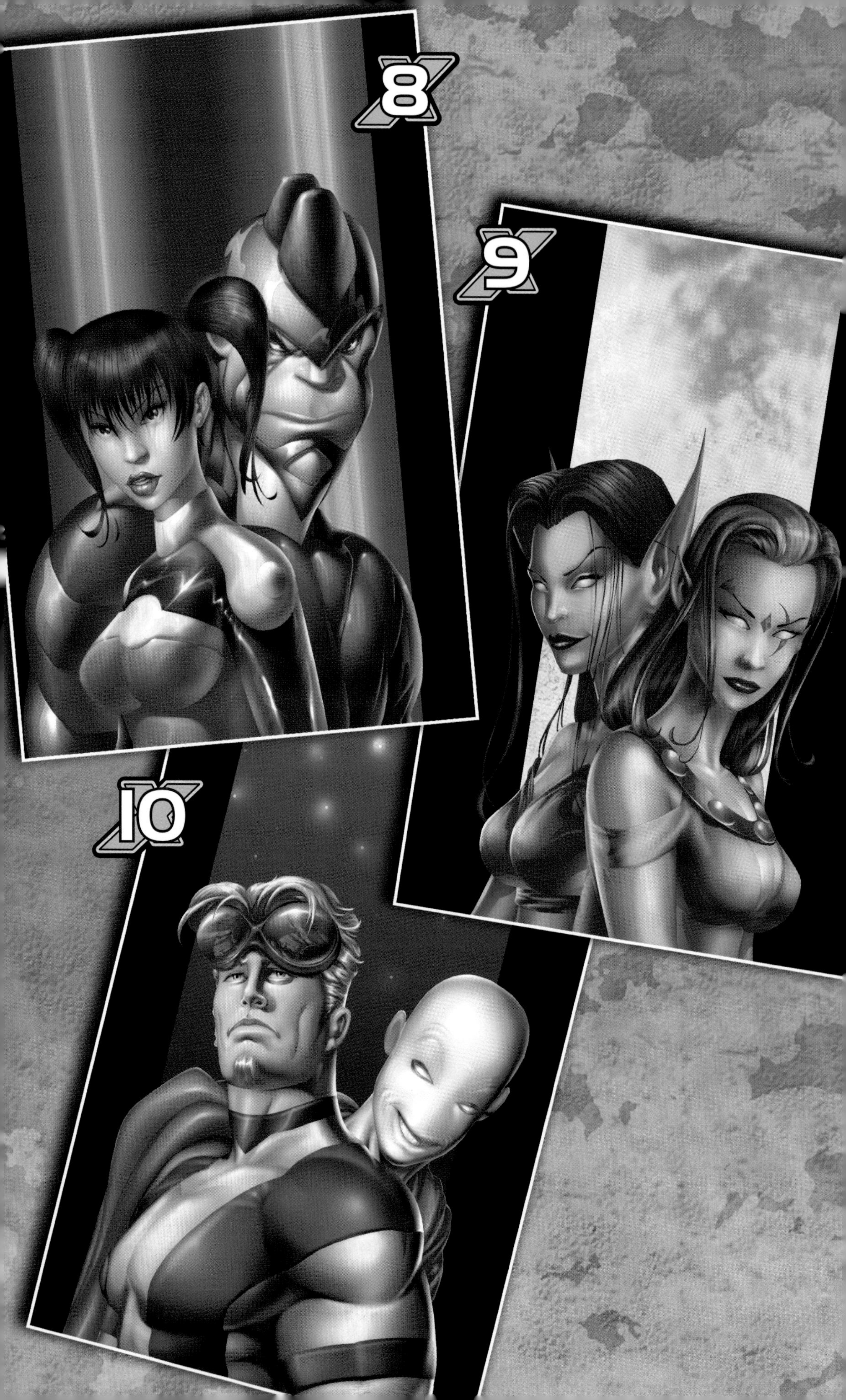
8
9
10

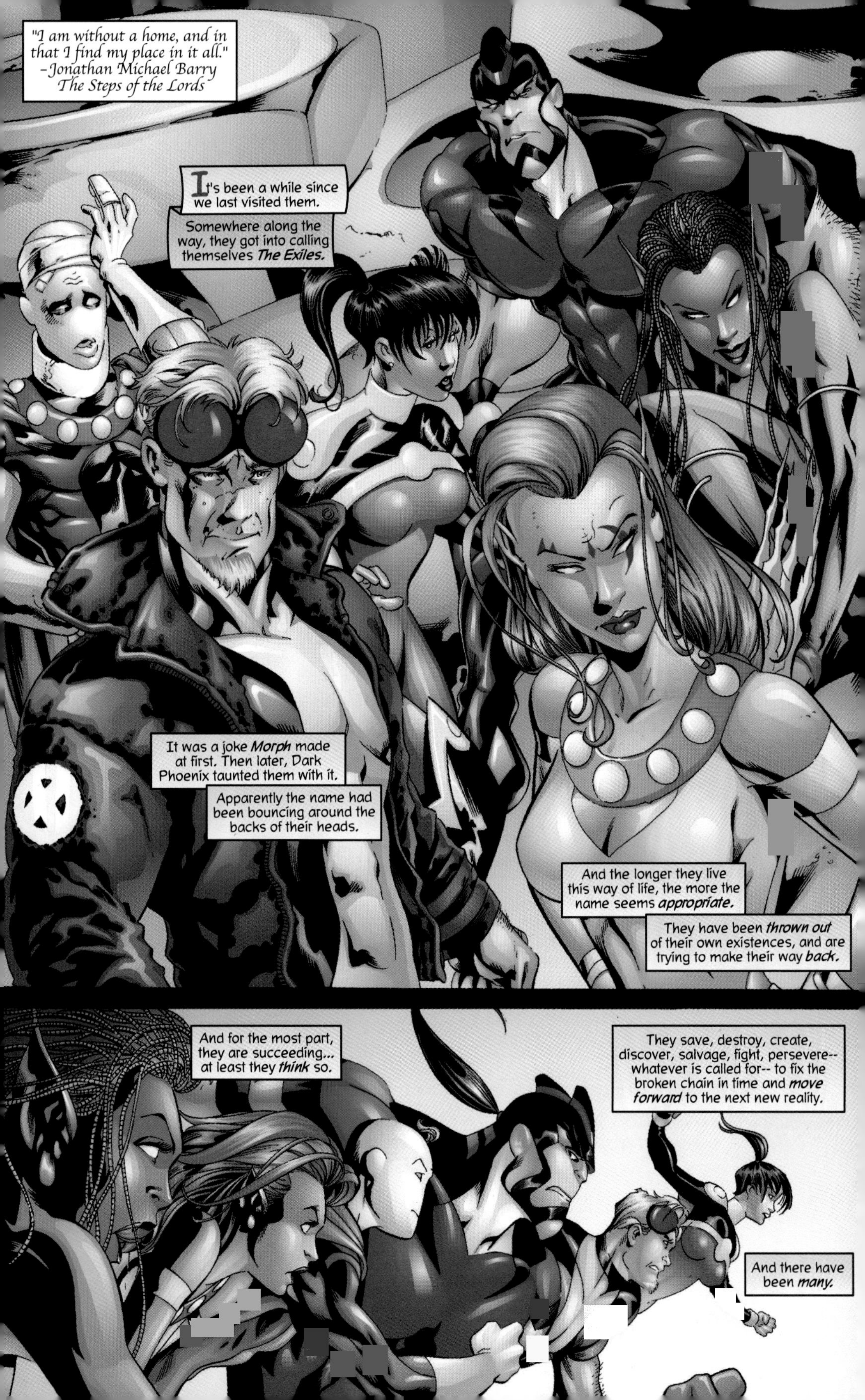
"I am without a home, and in that I find my place in it all."
–Jonathan Michael Barry
The Steps of the Lords
It's been a while since we last visited them.
Somewhere along the way, they got into calling themselves *The Exiles.*
It was a joke *Morph* made at first. Then later, Dark Phoenix taunted them with it.
Apparently the name had been bouncing around the backs of their heads.
And the longer they live this way of life, the more the name seems *appropriate.*
They have been *thrown out* of their own existences, and are trying to make their way *back.*
And for the most part, they are succeeding... at least they *think* so.
They save, destroy, create, discover, salvage, fight, persevere-- whatever is called for-- to fix the broken chain in time and *move forward* to the next new reality.
And there have been *many.*

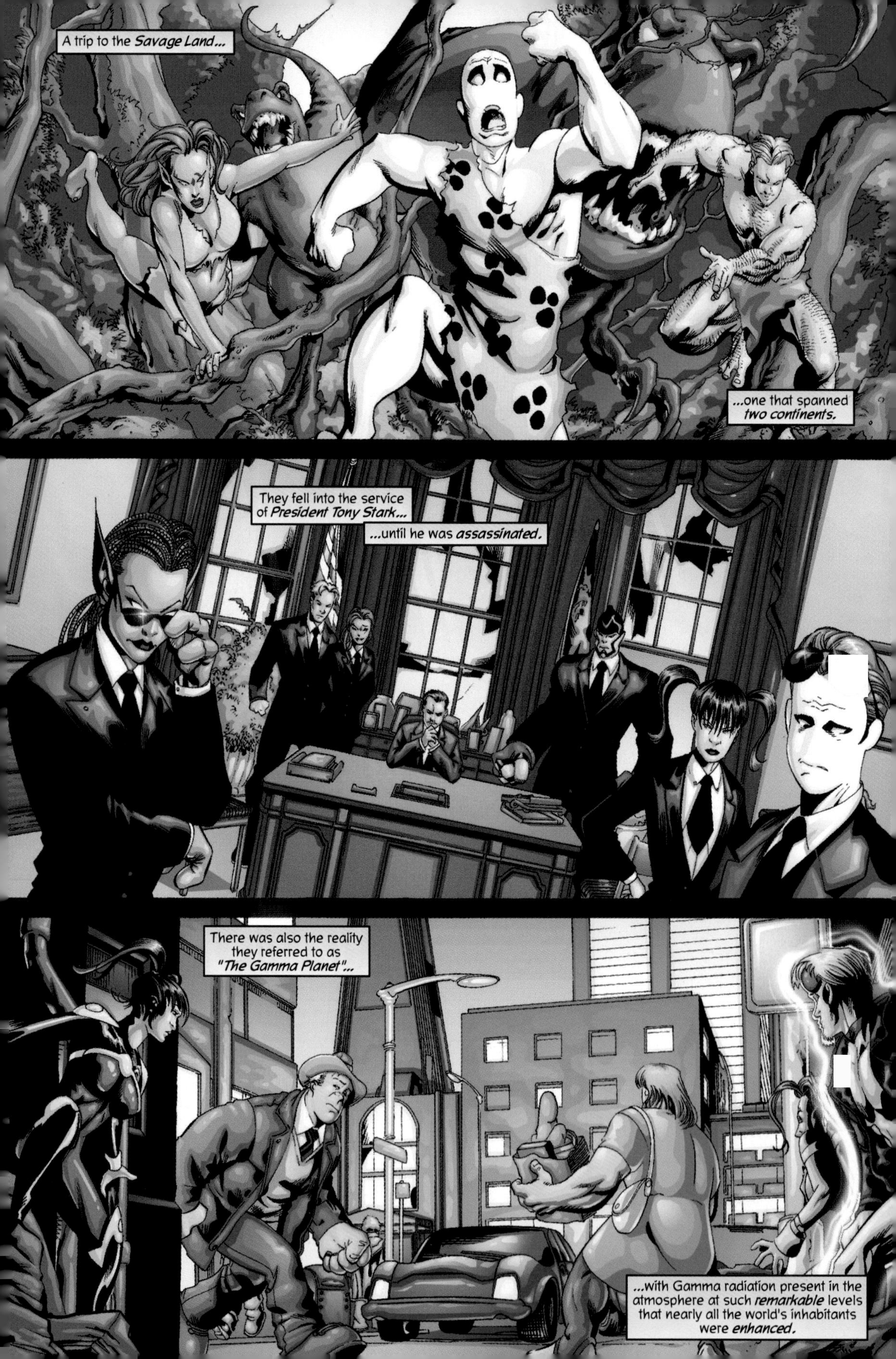
A trip to the *Savage Land...*
...one that spanned *two continents.*
They fell into the service of *President Tony Stark...*
...until he was *assassinated.*
There was also the reality they referred to as *"The Gamma Planet"...*
...with Gamma radiation present in the atmosphere at such *remarkable* levels that nearly all the world's inhabitants were *enhanced.*

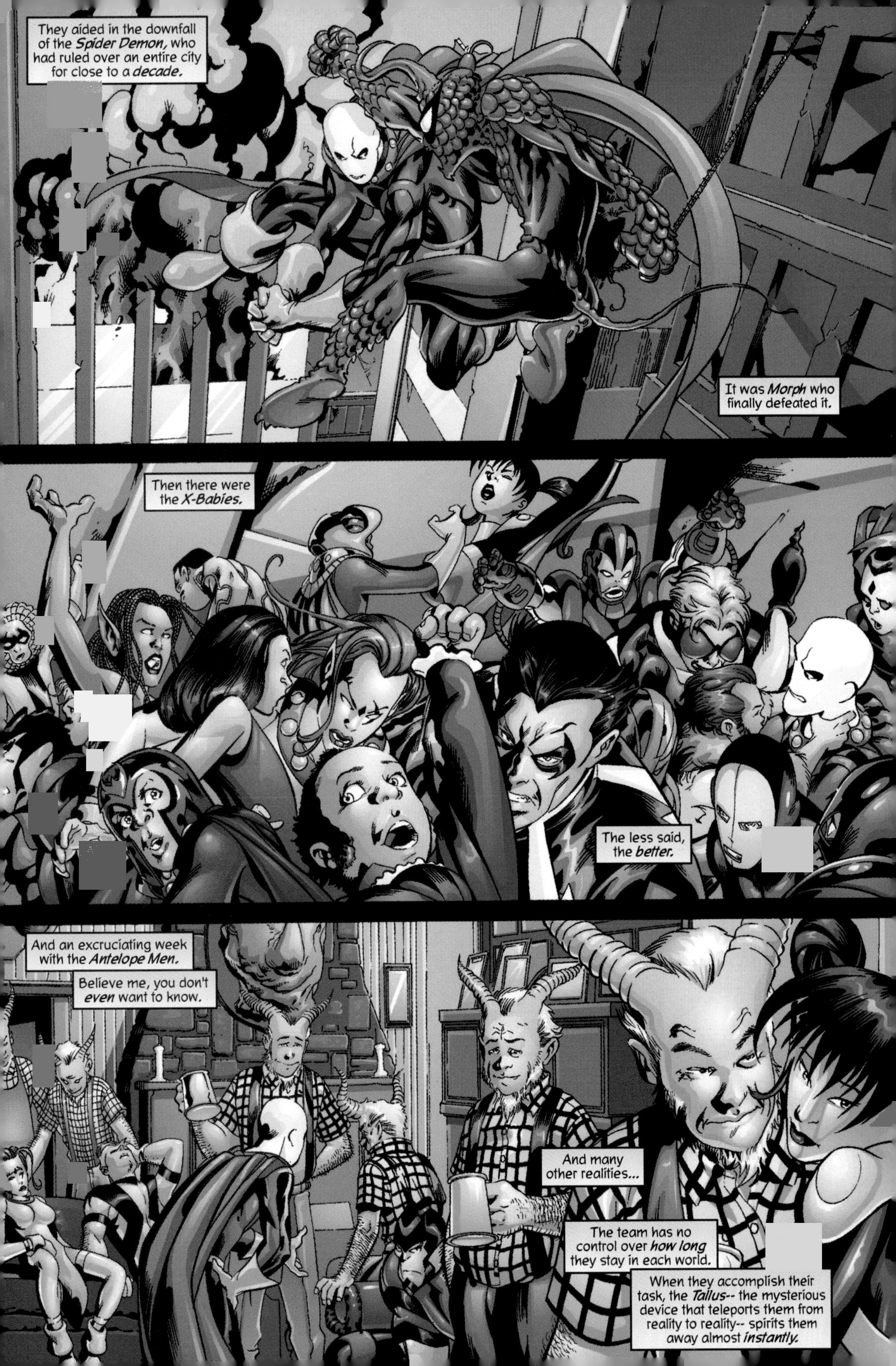
They aided in the downfall of the Spider Demon, who had ruled over an entire city for close to a decade.
It was Morph who finally defeated it.
Then there were the X-Babies.
The less said, the better.
And an excruciating week with the Antelope Men.
Believe me, you don't even want to know.
And many other realities...
The team has no control over how long they stay in each world.
When they accomplish their task, the Tallus-- the mysterious device that teleports them from reality to reality-- spirits them away almost instantly.

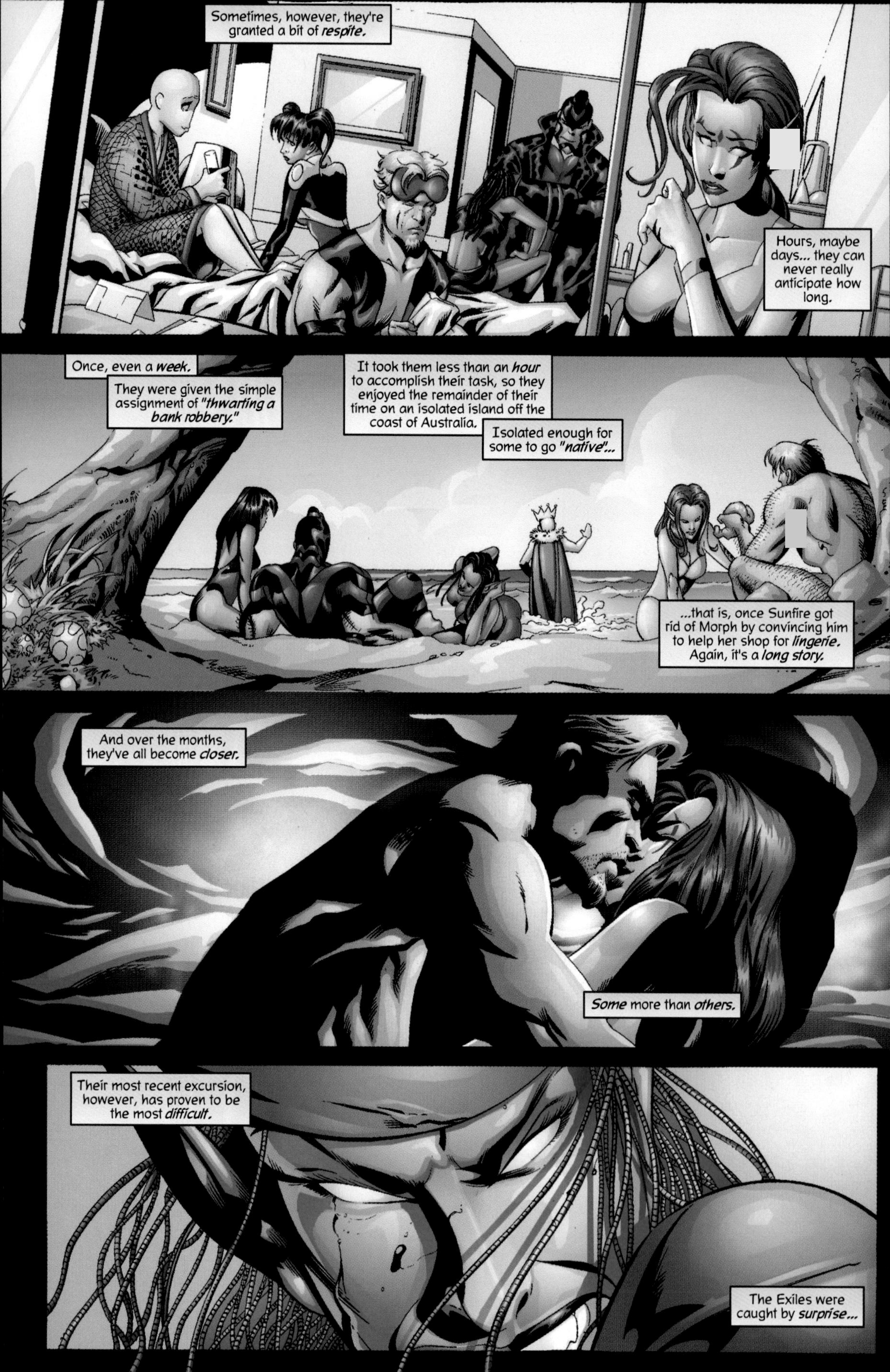
Sometimes, however, they're granted a bit of *respite.*
Hours, maybe days... they can never really anticipate how long.
Once, even a *week.*
They were given the simple assignment of *"thwarting a bank robbery."*
It took them less than an *hour* to accomplish their task, so they enjoyed the remainder of their time on an isolated island off the coast of Australia.
Isolated enough for some to go *"native"...*
...that is, once Sunfire got rid of Morph by convincing him to help her shop for *lingerie.* Again, it's a *long story.*
And over the months, they've all become *closer.*
Some more than *others.*
Their most recent excursion, however, has proven to be the most *difficult.*
The Exiles were caught by *surprise...*

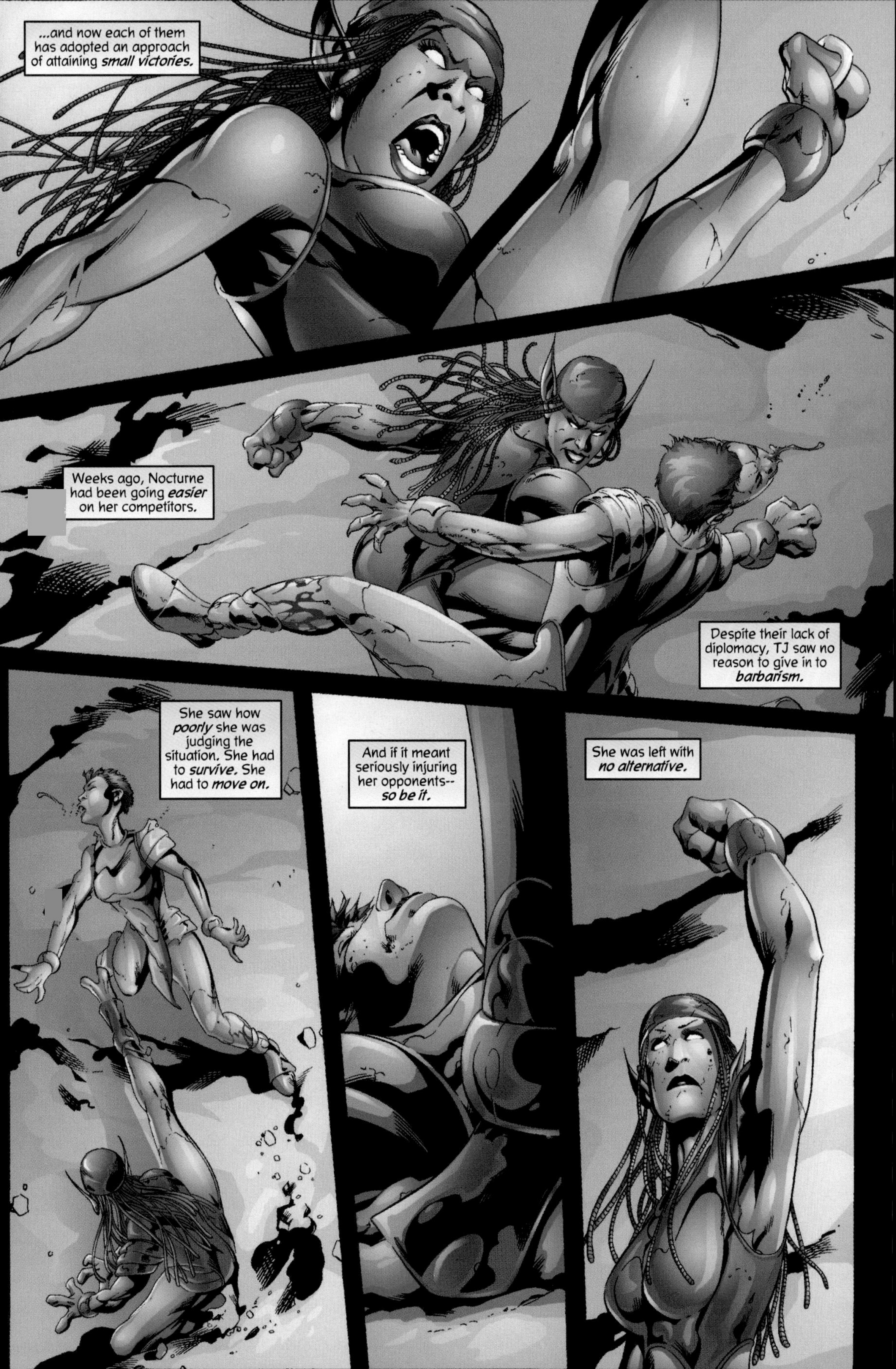
...and now each of them has adopted an approach of attaining small victories.
Weeks ago, Nocturne had been going easier on her competitors.
Despite their lack of diplomacy, TJ saw no reason to give in to barbarism.
She saw how poorly she was judging the situation. She had to survive. She had to move on.
And if it meant seriously injuring her opponents-- so be it.
She was left with no alternative.

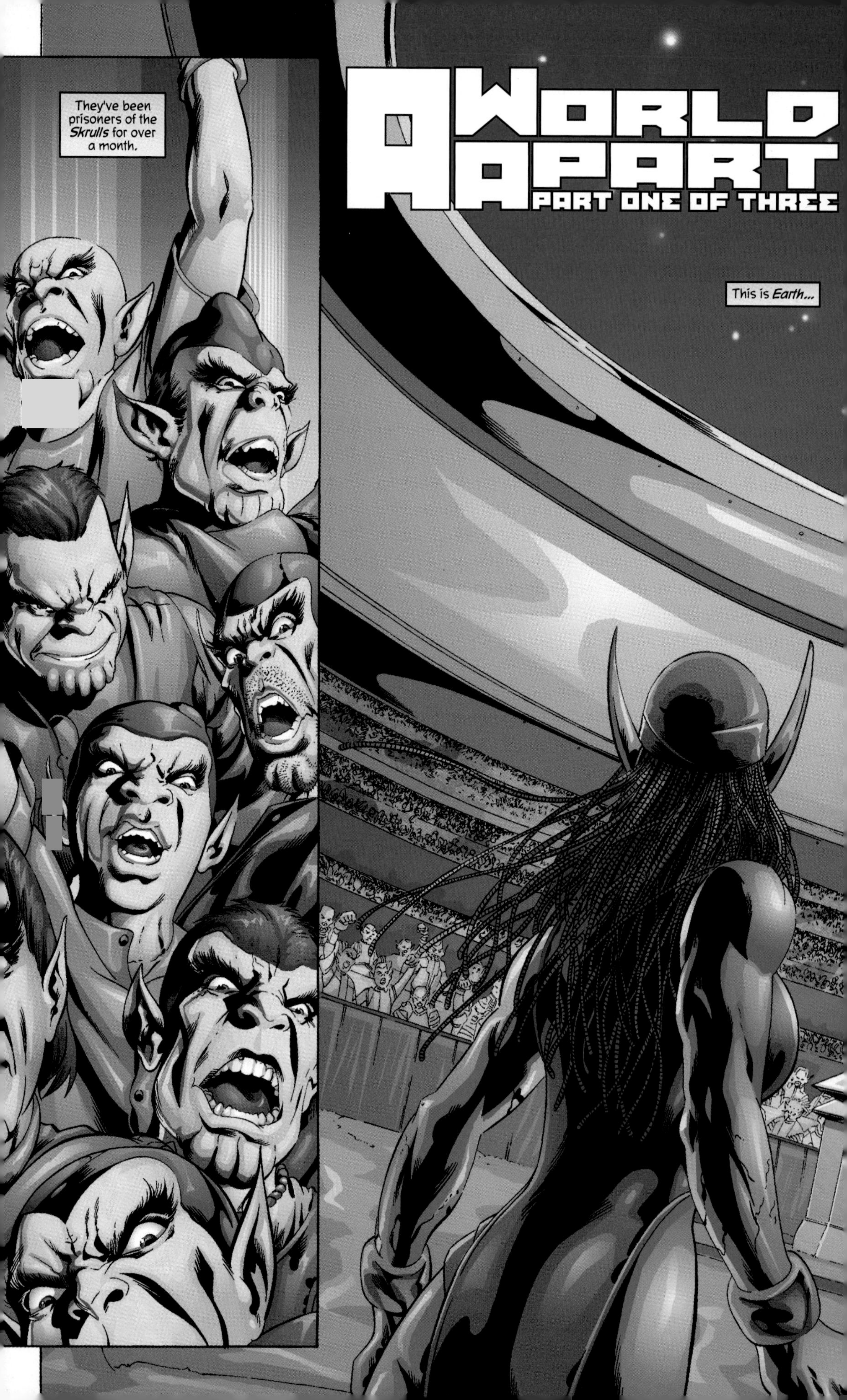
They've been prisoners of the *Skrulls* for over a month.
A WORLD APART
PART ONE OF THREE
This is *Earth*...

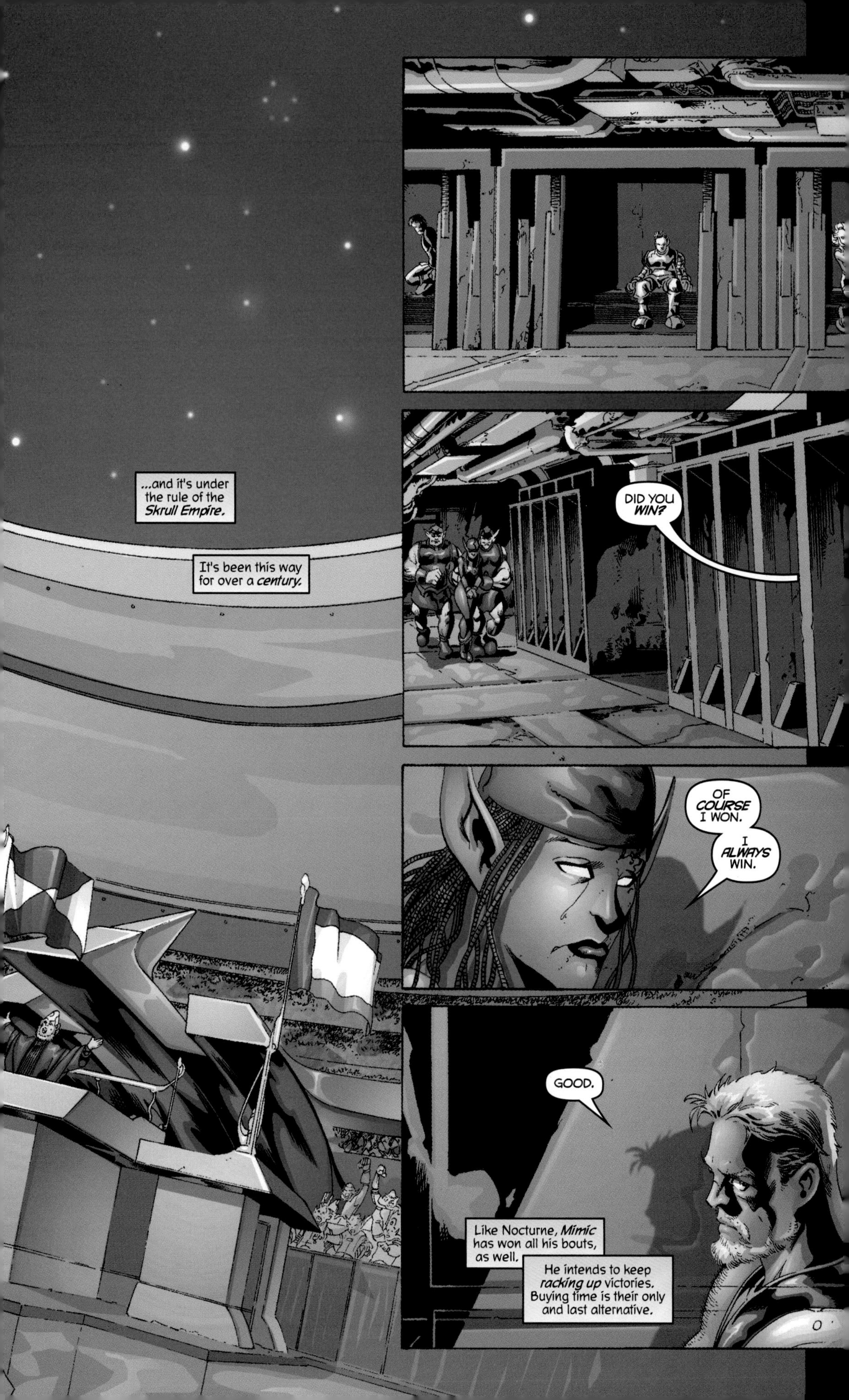
...and it's under the rule of the *Skrull Empire.*
It's been this way for over a *century.*
DID YOU *WIN?*
OF *COURSE* I WON.
I *ALWAYS* WIN.
GOOD.
Like Nocturne, *Mimic* has won all his bouts, as well.
He intends to keep *racking up* victories. Buying time is their only and last alternative.

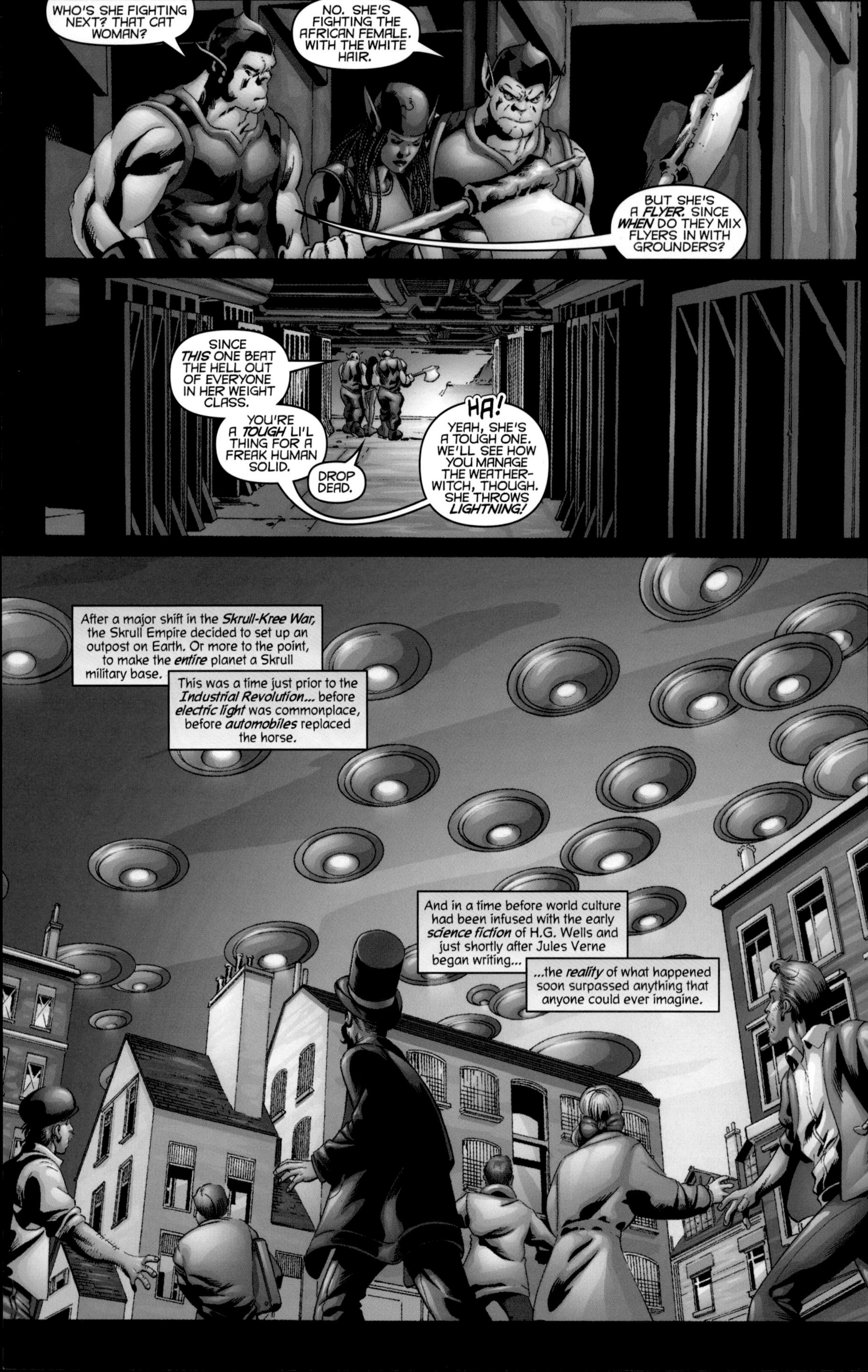
WHO'S SHE FIGHTING NEXT? THAT CAT WOMAN?
NO. SHE'S FIGHTING THE AFRICAN FEMALE. WITH THE WHITE HAIR.
BUT SHE'S A FLYER. SINCE WHEN DO THEY MIX FLYERS IN WITH GROUNDERS?
SINCE THIS ONE BEAT THE HELL OUT OF EVERYONE IN HER WEIGHT CLASS.
YOU'RE A TOUGH LI'L THING FOR A FREAK HUMAN SOLID.
DROP DEAD.
HA!
YEAH, SHE'S A TOUGH ONE. WE'LL SEE HOW YOU MANAGE THE WEATHER-WITCH, THOUGH. SHE THROWS LIGHTNING!
After a major shift in the Skrull-Kree War, the Skrull Empire decided to set up an outpost on Earth. Or more to the point, to make the entire planet a Skrull military base.
This was a time just prior to the Industrial Revolution... before electric light was commonplace, before automobiles replaced the horse.
And in a time before world culture had been infused with the early science fiction of H.G. Wells and just shortly after Jules Verne began writing...
...the reality of what happened soon surpassed anything that anyone could ever imagine.

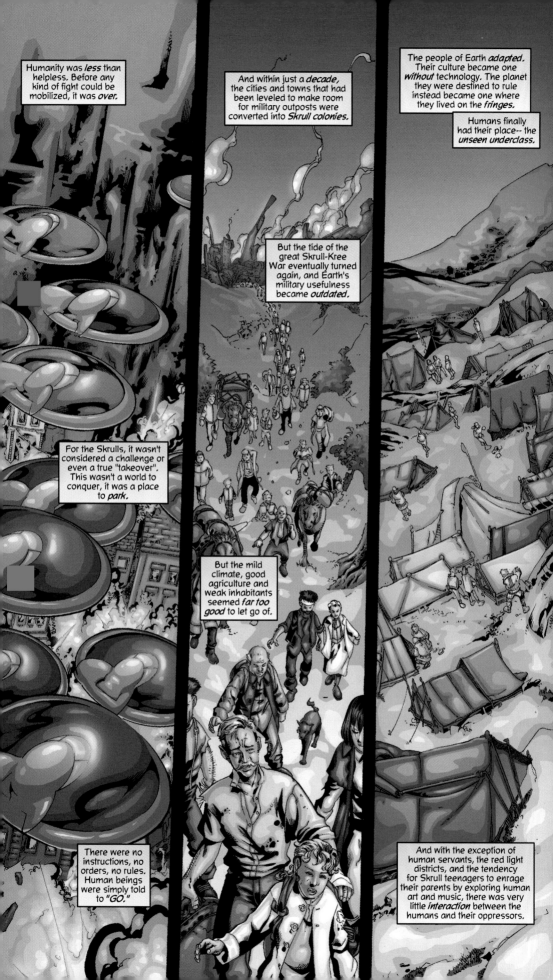

Humanity was *less* than helpless. Before any kind of fight could be mobilized, it was *over*.

And within just a *decade*, the cities and towns that had been leveled to make room for military outposts were converted into *Skrull colonies.*

The people of Earth *adapted.* Their culture became one *without* technology. The planet they were destined to rule instead became one where they lived on the *fringes.*

Humans finally had their place-- the *unseen underclass.*

But the tide of the great Skrull-Kree War eventually turned again, and Earth's military usefulness became *outdated.*

For the Skrulls, it wasn't considered a challenge or even a true "takeover". This wasn't a world to conquer, it was a place to *park.*

But the mild climate, good agriculture and weak inhabitants seemed *far too good* to let go of.

There were no instructions, no orders, no rules. Human beings were simply told to *"GO."*

And with the exception of human servants, the red light districts, and the tendency for Skrull teenagers to enrage their parents by exploring human art and music, there was very little *interaction* between the humans and their oppressors.

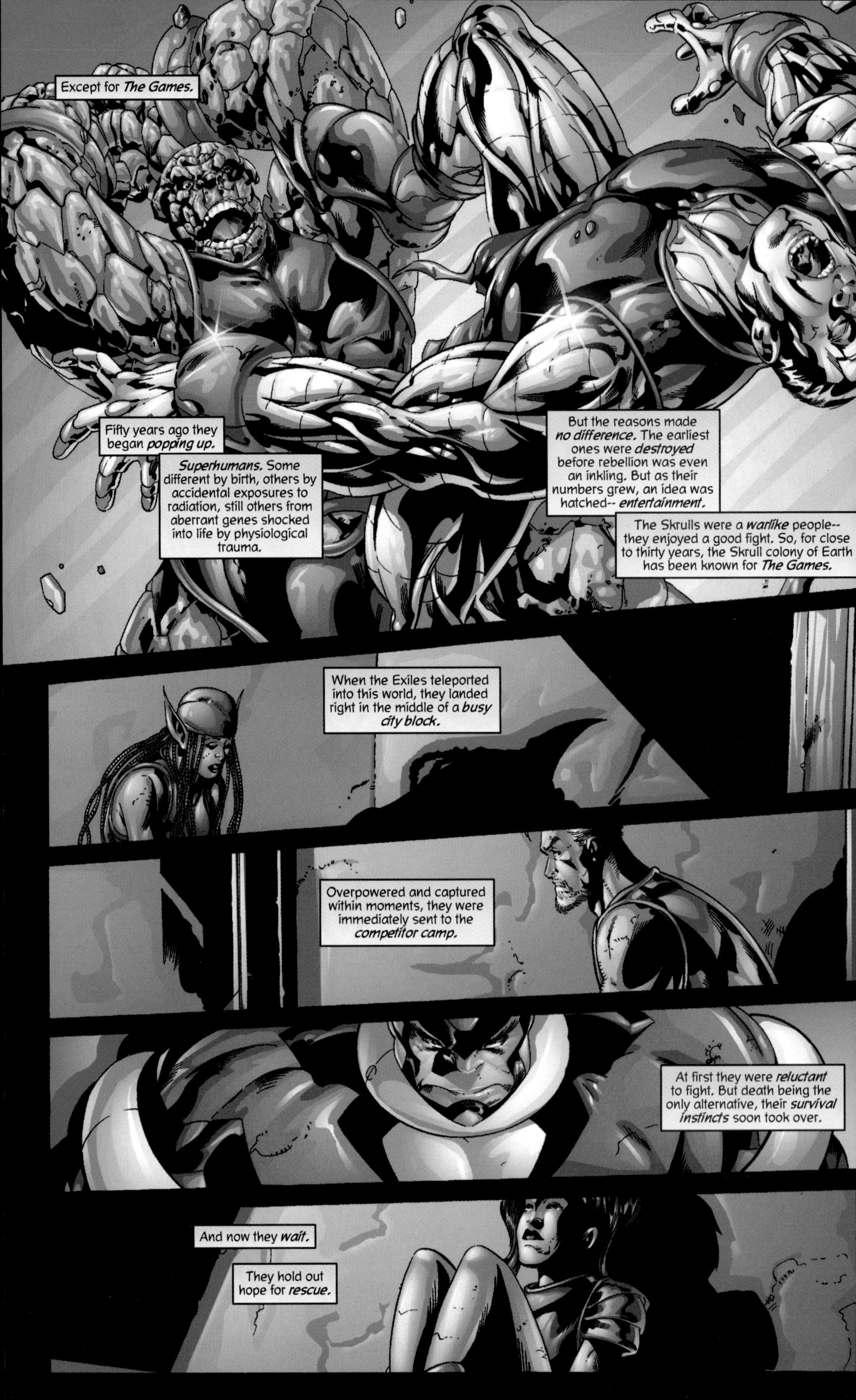

Except for *The Games.*
Fifty years ago they began *popping up.*
Superhumans. Some different by birth, others by accidental exposures to radiation, still others from aberrant genes shocked into life by physiological trauma.
But the reasons made *no difference.* The earliest ones were *destroyed* before rebellion was even an inkling. But as their numbers grew, an idea was hatched-- *entertainment.*
The Skrulls were a *warlike* people-- they enjoyed a good fight. So, for close to thirty years, the Skrull colony of Earth has been known for *The Games.*
When the Exiles teleported into this world, they landed right in the middle of a *busy city block.*
Overpowered and captured within moments, they were immediately sent to the *competitor camp.*
At first they were *reluctant* to fight. But death being the only alternative, their *survival instincts* soon took over.
And now they *wait.*
They hold out hope for *rescue.*

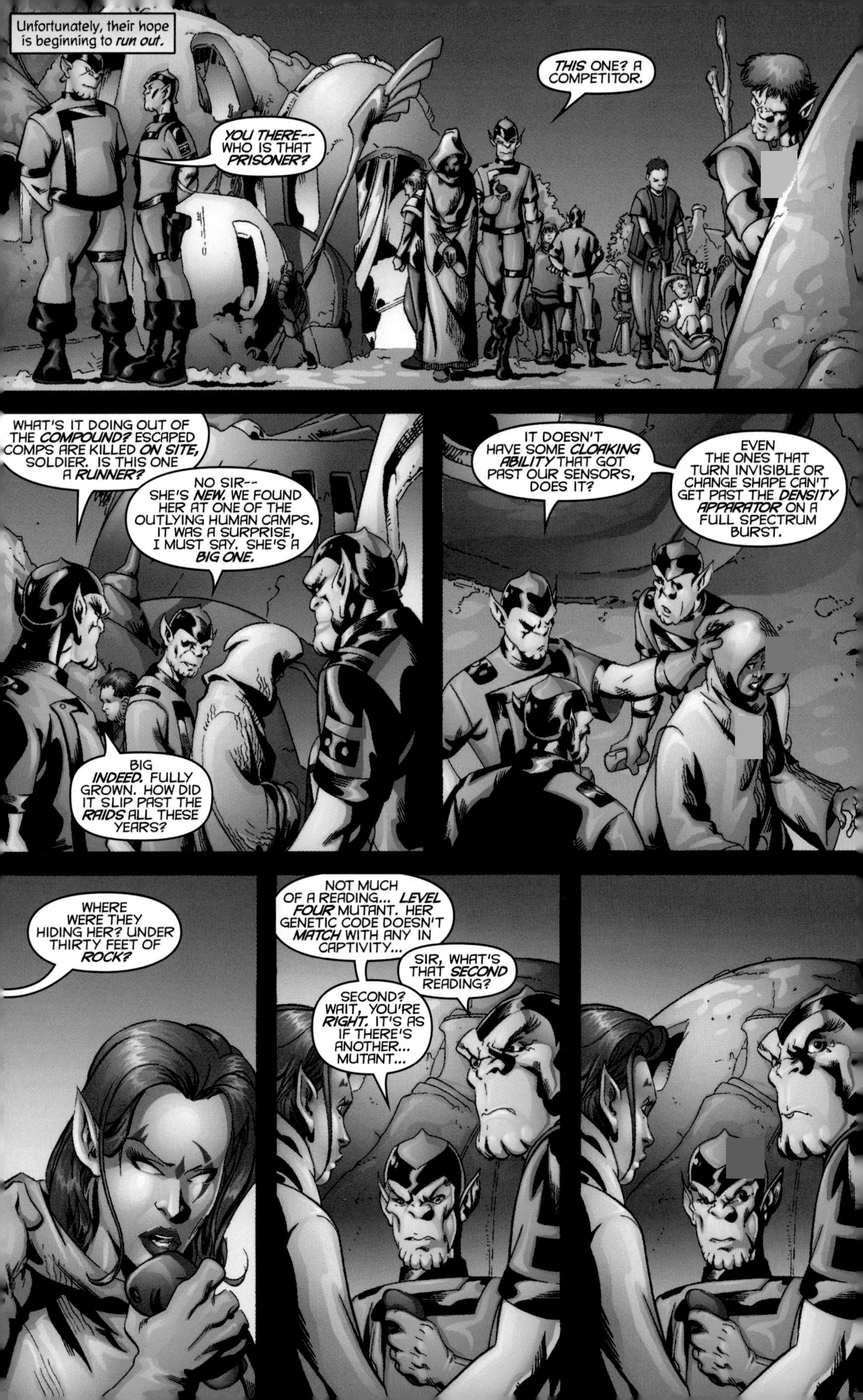

Unfortunately, their hope is beginning to *run out.*
YOU THERE-- WHO IS THAT PRISONER?
THIS ONE? A COMPETITOR.
WHAT'S IT DOING OUT OF THE COMPOUND? ESCAPED COMPS ARE KILLED ON SITE, SOLDIER. IS THIS ONE A RUNNER?
NO SIR-- SHE'S NEW. WE FOUND HER AT ONE OF THE OUTLYING HUMAN CAMPS. IT WAS A SURPRISE, I MUST SAY. SHE'S A BIG ONE.
BIG INDEED. FULLY GROWN. HOW DID IT SLIP PAST THE RAIDS ALL THESE YEARS?
IT DOESN'T HAVE SOME CLOAKING ABILITY THAT GOT PAST OUR SENSORS, DOES IT?
EVEN THE ONES THAT TURN INVISIBLE OR CHANGE SHAPE CAN'T GET PAST THE DENSITY APPARATOR ON A FULL SPECTRUM BURST.
WHERE WERE THEY HIDING HER? UNDER THIRTY FEET OF ROCK?
NOT MUCH OF A READING... LEVEL FOUR MUTANT. HER GENETIC CODE DOESN'T MATCH WITH ANY IN CAPTIVITY...
SIR, WHAT'S THAT SECOND READING?
SECOND? WAIT, YOU'RE RIGHT. IT'S AS IF THERE'S ANOTHER... MUTANT...

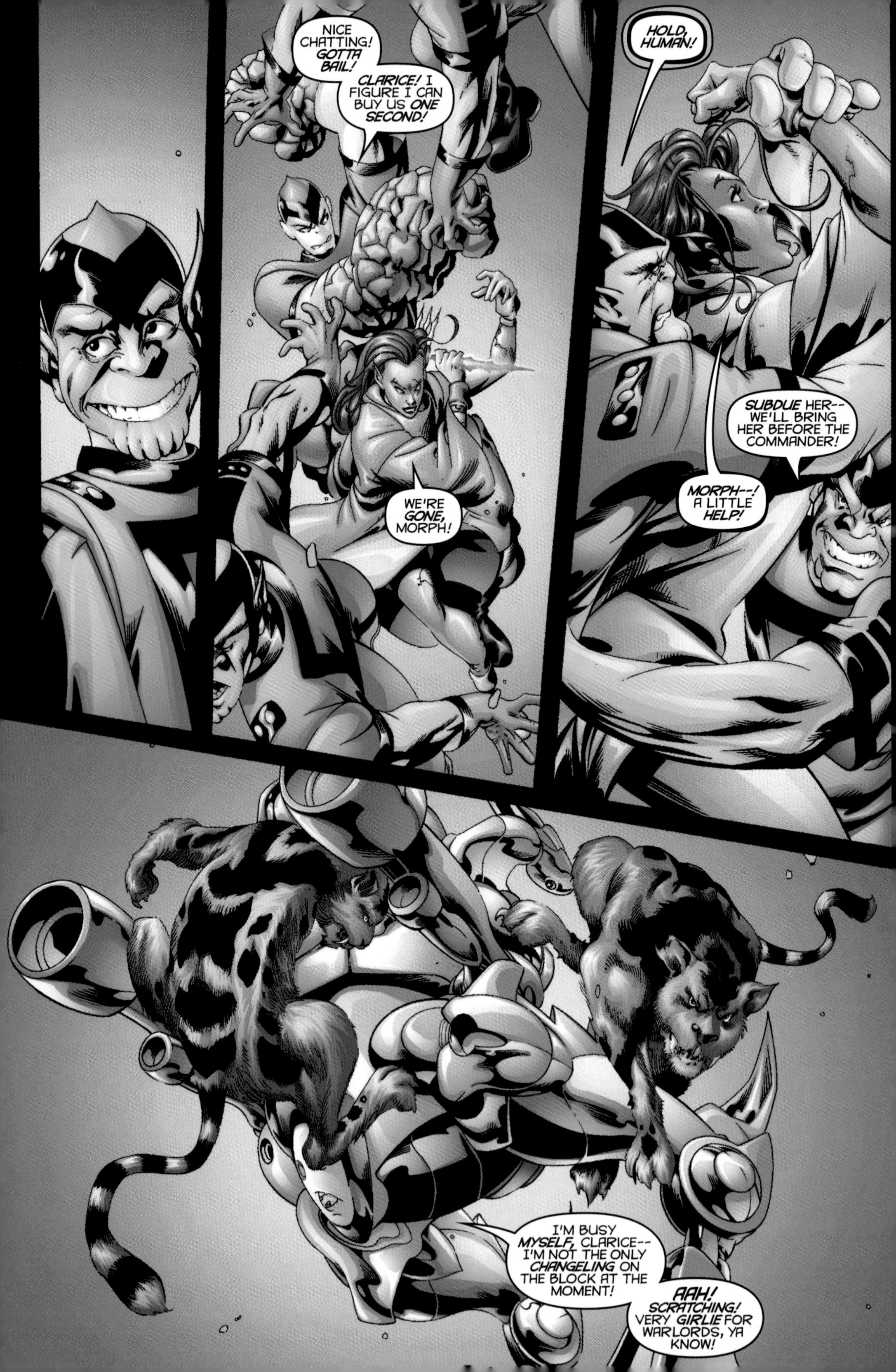
NICE CHATTING! GOTTA BAIL!
CLARICE! I FIGURE I CAN BUY US ONE SECOND!
WE'RE GONE, MORPH!
HOLD, HUMAN!
SUBDUE HER-- WE'LL BRING HER BEFORE THE COMMANDER!
MORPH--! A LITTLE HELP!
I'M BUSY MYSELF, CLARICE-- I'M NOT THE ONLY CHANGELING ON THE BLOCK AT THE MOMENT!
AAH! SCRATCHING! VERY GIRLIE FOR WARLORDS, YA KNOW!

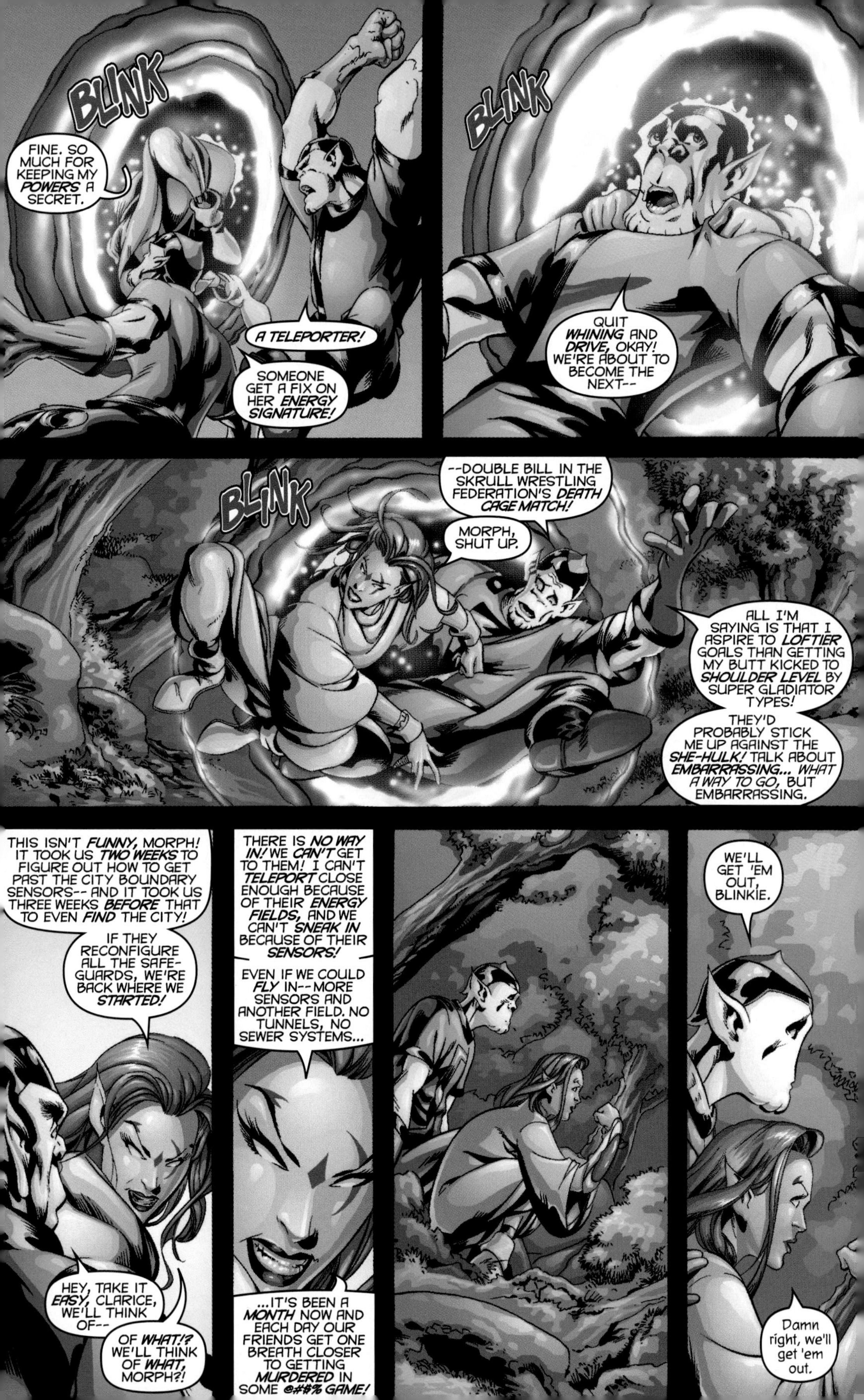
BLINK
FINE. SO MUCH FOR KEEPING MY POWERS A SECRET.
A TELEPORTER!
SOMEONE GET A FIX ON HER ENERGY SIGNATURE!
BLINK
QUIT WHINING AND DRIVE, OKAY! WE'RE ABOUT TO BECOME THE NEXT--
BLINK
--DOUBLE BILL IN THE SKRULL WRESTLING FEDERATION'S DEATH CAGE MATCH!
MORPH, SHUT UP.
ALL I'M SAYING IS THAT I ASPIRE TO LOFTIER GOALS THAN GETTING MY BUTT KICKED TO SHOULDER LEVEL BY SUPER GLADIATOR TYPES!
THEY'D PROBABLY STICK ME UP AGAINST THE SHE-HULK! TALK ABOUT EMBARRASSING... WHAT A WAY TO GO, BUT EMBARRASSING.
THIS ISN'T FUNNY, MORPH! IT TOOK US TWO WEEKS TO FIGURE OUT HOW TO GET PAST THE CITY BOUNDARY SENSORS-- AND IT TOOK US THREE WEEKS BEFORE THAT TO EVEN FIND THE CITY!
IF THEY RECONFIGURE ALL THE SAFE-GUARDS, WE'RE BACK WHERE WE STARTED!
HEY, TAKE IT EASY, CLARICE, WE'LL THINK OF--
OF WHAT!? WE'LL THINK OF WHAT, MORPH?!
THERE IS NO WAY IN! WE CAN'T GET TO THEM! I CAN'T TELEPORT CLOSE ENOUGH BECAUSE OF THEIR ENERGY FIELDS, AND WE CAN'T SNEAK IN BECAUSE OF THEIR SENSORS!
EVEN IF WE COULD FLY IN--MORE SENSORS AND ANOTHER FIELD. NO TUNNELS, NO SEWER SYSTEMS...
...IT'S BEEN A MONTH NOW AND EACH DAY OUR FRIENDS GET ONE BREATH CLOSER TO GETTING MURDERED IN SOME @#$% GAME!
WE'LL GET 'EM OUT, BLINKIE.
Damn right, we'll get 'em out.

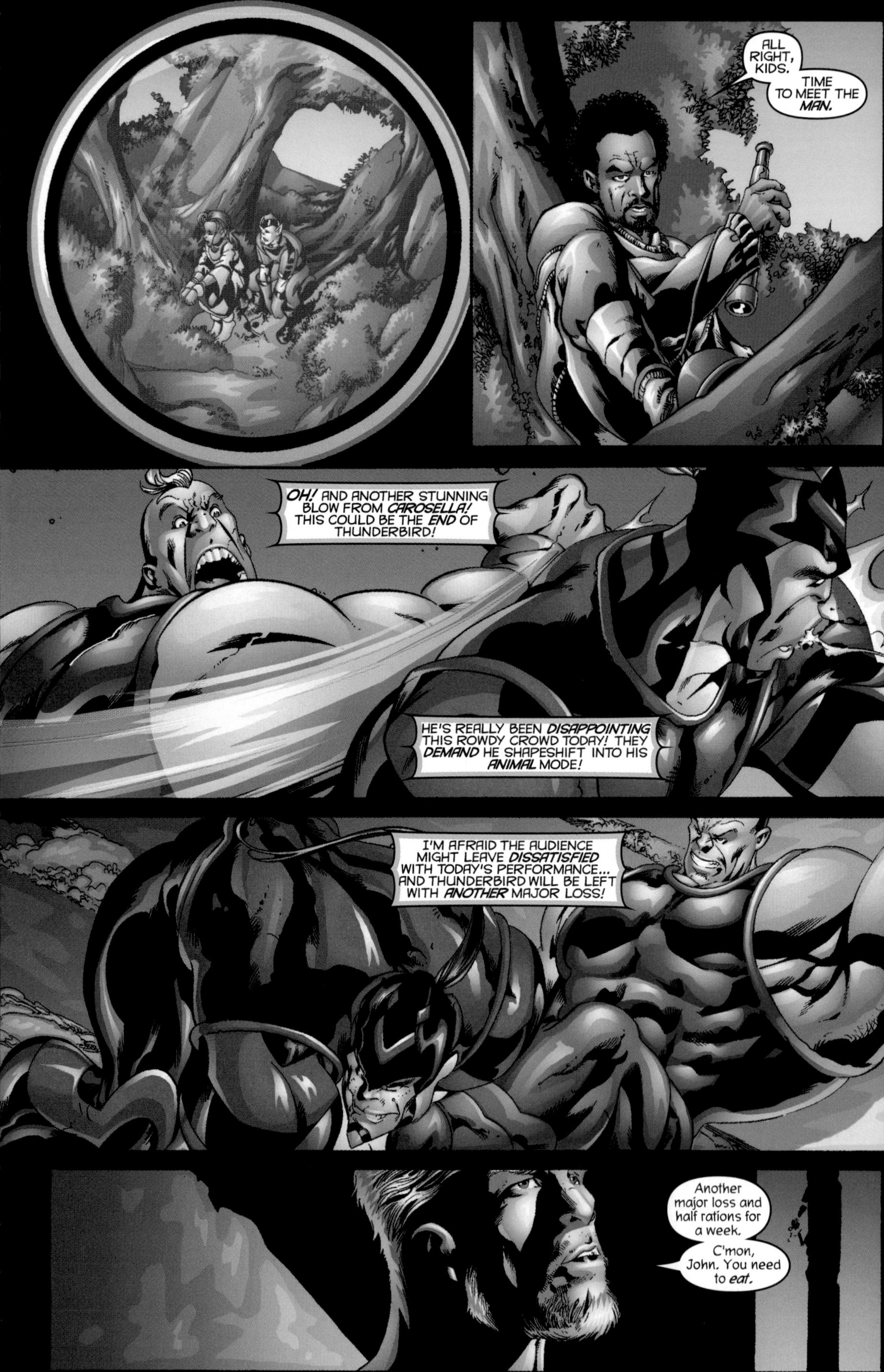
ALL RIGHT, KIDS.
TIME TO MEET THE *MAN.*
OH! AND ANOTHER STUNNING BLOW FROM *CAROSELLA!* THIS COULD BE THE *END* OF THUNDERBIRD!
HE'S REALLY BEEN *DISAPPOINTING* THIS ROWDY CROWD TODAY! THEY *DEMAND* HE SHAPESHIFT INTO HIS *ANIMAL* MODE!
I'M AFRAID THE AUDIENCE MIGHT LEAVE *DISSATISFIED* WITH TODAY'S PERFORMANCE... AND THUNDERBIRD WILL BE LEFT WITH *ANOTHER* MAJOR LOSS!
Another major loss and half rations for a week.
C'mon, John. You need to *eat.*

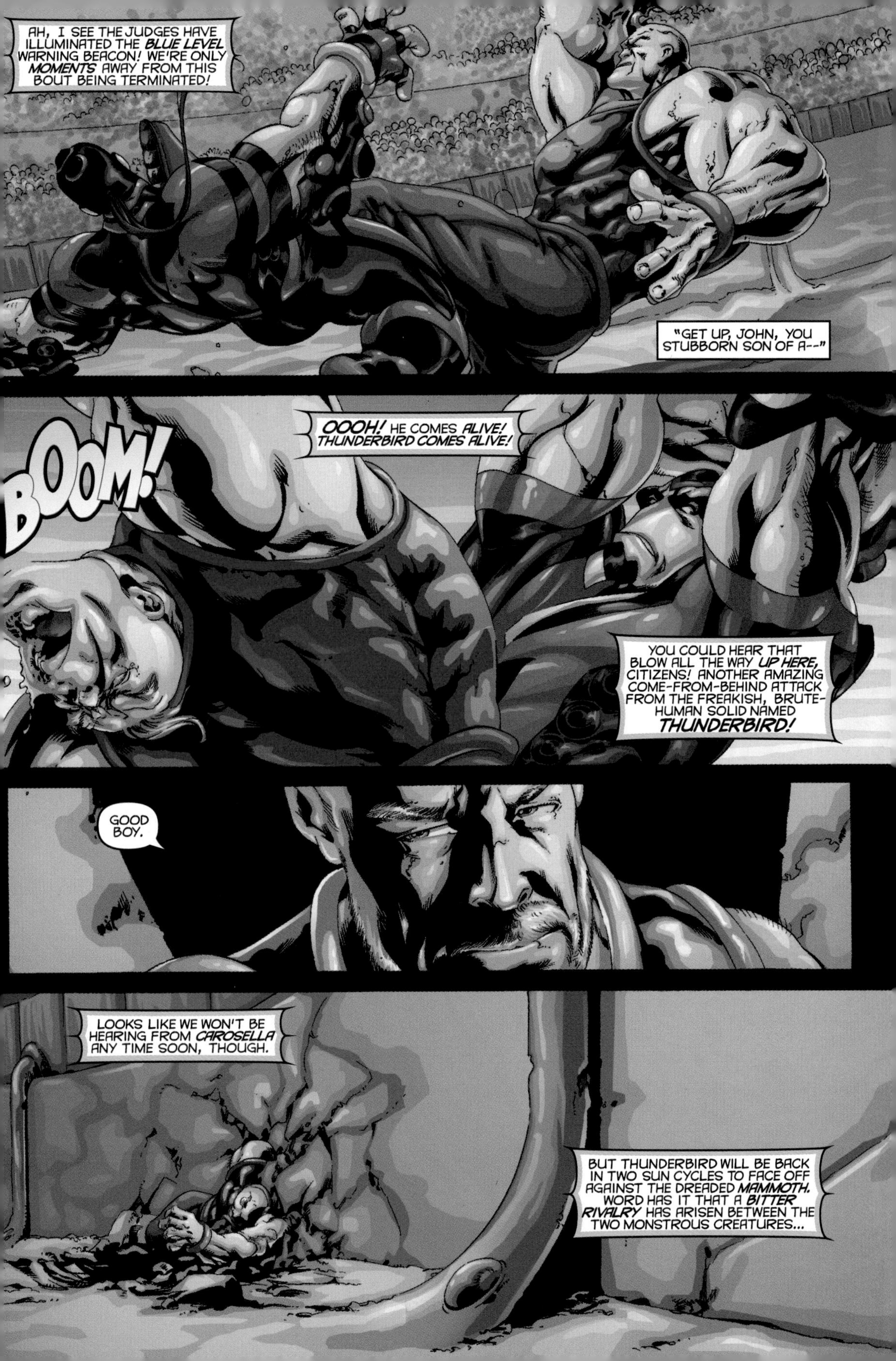
AH, I SEE THE JUDGES HAVE ILLUMINATED THE BLUE LEVEL WARNING BEACON! WE'RE ONLY MOMENTS AWAY FROM THIS BOUT BEING TERMINATED!
"GET UP, JOHN, YOU STUBBORN SON OF A--"
BOOM!
OOOH! HE COMES ALIVE! THUNDERBIRD COMES ALIVE!
YOU COULD HEAR THAT BLOW ALL THE WAY UP HERE, CITIZENS! ANOTHER AMAZING COME-FROM-BEHIND ATTACK FROM THE FREAKISH, BRUTE-HUMAN SOLID NAMED THUNDERBIRD!
GOOD BOY.
LOOKS LIKE WE WON'T BE HEARING FROM CAROSELLA ANY TIME SOON, THOUGH.
BUT THUNDERBIRD WILL BE BACK IN TWO SUN CYCLES TO FACE OFF AGAINST THE DREADED MAMMOTH. WORD HAS IT THAT A BITTER RIVALRY HAS ARISEN BETWEEN THE TWO MONSTROUS CREATURES...

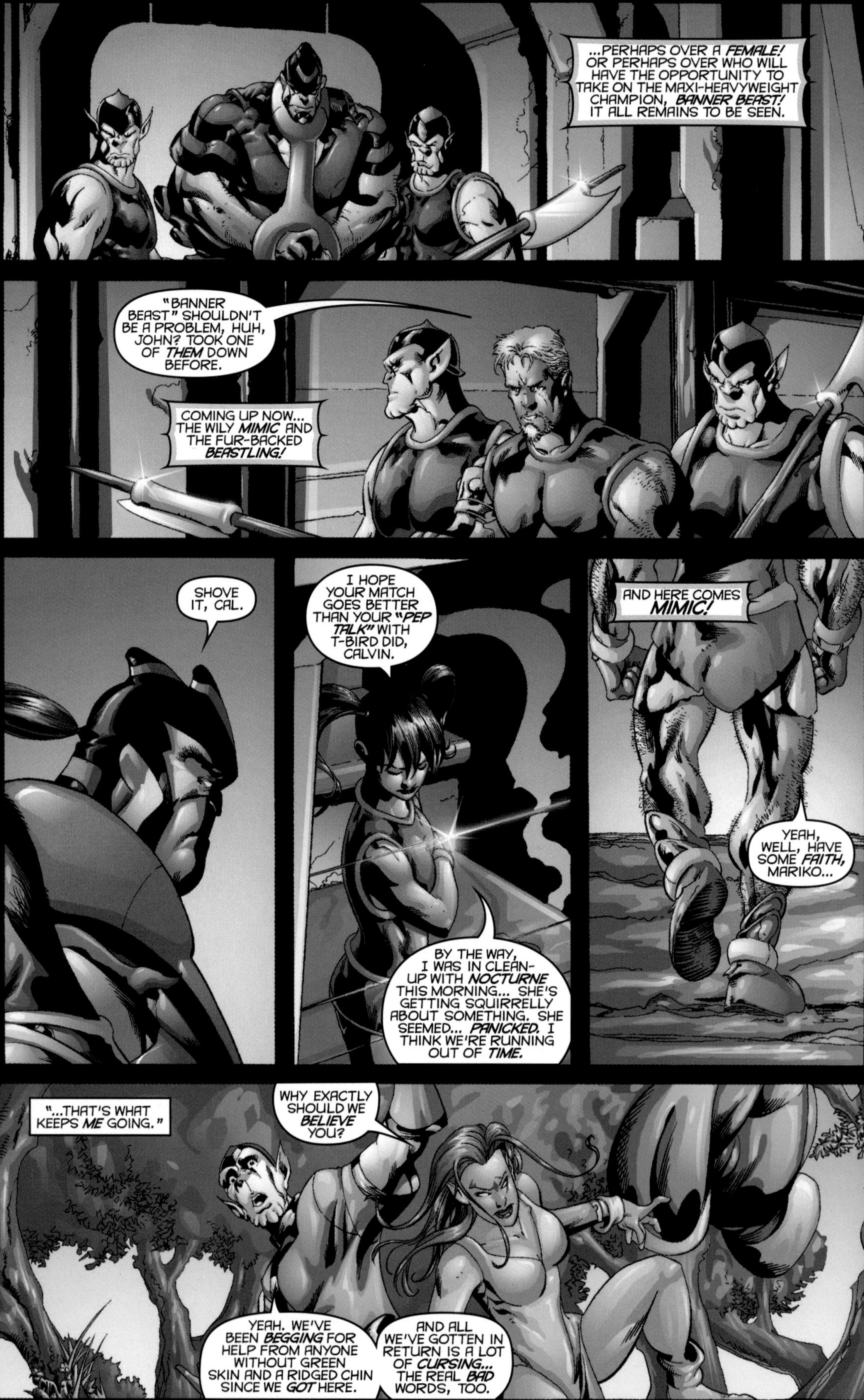
...PERHAPS OVER A *FEMALE!* OR PERHAPS OVER WHO WILL HAVE THE OPPORTUNITY TO TAKE ON THE MAXI-HEAVYWEIGHT CHAMPION, *BANNER BEAST!* IT ALL REMAINS TO BE SEEN.
"BANNER BEAST" SHOULDN'T BE A PROBLEM, HUH, JOHN? TOOK ONE OF *THEM* DOWN BEFORE.
COMING UP NOW... THE WILY *MIMIC* AND THE FUR-BACKED *BEASTLING!*
SHOVE IT, CAL.
I HOPE YOUR MATCH GOES BETTER THAN YOUR *"PEP TALK"* WITH T-BIRD DID, CALVIN.
BY THE WAY, I WAS IN CLEAN-UP WITH *NOCTURNE* THIS MORNING... SHE'S GETTING SQUIRRELLY ABOUT SOMETHING. SHE SEEMED... *PANICKED.* I THINK WE'RE RUNNING OUT OF *TIME.*
AND HERE COMES *MIMIC!*
YEAH, WELL, HAVE SOME *FAITH,* MARIKO...
"...THAT'S WHAT KEEPS *ME* GOING."
WHY EXACTLY SHOULD WE *BELIEVE* YOU?
YEAH. WE'VE BEEN *BEGGING* FOR HELP FROM ANYONE WITHOUT GREEN SKIN AND A RIDGED CHIN SINCE WE *GOT* HERE.
AND ALL WE'VE GOTTEN IN RETURN IS A LOT OF *CURSING...* THE REAL *BAD* WORDS, TOO.

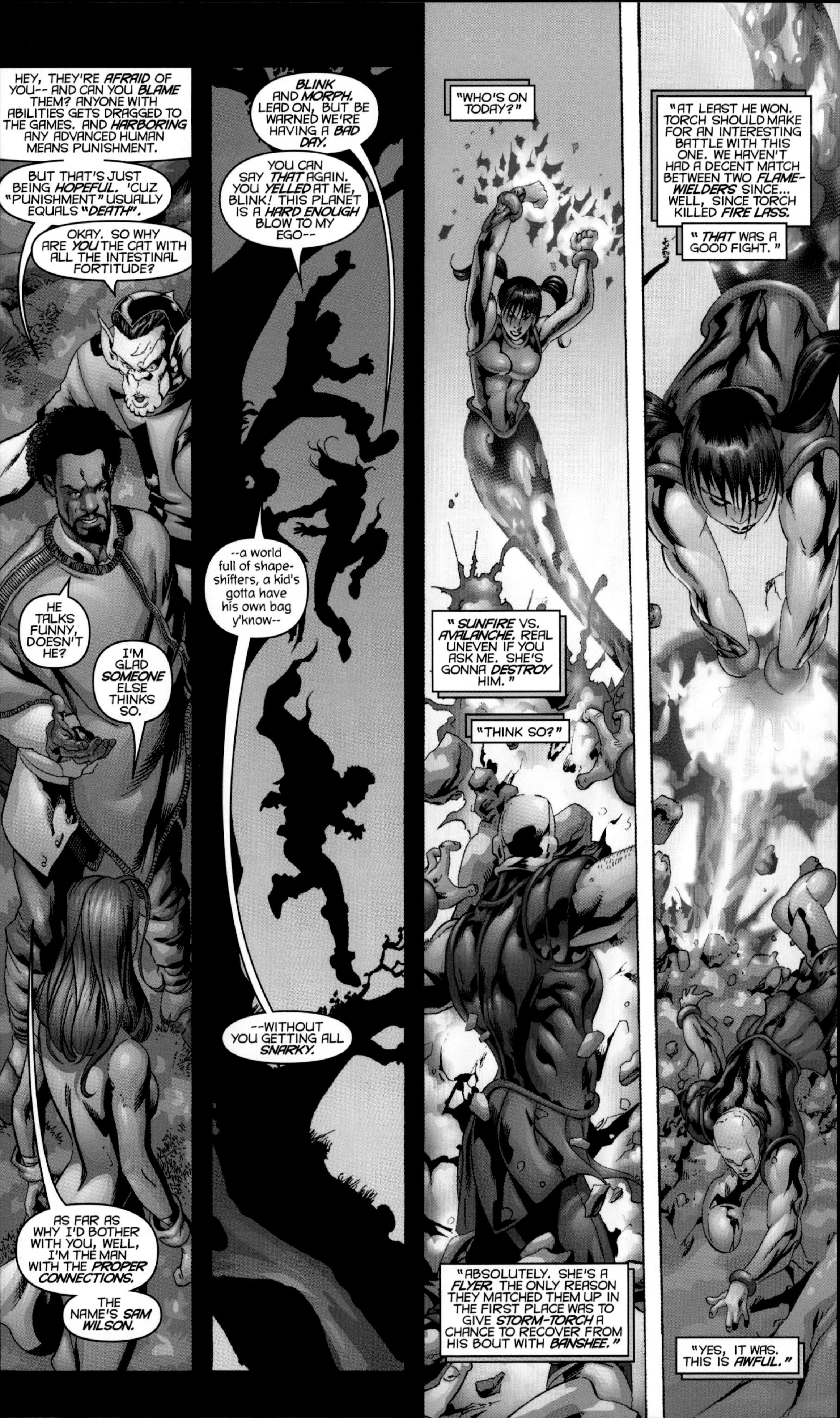

HEY, THEY'RE AFRAID OF YOU-- AND CAN YOU BLAME THEM? ANYONE WITH ABILITIES GETS DRAGGED TO THE GAMES. AND HARBORING ANY ADVANCED HUMAN MEANS PUNISHMENT.
BUT THAT'S JUST BEING HOPEFUL. 'CUZ "PUNISHMENT" USUALLY EQUALS "DEATH".
OKAY. SO WHY ARE YOU THE CAT WITH ALL THE INTESTINAL FORTITUDE?
HE TALKS FUNNY, DOESN'T HE?
I'M GLAD SOMEONE ELSE THINKS SO.
AS FAR AS WHY I'D BOTHER WITH YOU, WELL, I'M THE MAN WITH THE PROPER CONNECTIONS.
THE NAME'S SAM WILSON.
BLINK AND MORPH. LEAD ON, BUT BE WARNED WE'RE HAVING A BAD DAY.
YOU CAN SAY THAT AGAIN. YOU YELLED AT ME, BLINK! THIS PLANET IS A HARD ENOUGH BLOW TO MY EGO--
--a world full of shape-shifters, a kid's gotta have his own bag y'know--
--WITHOUT YOU GETTING ALL SNARKY.
"WHO'S ON TODAY?"
"SUNFIRE VS. AVALANCHE. REAL UNEVEN IF YOU ASK ME. SHE'S GONNA DESTROY HIM."
"THINK SO?"
"ABSOLUTELY. SHE'S A FLYER. THE ONLY REASON THEY MATCHED THEM UP IN THE FIRST PLACE WAS TO GIVE STORM-TORCH A CHANCE TO RECOVER FROM HIS BOUT WITH BANSHEE."
"AT LEAST HE WON. TORCH SHOULD MAKE FOR AN INTERESTING BATTLE WITH THIS ONE. WE HAVEN'T HAD A DECENT MATCH BETWEEN TWO FLAME-WIELDERS SINCE... WELL, SINCE TORCH KILLED FIRE LASS.
"THAT WAS A GOOD FIGHT."
"YES, IT WAS. THIS IS AWFUL."

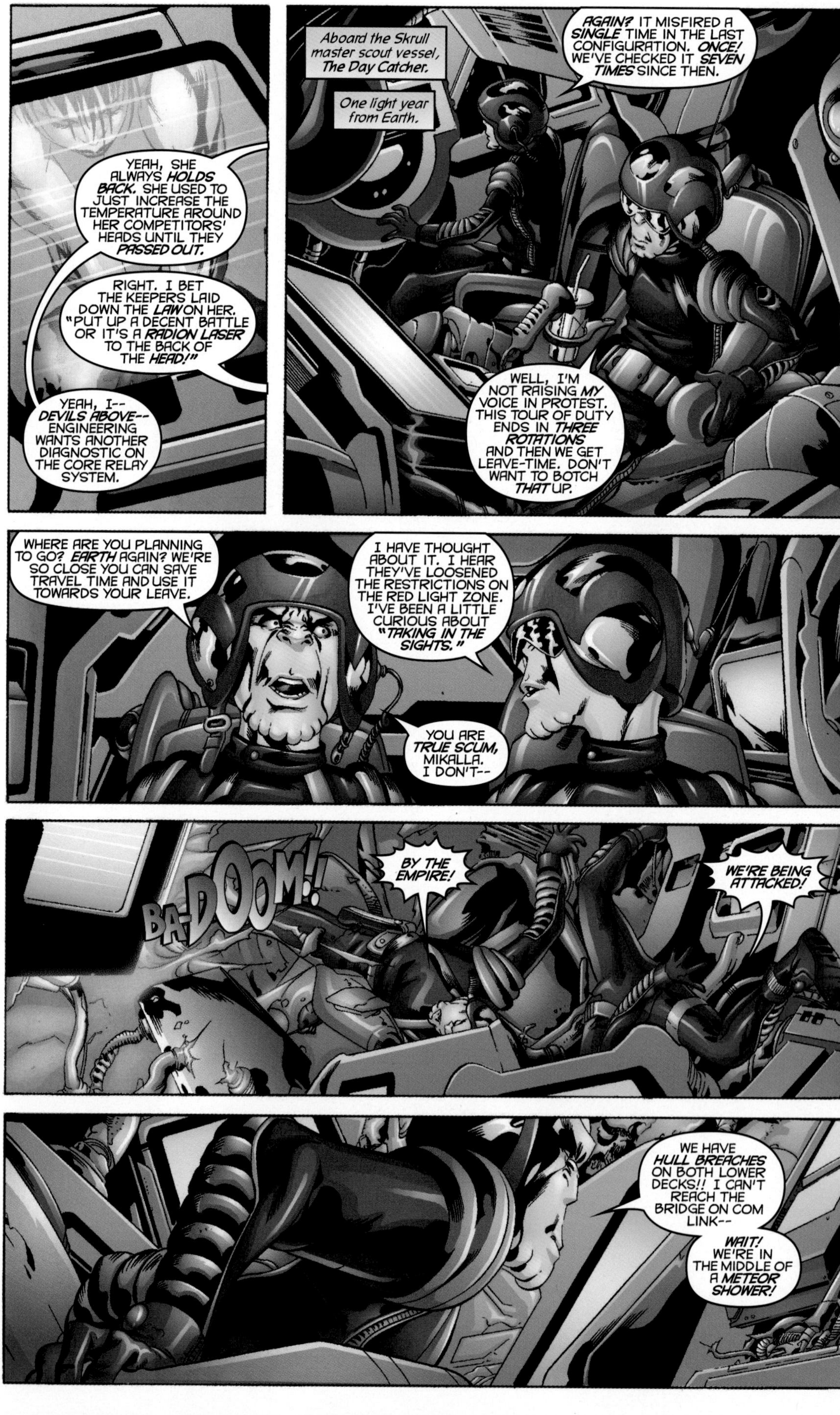
YEAH, SHE ALWAYS HOLDS BACK. SHE USED TO JUST INCREASE THE TEMPERATURE AROUND HER COMPETITORS' HEADS UNTIL THEY PASSED OUT.
RIGHT. I BET THE KEEPER'S LAID DOWN THE LAW ON HER. "PUT UP A DECENT BATTLE OR IT'S A RADION LASER TO THE BACK OF THE HEAD!"
YEAH, I-- DEVILS ABOVE-- ENGINEERING WANTS ANOTHER DIAGNOSTIC ON THE CORE RELAY SYSTEM.
Aboard the Skrull master scout vessel, The Day Catcher.
One light year from Earth.
AGAIN? IT MISFIRED A SINGLE TIME IN THE LAST CONFIGURATION. ONCE! WE'VE CHECKED IT SEVEN TIMES SINCE THEN.
WELL, I'M NOT RAISING MY VOICE IN PROTEST. THIS TOUR OF DUTY ENDS IN THREE ROTATIONS AND THEN WE GET LEAVE-TIME. DON'T WANT TO BOTCH THAT UP.
WHERE ARE YOU PLANNING TO GO? EARTH AGAIN? WE'RE SO CLOSE YOU CAN SAVE TRAVEL TIME AND USE IT TOWARDS YOUR LEAVE.
I HAVE THOUGHT ABOUT IT. I HEAR THEY'VE LOOSENED THE RESTRICTIONS ON THE RED LIGHT ZONE. I'VE BEEN A LITTLE CURIOUS ABOUT "TAKING IN THE SIGHTS."
YOU ARE TRUE SCUM, MIKALLA. I DON'T--
BA-DOOM!!
BY THE EMPIRE!
WE'RE BEING ATTACKED!
WE HAVE HULL BREACHES ON BOTH LOWER DECKS!! I CAN'T REACH THE BRIDGE ON COM LINK--
WAIT! WE'RE IN THE MIDDLE OF A METEOR SHOWER!

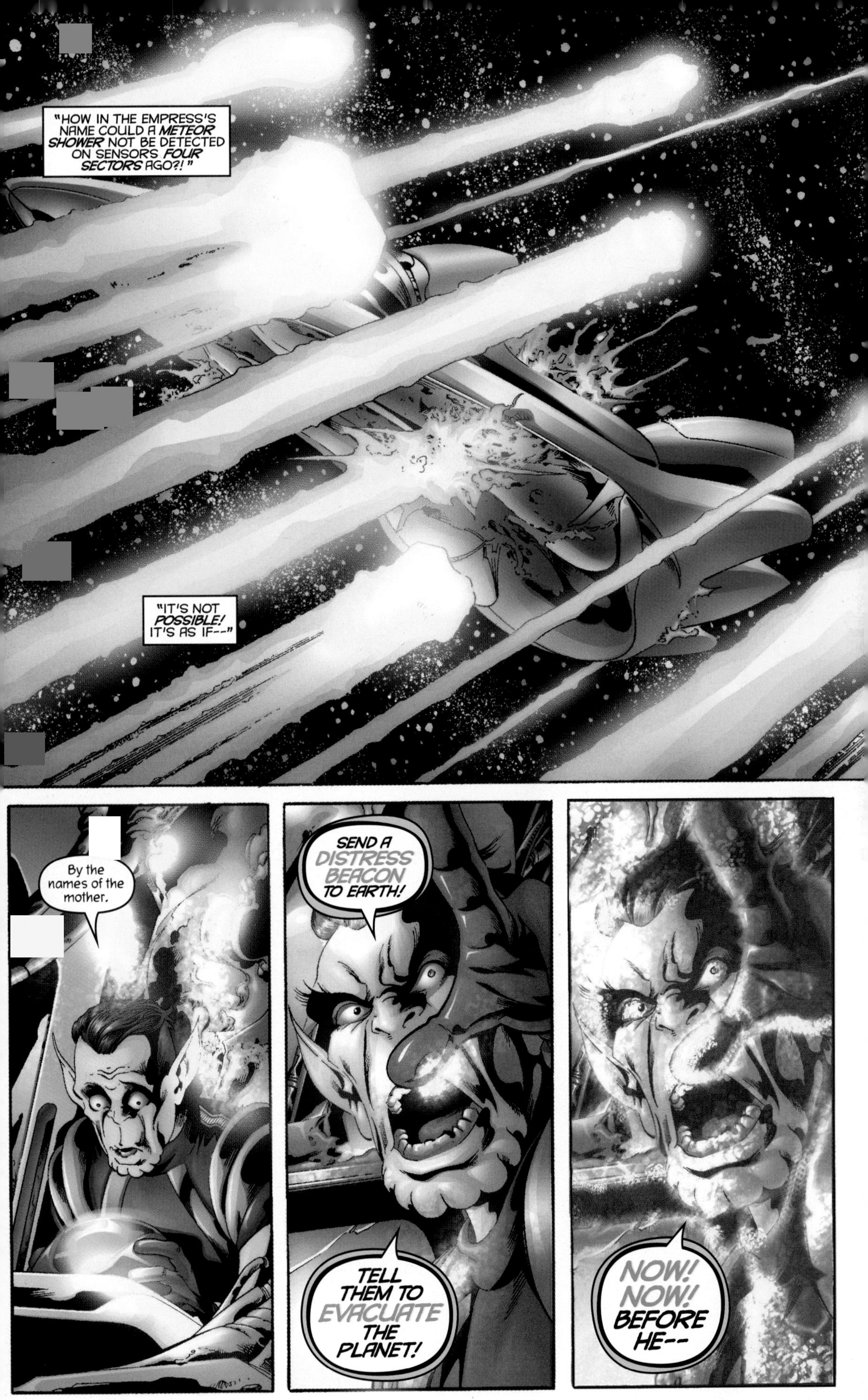
"HOW IN THE EMPRESS'S NAME COULD A METEOR SHOWER NOT BE DETECTED ON SENSORS FOUR SECTORS AGO?!"
"IT'S NOT POSSIBLE! IT'S AS IF--"
By the names of the mother.
SEND A DISTRESS BEACON TO EARTH!
TELL THEM TO EVACUATE THE PLANET!
NOW! NOW! BEFORE HE--

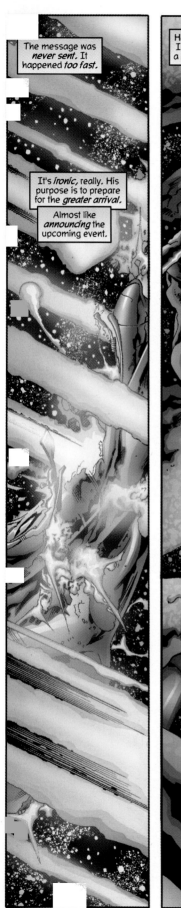

The message was *never sent*. It happened *too fast*.

It's *ironic*, really. His purpose is to prepare for the *greater arrival*.

Almost like *announcing* the upcoming event.

He is *Terrax the Tamer*. In his past life he was a *warrior*. A *ruler*.

He answered to nothing but his *own will*.

Now, he is a *Herald*.

He seeks out *sustenance* for his *master*.

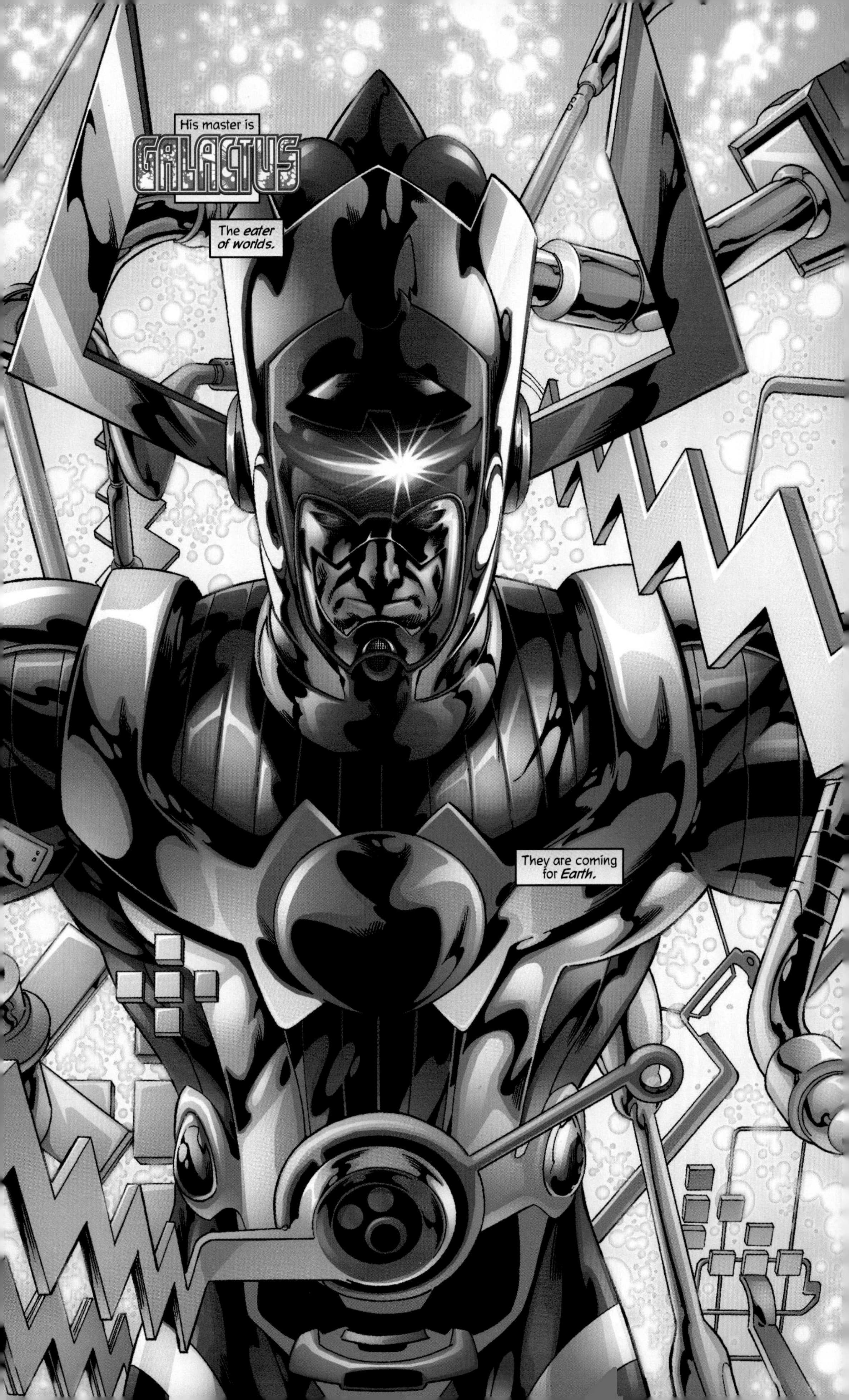
His master is
GALACTUS
The eater of worlds.
They are coming for Earth.

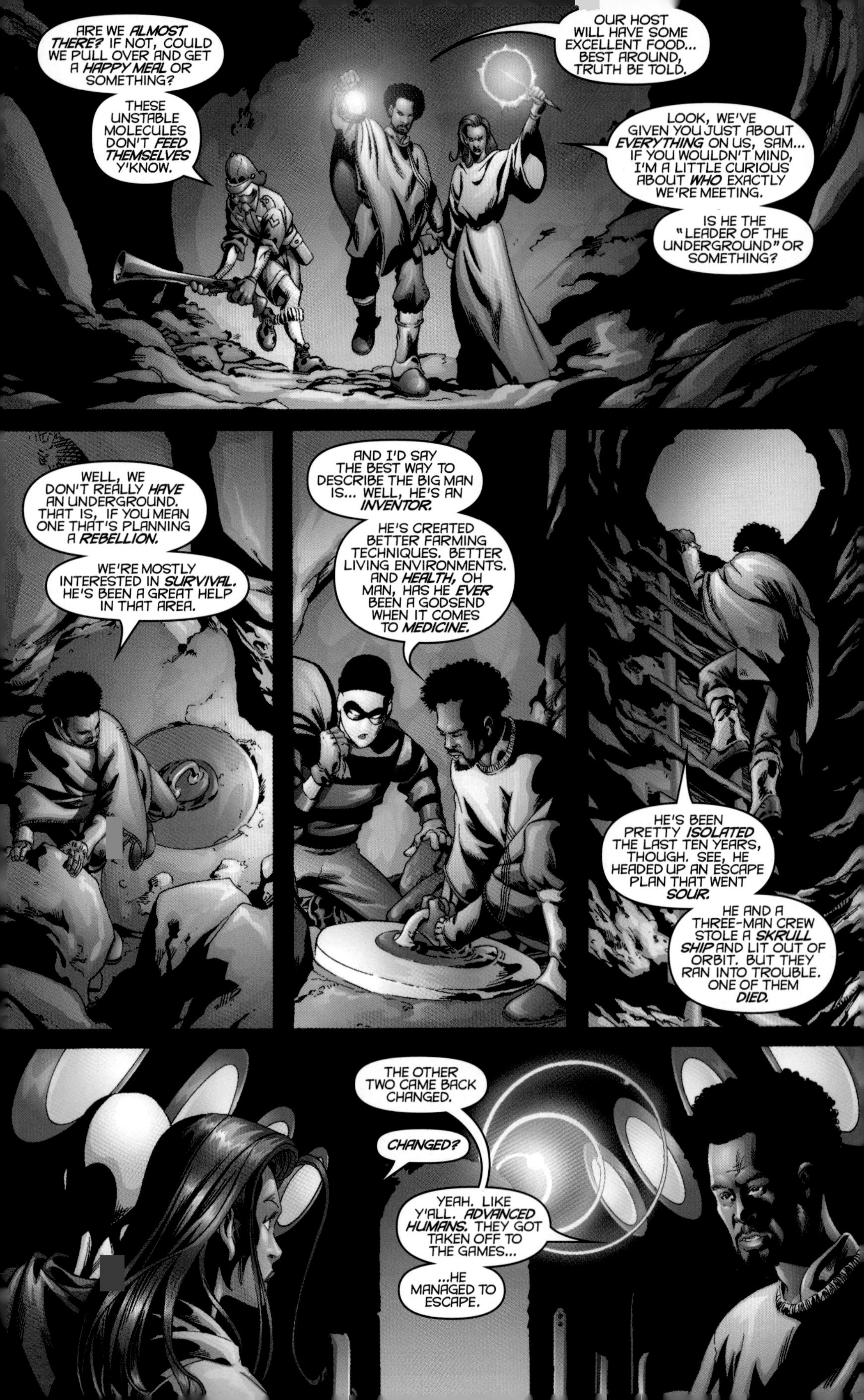
ARE WE ALMOST THERE? IF NOT, COULD WE PULL OVER AND GET A HAPPY MEAL OR SOMETHING?
THESE UNSTABLE MOLECULES DON'T FEED THEMSELVES Y'KNOW.
OUR HOST WILL HAVE SOME EXCELLENT FOOD... BEST AROUND, TRUTH BE TOLD.
LOOK, WE'VE GIVEN YOU JUST ABOUT EVERYTHING ON US, SAM... IF YOU WOULDN'T MIND, I'M A LITTLE CURIOUS ABOUT WHO EXACTLY WE'RE MEETING.
IS HE THE "LEADER OF THE UNDERGROUND" OR SOMETHING?
WELL, WE DON'T REALLY HAVE AN UNDERGROUND. THAT IS, IF YOU MEAN ONE THAT'S PLANNING A REBELLION.
WE'RE MOSTLY INTERESTED IN SURVIVAL. HE'S BEEN A GREAT HELP IN THAT AREA.
AND I'D SAY THE BEST WAY TO DESCRIBE THE BIG MAN IS... WELL, HE'S AN INVENTOR.
HE'S CREATED BETTER FARMING TECHNIQUES. BETTER LIVING ENVIRONMENTS. AND HEALTH, OH MAN, HAS HE EVER BEEN A GODSEND WHEN IT COMES TO MEDICINE.
HE'S BEEN PRETTY ISOLATED THE LAST TEN YEARS, THOUGH. SEE, HE HEADED UP AN ESCAPE PLAN THAT WENT SOUR.
HE AND A THREE-MAN CREW STOLE A SKRULL SHIP AND LIT OUT OF ORBIT. BUT THEY RAN INTO TROUBLE. ONE OF THEM DIED.
THE OTHER TWO CAME BACK CHANGED.
CHANGED?
YEAH. LIKE Y'ALL. ADVANCED HUMANS. THEY GOT TAKEN OFF TO THE GAMES...
...HE MANAGED TO ESCAPE.

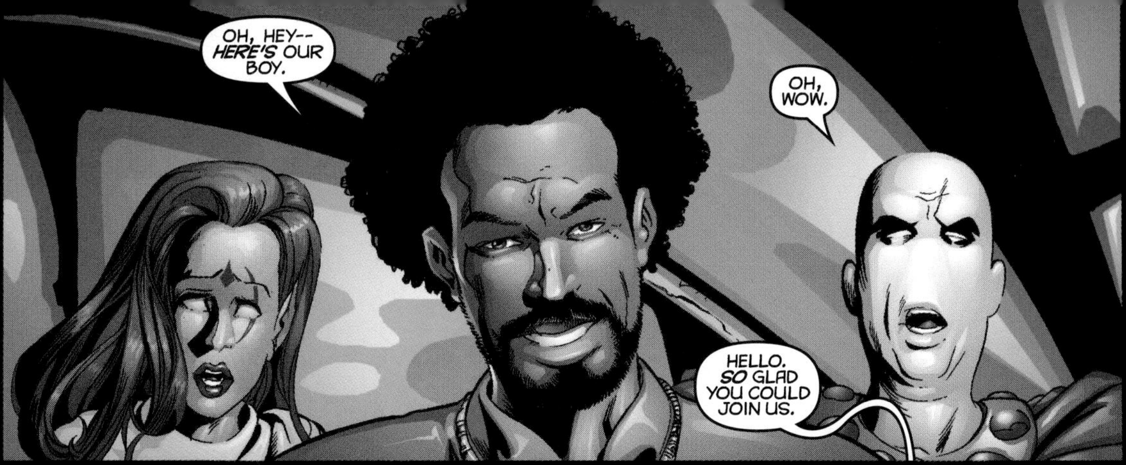

OH, HEY-- *HERE'S* OUR BOY.
OH, WOW.
HELLO. *SO* GLAD YOU COULD JOIN US.

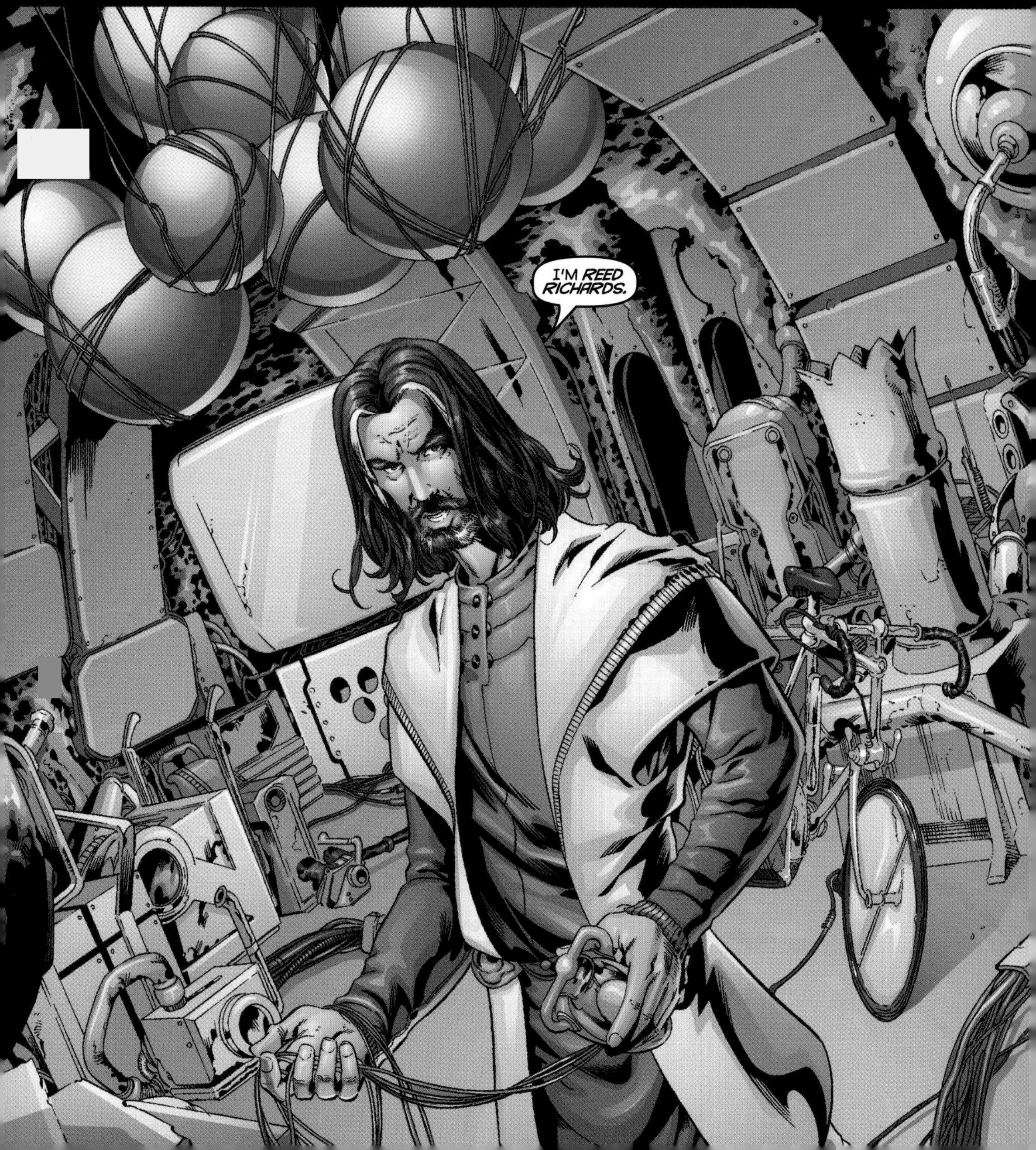

I'M *REED RICHARDS.*

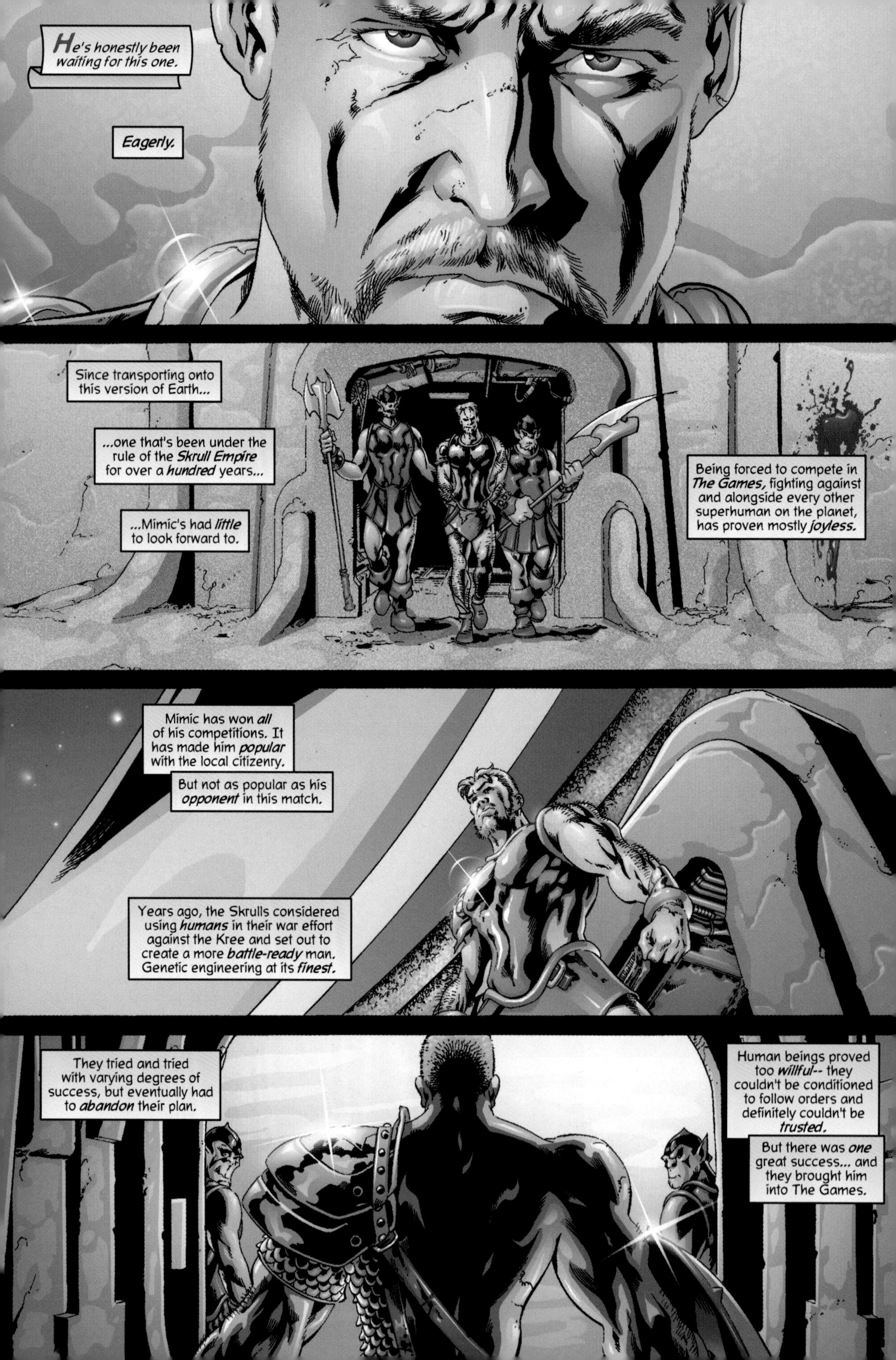
He's honestly been waiting for this one.
Eagerly.
Since transporting onto this version of Earth...
...one that's been under the rule of the Skrull Empire for over a hundred years...
...Mimic's had little to look forward to.
Being forced to compete in The Games, fighting against and alongside every other superhuman on the planet, has proven mostly joyless.
Mimic has won all of his competitions. It has made him popular with the local citizenry.
But not as popular as his opponent in this match.
Years ago, the Skrulls considered using humans in their war effort against the Kree and set out to create a more battle-ready man. Genetic engineering at its finest.
They tried and tried with varying degrees of success, but eventually had to abandon their plan.
Human beings proved too willful-- they couldn't be conditioned to follow orders and definitely couldn't be trusted.
But there was one great success... and they brought him into The Games.

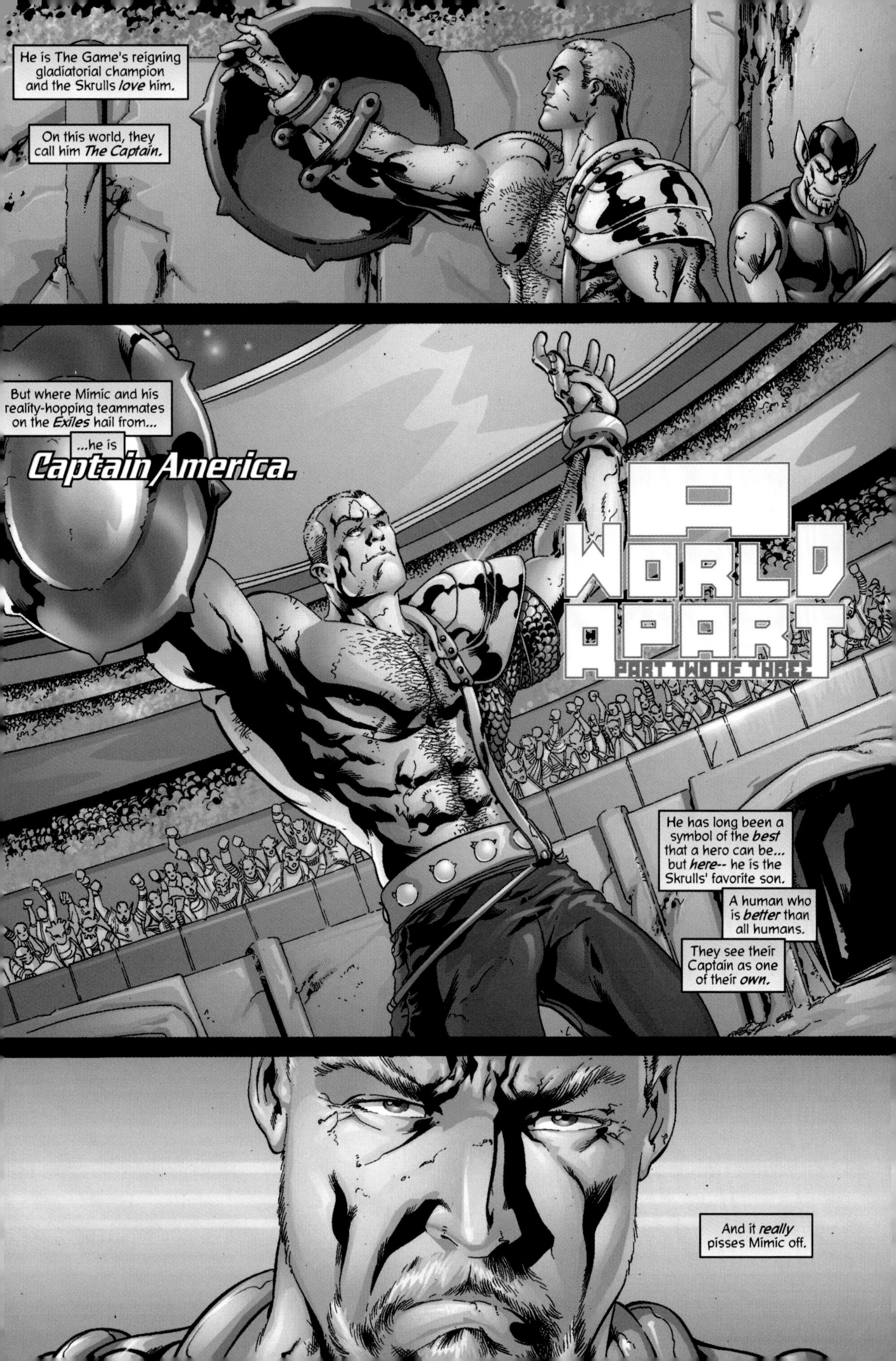
He is The Game's reigning gladiatorial champion and the Skrulls *love* him.
On this world, they call him *The Captain.*
But where Mimic and his reality-hopping teammates on the *Exiles* hail from...
...he is
Captain America.
A WORLD APART
PART TWO OF THREE
He has long been a symbol of the *best* that a hero can be... but *here--* he is the Skrulls' favorite son.
A human who is *better* than all humans.
They see their Captain as one of their *own.*
And it *really* pisses Mimic off.

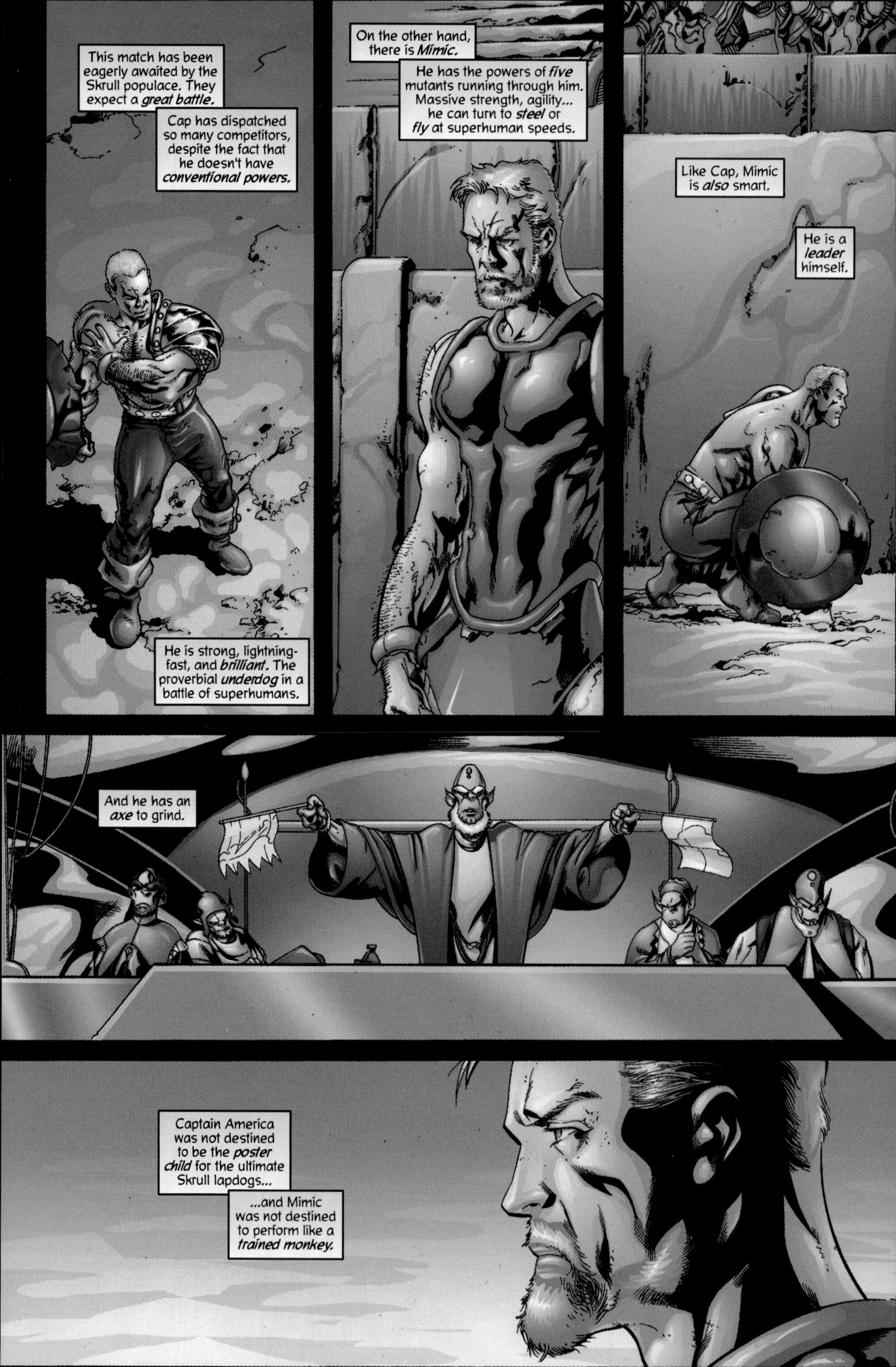

This match has been eagerly awaited by the Skrull populace. They expect a *great battle.*
Cap has dispatched so many competitors, despite the fact that he doesn't have *conventional powers.*
He is strong, lightning-fast, and *brilliant.* The proverbial *underdog* in a battle of superhumans.
On the other hand, there is *Mimic.*
He has the powers of *five* mutants running through him. Massive strength, agility... he can turn to *steel* or *fly* at superhuman speeds.
Like Cap, Mimic is *also* smart.
He is a *leader* himself.
And he has an *axe* to grind.
Captain America was not destined to be the *poster child* for the ultimate Skrull lapdogs...
...and Mimic was not destined to perform like a *trained monkey.*

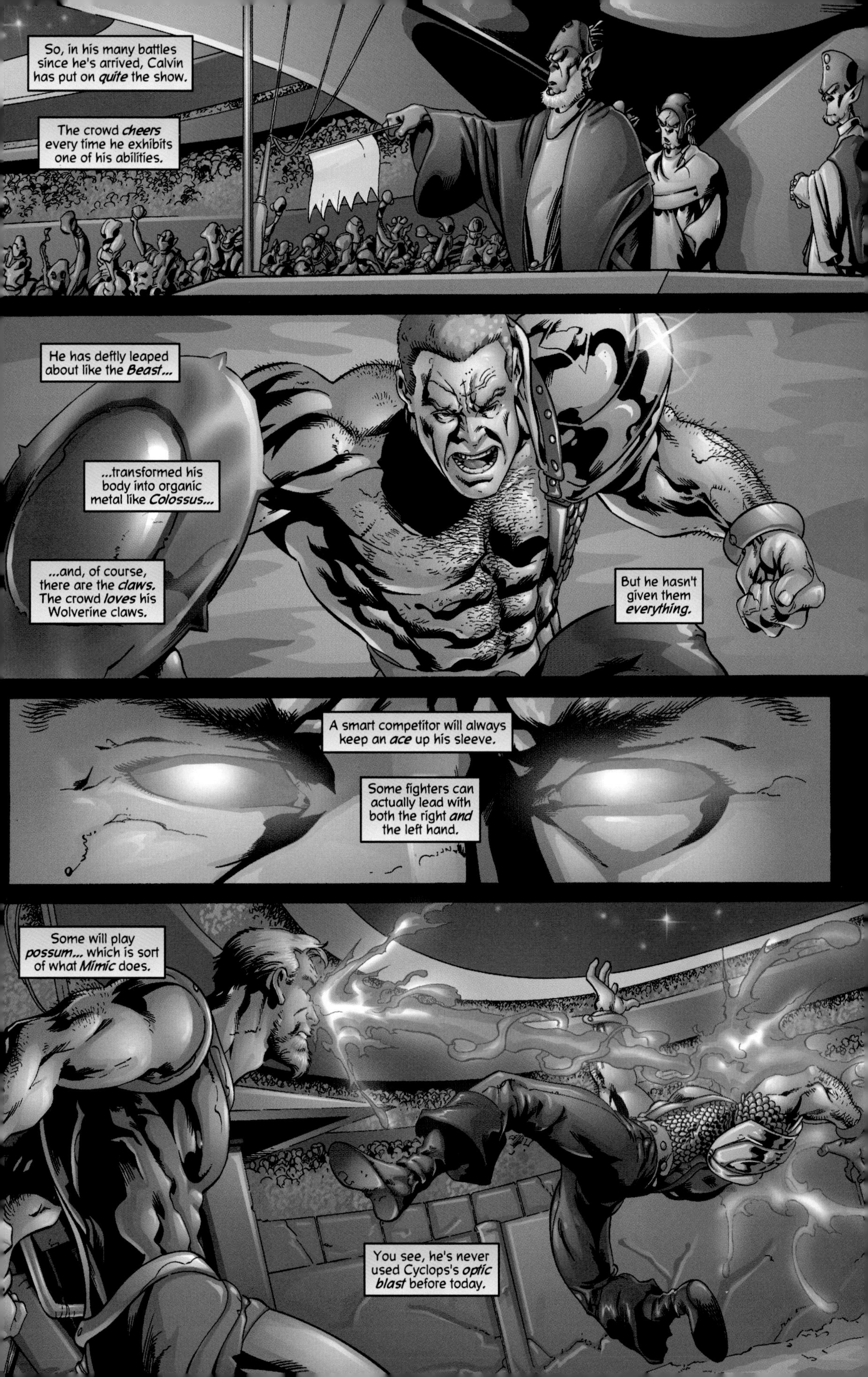
So, in his many battles since he's arrived, Calvin has put on *quite* the show.
The crowd *cheers* every time he exhibits one of his abilities.
He has deftly leaped about like the *Beast...*
...transformed his body into organic metal like *Colossus...*
...and, of course, there are the *claws.* The crowd *loves* his Wolverine claws.
But he hasn't given them *everything.*
A smart competitor will always keep an *ace* up his sleeve.
Some fighters can actually lead with both the right *and* the left hand.
Some will play *possum...* which is sort of what *Mimic* does.
You see, he's never used Cyclops's *optic blast* before today.

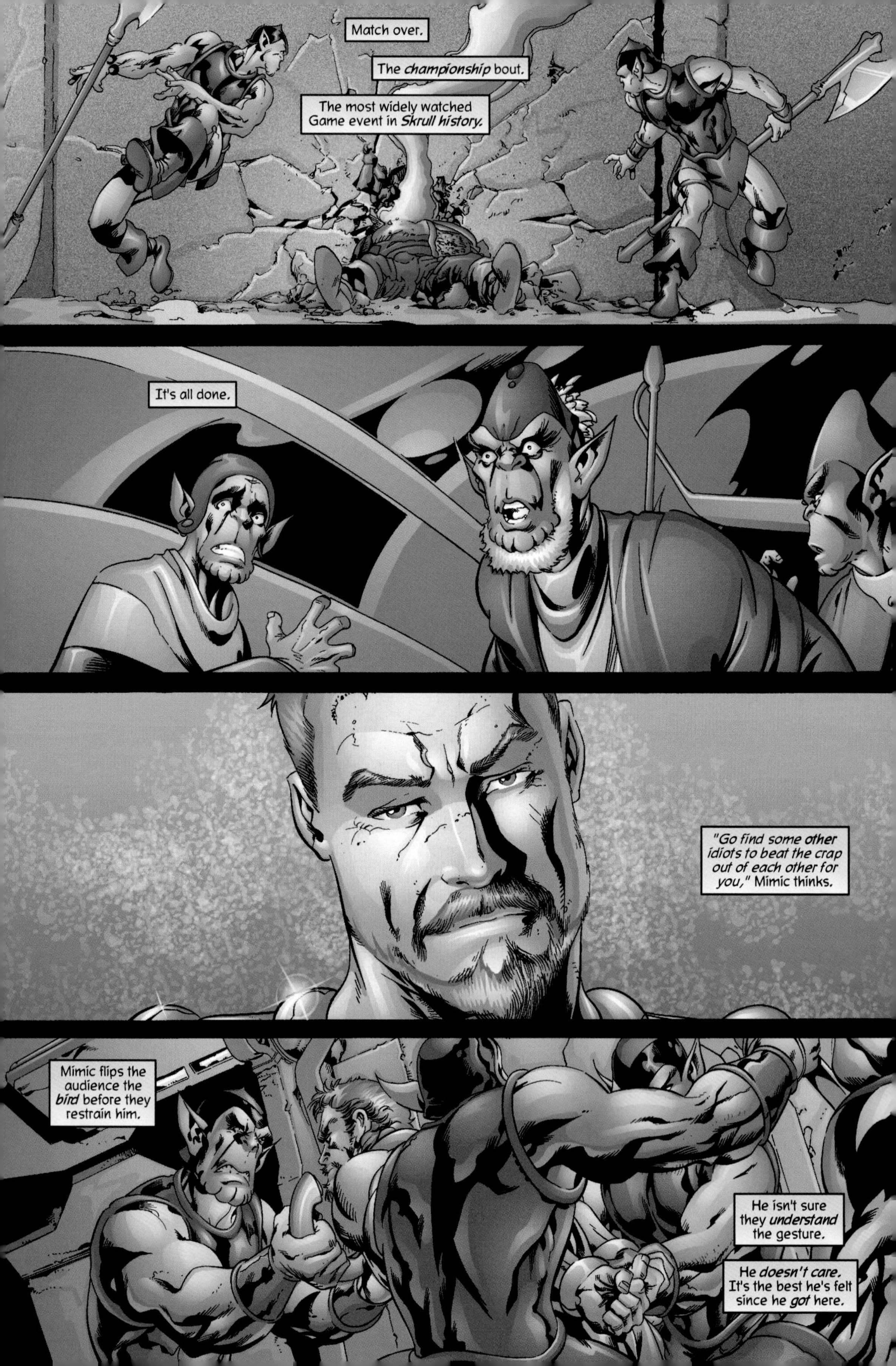
Match over.
The *championship* bout.
The most widely watched Game event in *Skrull history.*
It's all done.
"Go find some other idiots to beat the crap out of each other for you," Mimic thinks.
Mimic flips the audience the *bird* before they restrain him.
He isn't sure they *understand* the gesture.
He *doesn't care.* It's the best he's felt since he *got* here.

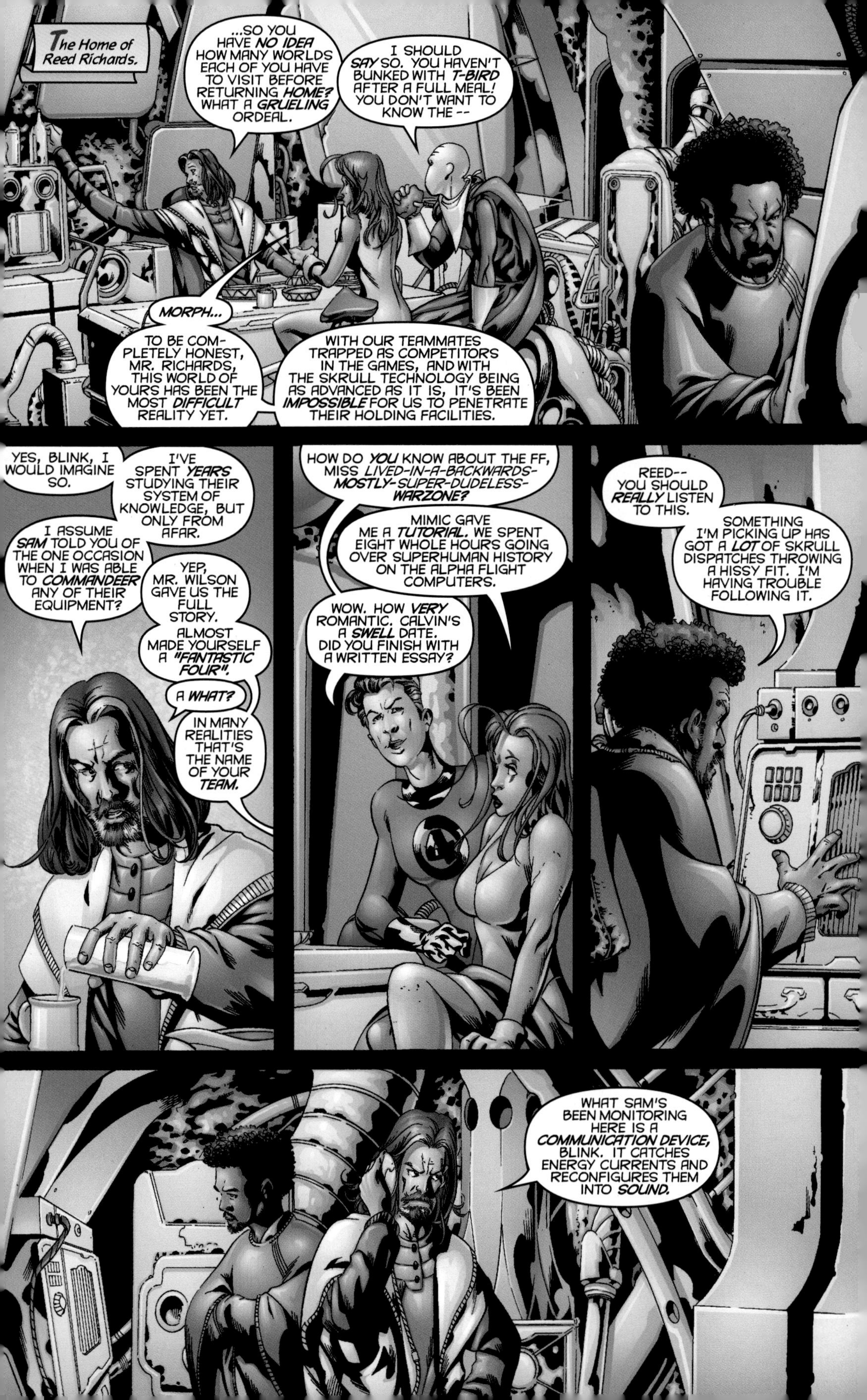
The Home of Reed Richards.
...SO YOU HAVE NO IDEA HOW MANY WORLDS EACH OF YOU HAVE TO VISIT BEFORE RETURNING HOME? WHAT A GRUELING ORDEAL.
I SHOULD SAY SO. YOU HAVEN'T BUNKED WITH T-BIRD AFTER A FULL MEAL! YOU DON'T WANT TO KNOW THE --
MORPH...
TO BE COMPLETELY HONEST, MR. RICHARDS, THIS WORLD OF YOURS HAS BEEN THE MOST DIFFICULT REALITY YET.
WITH OUR TEAMMATES TRAPPED AS COMPETITORS IN THE GAMES, AND WITH THE SKRULL TECHNOLOGY BEING AS ADVANCED AS IT IS, IT'S BEEN IMPOSSIBLE FOR US TO PENETRATE THEIR HOLDING FACILITIES.
YES, BLINK, I WOULD IMAGINE SO.
I'VE SPENT YEARS STUDYING THEIR SYSTEM OF KNOWLEDGE, BUT ONLY FROM AFAR.
I ASSUME SAM TOLD YOU OF THE ONE OCCASION WHEN I WAS ABLE TO COMMANDEER ANY OF THEIR EQUIPMENT?
YEP, MR. WILSON GAVE US THE FULL STORY.
ALMOST MADE YOURSELF A "FANTASTIC FOUR".
A WHAT?
IN MANY REALITIES THAT'S THE NAME OF YOUR TEAM.
HOW DO YOU KNOW ABOUT THE FF, MISS LIVED-IN-A-BACKWARDS-MOSTLY-SUPER-DUDELESS-WARZONE?
MIMIC GAVE ME A TUTORIAL. WE SPENT EIGHT WHOLE HOURS GOING OVER SUPERHUMAN HISTORY ON THE ALPHA FLIGHT COMPUTERS.
WOW. HOW VERY ROMANTIC. CALVIN'S A SWELL DATE. DID YOU FINISH WITH A WRITTEN ESSAY?
REED-- YOU SHOULD REALLY LISTEN TO THIS.
SOMETHING I'M PICKING UP HAS GOT A LOT OF SKRULL DISPATCHES THROWING A HISSY FIT. I'M HAVING TROUBLE FOLLOWING IT.
WHAT SAM'S BEEN MONITORING HERE IS A COMMUNICATION DEVICE, BLINK. IT CATCHES ENERGY CURRENTS AND RECONFIGURES THEM INTO SOUND.

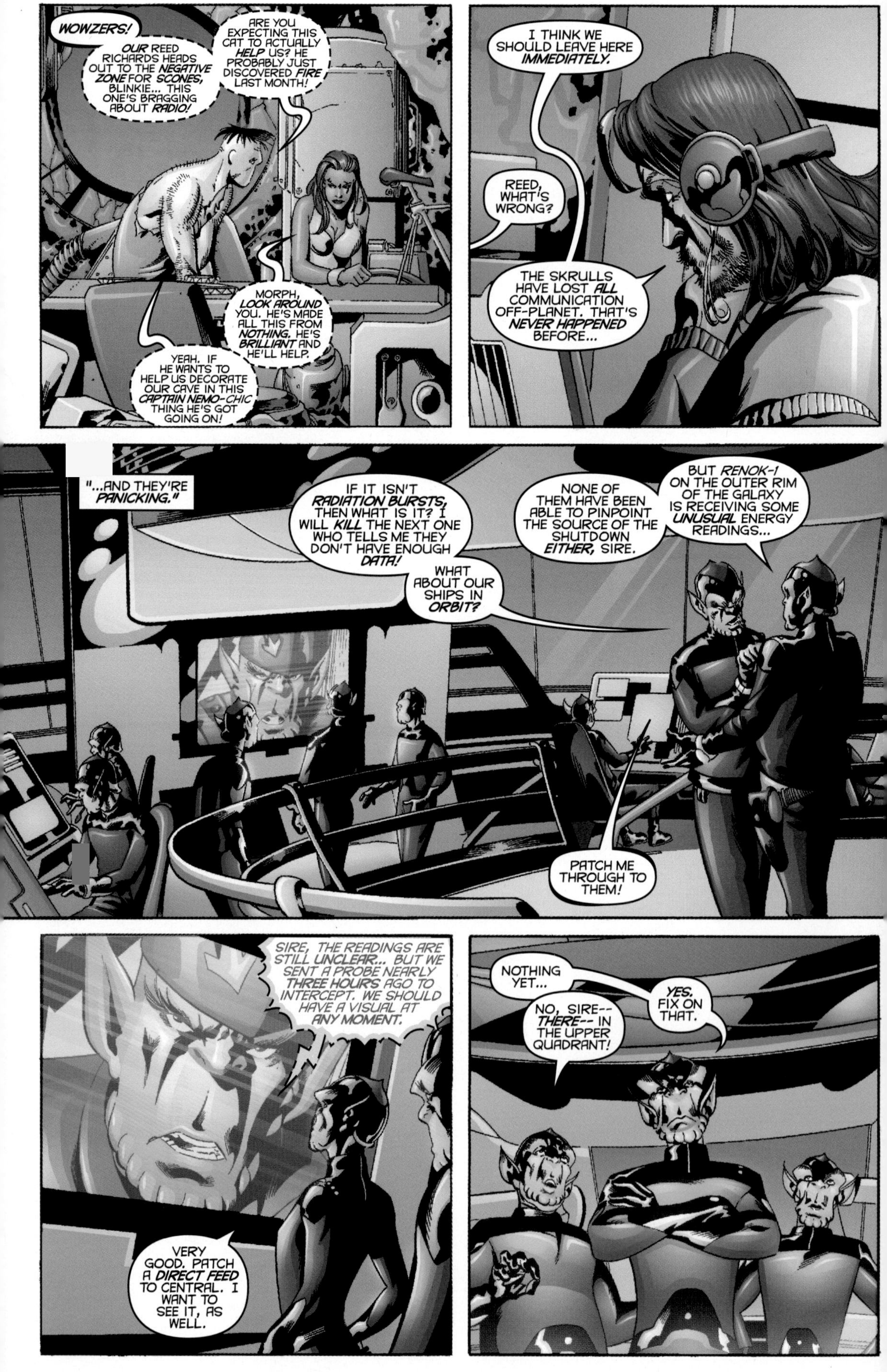
WOWZERS!
OUR REED RICHARDS HEADS OUT TO THE NEGATIVE ZONE FOR SCONES, BLINKIE... THIS ONE'S BRAGGING ABOUT RADIO!
ARE YOU EXPECTING THIS CAT TO ACTUALLY HELP US? HE PROBABLY JUST DISCOVERED FIRE LAST MONTH!
MORPH, LOOK AROUND YOU. HE'S MADE ALL THIS FROM NOTHING. HE'S BRILLIANT AND HE'LL HELP.
YEAH. IF HE WANTS TO HELP US DECORATE OUR CAVE IN THIS CAPTAIN NEMO-CHIC THING HE'S GOT GOING ON!
I THINK WE SHOULD LEAVE HERE IMMEDIATELY.
REED, WHAT'S WRONG?
THE SKRULLS HAVE LOST ALL COMMUNICATION OFF-PLANET. THAT'S NEVER HAPPENED BEFORE...
"...AND THEY'RE PANICKING."
IF IT ISN'T RADIATION BURSTS, THEN WHAT IS IT? I WILL KILL THE NEXT ONE WHO TELLS ME THEY DON'T HAVE ENOUGH DATA!
WHAT ABOUT OUR SHIPS IN ORBIT?
NONE OF THEM HAVE BEEN ABLE TO PINPOINT THE SOURCE OF THE SHUTDOWN EITHER, SIRE.
BUT RENOK-I ON THE OUTER RIM OF THE GALAXY IS RECEIVING SOME UNUSUAL ENERGY READINGS...
PATCH ME THROUGH TO THEM!
SIRE, THE READINGS ARE STILL UNCLEAR... BUT WE SENT A PROBE NEARLY THREE HOURS AGO TO INTERCEPT. WE SHOULD HAVE A VISUAL AT ANY MOMENT.
VERY GOOD. PATCH A DIRECT FEED TO CENTRAL. I WANT TO SEE IT, AS WELL.
NOTHING YET...
NO, SIRE-- THERE-- IN THE UPPER QUADRANT!
YES. FIX ON THAT.

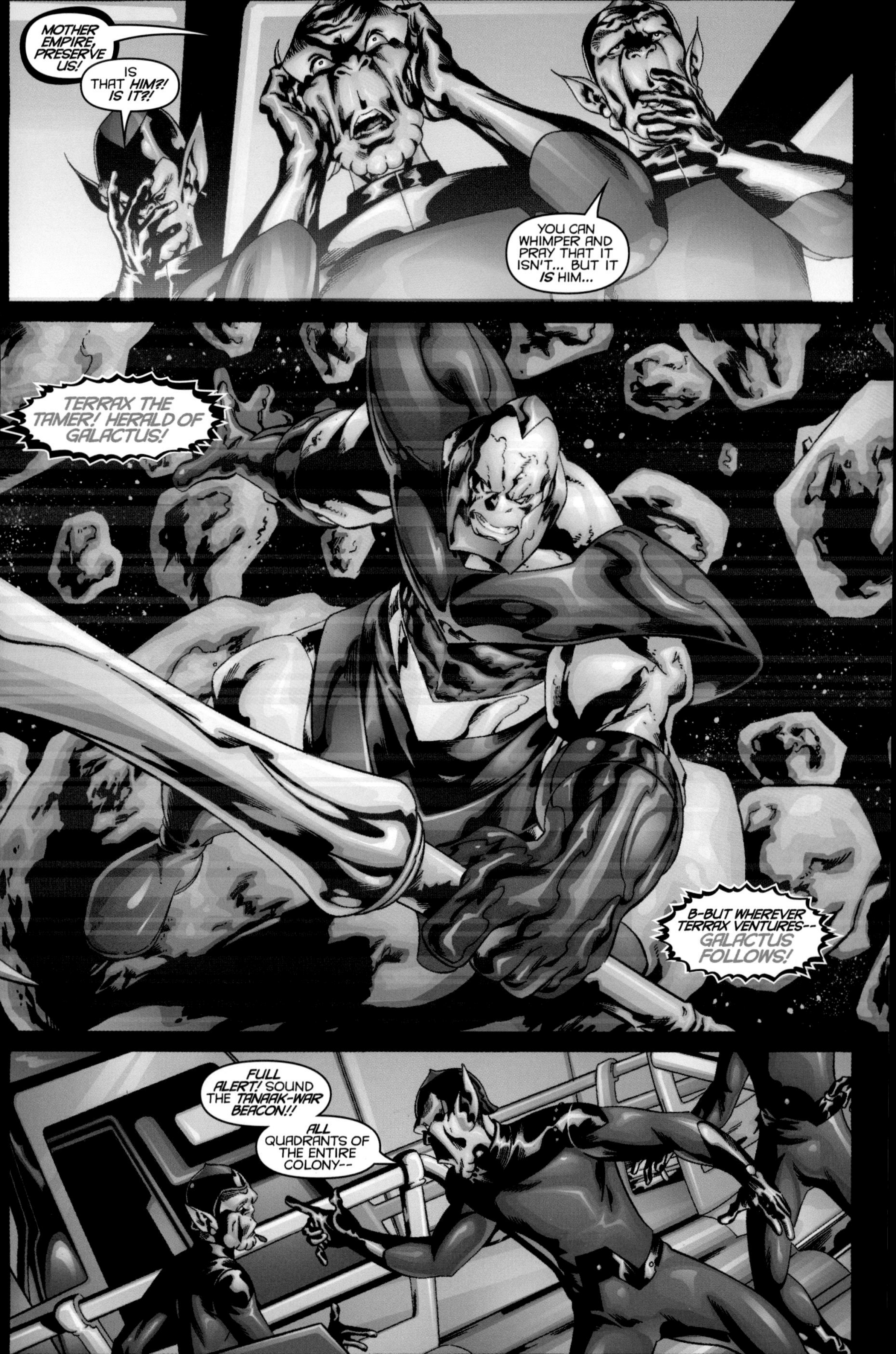
MOTHER EMPIRE, PRESERVE US!
IS THAT HIM?! IS IT?!
YOU CAN WHIMPER AND PRAY THAT IT ISN'T... BUT IT IS HIM...
TERRAX THE TAMER! HERALD OF GALACTUS!
B-BUT WHEREVER TERRAX VENTURES-- GALACTUS FOLLOWS!
FULL ALERT! SOUND THE TANAAK-WAR BEACON!!
ALL QUADRANTS OF THE ENTIRE COLONY--

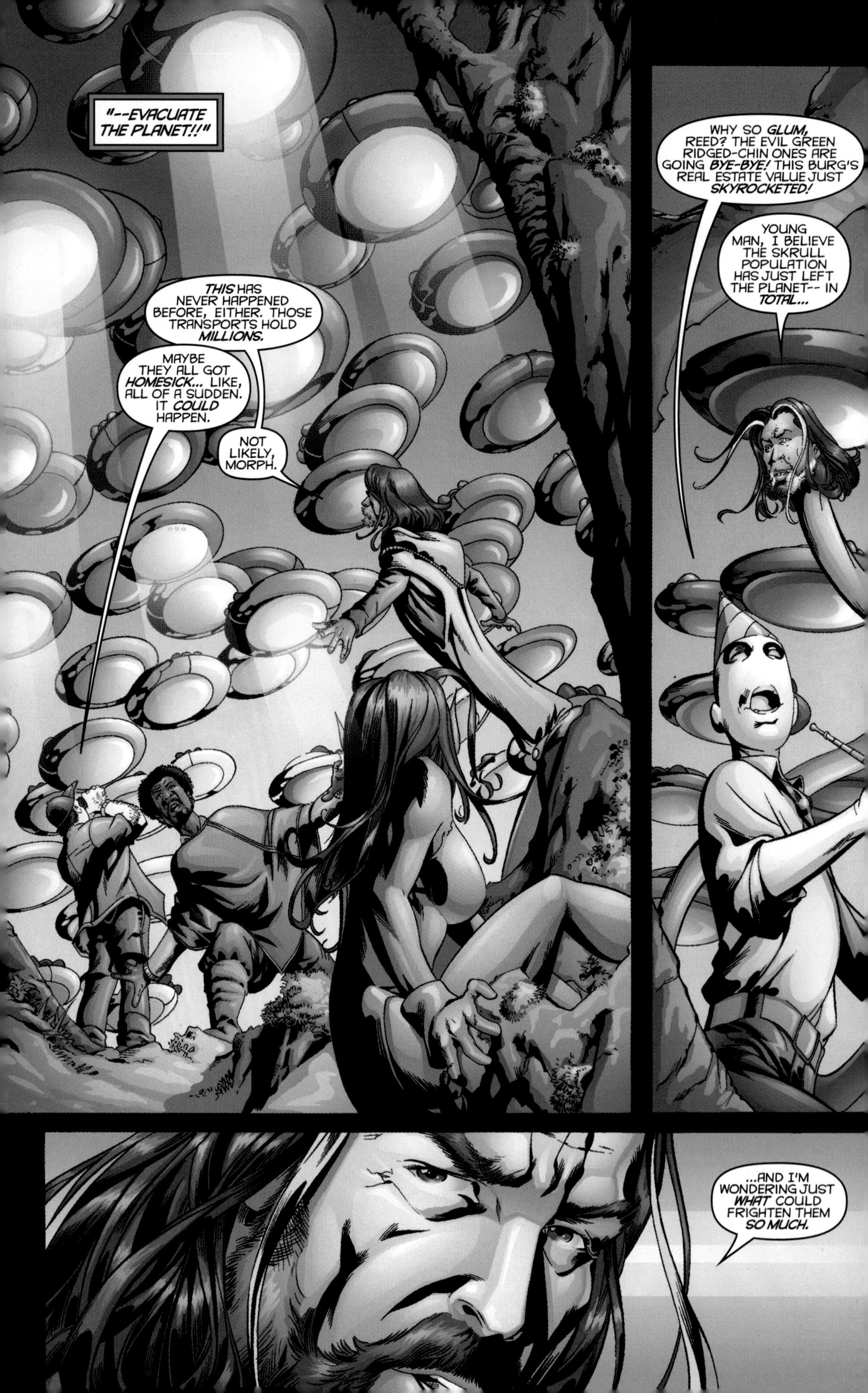
"--EVACUATE THE PLANET!!"
THIS HAS NEVER HAPPENED BEFORE, EITHER. THOSE TRANSPORTS HOLD MILLIONS.
MAYBE THEY ALL GOT HOMESICK... LIKE, ALL OF A SUDDEN. IT COULD HAPPEN.
NOT LIKELY, MORPH.
WHY SO GLUM, REED? THE EVIL GREEN RIDGED-CHIN ONES ARE GOING BYE-BYE! THIS BURG'S REAL ESTATE VALUE JUST SKYROCKETED!
YOUNG MAN, I BELIEVE THE SKRULL POPULATION HAS JUST LEFT THE PLANET-- IN TOTAL...
...AND I'M WONDERING JUST WHAT COULD FRIGHTEN THEM SO MUCH.

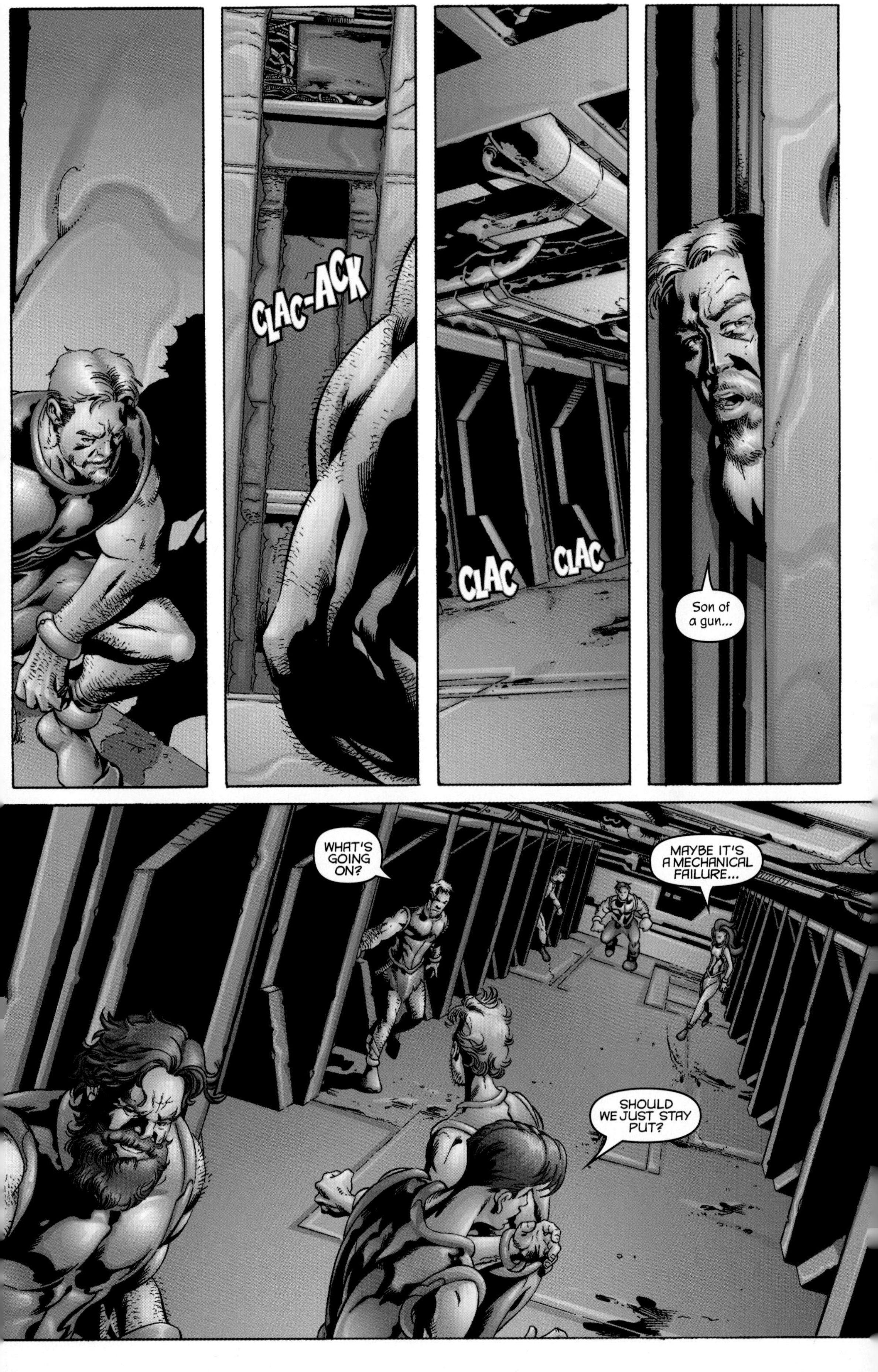

CLAC-ACK
CLAC
CLAC
Son of a gun...
WHAT'S GOING ON?
MAYBE IT'S A MECHANICAL FAILURE...
SHOULD WE JUST STAY PUT?

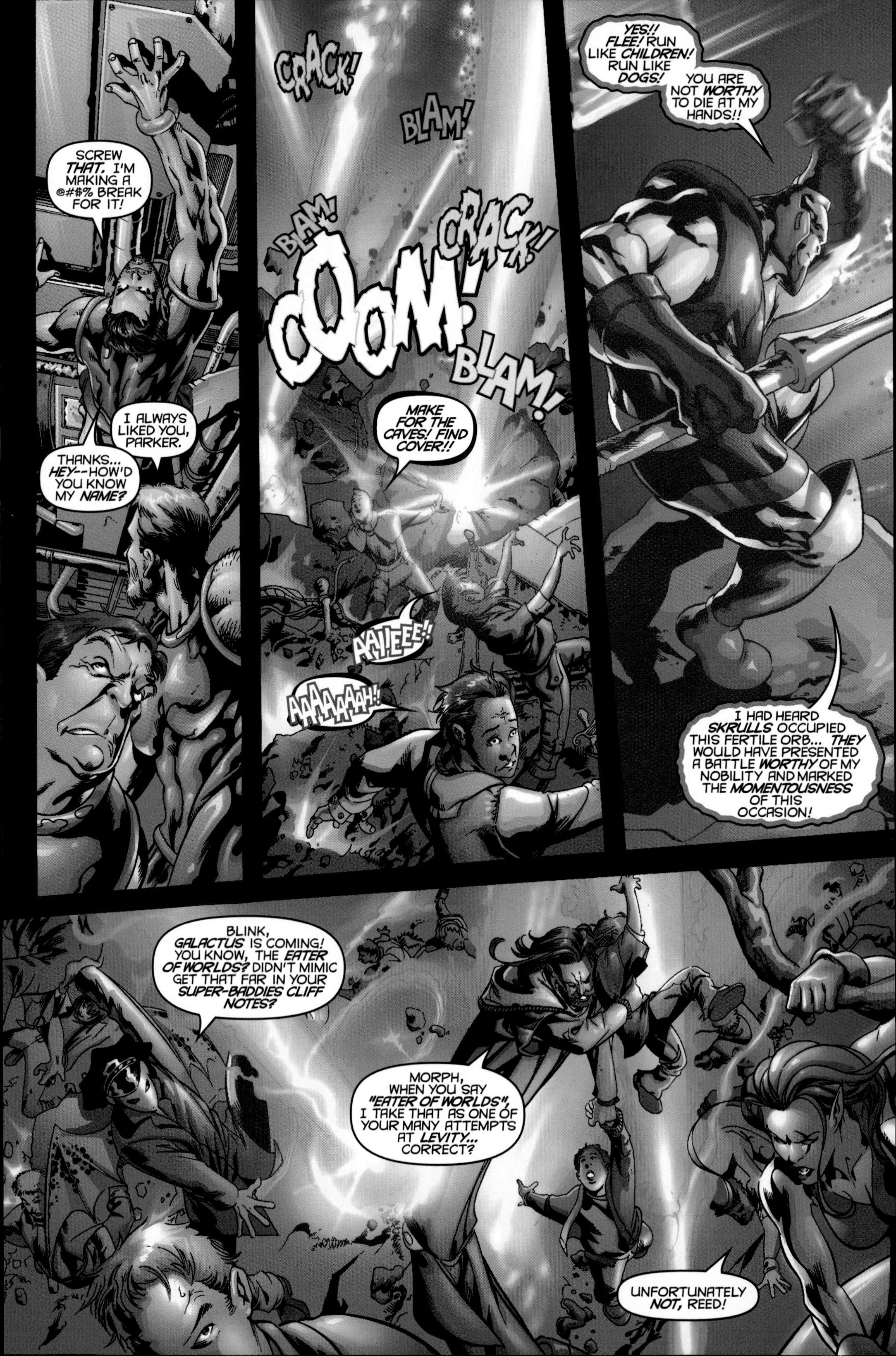
SCREW THAT. I'M MAKING A @#$% BREAK FOR IT!
I ALWAYS LIKED YOU, PARKER.
THANKS... HEY--HOW'D YOU KNOW MY NAME?
CRACK!
BLAM!
BLAM!
CRACK!
COOM!
BLAM!
MAKE FOR THE CAVES! FIND COVER!!
AAIEEE!!
AAAAAAAH!!
YES!! FLEE! RUN LIKE CHILDREN! RUN LIKE DOGS!
YOU ARE NOT WORTHY TO DIE AT MY HANDS!!
I HAD HEARD SKRULLS OCCUPIED THIS FERTILE ORB... THEY WOULD HAVE PRESENTED A BATTLE WORTHY OF MY NOBILITY AND MARKED THE MOMENTOUSNESS OF THIS OCCASION!
BLINK, GALACTUS IS COMING! YOU KNOW, THE EATER OF WORLDS? DIDN'T MIMIC GET THAT FAR IN YOUR SUPER-BADDIES CLIFF NOTES?
MORPH, WHEN YOU SAY "EATER OF WORLDS", I TAKE THAT AS ONE OF YOUR MANY ATTEMPTS AT LEVITY... CORRECT?
UNFORTUNATELY NOT, REED!

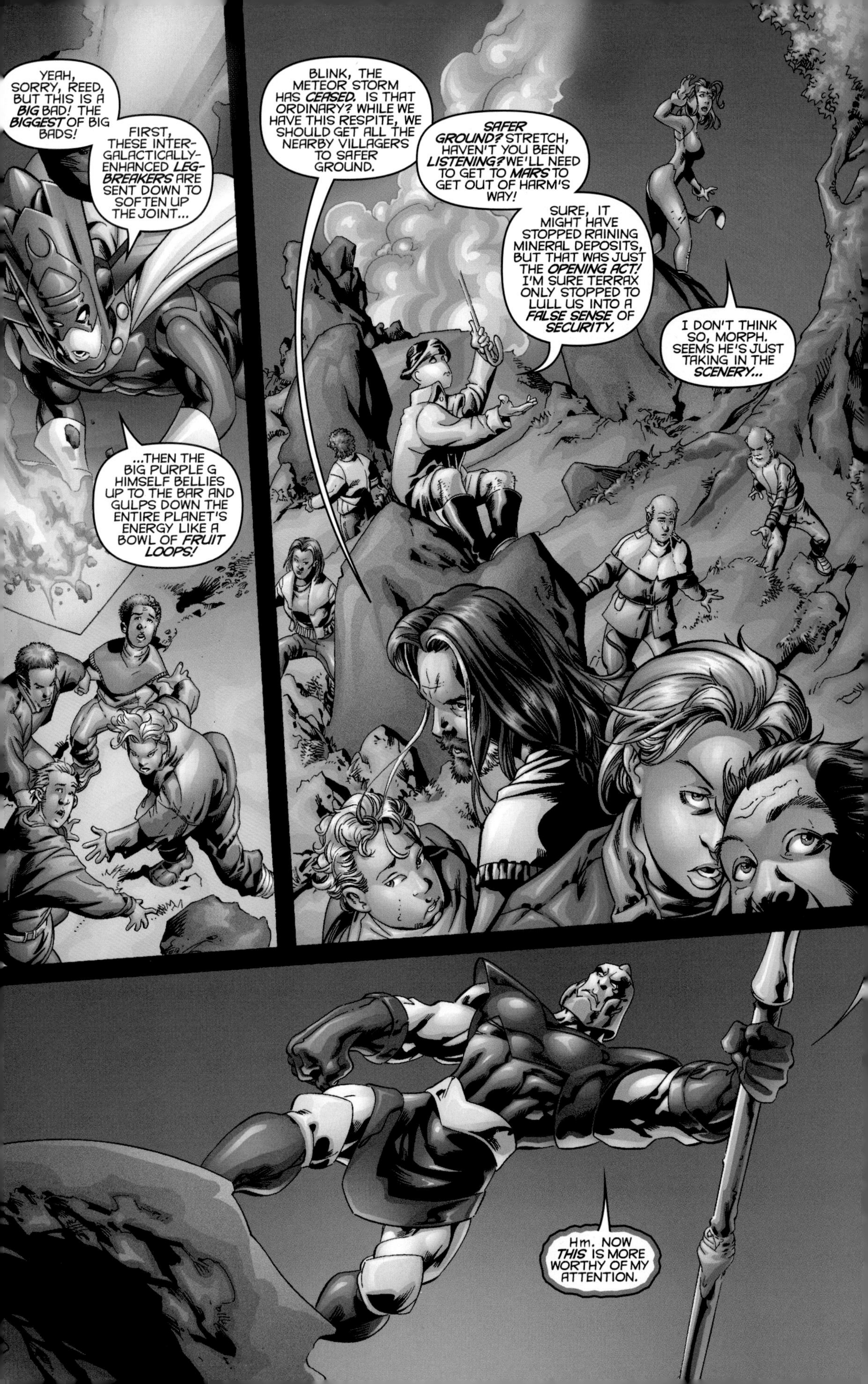
YEAH, SORRY, REED, BUT THIS IS A BIG BAD! THE BIGGEST OF BIG BADS!
FIRST, THESE INTER-GALACTICALLY-ENHANCED LEG-BREAKERS ARE SENT DOWN TO SOFTEN UP THE JOINT...
...THEN THE BIG PURPLE G HIMSELF BELLIES UP TO THE BAR AND GULPS DOWN THE ENTIRE PLANET'S ENERGY LIKE A BOWL OF FRUIT LOOPS!
BLINK, THE METEOR STORM HAS CEASED. IS THAT ORDINARY? WHILE WE HAVE THIS RESPITE, WE SHOULD GET ALL THE NEARBY VILLAGERS TO SAFER GROUND.
SAFER GROUND? STRETCH, HAVEN'T YOU BEEN LISTENING? WE'LL NEED TO GET TO MARS TO GET OUT OF HARM'S WAY!
SURE, IT MIGHT HAVE STOPPED RAINING MINERAL DEPOSITS, BUT THAT WAS JUST THE OPENING ACT! I'M SURE TERRAX ONLY STOPPED TO LULL US INTO A FALSE SENSE OF SECURITY.
I DON'T THINK SO, MORPH. SEEMS HE'S JUST TAKING IN THE SCENERY...
Hm. NOW THIS IS MORE WORTHY OF MY ATTENTION.

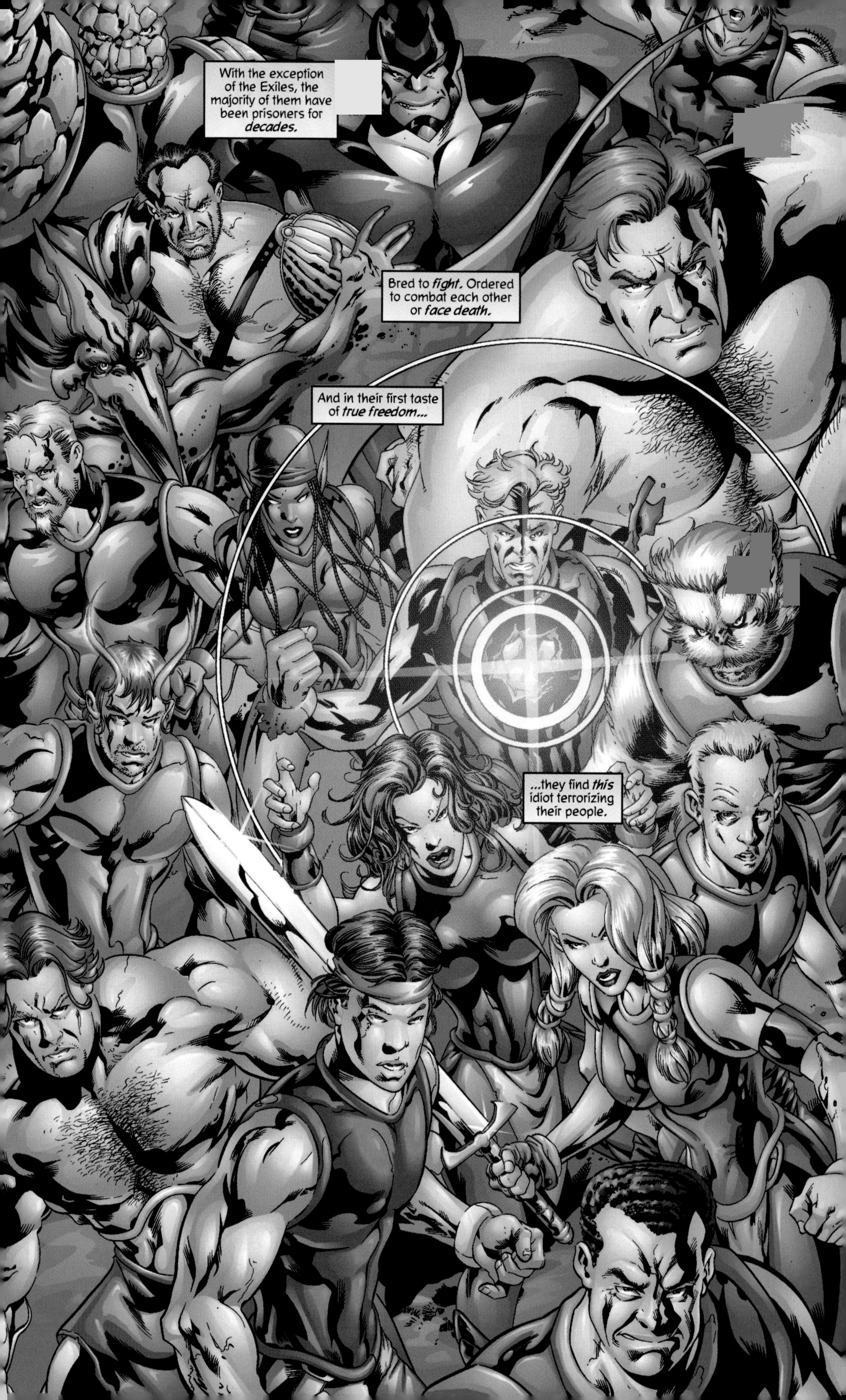
With the exception of the Exiles, the majority of them have been prisoners for *decades.*
Bred to *fight.* Ordered to combat each other or *face death.*
And in their first taste of *true freedom...*
...they find *this* idiot terrorizing their people.

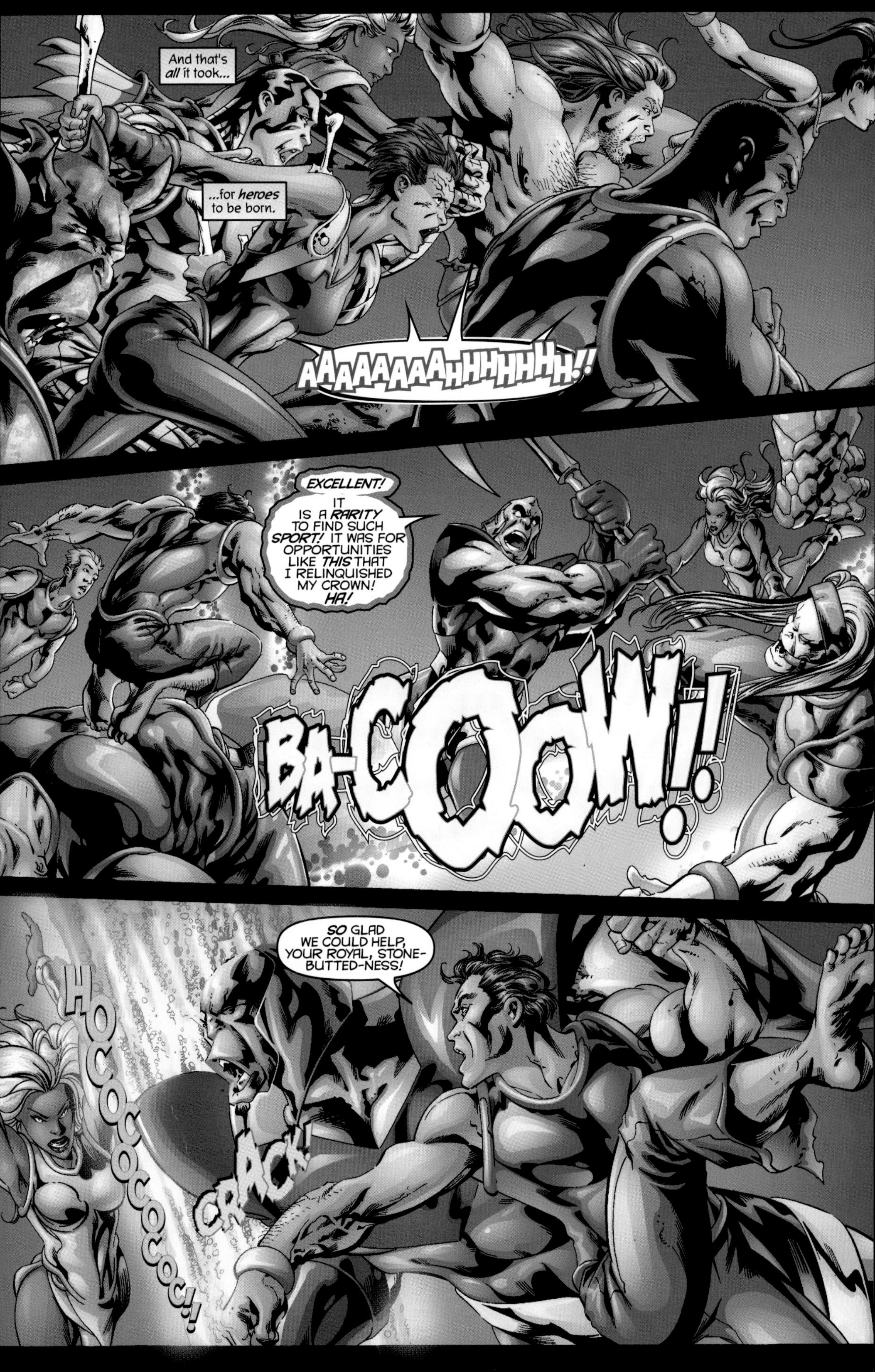
And that's *all* it took...
...for *heroes* to be born.
AAAAAAAAHHHHHHH!!
EXCELLENT! IT IS A *RARITY* TO FIND SUCH *SPORT!* IT WAS FOR OPPORTUNITIES LIKE *THIS* THAT I RELINQUISHED MY CROWN! *HA!*
BA-COOOM!!
SO GLAD WE COULD HELP, YOUR ROYAL, STONE-BUTTED-NESS!
HOOOOOOOC!!
CRACK!

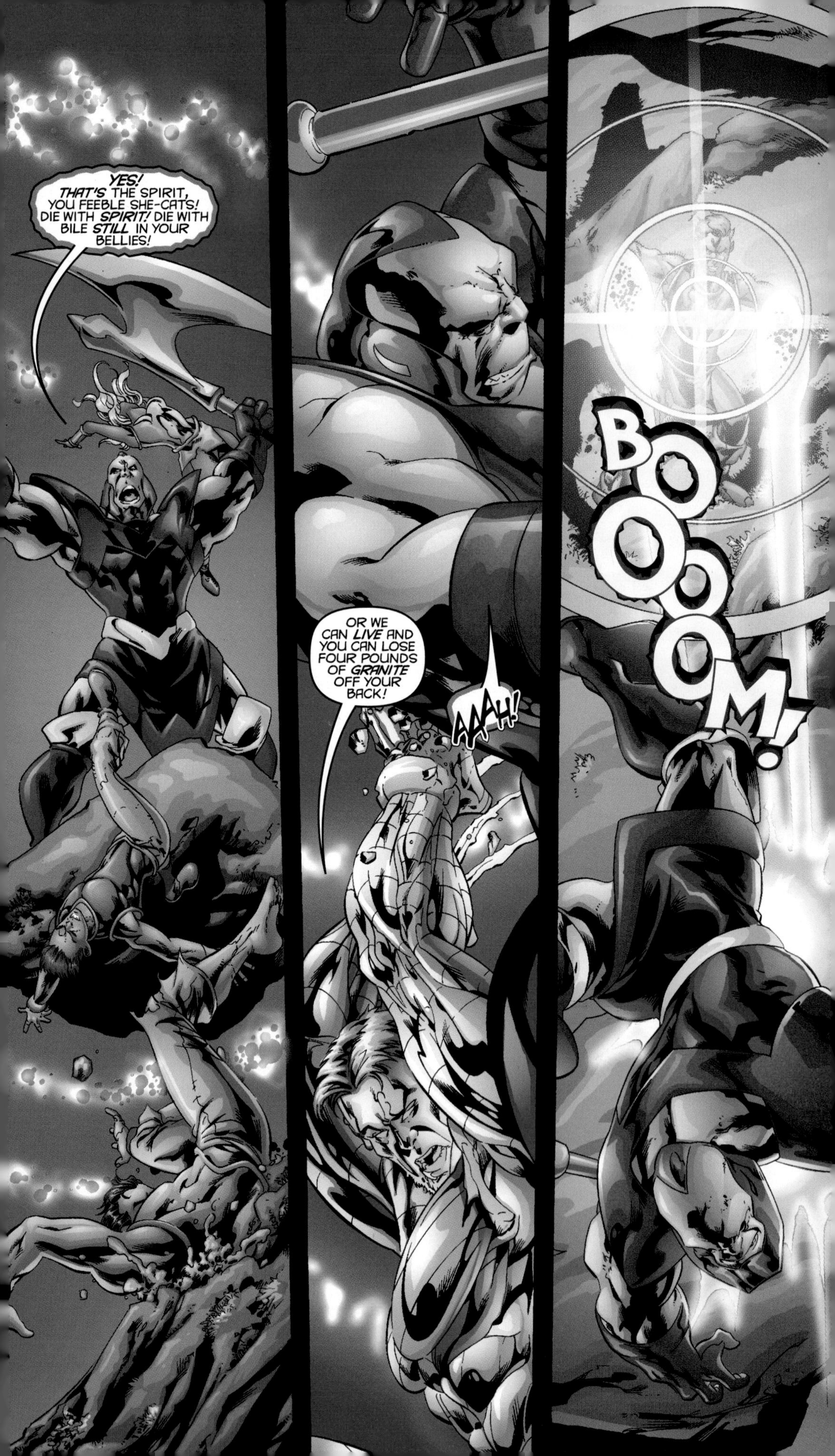
YES! THAT'S THE SPIRIT, YOU FEEBLE SHE-CATS! DIE WITH SPIRIT! DIE WITH BILE STILL IN YOUR BELLIES!
OR WE CAN LIVE AND YOU CAN LOSE FOUR POUNDS OF GRANITE OFF YOUR BACK!
AAAH!
BOOOOOM!

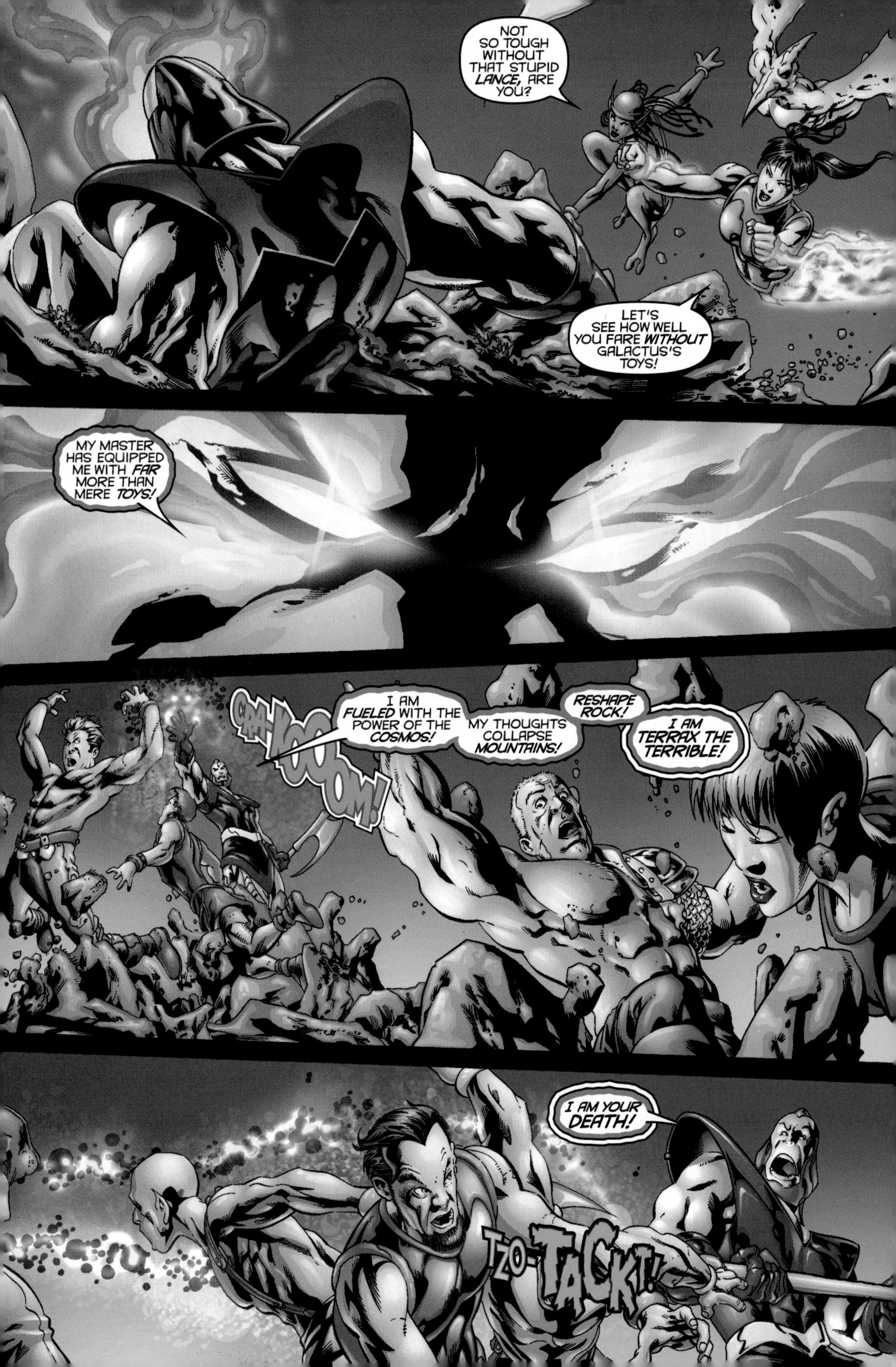
NOT SO TOUGH WITHOUT THAT STUPID *LANCE,* ARE YOU?
LET'S SEE HOW WELL YOU FARE *WITHOUT* GALACTUS'S TOYS!
MY MASTER HAS EQUIPPED ME WITH *FAR* MORE THAN MERE *TOYS!*
CRA-KOOOOM!
I AM *FUELED* WITH THE POWER OF THE *COSMOS!*
MY THOUGHTS COLLAPSE *MOUNTAINS!*
RESHAPE ROCK!
I AM TERRAX THE TERRIBLE!
I AM YOUR DEATH!
TZO-TACKT!

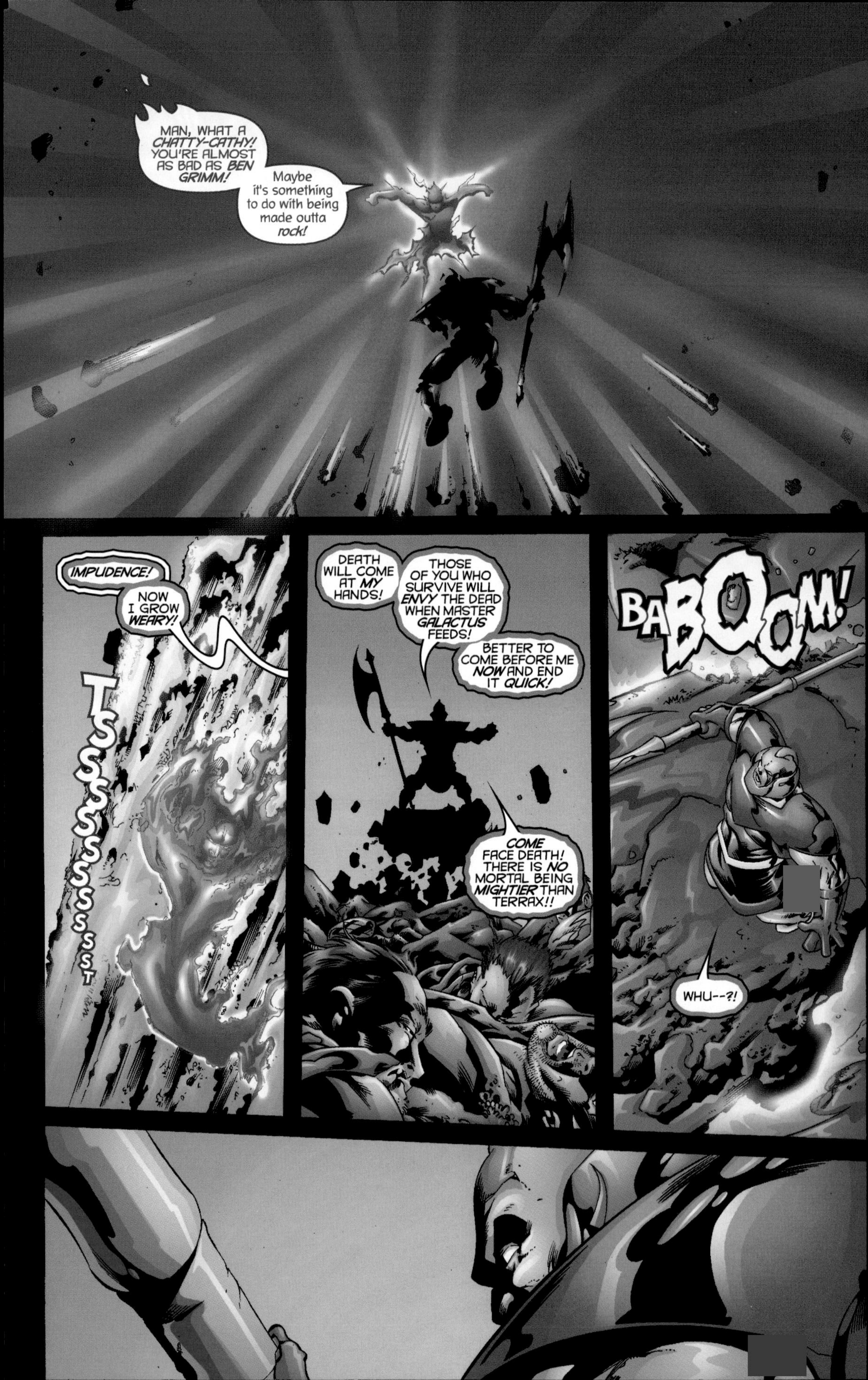
MAN, WHAT A CHATTY-CATHY! YOU'RE ALMOST AS BAD AS BEN GRIMM!
Maybe it's something to do with being made outta rock!
IMPUDENCE!
NOW I GROW WEARY!
TSSSSSSSSST
DEATH WILL COME AT MY HANDS!
THOSE OF YOU WHO SURVIVE WILL ENVY THE DEAD WHEN MASTER GALACTUS FEEDS!
BETTER TO COME BEFORE ME NOW AND END IT QUICK!
COME FACE DEATH! THERE IS NO MORTAL BEING MIGHTIER THAN TERRAX!!
BABOOM!
WHU--?!

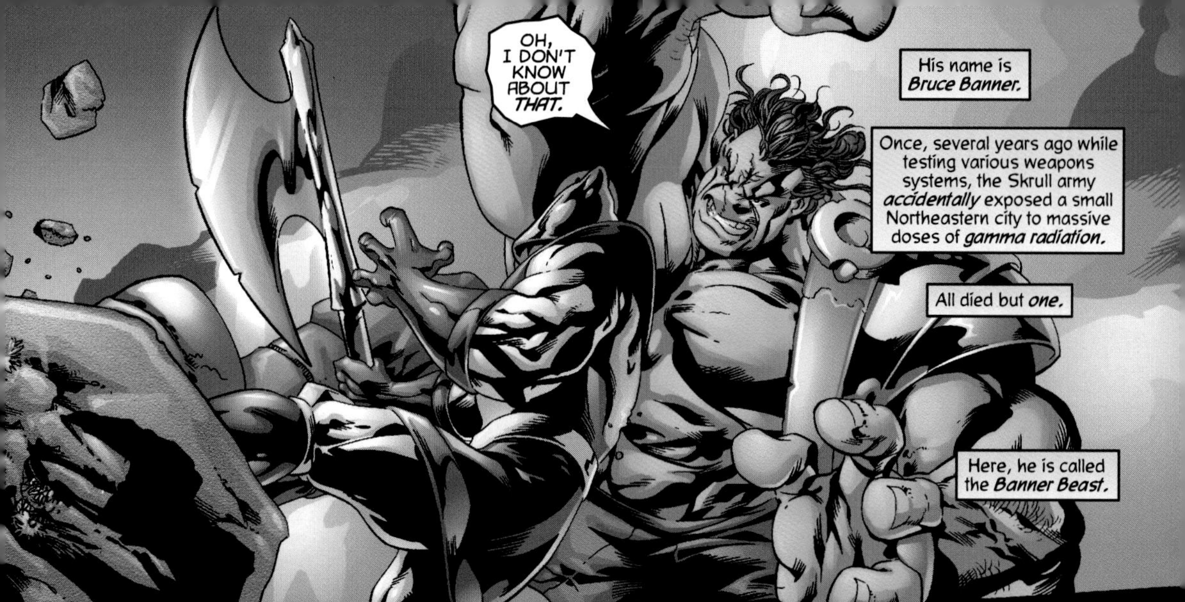

OH, I DON'T KNOW ABOUT *THAT.*
His name is *Bruce Banner.*
Once, several years ago while testing various weapons systems, the Skrull army *accidentally* exposed a small Northeastern city to massive doses of *gamma radiation.*
All died but *one.*
Here, he is called the *Banner Beast.*

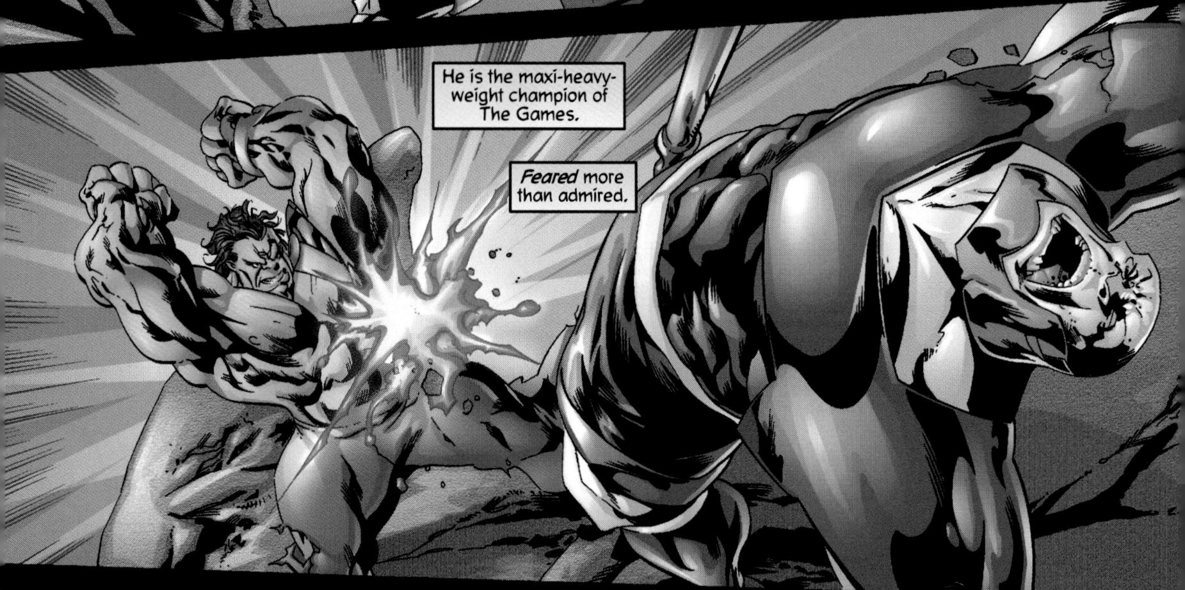

He is the maxi-heavy-weight champion of The Games.
Feared more than admired.

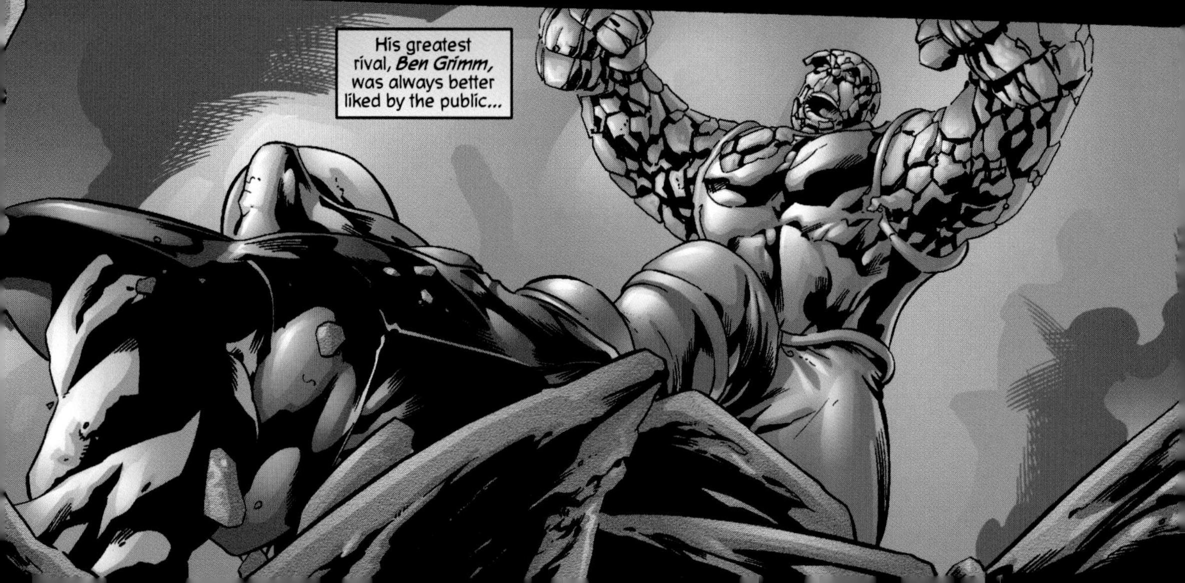

His greatest rival, *Ben Grimm,* was always better liked by the public...

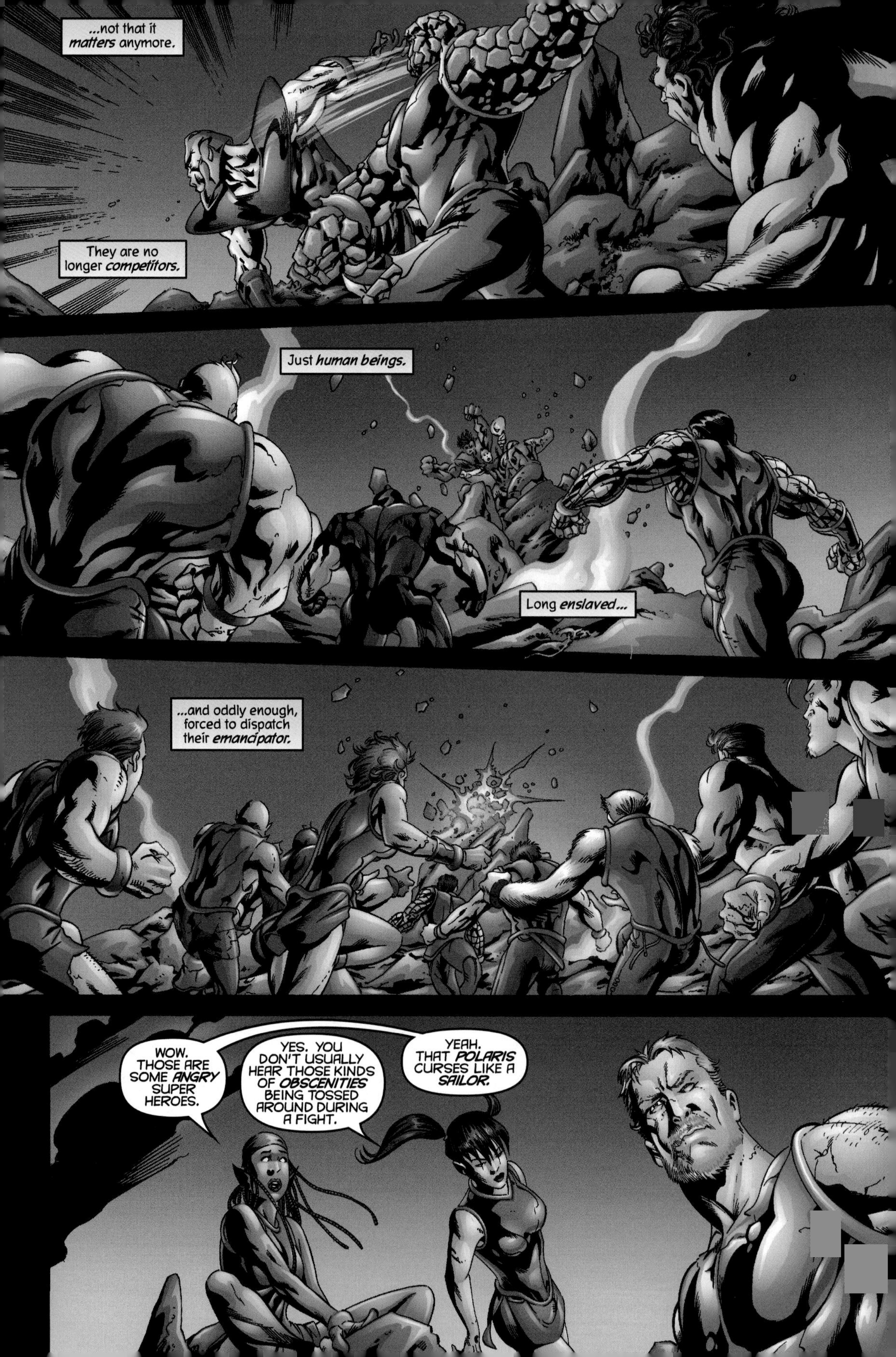
...not that it matters anymore.
They are no longer competitors.
Just human beings.
Long enslaved...
...and oddly enough, forced to dispatch their emancipator.
WOW. THOSE ARE SOME ANGRY SUPER HEROES.
YES. YOU DON'T USUALLY HEAR THOSE KINDS OF OBSCENITIES BEING TOSSED AROUND DURING A FIGHT.
YEAH. THAT POLARIS CURSES LIKE A SAILOR.

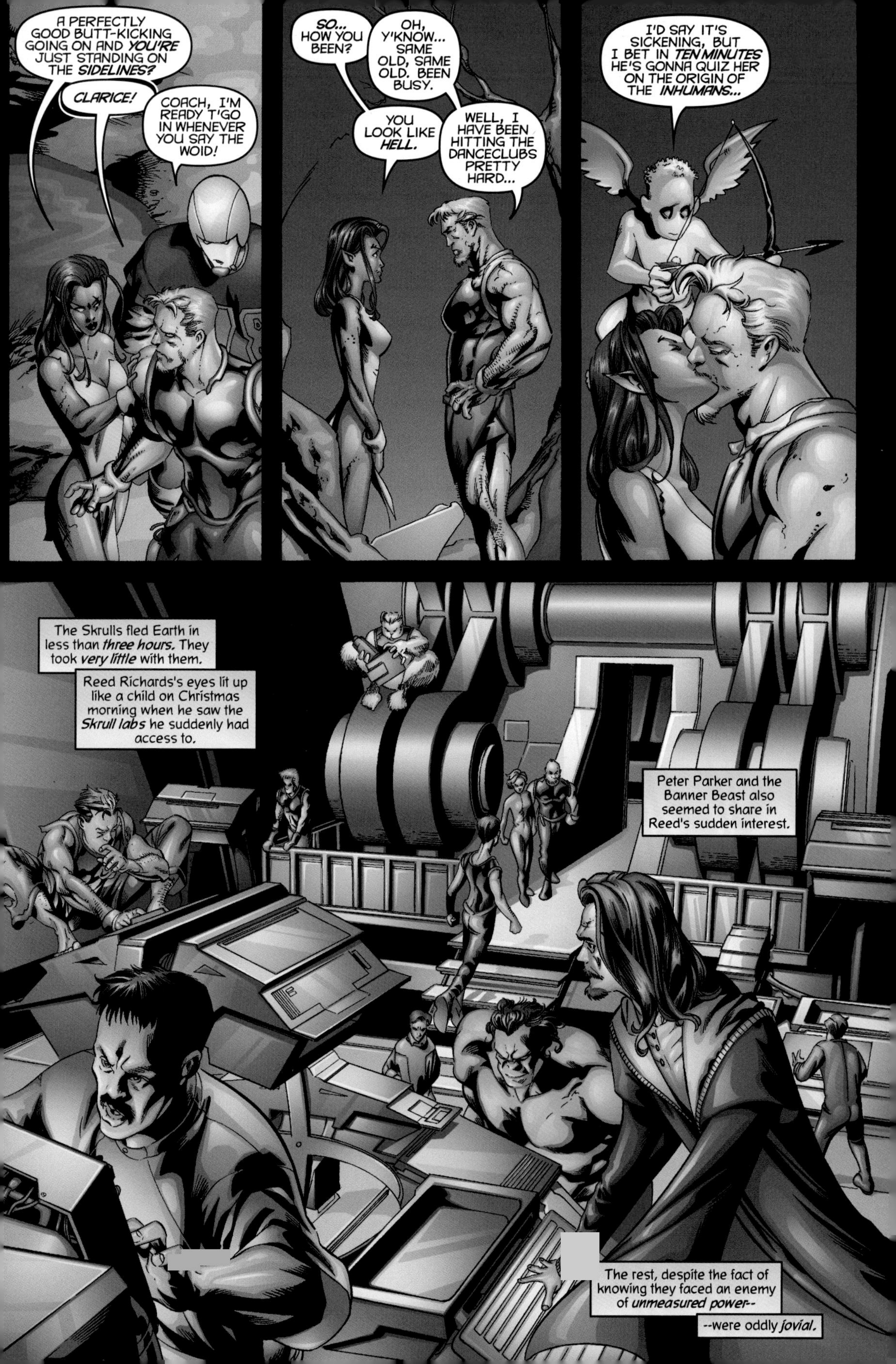
A PERFECTLY GOOD BUTT-KICKING GOING ON AND *YOU'RE* JUST STANDING ON THE *SIDELINES?*
CLARICE!
COACH, I'M READY T'GO IN WHENEVER YOU SAY THE WOID!
SO... HOW YOU BEEN?
OH, Y'KNOW... SAME OLD, SAME OLD. BEEN BUSY.
YOU LOOK LIKE *HELL.*
WELL, I HAVE BEEN HITTING THE DANCECLUBS PRETTY HARD...
I'D SAY IT'S SICKENING, BUT I BET IN *TEN MINUTES* HE'S GONNA QUIZ HER ON THE ORIGIN OF THE *INHUMANS...*
The Skrulls fled Earth in less than *three hours.* They took *very little* with them.
Reed Richards's eyes lit up like a child on Christmas morning when he saw the *Skrull labs* he suddenly had access to.
Peter Parker and the Banner Beast also seemed to share in Reed's sudden interest.
The rest, despite the fact of knowing they faced an enemy of *unmeasured power--*
--were oddly *jovial.*

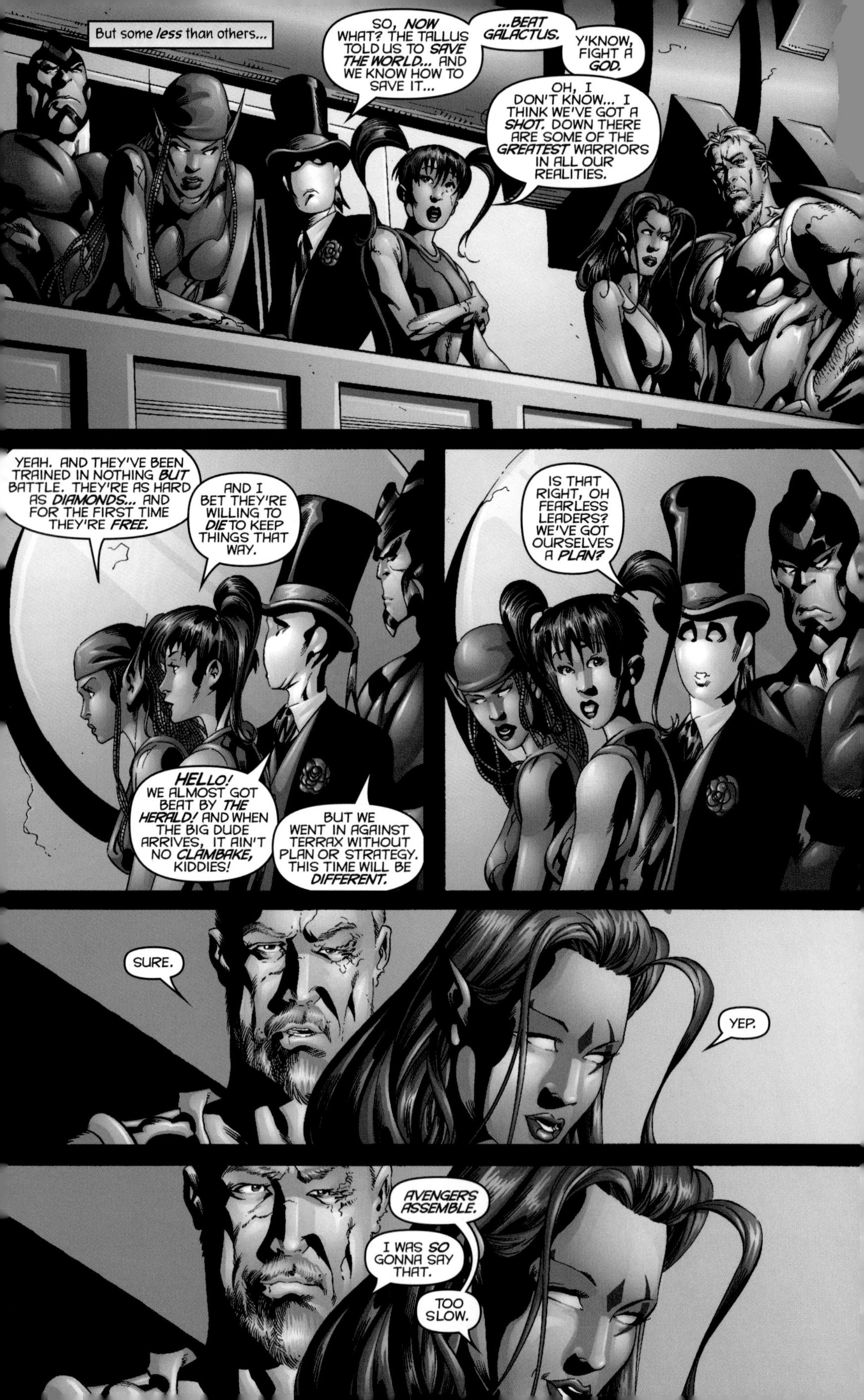

But some *less* than others...
SO, *NOW* WHAT? THE TALLUS TOLD US TO *SAVE THE WORLD...* AND WE KNOW HOW TO SAVE IT...
...*BEAT GALACTUS.*
Y'KNOW, FIGHT A *GOD.*
OH, I DON'T KNOW... I THINK WE'VE GOT A *SHOT.* DOWN THERE ARE SOME OF THE *GREATEST* WARRIORS IN ALL OUR REALITIES.
YEAH. AND THEY'VE BEEN TRAINED IN NOTHING *BUT* BATTLE. THEY'RE AS HARD AS *DIAMONDS...* AND FOR THE FIRST TIME THEY'RE *FREE.*
AND I BET THEY'RE WILLING TO *DIE* TO KEEP THINGS THAT WAY.
HELLO! WE ALMOST GOT BEAT BY *THE HERALD!* AND WHEN THE BIG DUDE ARRIVES, IT AIN'T NO *CLAMBAKE,* KIDDIES!
BUT WE WENT IN AGAINST TERRAX WITHOUT PLAN OR STRATEGY. THIS TIME WILL BE *DIFFERENT.*
IS THAT RIGHT, OH FEARLESS LEADERS? WE'VE GOT OURSELVES A *PLAN?*
SURE.
YEP.
AVENGERS ASSEMBLE.
I WAS *SO* GONNA SAY THAT.
TOO SLOW.

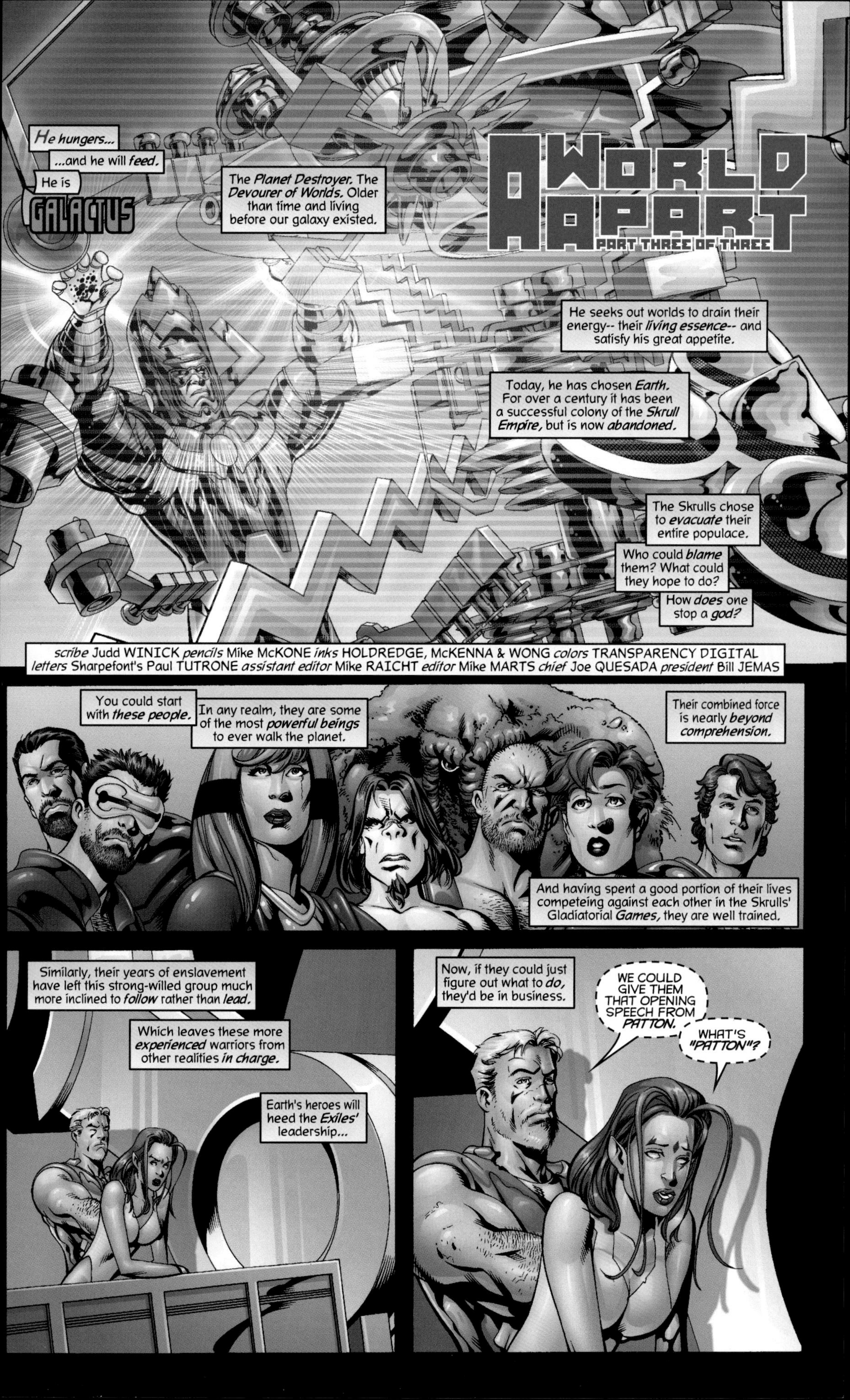
He hungers...
...and he will feed.
He is
GALACTUS
The Planet Destroyer. The Devourer of Worlds. Older than time and living before our galaxy existed.
A WORLD APART
PART THREE OF THREE
He seeks out worlds to drain their energy-- their living essence-- and satisfy his great appetite.
Today, he has chosen Earth. For over a century it has been a successful colony of the Skrull Empire, but is now abandoned.
The Skrulls chose to evacuate their entire populace.
Who could blame them? What could they hope to do?
How does one stop a god?
scribe Judd WINICK pencils Mike McKONE inks HOLDREDGE, McKENNA & WONG colors TRANSPARENCY DIGITAL letters Sharpefont's Paul TUTRONE assistant editor Mike RAICHT editor Mike MARTS chief Joe QUESADA president Bill JEMAS
You could start with these people.
In any realm, they are some of the most powerful beings to ever walk the planet.
Their combined force is nearly beyond comprehension.
And having spent a good portion of their lives competeing against each other in the Skrulls' Gladiatorial Games, they are well trained.
Similarly, their years of enslavement have left this strong-willed group much more inclined to follow rather than lead.
Which leaves these more experienced warriors from other realities in charge.
Earth's heroes will heed the Exiles' leadership...
Now, if they could just figure out what to do, they'd be in business.
WE COULD GIVE THEM THAT OPENING SPEECH FROM PATTON.
WHAT'S "PATTON"?

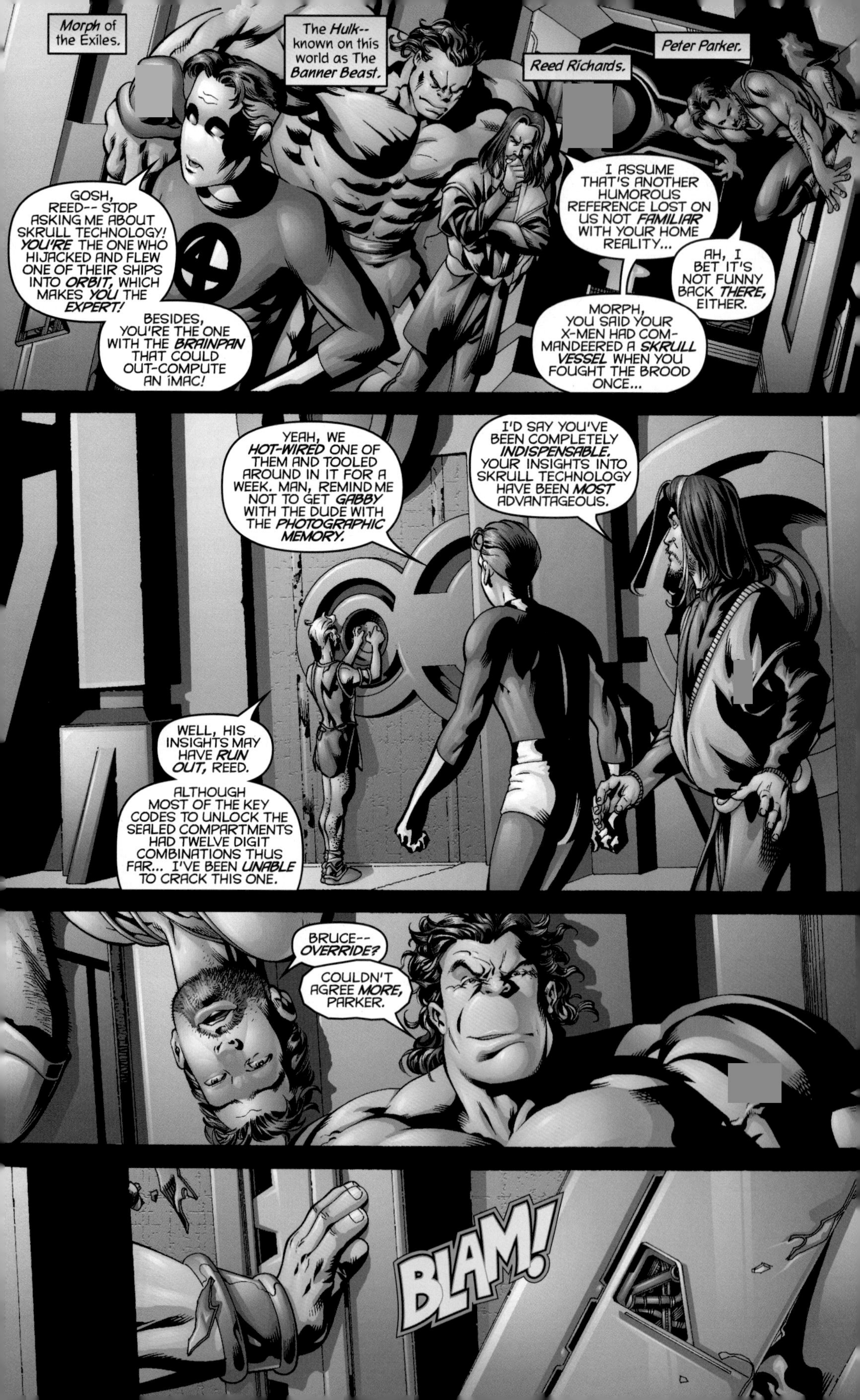

Morph of the Exiles.
The Hulk-- known on this world as The Banner Beast.
Reed Richards.
Peter Parker.
GOSH, REED-- STOP ASKING ME ABOUT SKRULL TECHNOLOGY! YOU'RE THE ONE WHO HIJACKED AND FLEW ONE OF THEIR SHIPS INTO ORBIT, WHICH MAKES YOU THE EXPERT!
BESIDES, YOU'RE THE ONE WITH THE BRAINPAN THAT COULD OUT-COMPUTE AN iMAC!
I ASSUME THAT'S ANOTHER HUMOROUS REFERENCE LOST ON US NOT FAMILIAR WITH YOUR HOME REALITY...
AH, I BET IT'S NOT FUNNY BACK THERE, EITHER.
MORPH, YOU SAID YOUR X-MEN HAD COM-MANDEERED A SKRULL VESSEL WHEN YOU FOUGHT THE BROOD ONCE...
YEAH, WE HOT-WIRED ONE OF THEM AND TOOLED AROUND IN IT FOR A WEEK. MAN, REMIND ME NOT TO GET GABBY WITH THE DUDE WITH THE PHOTOGRAPHIC MEMORY.
I'D SAY YOU'VE BEEN COMPLETELY INDISPENSABLE. YOUR INSIGHTS INTO SKRULL TECHNOLOGY HAVE BEEN MOST ADVANTAGEOUS.
WELL, HIS INSIGHTS MAY HAVE RUN OUT, REED.
ALTHOUGH MOST OF THE KEY CODES TO UNLOCK THE SEALED COMPARTMENTS HAD TWELVE DIGIT COMBINATIONS THUS FAR... I'VE BEEN UNABLE TO CRACK THIS ONE.
BRUCE-- OVERRIDE?
COULDN'T AGREE MORE, PARKER.
BLAM!

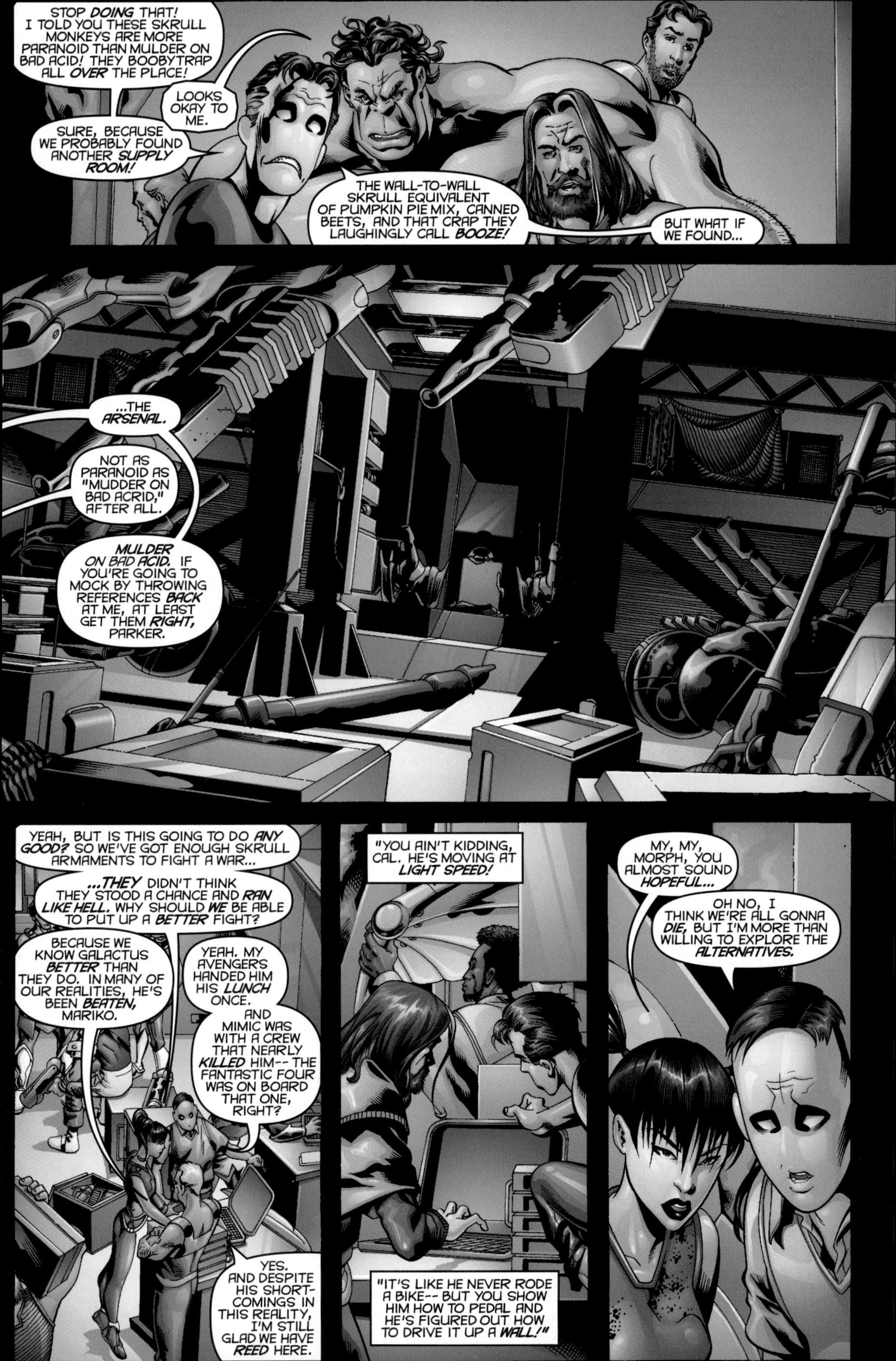

STOP DOING THAT! I TOLD YOU THESE SKRULL MONKEYS ARE MORE PARANOID THAN MULDER ON BAD ACID! THEY BOOBYTRAP ALL OVER THE PLACE!
LOOKS OKAY TO ME.
SURE, BECAUSE WE PROBABLY FOUND ANOTHER SUPPLY ROOM!
THE WALL-TO-WALL SKRULL EQUIVALENT OF PUMPKIN PIE MIX, CANNED BEETS, AND THAT CRAP THEY LAUGHINGLY CALL BOOZE!
BUT WHAT IF WE FOUND...
...THE ARSENAL.
NOT AS PARANOID AS "MUDDER ON BAD ACRID," AFTER ALL.
MULDER ON BAD ACID. IF YOU'RE GOING TO MOCK BY THROWING REFERENCES BACK AT ME, AT LEAST GET THEM RIGHT, PARKER.
YEAH, BUT IS THIS GOING TO DO ANY GOOD? SO WE'VE GOT ENOUGH SKRULL ARMAMENTS TO FIGHT A WAR...
...THEY DIDN'T THINK THEY STOOD A CHANCE AND RAN LIKE HELL. WHY SHOULD WE BE ABLE TO PUT UP A BETTER FIGHT?
BECAUSE WE KNOW GALACTUS BETTER THAN THEY DO. IN MANY OF OUR REALITIES, HE'S BEEN BEATEN, MARIKO.
YEAH. MY AVENGERS HANDED HIM HIS LUNCH ONCE.
AND MIMIC WAS WITH A CREW THAT NEARLY KILLED HIM-- THE FANTASTIC FOUR WAS ON BOARD THAT ONE, RIGHT?
YES. AND DESPITE HIS SHORT-COMINGS IN THIS REALITY, I'M STILL GLAD WE HAVE REED HERE.
"YOU AIN'T KIDDING, CAL. HE'S MOVING AT LIGHT SPEED!
"IT'S LIKE HE NEVER RODE A BIKE-- BUT YOU SHOW HIM HOW TO PEDAL AND HE'S FIGURED OUT HOW TO DRIVE IT UP A WALL!"
MY, MY, MORPH, YOU ALMOST SOUND HOPEFUL...
OH NO, I THINK WE'RE ALL GONNA DIE, BUT I'M MORE THAN WILLING TO EXPLORE THE ALTERNATIVES.

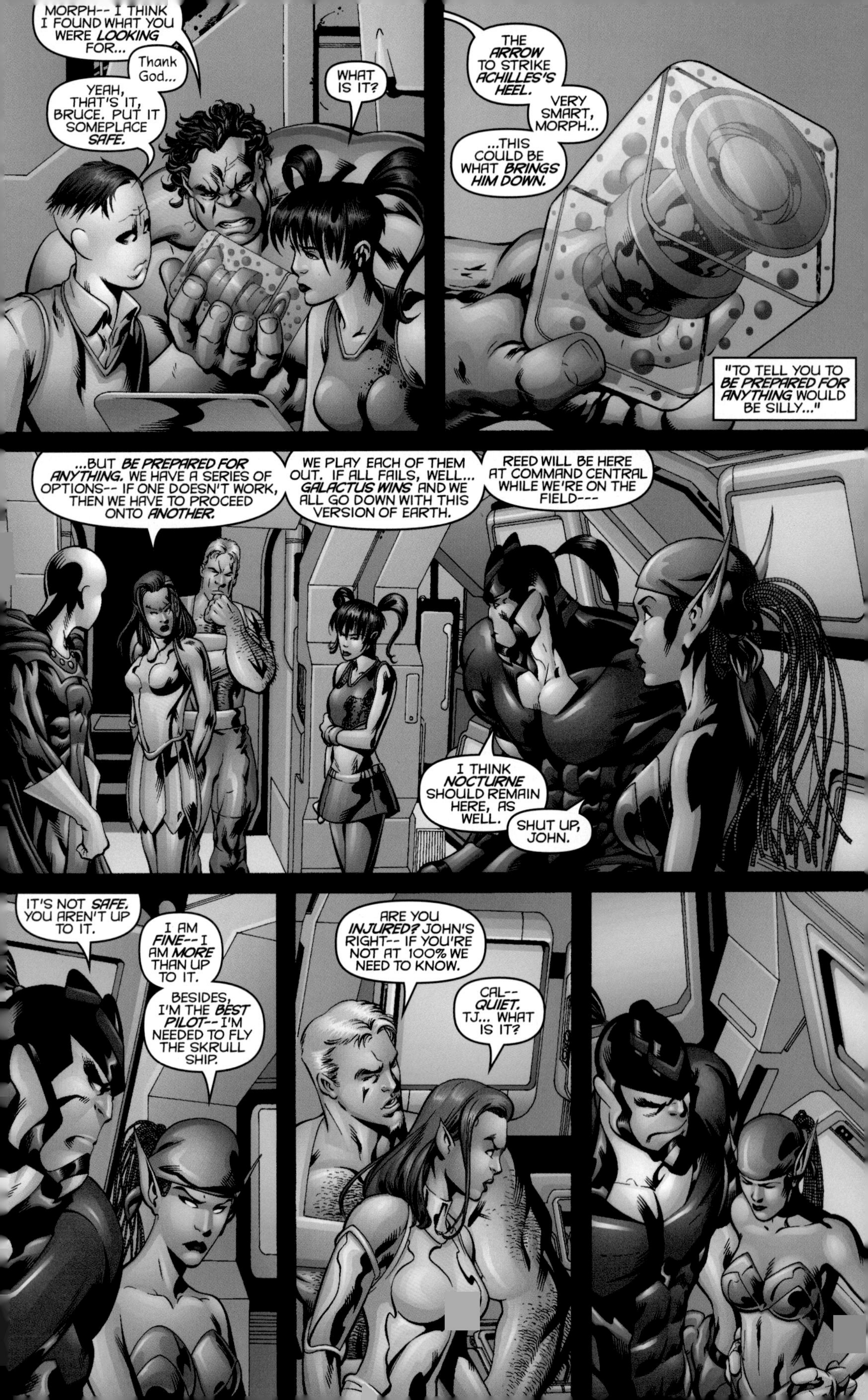

MORPH-- I THINK I FOUND WHAT YOU WERE *LOOKING* FOR...
Thank God...
YEAH, THAT'S IT, BRUCE. PUT IT SOMEPLACE *SAFE.*
WHAT IS IT?
THE *ARROW* TO STRIKE *ACHILLES'S HEEL.*
VERY SMART, MORPH...
...THIS COULD BE WHAT *BRINGS HIM DOWN.*
"TO TELL YOU TO *BE PREPARED FOR ANYTHING* WOULD BE SILLY..."
...BUT *BE PREPARED FOR ANYTHING.* WE HAVE A SERIES OF OPTIONS-- IF ONE DOESN'T WORK, THEN WE HAVE TO PROCEED ONTO *ANOTHER.*
WE PLAY EACH OF THEM OUT. IF ALL FAILS, WELL... *GALACTUS WINS* AND WE ALL GO DOWN WITH THIS VERSION OF EARTH.
REED WILL BE HERE AT COMMAND CENTRAL WHILE WE'RE ON THE FIELD---
I THINK *NOCTURNE* SHOULD REMAIN HERE, AS WELL.
SHUT UP, JOHN.
IT'S NOT *SAFE.* YOU AREN'T UP TO IT.
I AM *FINE--* I AM *MORE* THAN UP TO IT.
BESIDES, I'M THE *BEST PILOT--* I'M NEEDED TO FLY THE SKRULL SHIP.
ARE YOU *INJURED?* JOHN'S RIGHT-- IF YOU'RE NOT AT 100% WE NEED TO KNOW.
CAL-- *QUIET.* TJ... WHAT IS IT?

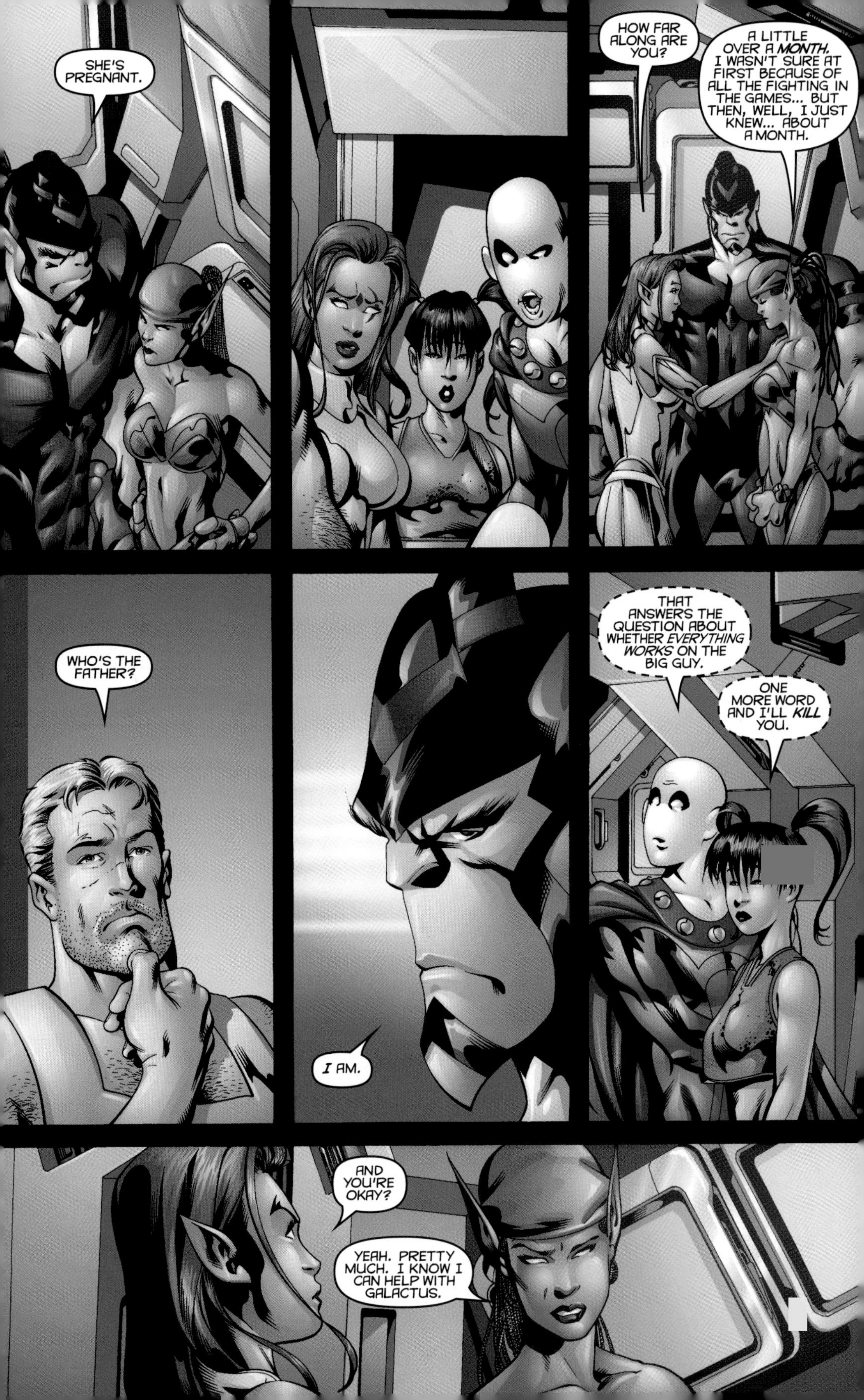
SHE'S PREGNANT.
HOW FAR ALONG ARE YOU?
A LITTLE OVER A MONTH. I WASN'T SURE AT FIRST BECAUSE OF ALL THE FIGHTING IN THE GAMES... BUT THEN, WELL, I JUST KNEW... ABOUT A MONTH.
WHO'S THE FATHER?
I AM.
THAT ANSWERS THE QUESTION ABOUT WHETHER EVERYTHING WORKS ON THE BIG GUY.
ONE MORE WORD AND I'LL KILL YOU.
AND YOU'RE OKAY?
YEAH. PRETTY MUCH. I KNOW I CAN HELP WITH GALACTUS.

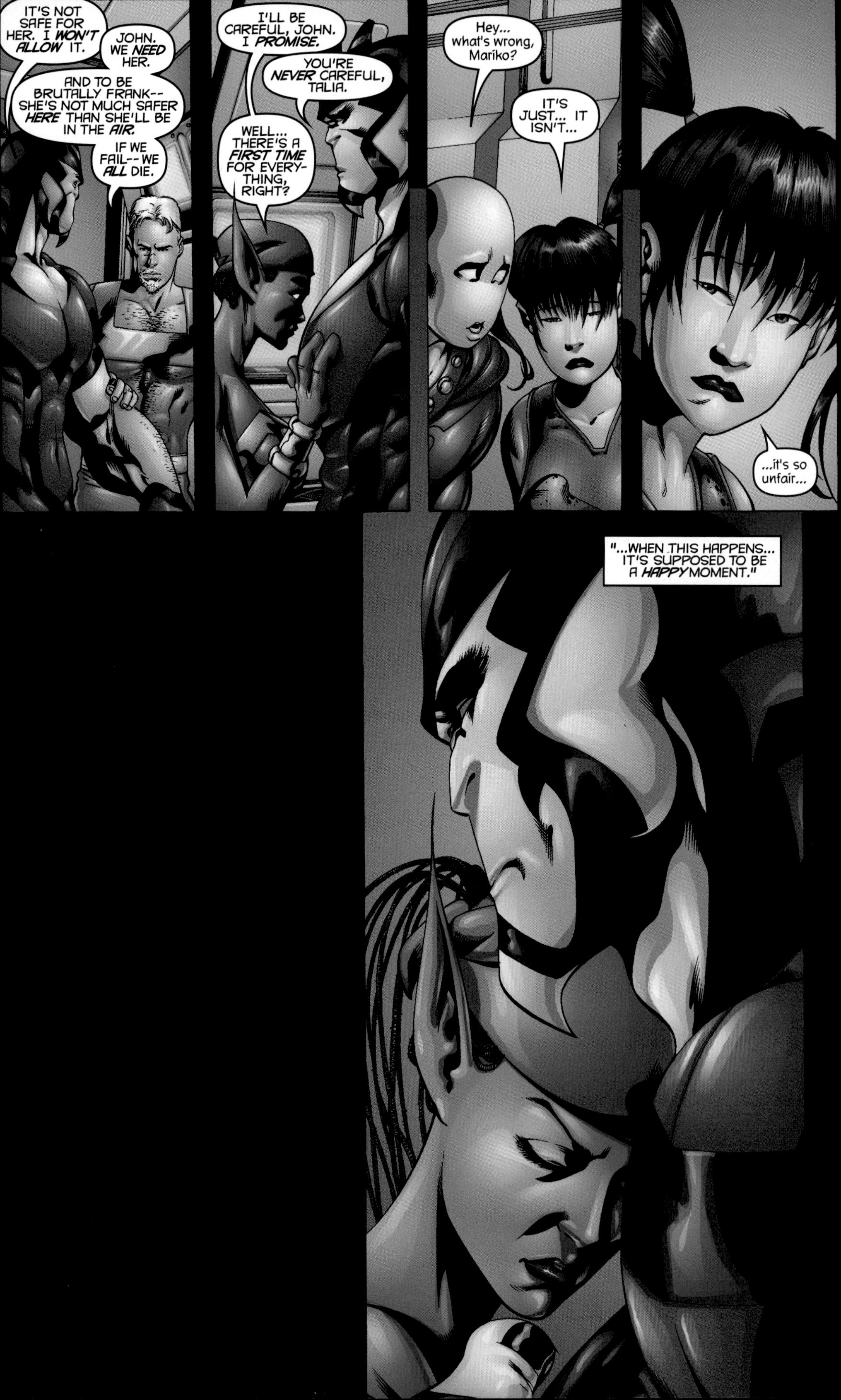

IT'S NOT SAFE FOR HER. I *WON'T ALLOW* IT.
JOHN. WE *NEED* HER.
AND TO BE BRUTALLY FRANK-- SHE'S NOT MUCH SAFER *HERE* THAN SHE'LL BE IN THE *AIR.*
IF WE FAIL-- WE *ALL* DIE.
I'LL BE CAREFUL, JOHN. I *PROMISE.*
YOU'RE *NEVER* CAREFUL, TALIA.
WELL... THERE'S A *FIRST TIME* FOR EVERY-THING, RIGHT?
Hey... what's wrong, Mariko?
IT'S JUST... IT ISN'T...
...it's so unfair...
"...WHEN THIS HAPPENS... IT'S SUPPOSED TO BE A *HAPPY* MOMENT."

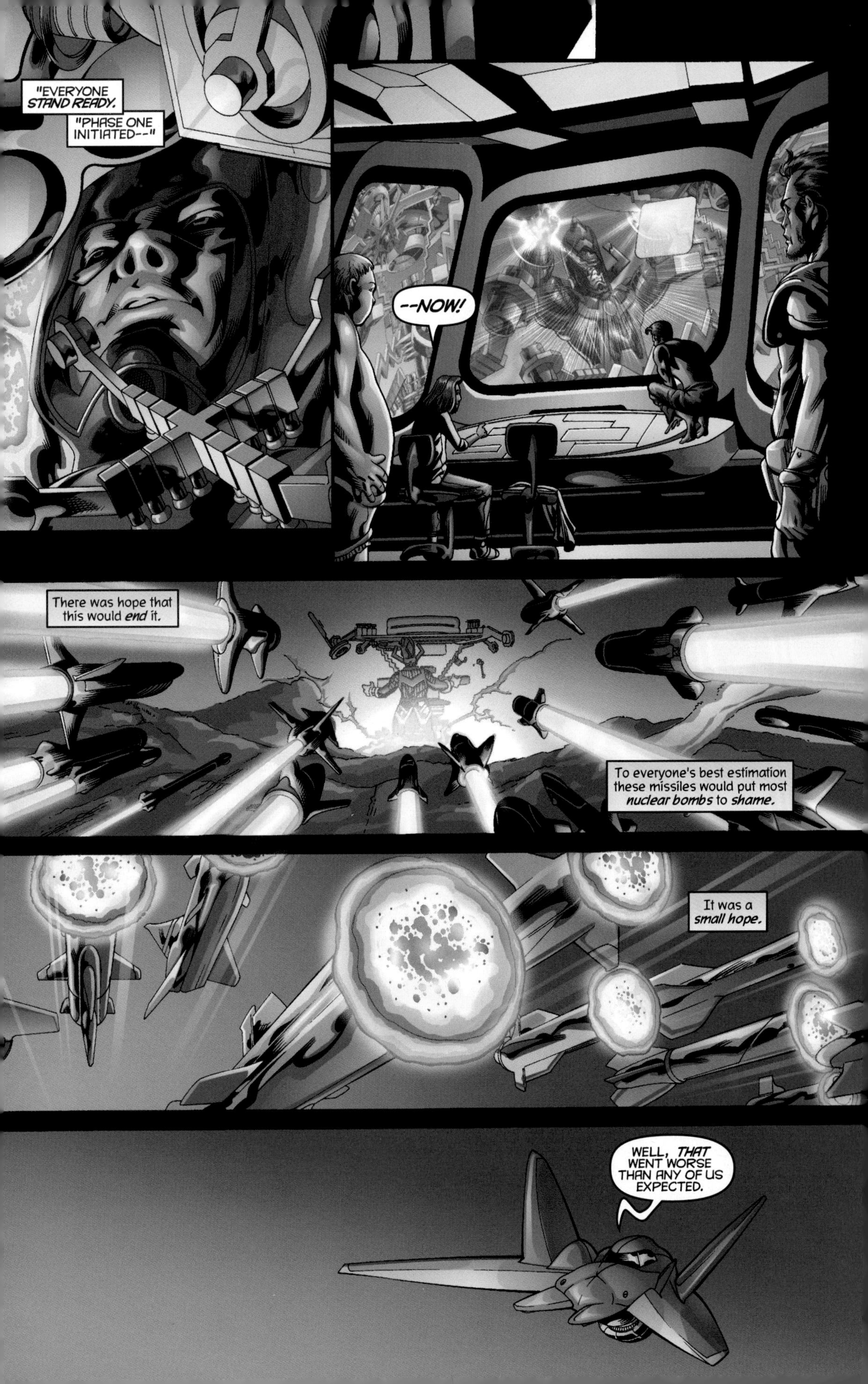
"EVERYONE STAND READY.
"PHASE ONE INITIATED--"
--NOW!
There was hope that this would end it.
To everyone's best estimation these missiles would put most nuclear bombs to shame.
It was a small hope.
WELL, THAT WENT WORSE THAN ANY OF US EXPECTED.

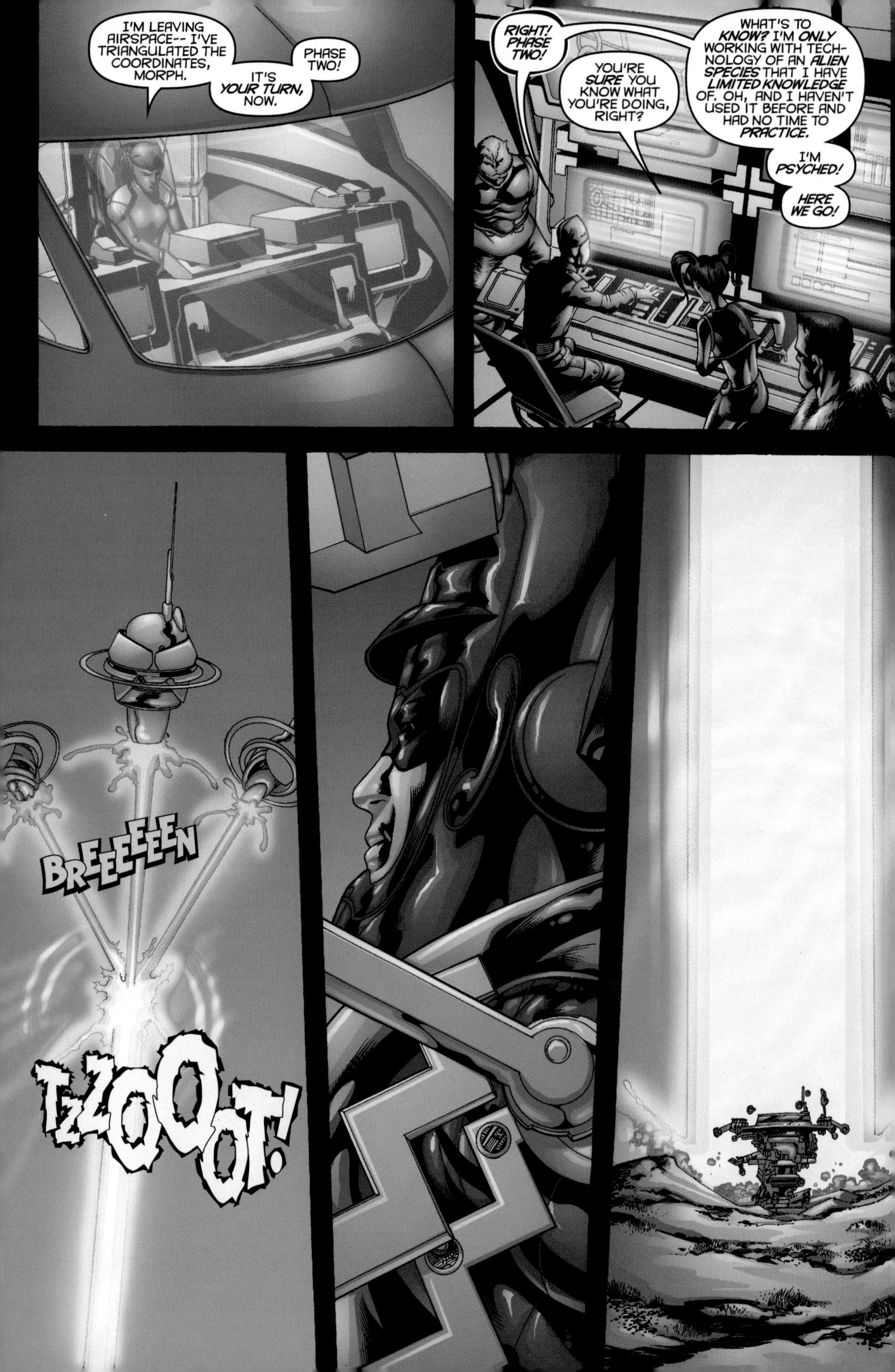
I'M LEAVING AIRSPACE-- I'VE TRIANGULATED THE COORDINATES, MORPH.
IT'S YOUR TURN, NOW.
PHASE TWO!
RIGHT! PHASE TWO!
YOU'RE SURE YOU KNOW WHAT YOU'RE DOING, RIGHT?
WHAT'S TO KNOW? I'M ONLY WORKING WITH TECHNOLOGY OF AN ALIEN SPECIES THAT I HAVE LIMITED KNOWLEDGE OF. OH, AND I HAVEN'T USED IT BEFORE AND HAD NO TIME TO PRACTICE.
I'M PSYCHED!
HERE WE GO!
BREEEEEN
TZZOOOOT!

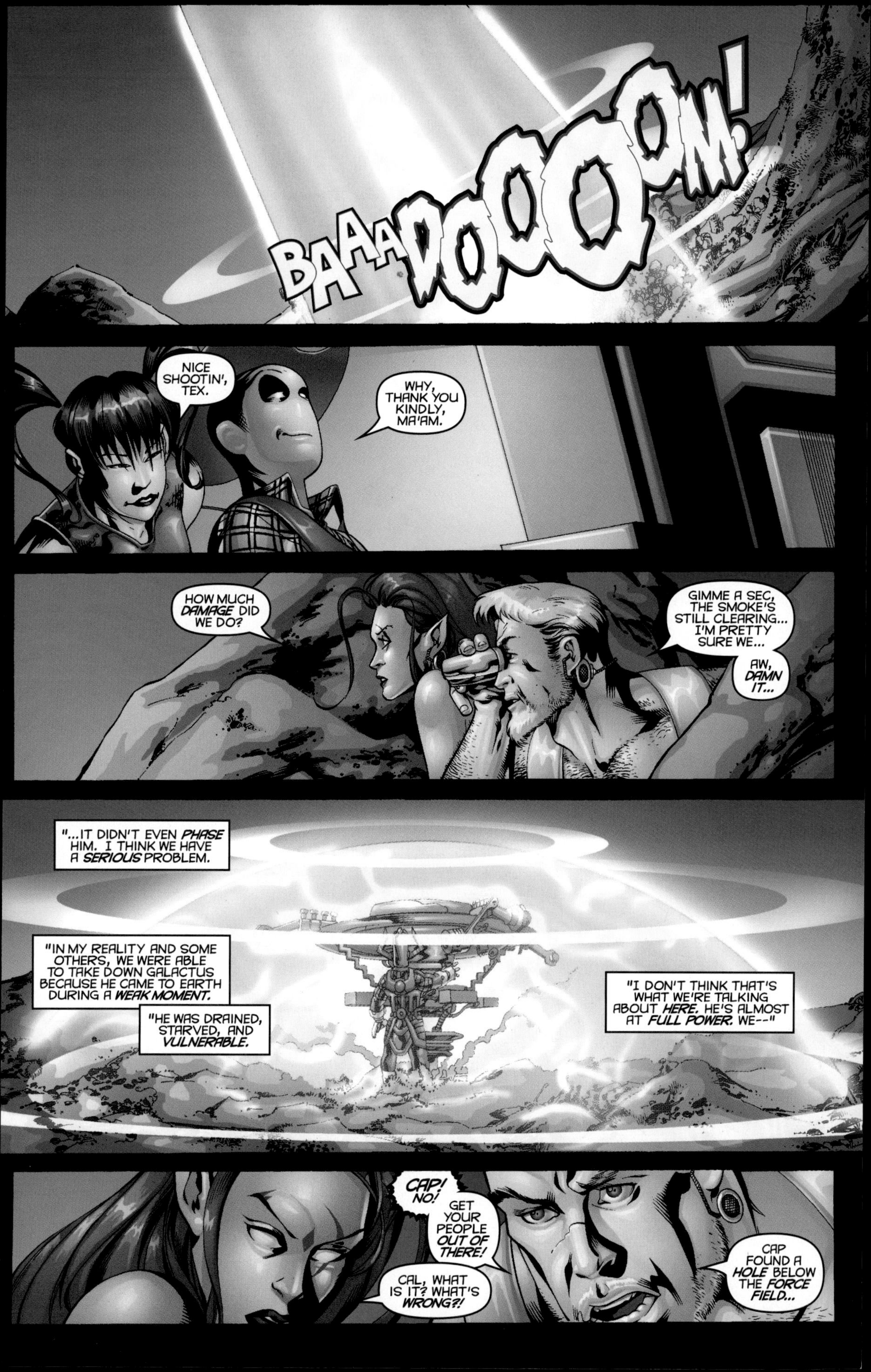
BAAADOOOOOM!
NICE SHOOTIN', TEX.
WHY, THANK YOU KINDLY, MA'AM.
HOW MUCH DAMAGE DID WE DO?
GIMME A SEC, THE SMOKE'S STILL CLEARING... I'M PRETTY SURE WE...
AW, DAMN IT...
"...IT DIDN'T EVEN PHASE HIM. I THINK WE HAVE A SERIOUS PROBLEM.
"IN MY REALITY AND SOME OTHERS, WE WERE ABLE TO TAKE DOWN GALACTUS BECAUSE HE CAME TO EARTH DURING A WEAK MOMENT.
"HE WAS DRAINED, STARVED, AND VULNERABLE.
"I DON'T THINK THAT'S WHAT WE'RE TALKING ABOUT HERE. HE'S ALMOST AT FULL POWER. WE--"
CAP! NO!
GET YOUR PEOPLE OUT OF THERE!
CAL, WHAT IS IT? WHAT'S WRONG?!
CAP FOUND A HOLE BELOW THE FORCE FIELD...

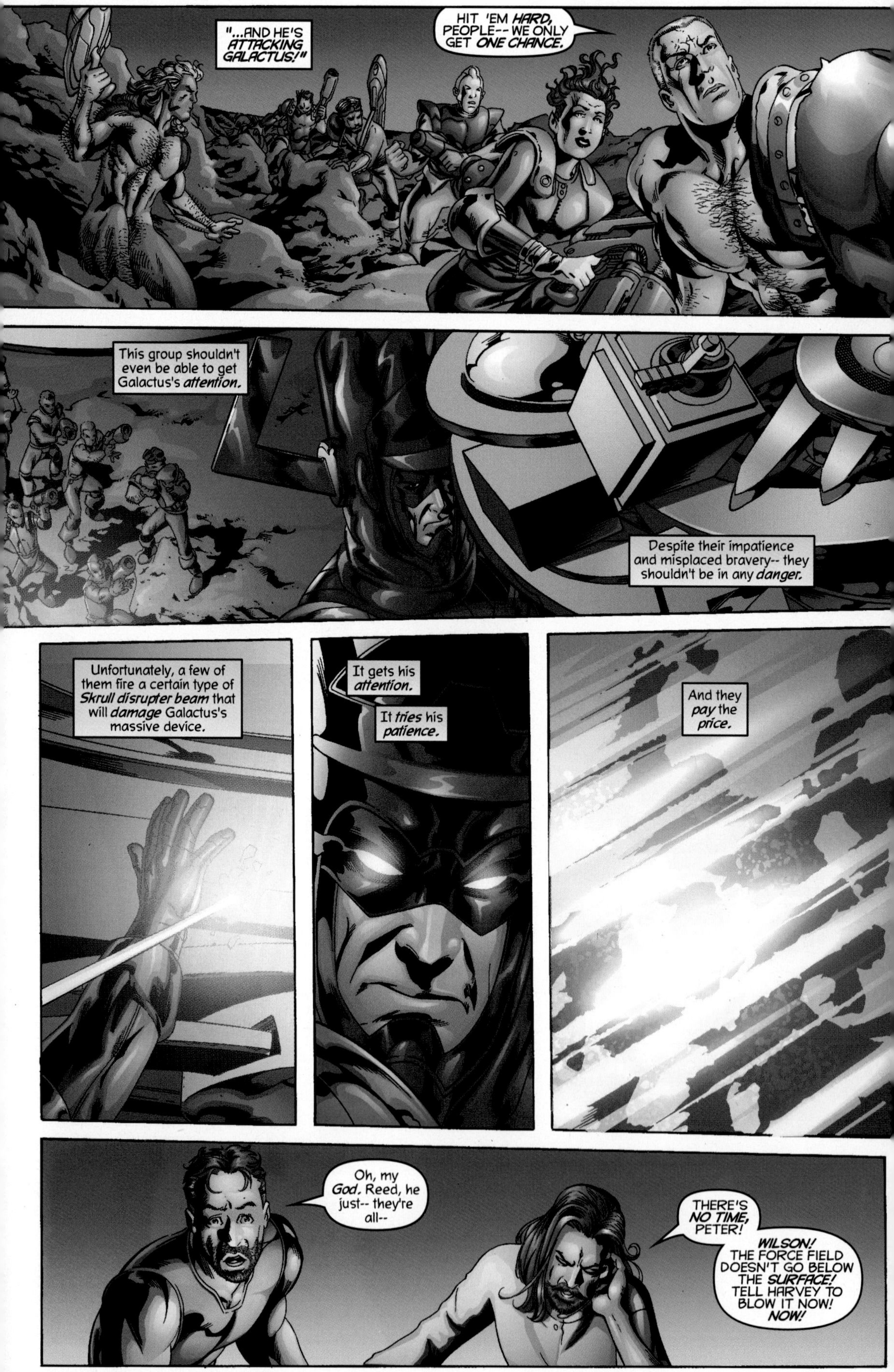
"...AND HE'S ATTACKING GALACTUS!"
HIT 'EM HARD, PEOPLE-- WE ONLY GET ONE CHANCE.
This group shouldn't even be able to get Galactus's attention.
Despite their impatience and misplaced bravery-- they shouldn't be in any danger.
Unfortunately, a few of them fire a certain type of Skrull disrupter beam that will damage Galactus's massive device.
It gets his attention.
It tries his patience.
And they pay the price.
Oh, my God. Reed, he just-- they're all--
THERE'S NO TIME, PETER!
WILSON! THE FORCE FIELD DOESN'T GO BELOW THE SURFACE! TELL HARVEY TO BLOW IT NOW! NOW!

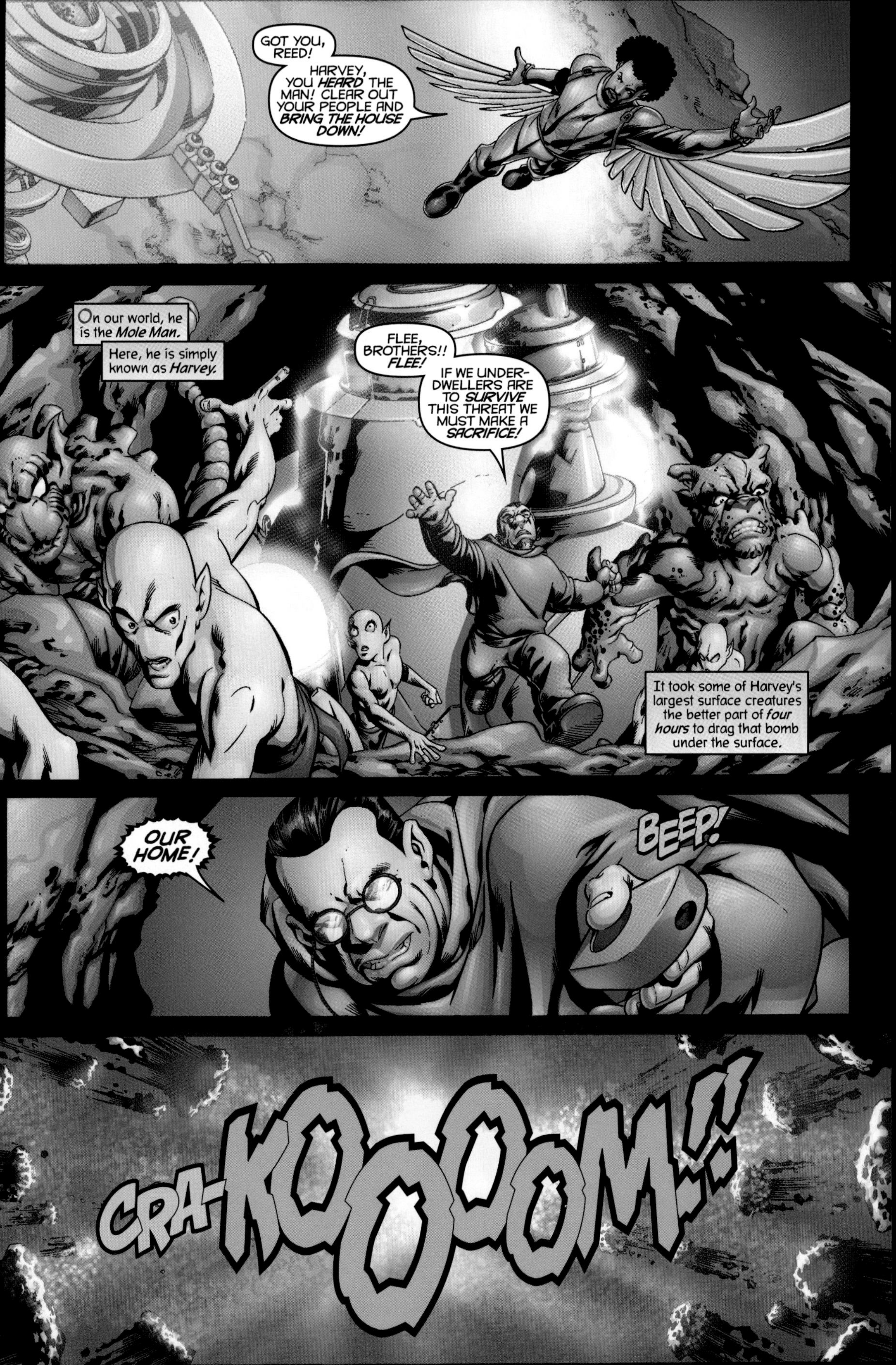
GOT YOU, REED!
HARVEY, YOU *HEARD* THE MAN! CLEAR OUT YOUR PEOPLE AND *BRING THE HOUSE DOWN!*
On our world, he is the *Mole Man.*
Here, he is simply known as *Harvey.*
FLEE, BROTHERS!! *FLEE!*
IF WE UNDER-DWELLERS ARE TO *SURVIVE* THIS THREAT WE MUST MAKE A *SACRIFICE!*
It took some of Harvey's largest surface creatures the better part of *four hours* to drag that bomb under the surface.
OUR HOME!
BEEP!
CRA-KOOOOM!!

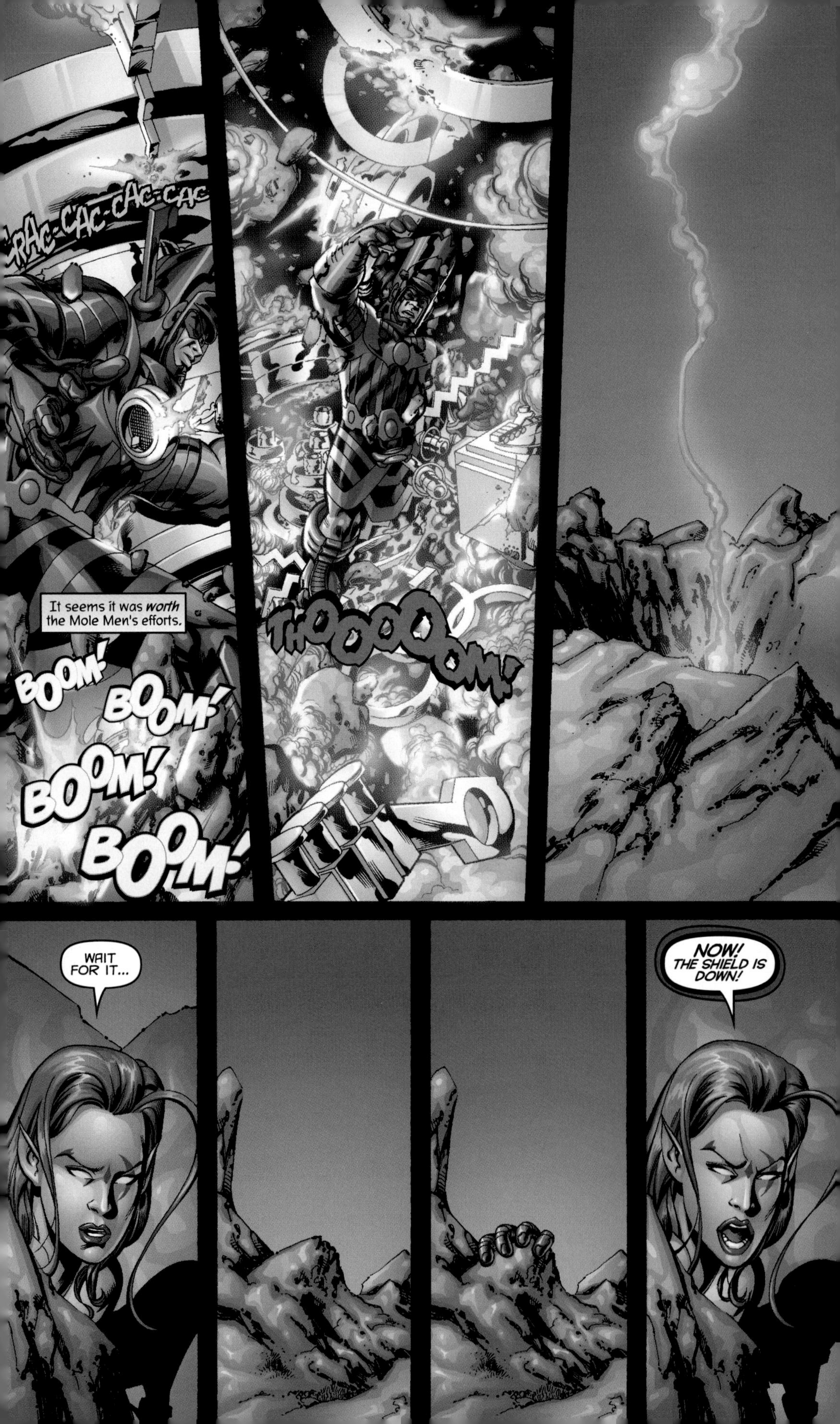
CRAC-CAC-CAC-CAC
It seems it was *worth* the Mole Men's efforts.
BOOM!
BOOM!
BOOM!
BOOM!
THOOOOOOM!
WAIT FOR IT...
NOW! THE SHIELD IS DOWN!

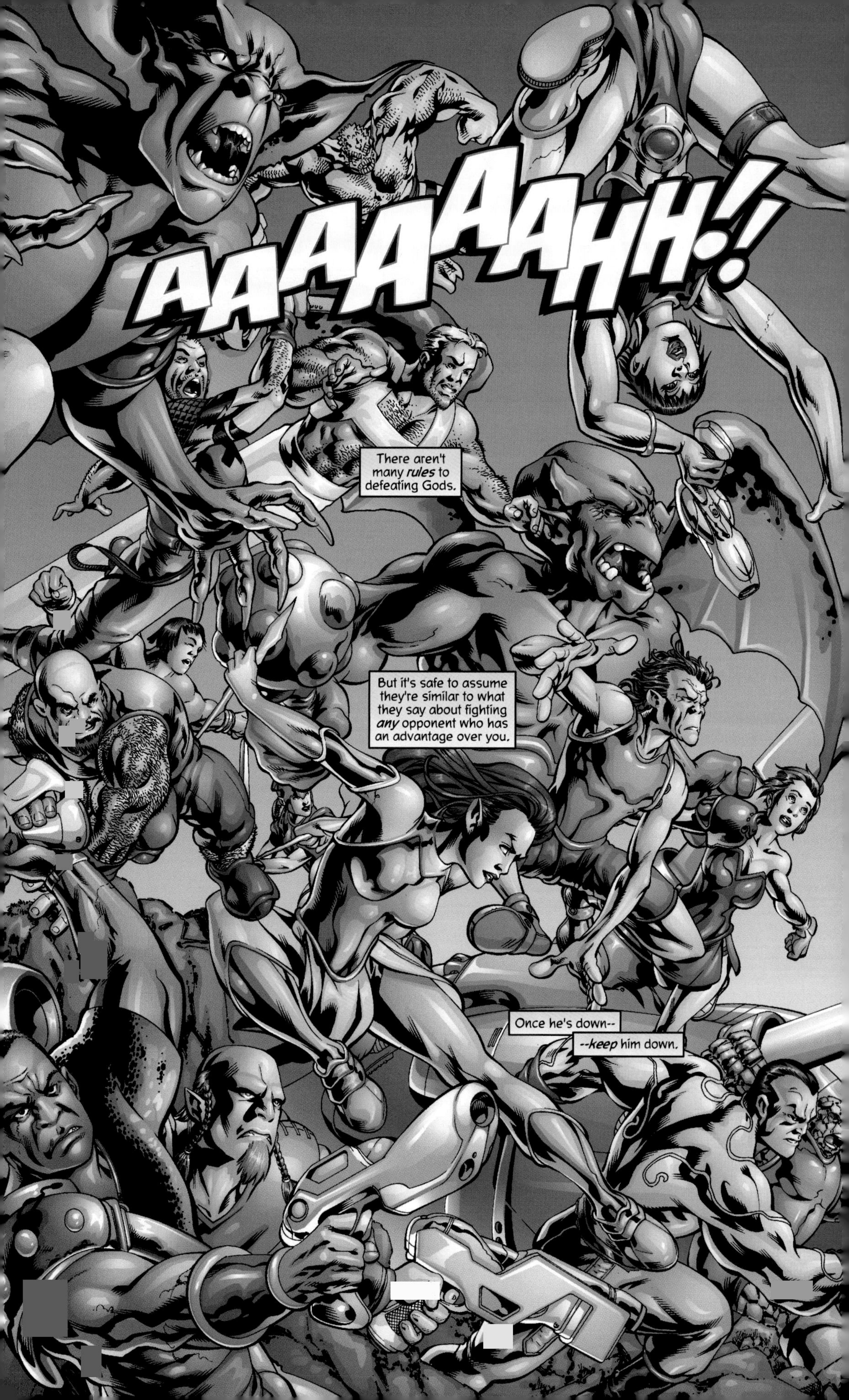
AAAAAAHH!!
There aren't many *rules* to defeating Gods.
But it's safe to assume they're similar to what they say about fighting *any* opponent who has an advantage over you.
Once he's down--
--*keep* him down.

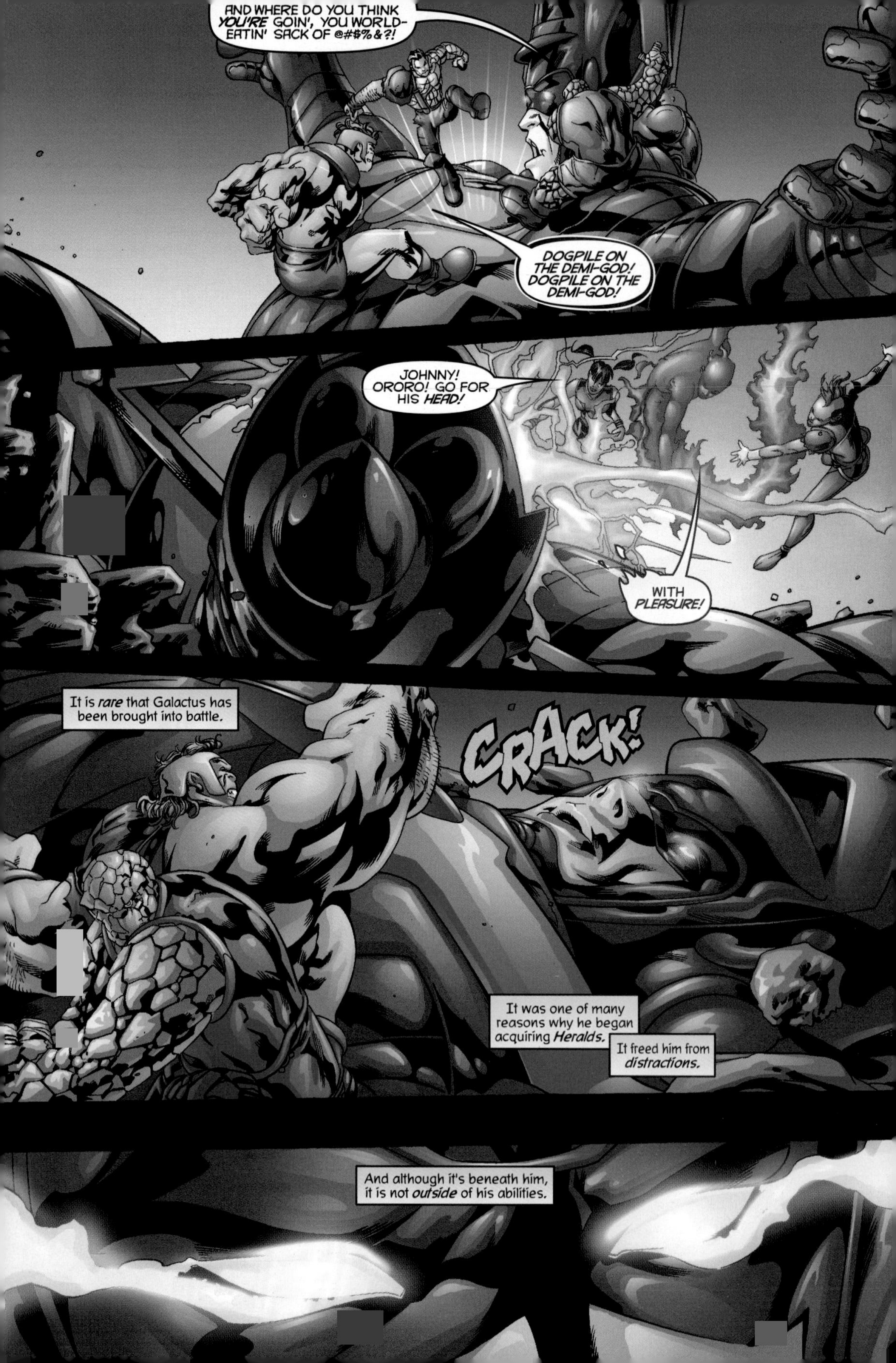
AND WHERE DO YOU THINK *YOU'RE* GOIN', YOU WORLD-EATIN' SACK OF @#$%&?!
DOGPILE ON THE DEMI-GOD! DOGPILE ON THE DEMI-GOD!
JOHNNY! ORORO! GO FOR HIS *HEAD!*
WITH *PLEASURE!*
It is *rare* that Galactus has been brought into battle.
CRACK!
It was one of many reasons why he began acquiring *Heralds.*
It freed him from *distractions.*
And although it's beneath him, it is not *outside* of his abilities.

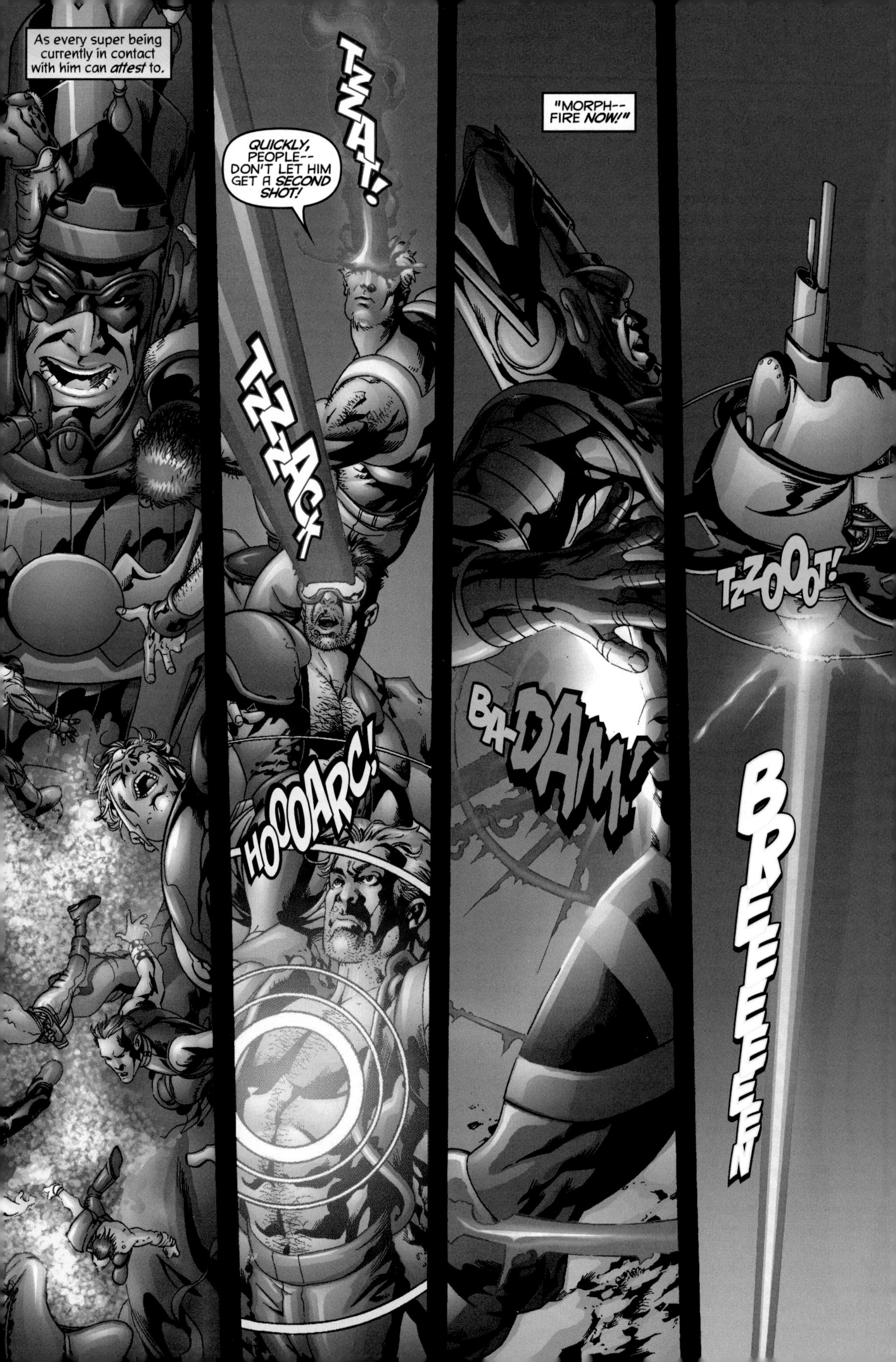

As every super being currently in contact with him can *attest* to.
TZZAT!
QUICKLY, PEOPLE-- DON'T LET HIM GET A *SECOND* SHOT!
TZZZACK
THOOOARC!
"MORPH-- FIRE *NOW!*"
BA-DAM!
TZZOOOT!
BREEEEEEN

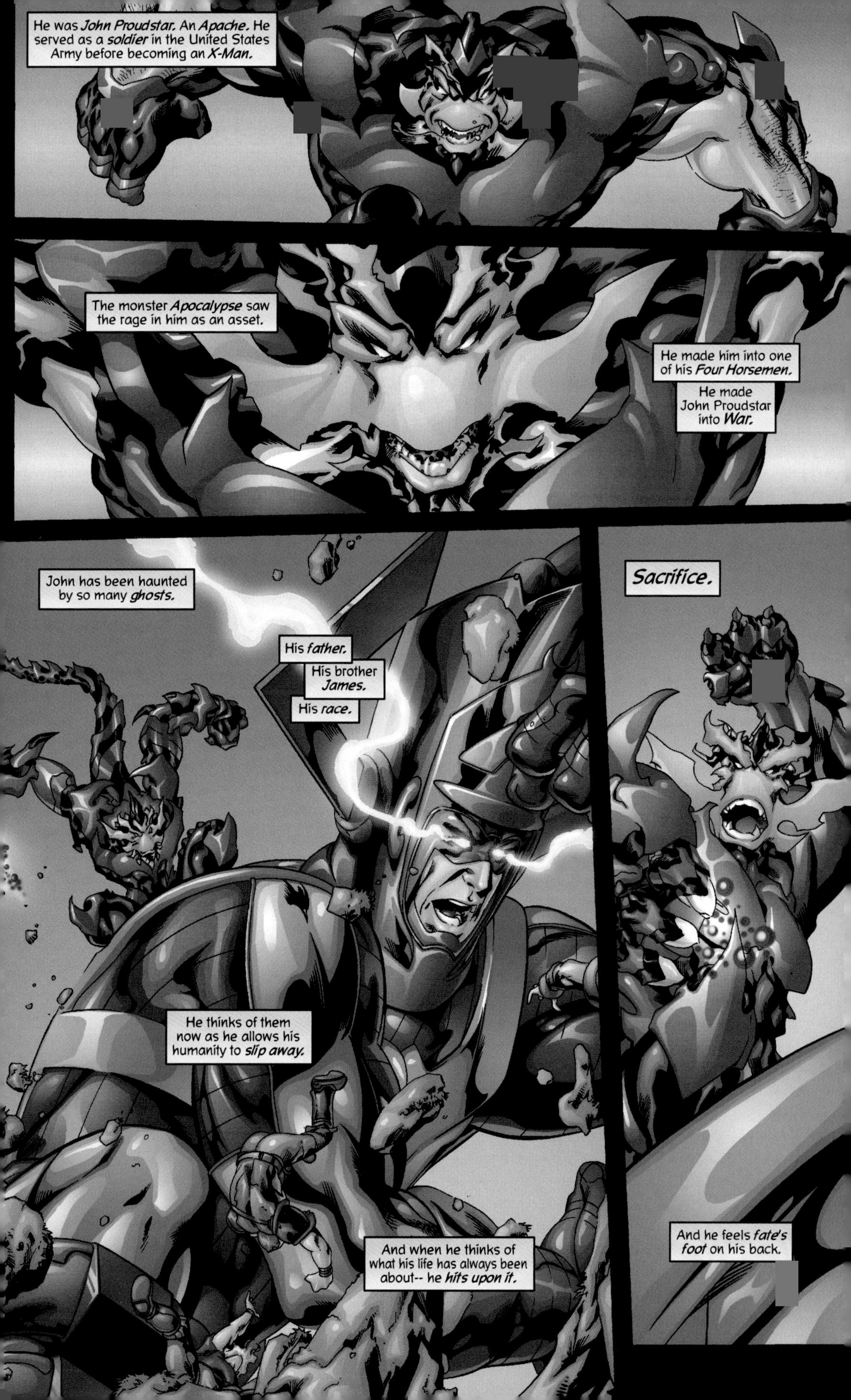
He was *John Proudstar*. An *Apache.* He served as a *soldier* in the United States Army before becoming an *X-Man.*
The monster *Apocalypse* saw the rage in him as an asset.
He made him into one of his *Four Horsemen.*
He made John Proudstar into *War.*
John has been haunted by so many *ghosts.*
His *father.*
His brother *James.*
His *race.*
He thinks of them now as he allows his humanity to *slip away.*
And when he thinks of what his life has always been about-- he *hits upon it.*
Sacrifice.
And he feels *fate's foot* on his back.

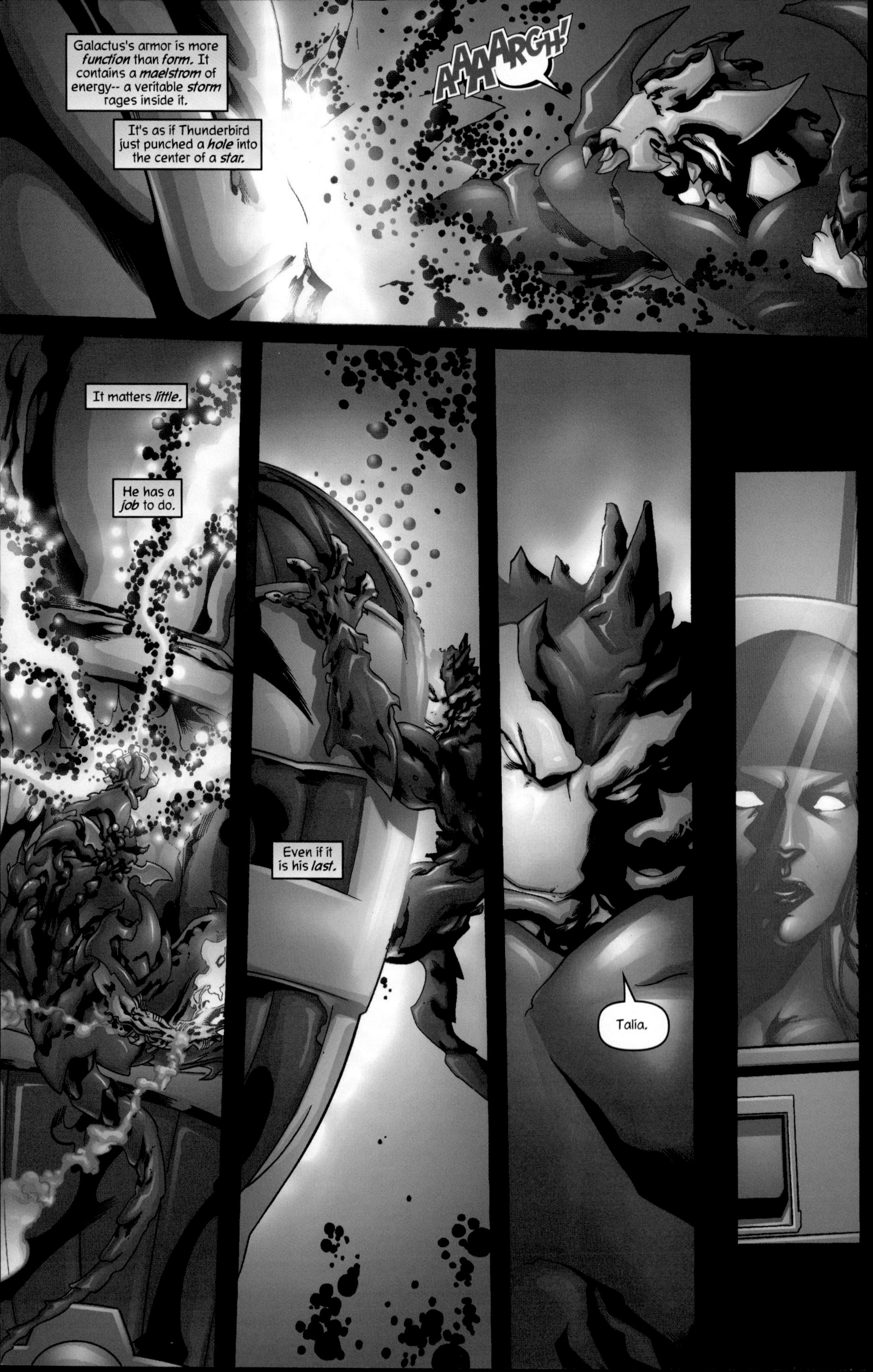
Galactus's armor is more function than form. It contains a maelstrom of energy-- a veritable storm rages inside it.
It's as if Thunderbird just punched a hole into the center of a star.
AAAARGH!
It matters little.
He has a job to do.
Even if it is his last.
Talia.

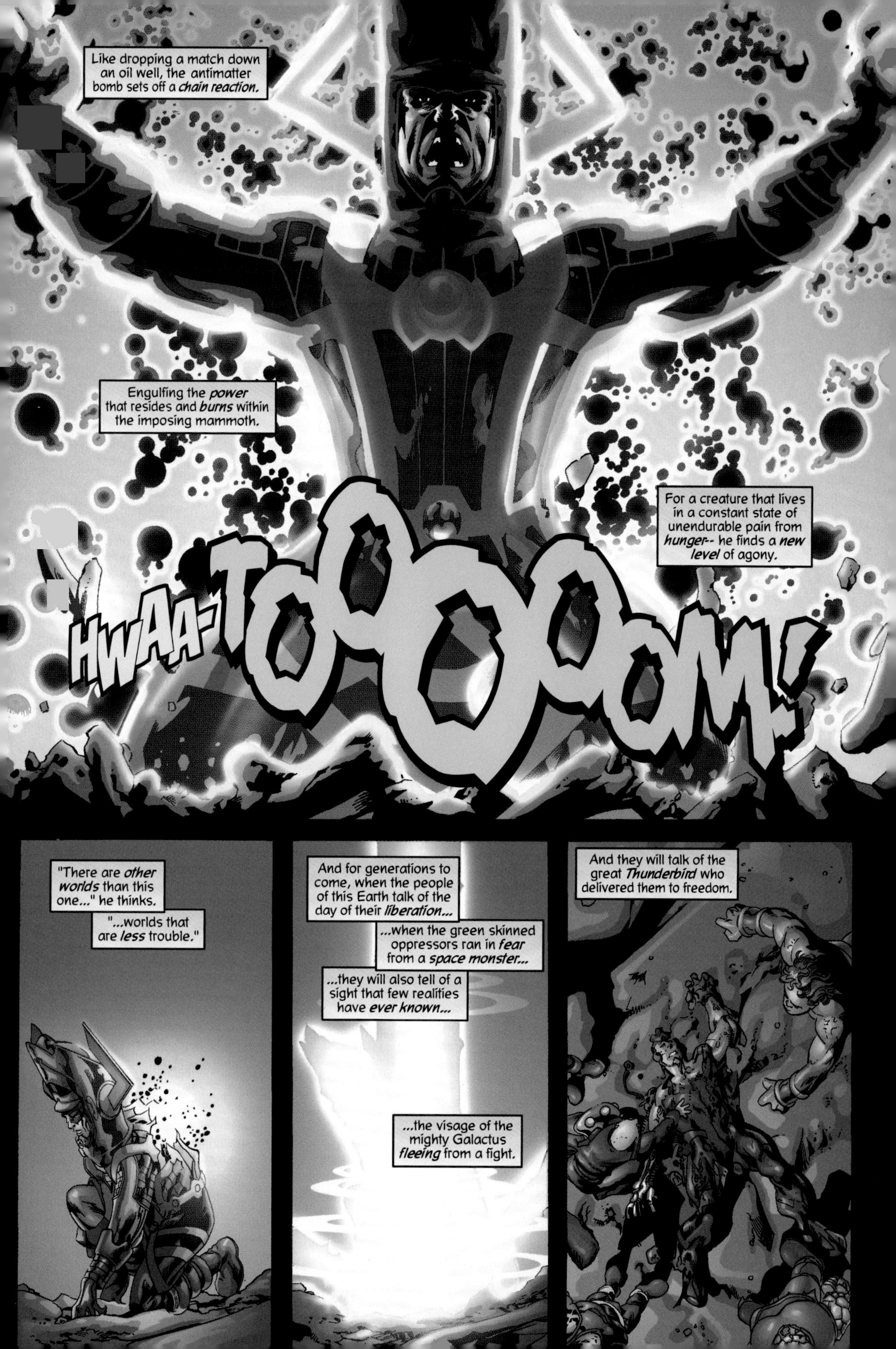

Like dropping a match down an oil well, the antimatter bomb sets off a *chain reaction.*
Engulfing the *power* that resides and *burns* within the imposing mammoth.
For a creature that lives in a constant state of unendurable pain from *hunger--* he finds a *new level* of agony.
HWAA-TOOOOOM!
"There are *other worlds* than this one..." he thinks.
"...worlds that are *less* trouble."
And for generations to come, when the people of this Earth talk of the day of their *liberation...*
...when the green skinned oppressors ran in *fear* from a *space monster...*
...they will also tell of a sight that few realities have *ever known...*
...the visage of the mighty Galactus *fleeing* from a fight.
And they will talk of the great *Thunderbird* who delivered them to freedom.

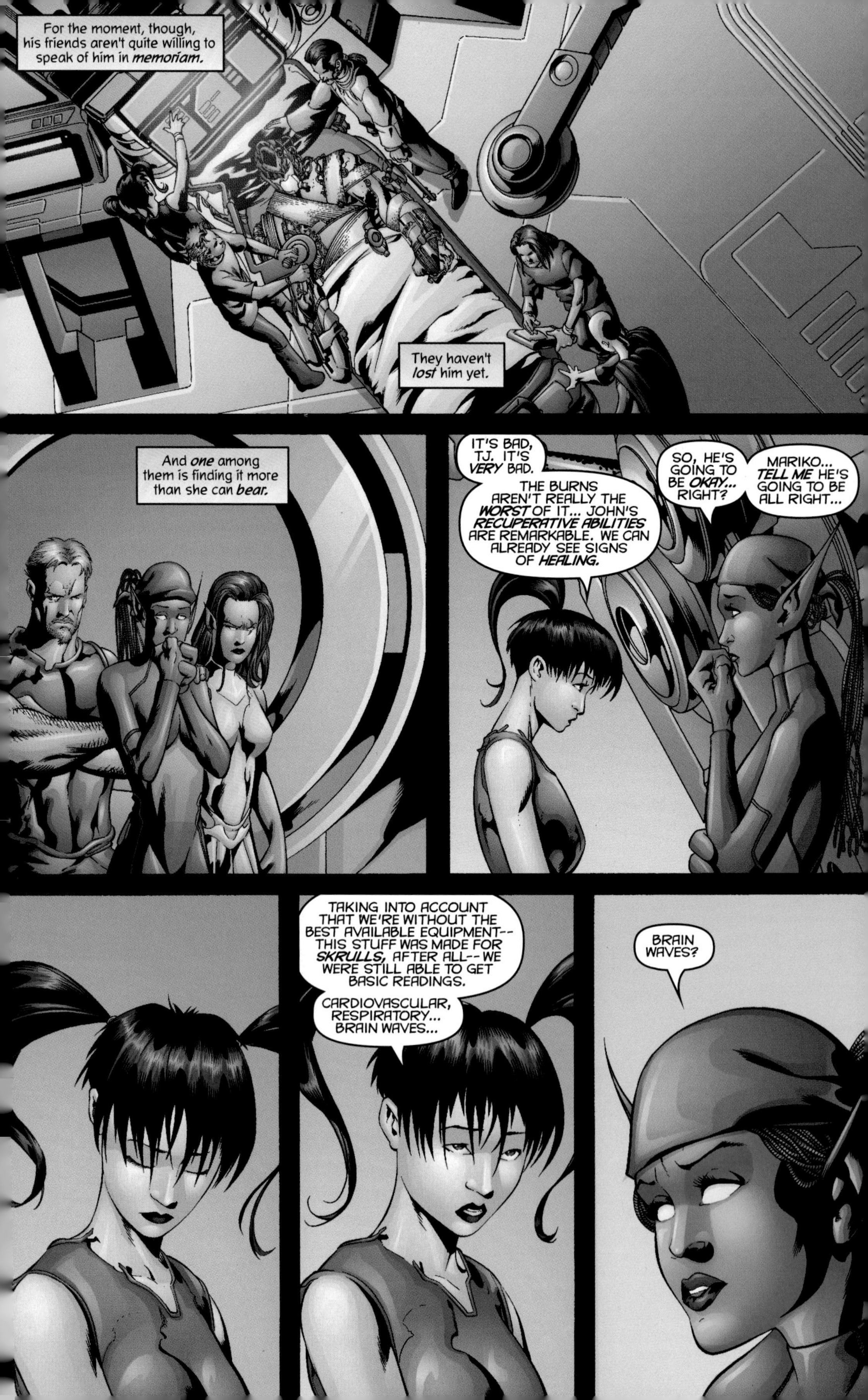
For the moment, though, his friends aren't quite willing to speak of him in *memoriam.*
They haven't *lost* him yet.
And *one* among them is finding it more than she can *bear.*
IT'S BAD, TJ. IT'S *VERY* BAD.
THE BURNS AREN'T REALLY THE *WORST* OF IT... JOHN'S *RECUPERATIVE ABILITIES* ARE REMARKABLE. WE CAN ALREADY SEE SIGNS OF *HEALING.*
SO, HE'S GOING TO BE *OKAY...* RIGHT?
MARIKO... *TELL ME* HE'S GOING TO BE ALL RIGHT...
TAKING INTO ACCOUNT THAT WE'RE WITHOUT THE BEST AVAILABLE EQUIPMENT-- THIS STUFF WAS MADE FOR *SKRULLS,* AFTER ALL-- WE WERE STILL ABLE TO GET BASIC READINGS.
CARDIOVASCULAR, RESPIRATORY... BRAIN WAVES...
BRAIN WAVES?

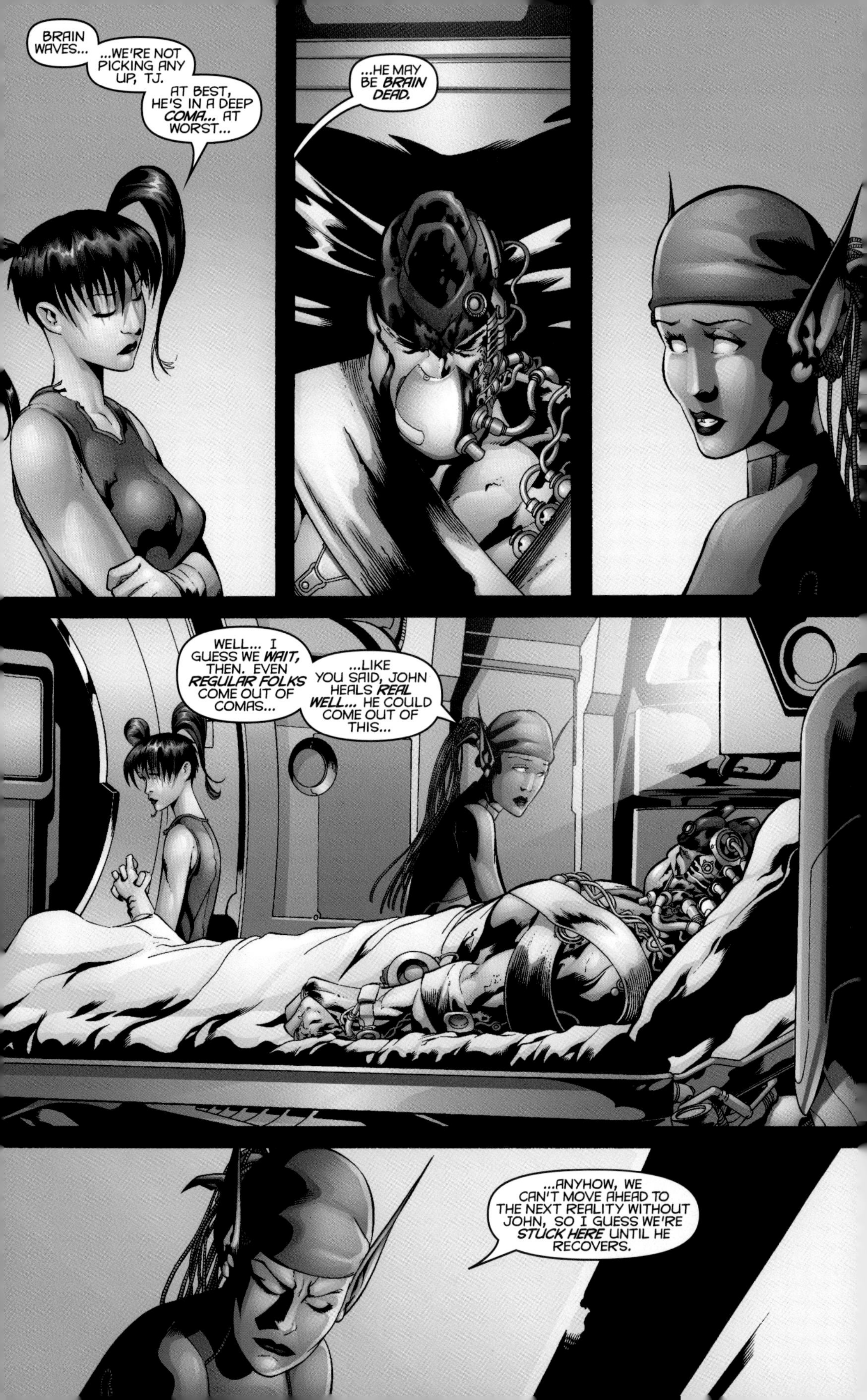
BRAIN WAVES...
...WE'RE NOT PICKING ANY UP, TJ.
AT BEST, HE'S IN A DEEP COMA... AT WORST...
...HE MAY BE BRAIN DEAD.
WELL... I GUESS WE WAIT, THEN. EVEN REGULAR FOLKS COME OUT OF COMAS...
...LIKE YOU SAID, JOHN HEALS REAL WELL... HE COULD COME OUT OF THIS...
...ANYHOW, WE CAN'T MOVE AHEAD TO THE NEXT REALITY WITHOUT JOHN, SO I GUESS WE'RE STUCK HERE UNTIL HE RECOVERS.

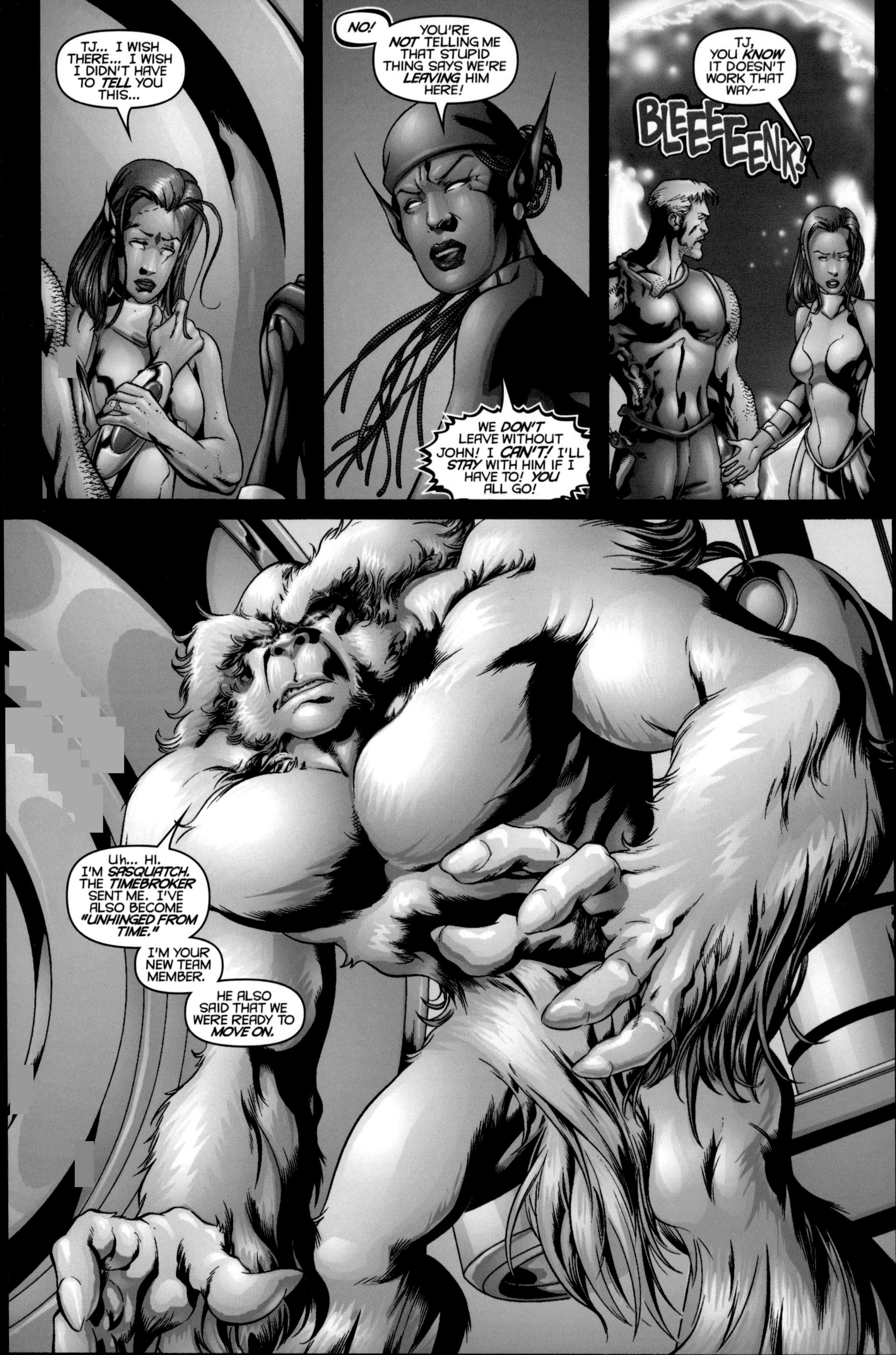

TJ... I WISH THERE... I WISH I DIDN'T HAVE TO TELL YOU THIS...
NO!
YOU'RE NOT TELLING ME THAT STUPID THING SAYS WE'RE LEAVING HIM HERE!
WE DON'T LEAVE WITHOUT JOHN! I CAN'T! I'LL STAY WITH HIM IF I HAVE TO! YOU ALL GO!
TJ, YOU KNOW IT DOESN'T WORK THAT WAY--
BLEEEEENK!
Uh... HI. I'M SASQUATCH. THE TIMEBROKER SENT ME. I'VE ALSO BECOME "UNHINGED FROM TIME."
I'M YOUR NEW TEAM MEMBER.
HE ALSO SAID THAT WE WERE READY TO MOVE ON.

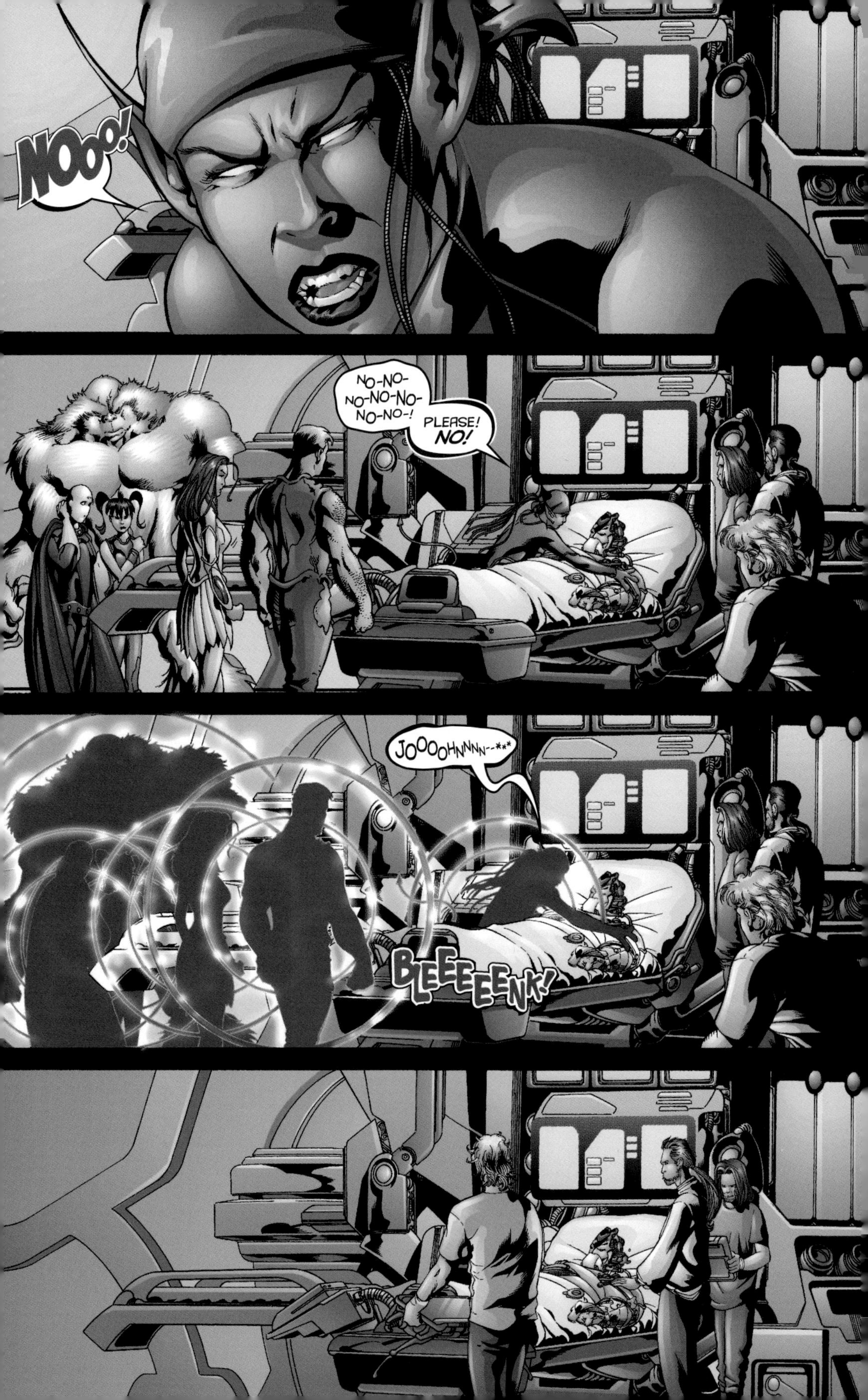
NOOO!
NO-NO-NO-NO-NO-NO-NO-!
PLEASE! NO!
JOOOOHNNNN--***
BLEEEEENK!

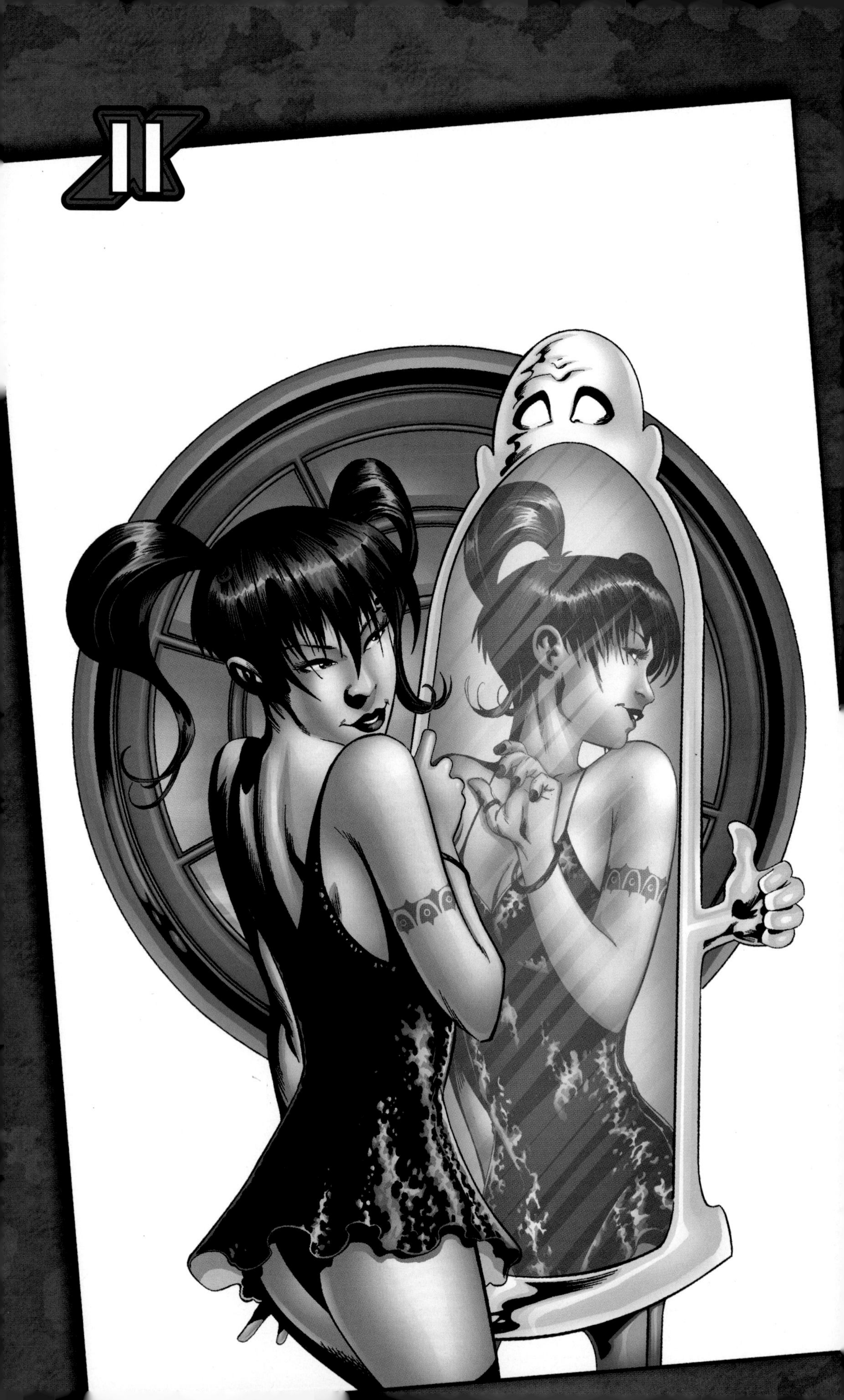

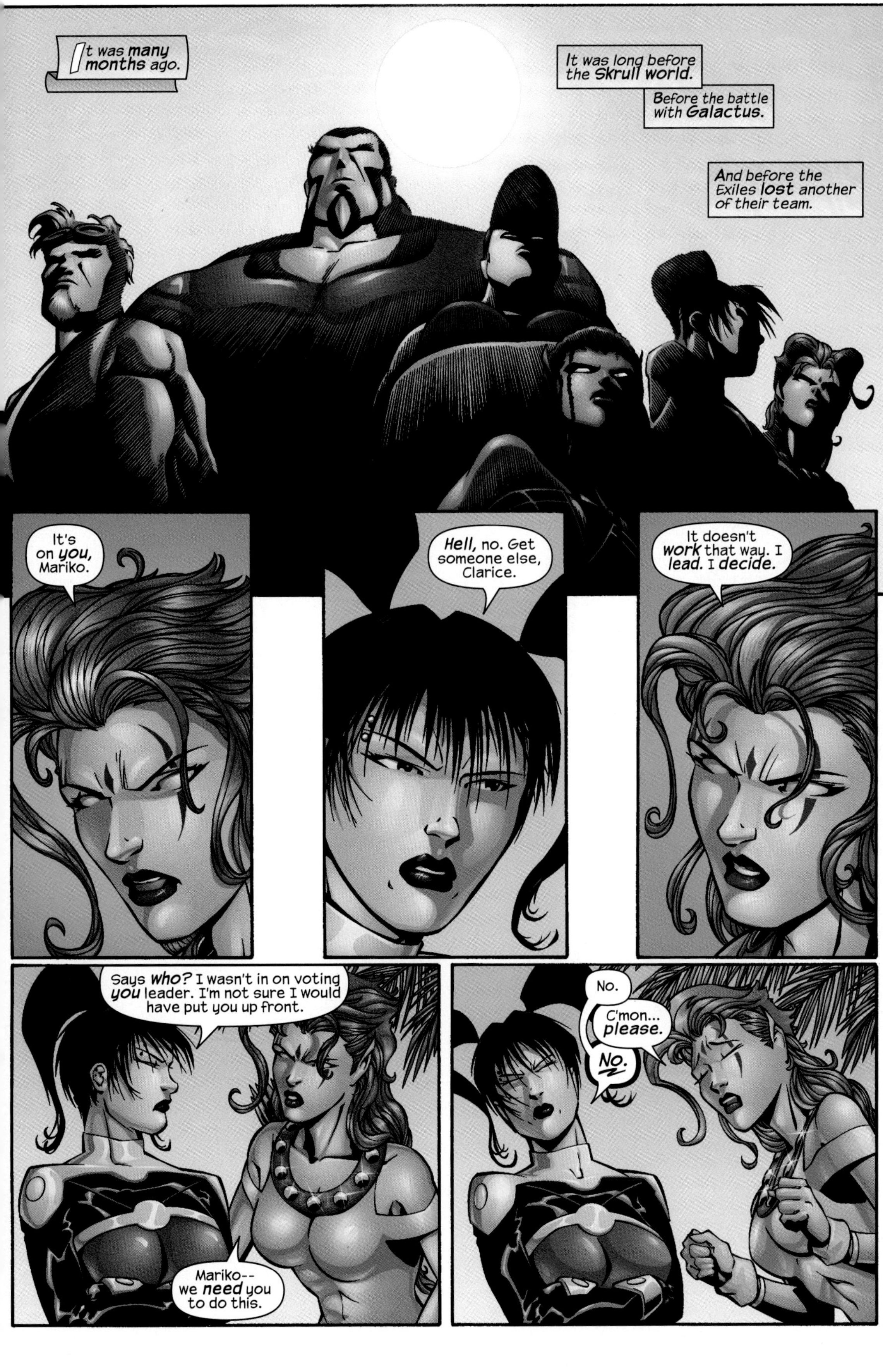
It was many months ago.
It was long before the Skrull world.
Before the battle with Galactus.
And before the Exiles lost another of their team.
It's on you, Mariko.
Hell, no. Get someone else, Clarice.
It doesn't work that way. I lead. I decide.
Says who? I wasn't in on voting you leader. I'm not sure I would have put you up front.
Mariko-- we need you to do this.
No.
C'mon... please.
No.

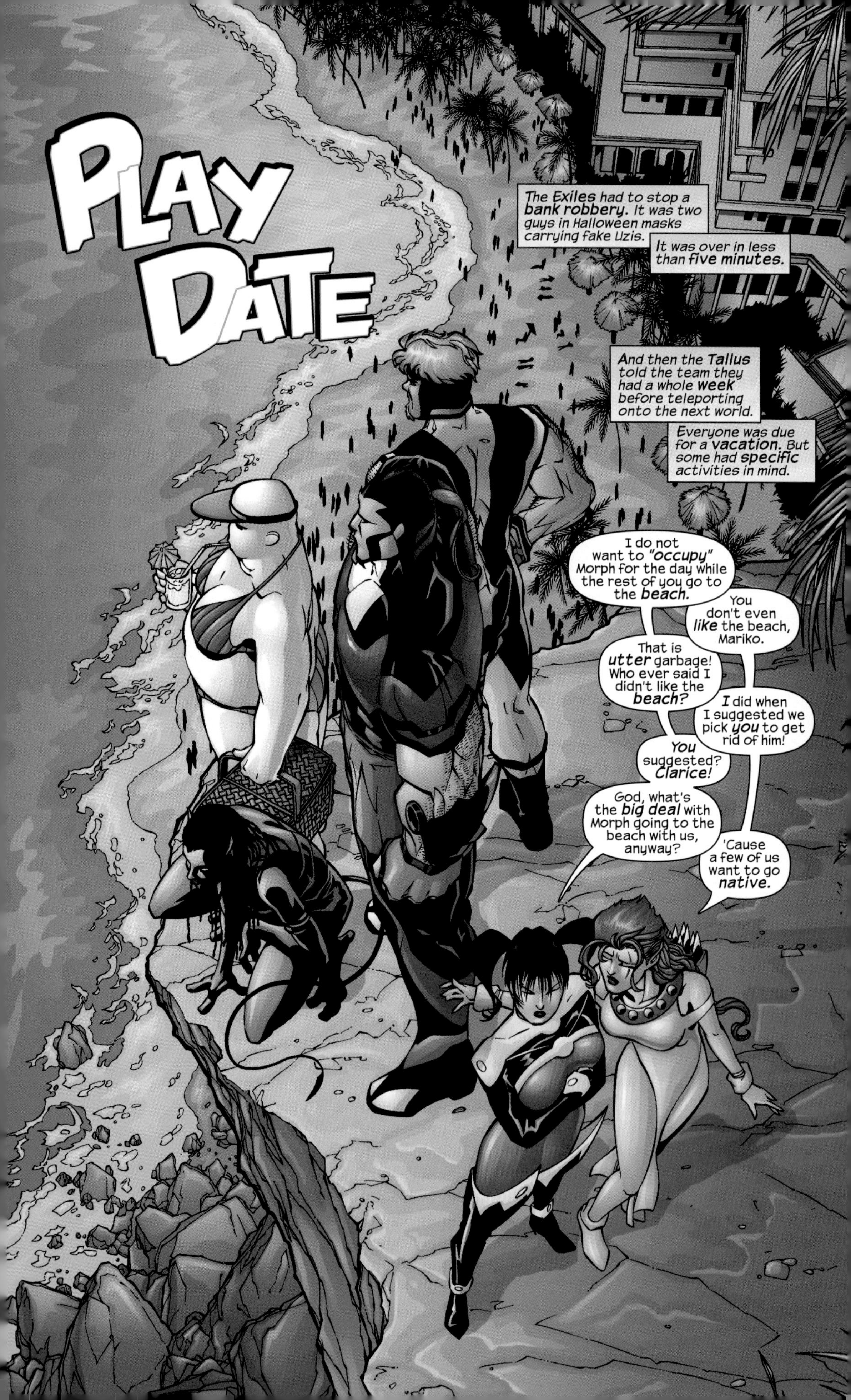
PLAY DATE
The Exiles had to stop a bank robbery. It was two guys in Halloween masks carrying fake Uzis.
It was over in less than five minutes.
And then the Tallus told the team they had a whole week before teleporting onto the next world.
Everyone was due for a vacation. But some had specific activities in mind.
I do not want to "occupy" Morph for the day while the rest of you go to the beach.
You don't even like the beach, Mariko.
That is utter garbage! Who ever said I didn't like the beach?
I did when I suggested we pick you to get rid of him!
You suggested? Clarice!
God, what's the big deal with Morph going to the beach with us, anyway?
'Cause a few of us want to go native.

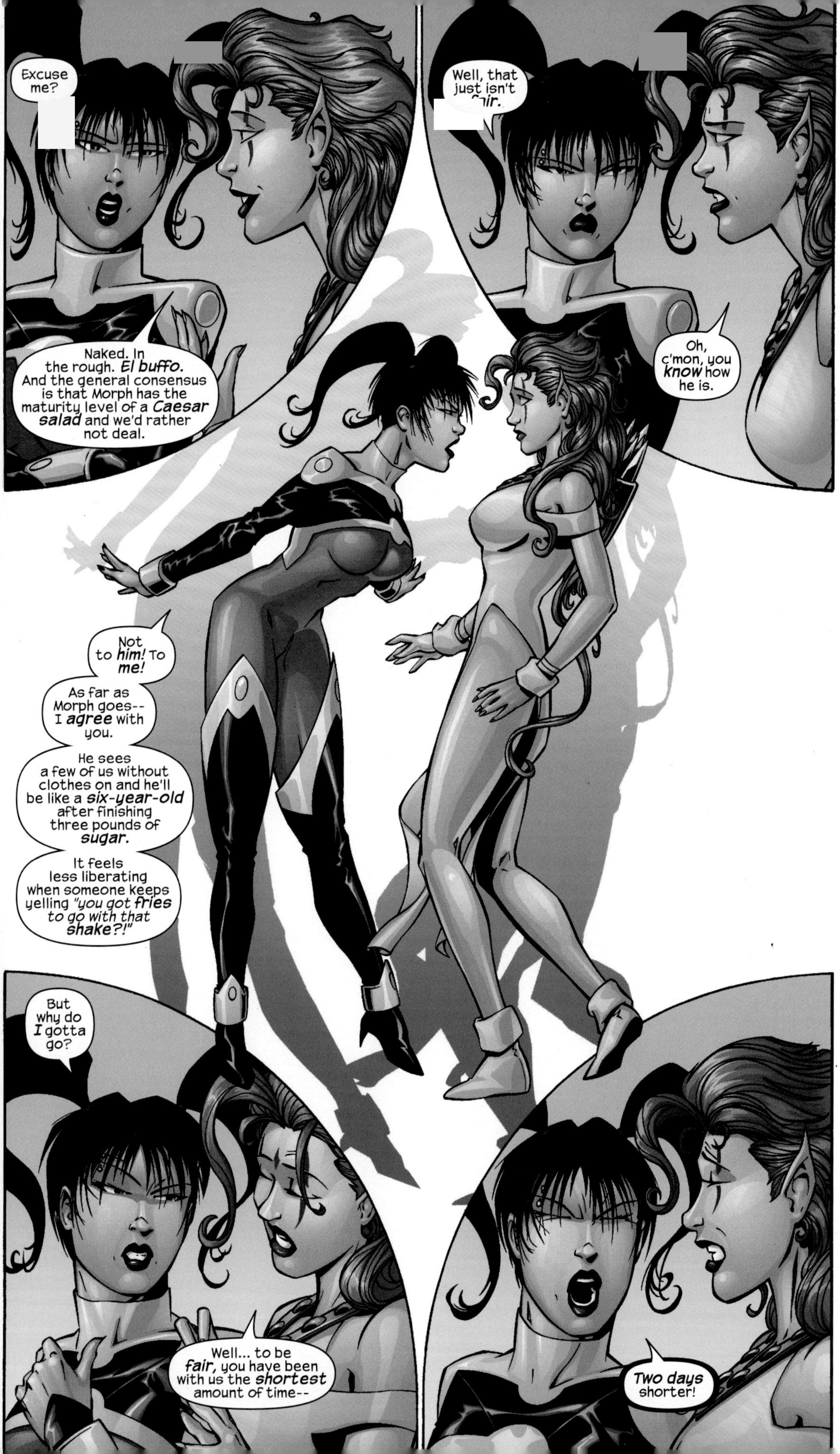

Excuse me?
Naked. In the rough. *El buffo.* And the general consensus is that Morph has the maturity level of a *Caesar salad* and we'd rather not deal.
Well, that just isn't fair.
Oh, c'mon, you ***know*** how he is.
Not to *him!* To *me!*
As far as Morph goes-- I ***agree*** with you.
He sees a few of us without clothes on and he'll be like a ***six-year-old*** after finishing three pounds of ***sugar.***
It feels less liberating when someone keeps yelling *"you got **fries** to go with that **shake**?!"*
But why do *I* gotta go?
Well... to be *fair,* you have been with us the ***shortest*** amount of time--
Two days shorter!

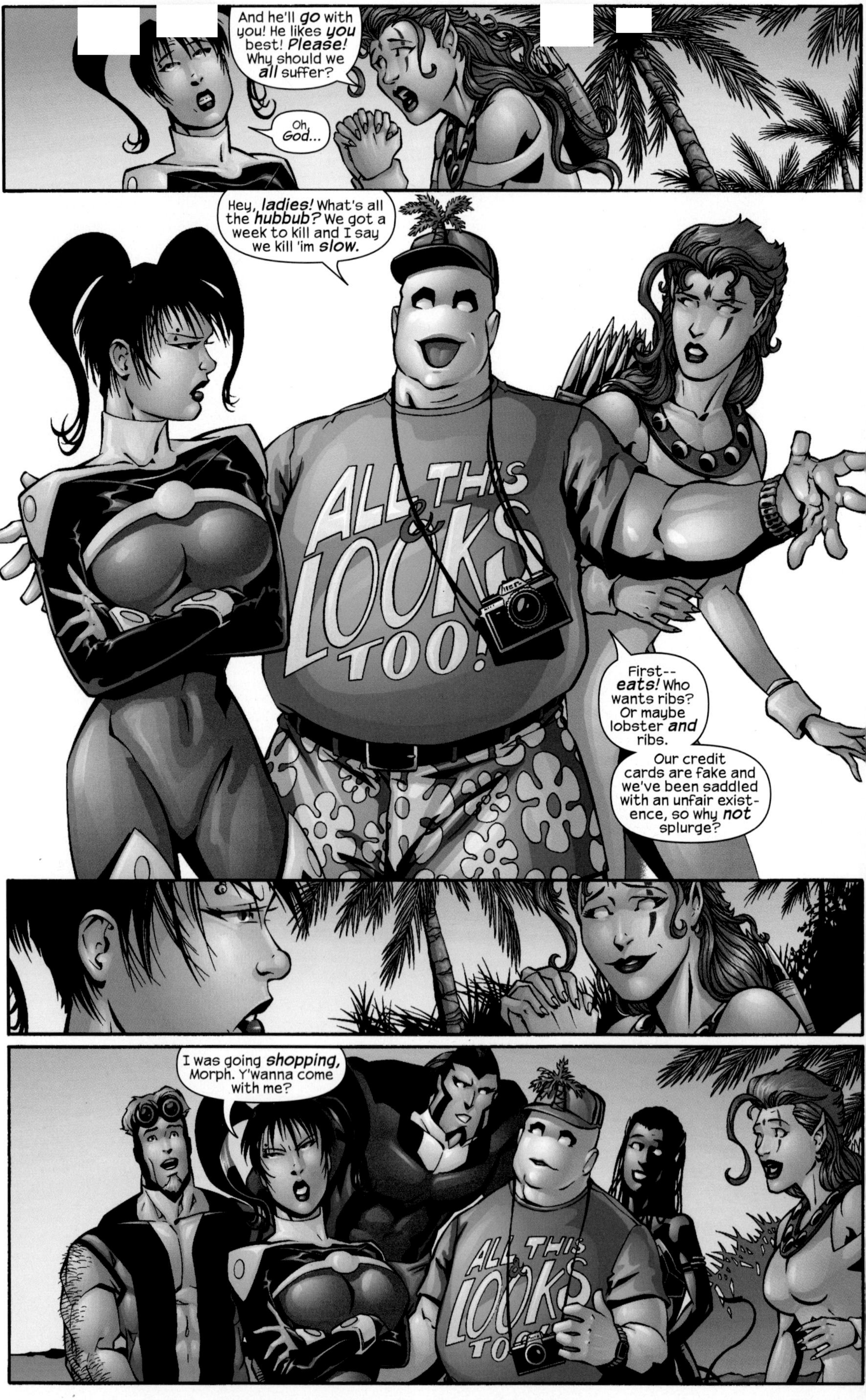
And he'll go with you! He likes you best! Please! Why should we all suffer?
Oh, God...
Hey, ladies! What's all the hubbub? We got a week to kill and I say we kill 'im slow.
First-- eats! Who wants ribs? Or maybe lobster and ribs.
Our credit cards are fake and we've been saddled with an unfair existence, so why not splurge?
ALL THIS & LOOKS TOO!
I was going shopping, Morph. Y'wanna come with me?
ALL THIS & LOOKS

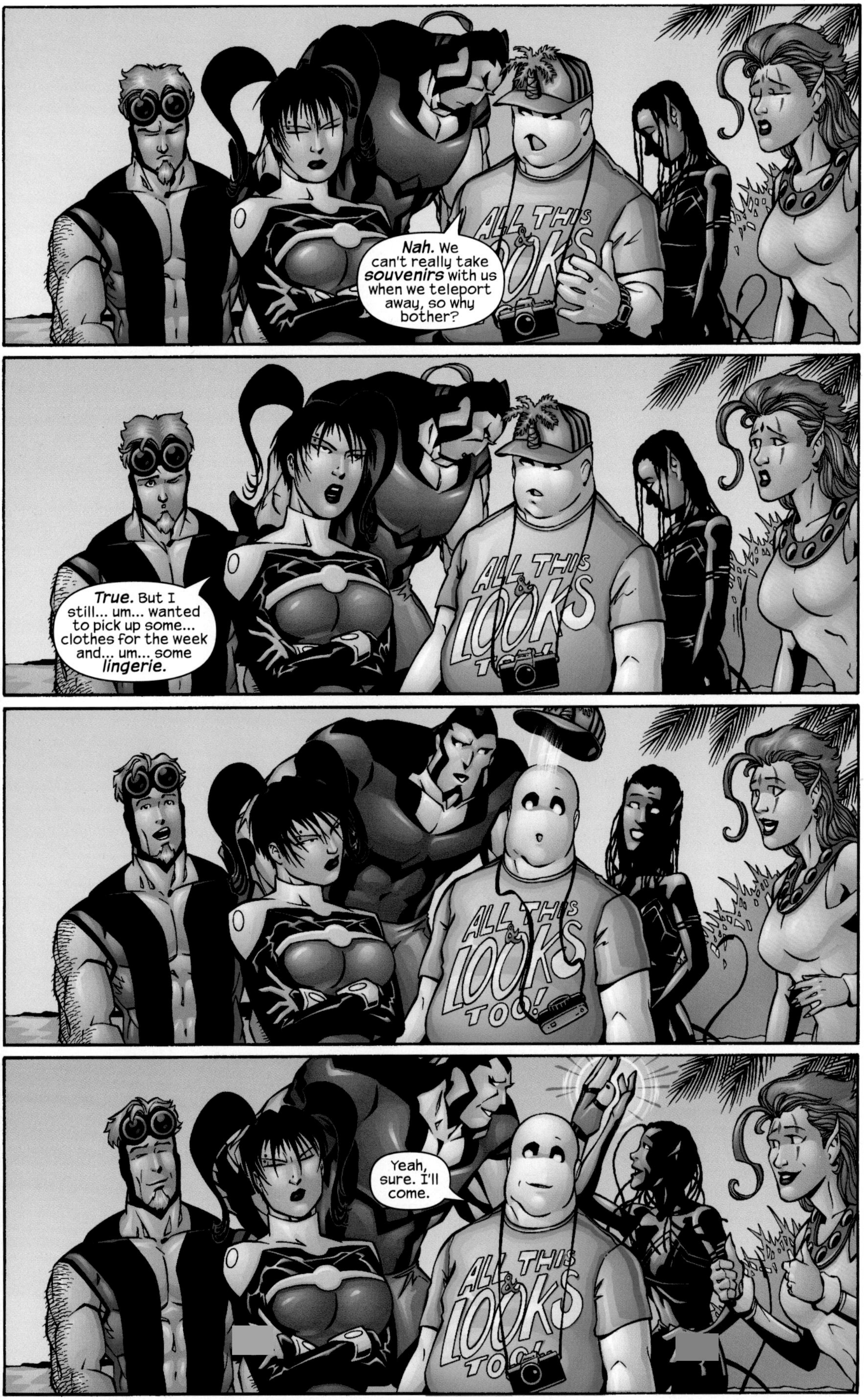
Nah. We can't really take souvenirs with us when we teleport away, so why bother?
True. But I still... um... wanted to pick up some... clothes for the week and... um... some lingerie.
Yeah, sure. I'll come.

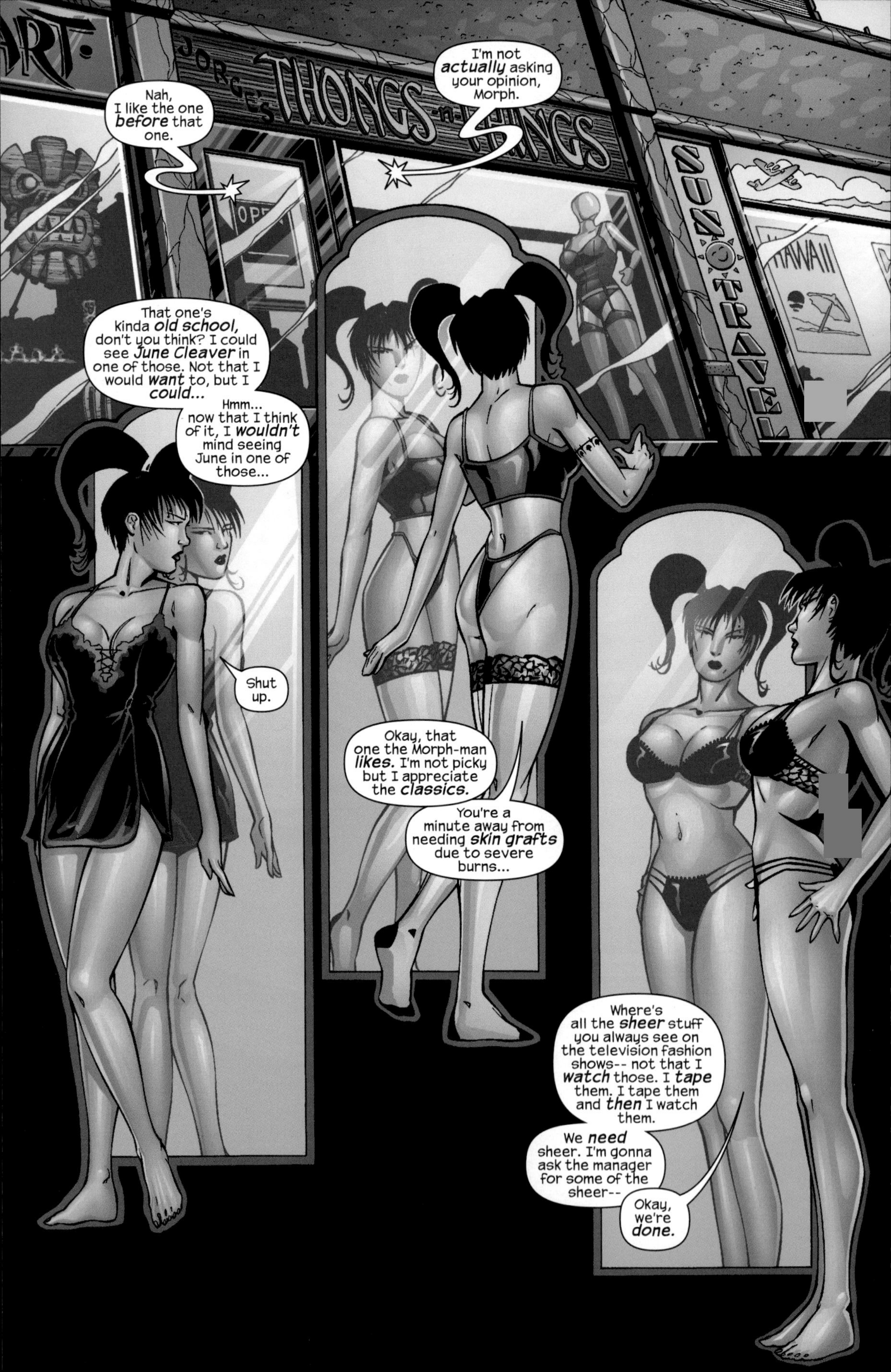

ART
JORGE'S THONGS-n-THINGS
OPEN
SUN TRAVEL
HAWAII
Nah, I like the one before that one.
I'm not actually asking your opinion, Morph.
That one's kinda old school, don't you think? I could see June Cleaver in one of those. Not that I would want to, but I could...
Hmm... now that I think of it, I wouldn't mind seeing June in one of those...
Shut up.
Okay, that one the Morph-man likes. I'm not picky but I appreciate the classics.
You're a minute away from needing skin grafts due to severe burns...
Where's all the sheer stuff you always see on the television fashion shows-- not that I watch those. I tape them. I tape them and then I watch them.
We need sheer. I'm gonna ask the manager for some of the sheer--
Okay, we're done.

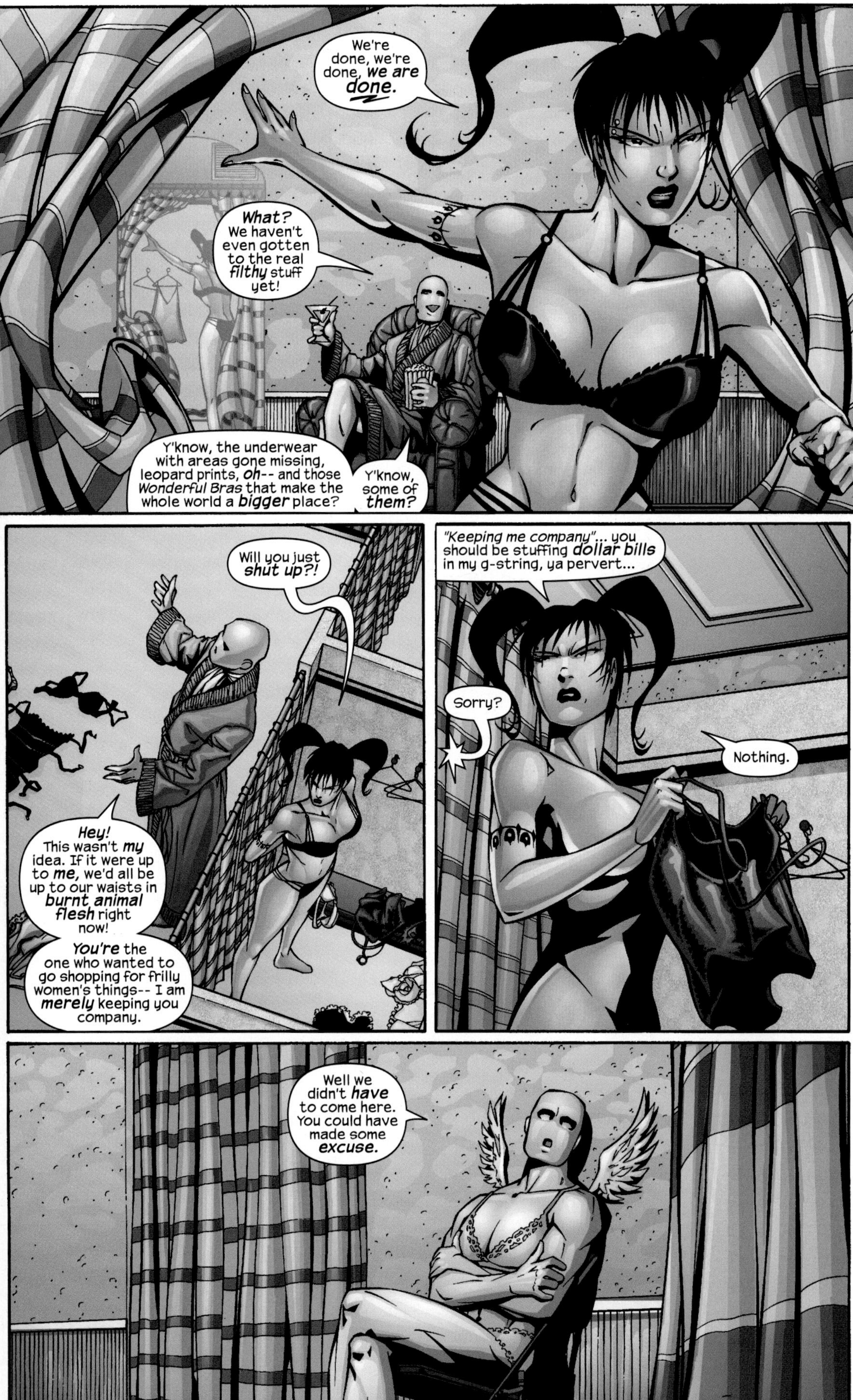
We're done, we're done, we are done.
What? We haven't even gotten to the real filthy stuff yet!
Y'know, the underwear with areas gone missing, leopard prints, oh-- and those Wonderful Bras that make the whole world a bigger place?
Y'know, some of them?
Will you just shut up?!
Hey! This wasn't my idea. If it were up to me, we'd all be up to our waists in burnt animal flesh right now!
You're the one who wanted to go shopping for frilly women's things-- I am merely keeping you company.
"Keeping me company"... you should be stuffing dollar bills in my g-string, ya pervert...
Sorry?
Nothing.
Well we didn't have to come here. You could have made some excuse.

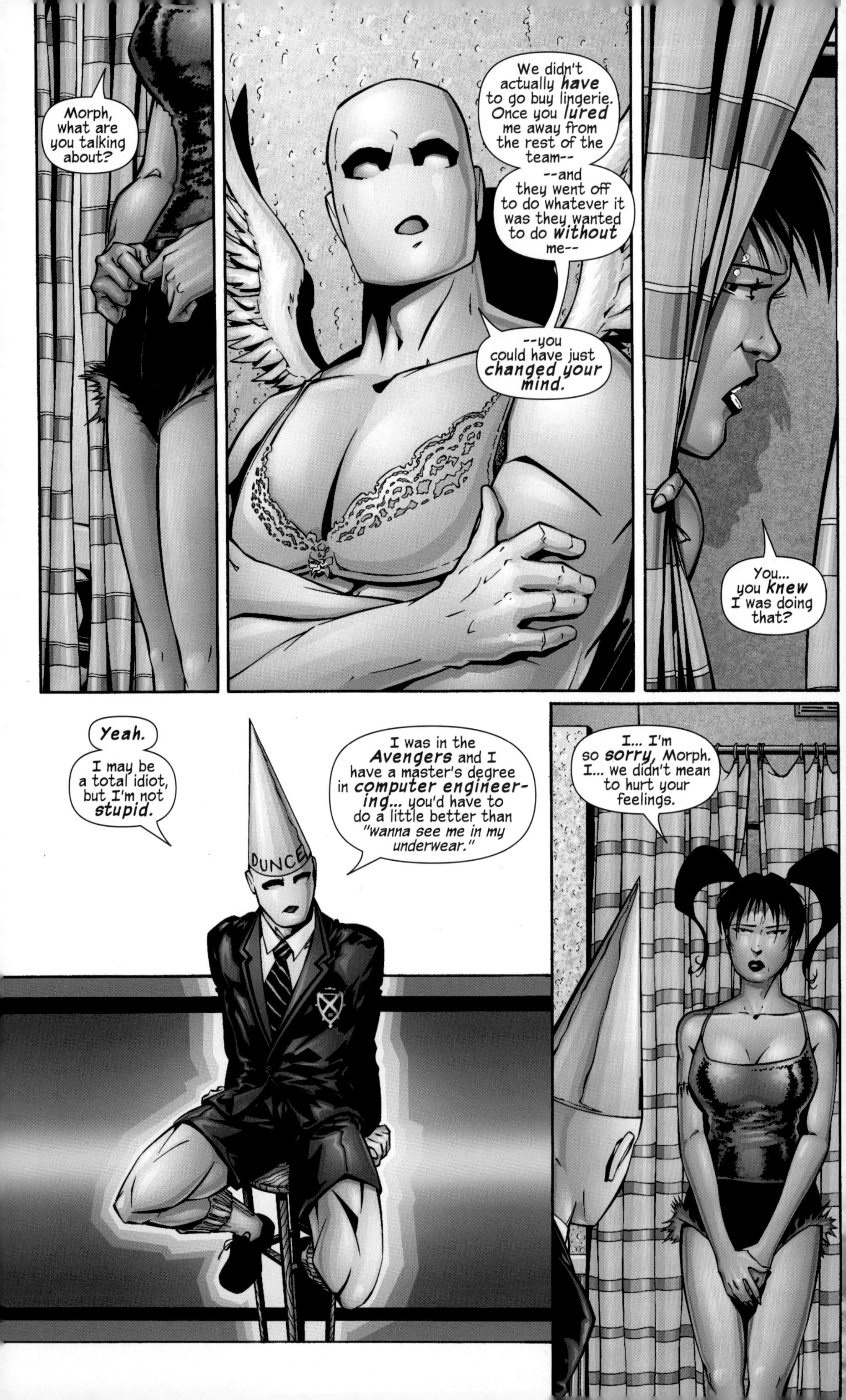
Morph, what are you talking about?
We didn't actually have to go buy lingerie. Once you lured me away from the rest of the team--
--and they went off to do whatever it was they wanted to do without me--
--you could have just changed your mind.
You... you knew I was doing that?
Yeah.
I may be a total idiot, but I'm not stupid.
DUNCE
I was in the Avengers and I have a master's degree in computer engineering... you'd have to do a little better than "wanna see me in my underwear."
I... I'm so sorry, Morph. I... we didn't mean to hurt your feelings.

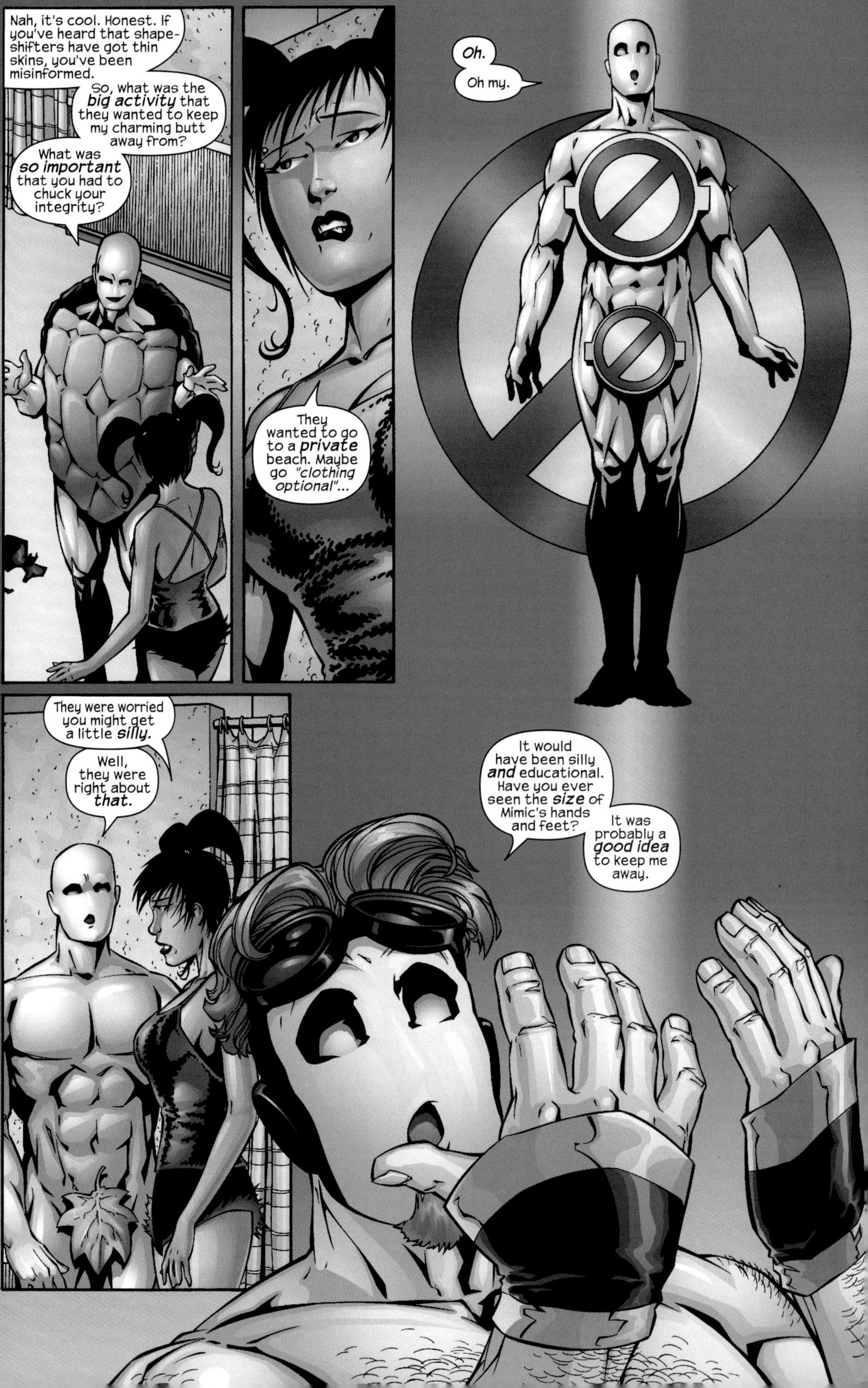
Nah, it's cool. Honest. If you've heard that shape-shifters have got thin skins, you've been misinformed.
So, what was the big activity that they wanted to keep my charming butt away from?
What was so important that you had to chuck your integrity?
They wanted to go to a private beach. Maybe go "clothing optional"...
Oh.
Oh my.
They were worried you might get a little silly.
Well, they were right about that.
It would have been silly and educational. Have you ever seen the size of Mimic's hands and feet?
It was probably a good idea to keep me away.

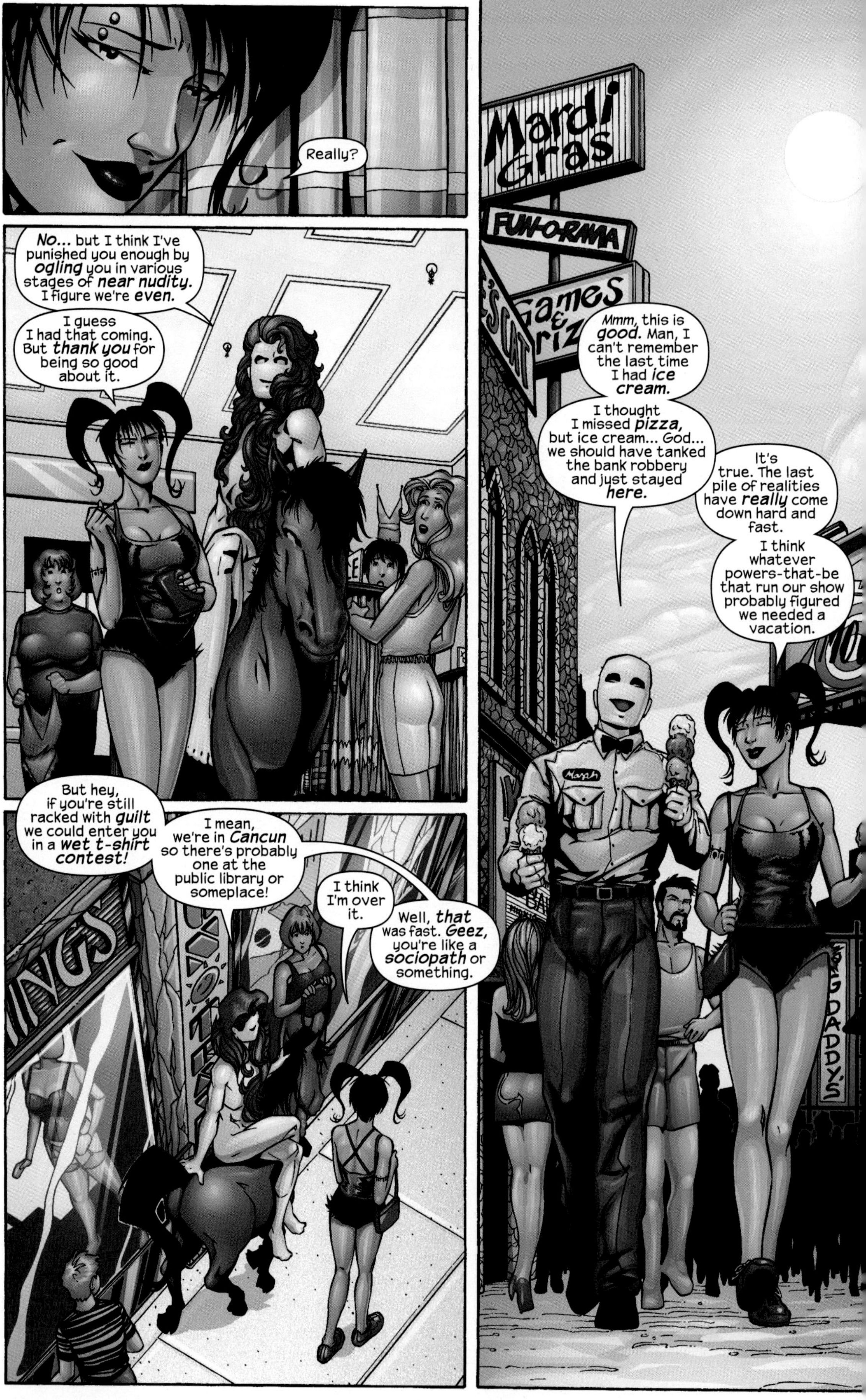
Really?
No... but I think I've punished you enough by ogling you in various stages of near nudity. I figure we're even.
I guess I had that coming. But thank you for being so good about it.
But hey, if you're still racked with guilt we could enter you in a wet t-shirt contest!
I mean, we're in Cancun so there's probably one at the public library or someplace!
I think I'm over it.
Well, that was fast. Geez, you're like a sociopath or something.
Mardi Gras
FUN-O-RAMA
Games
Mmm, this is good. Man, I can't remember the last time I had ice cream.
I thought I missed pizza, but ice cream... God... we should have tanked the bank robbery and just stayed here.
It's true. The last pile of realities have really come down hard and fast.
I think whatever powers-that-be that run our show probably figured we needed a vacation.

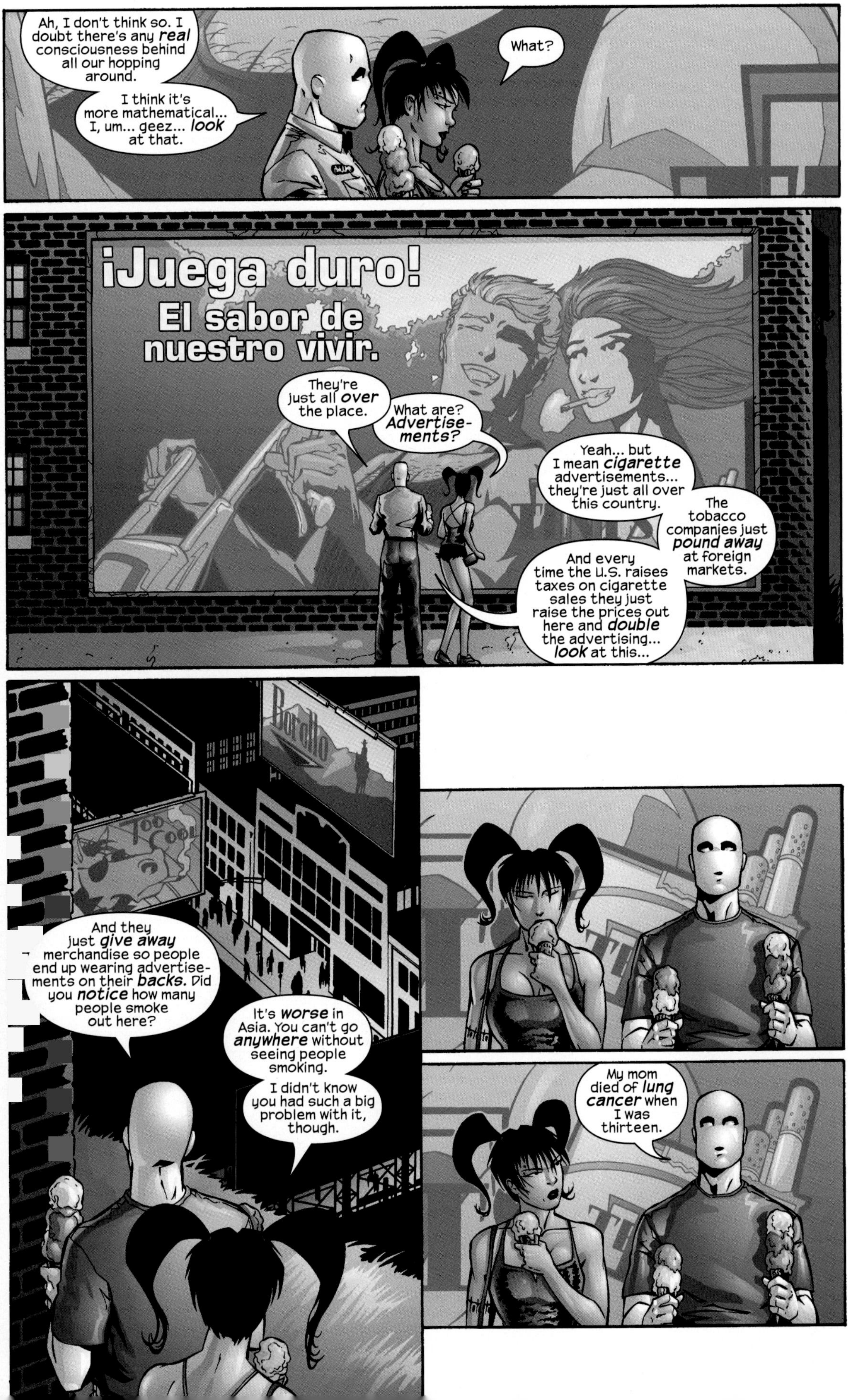

Ah, I don't think so. I doubt there's any real consciousness behind all our hopping around.
I think it's more mathematical... I, um... geez... look at that.
What?
¡Juega duro!
El sabor de nuestro vivir.
They're just all over the place.
What are? Advertise-ments?
Yeah... but I mean cigarette advertisements... they're just all over this country.
The tobacco companies just pound away at foreign markets.
And every time the U.S. raises taxes on cigarette sales they just raise the prices out here and double the advertising... look at this...
Borello
Too Cool
And they just give away merchandise so people end up wearing advertise-ments on their backs. Did you notice how many people smoke out here?
It's worse in Asia. You can't go anywhere without seeing people smoking.
I didn't know you had such a big problem with it, though.
My mom died of lung cancer when I was thirteen.

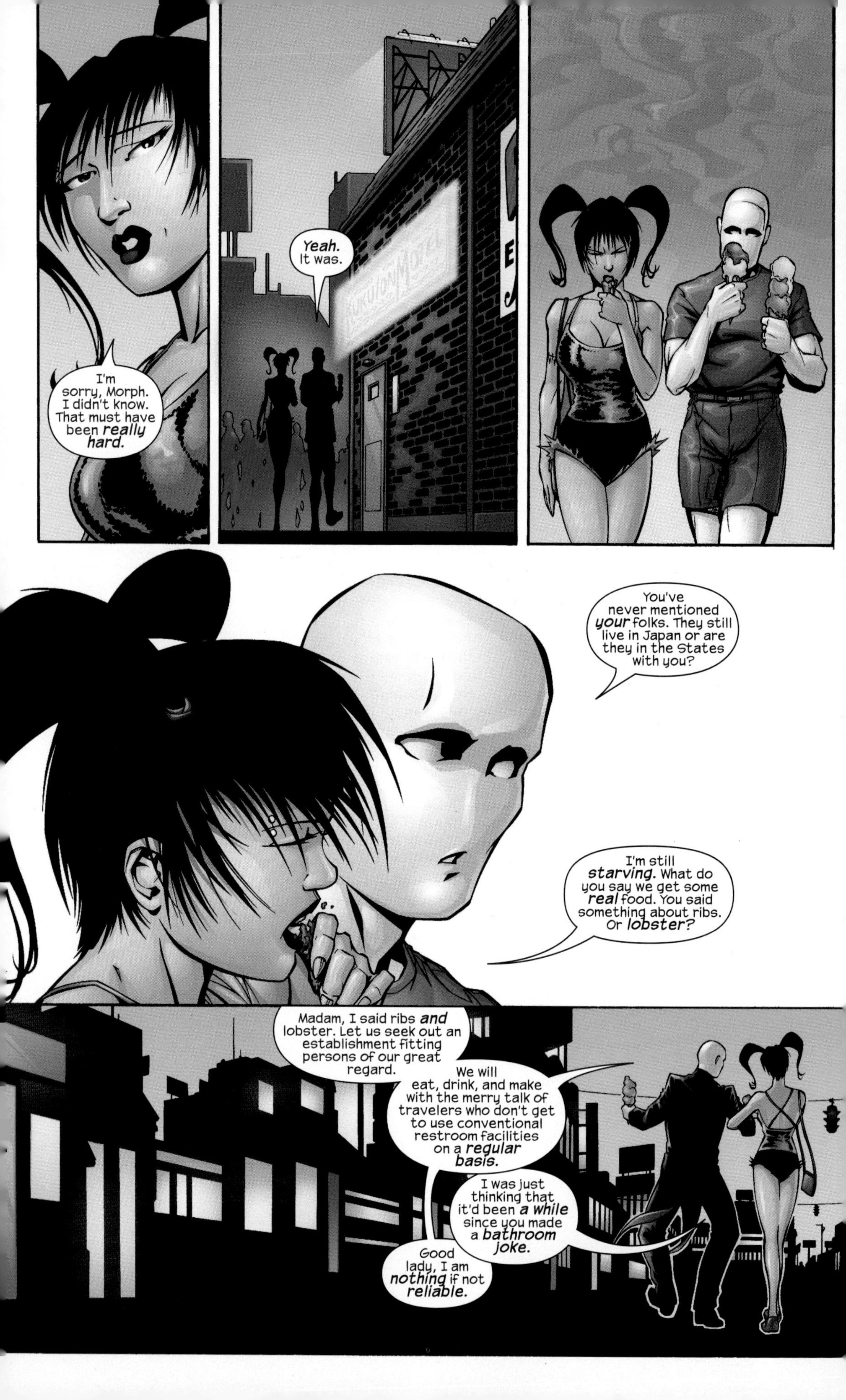
I'm sorry, Morph. I didn't know. That must have been really hard.
Yeah. It was.
KUKULON MOTEL
You've never mentioned your folks. They still live in Japan or are they in the States with you?
I'm still starving. What do you say we get some real food. You said something about ribs. Or lobster?
Madam, I said ribs and lobster. Let us seek out an establishment fitting persons of our great regard.
We will eat, drink, and make with the merry talk of travelers who don't get to use conventional restroom facilities on a regular basis.
I was just thinking that it'd been a while since you made a bathroom joke.
Good lady, I am nothing if not reliable.

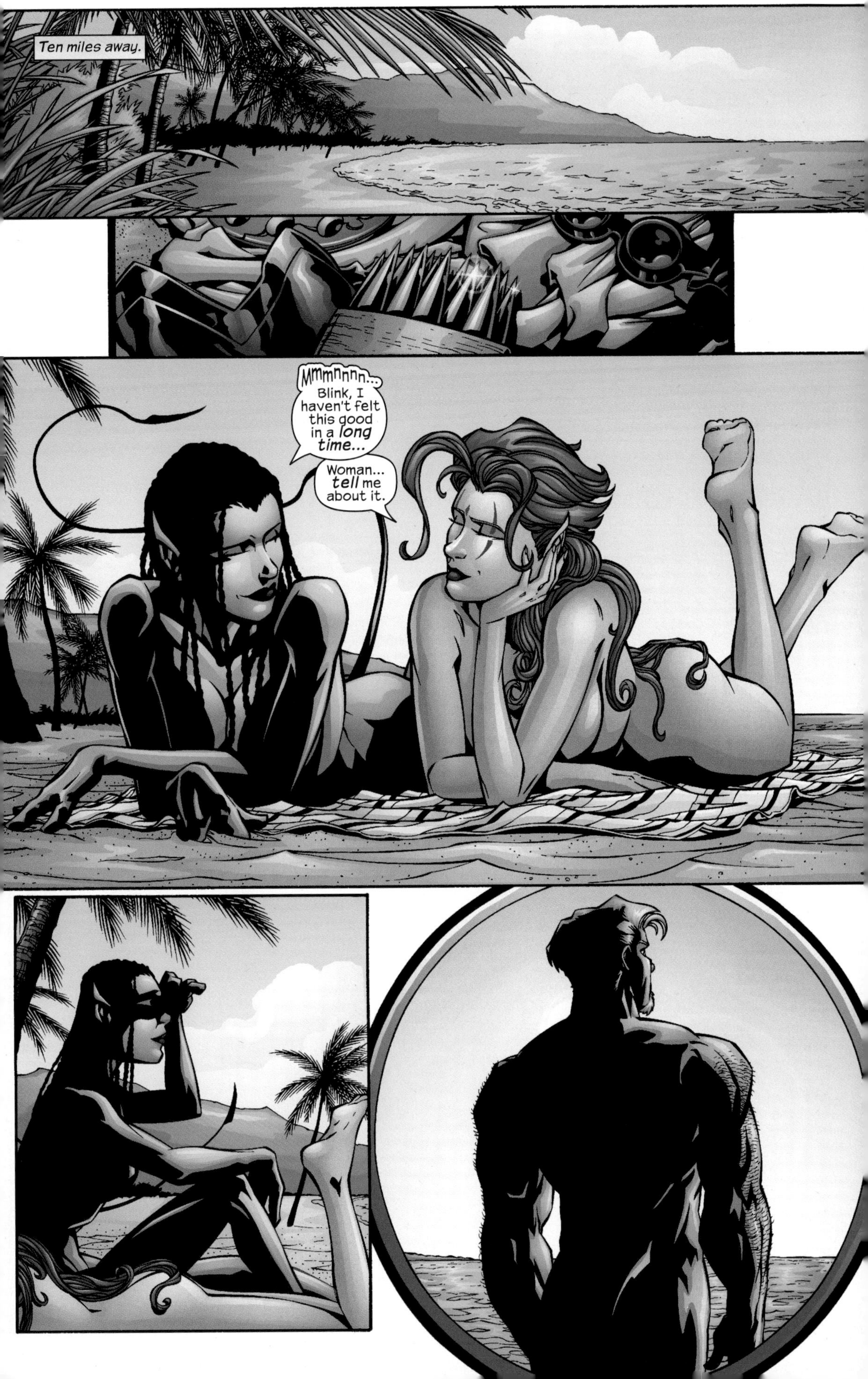
Ten miles away.
Mmmnnnn... Blink, I haven't felt this good in a long time...
Woman... tell me about it.

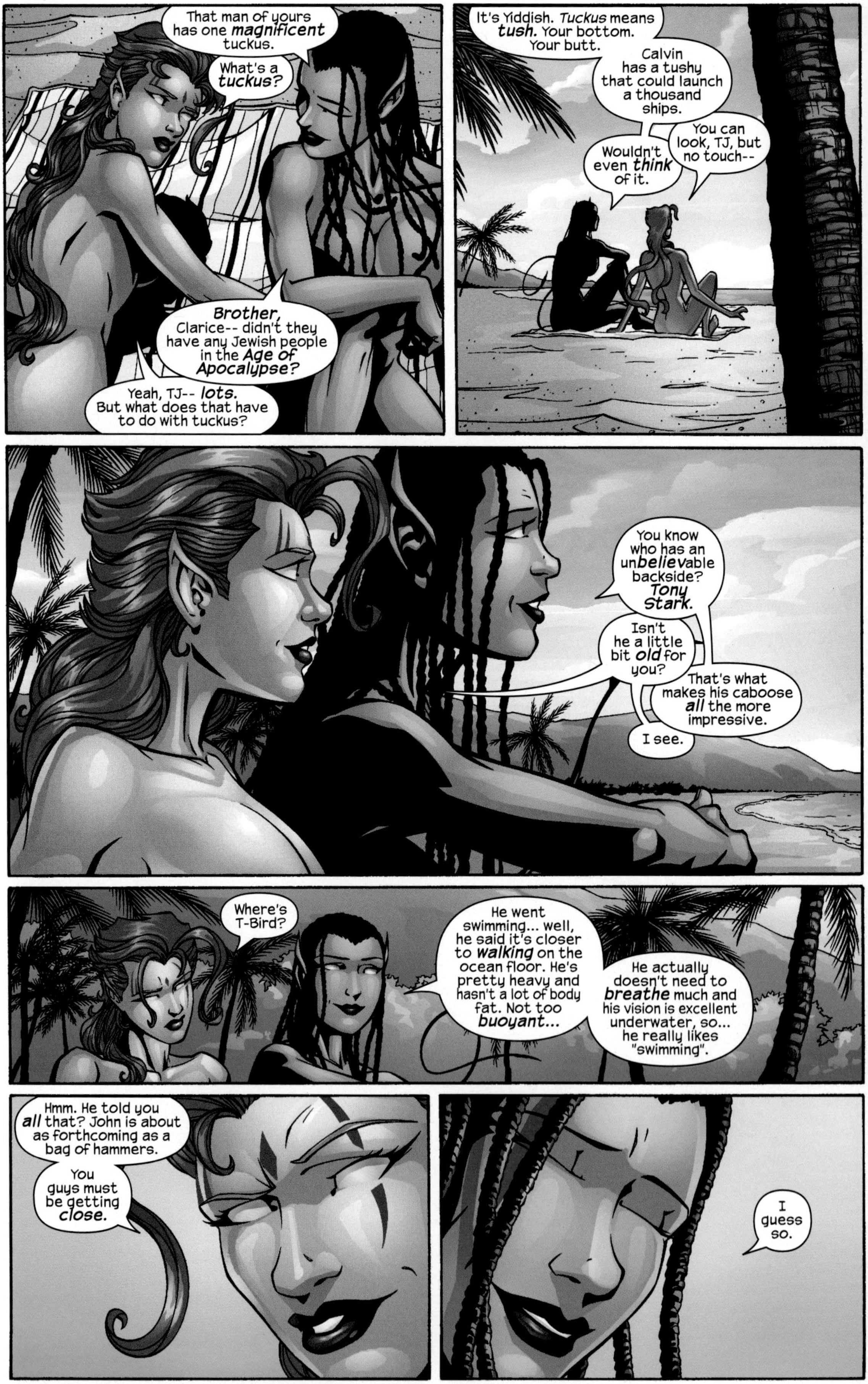
That man of yours has one magnificent tuckus.
What's a tuckus?
Brother, Clarice-- didn't they have any Jewish people in the Age of Apocalypse?
Yeah, TJ-- lots. But what does that have to do with tuckus?
It's Yiddish. Tuckus means tush. Your bottom. Your butt.
Calvin has a tushy that could launch a thousand ships.
Wouldn't even think of it.
You can look, TJ, but no touch--
You know who has an unbelievable backside? Tony Stark.
Isn't he a little bit old for you?
That's what makes his caboose all the more impressive.
I see.
Where's T-Bird?
He went swimming... well, he said it's closer to walking on the ocean floor. He's pretty heavy and hasn't a lot of body fat. Not too buoyant...
He actually doesn't need to breathe much and his vision is excellent underwater, so... he really likes "swimming".
Hmm. He told you all that? John is about as forthcoming as a bag of hammers.
You guys must be getting close.
I guess so.

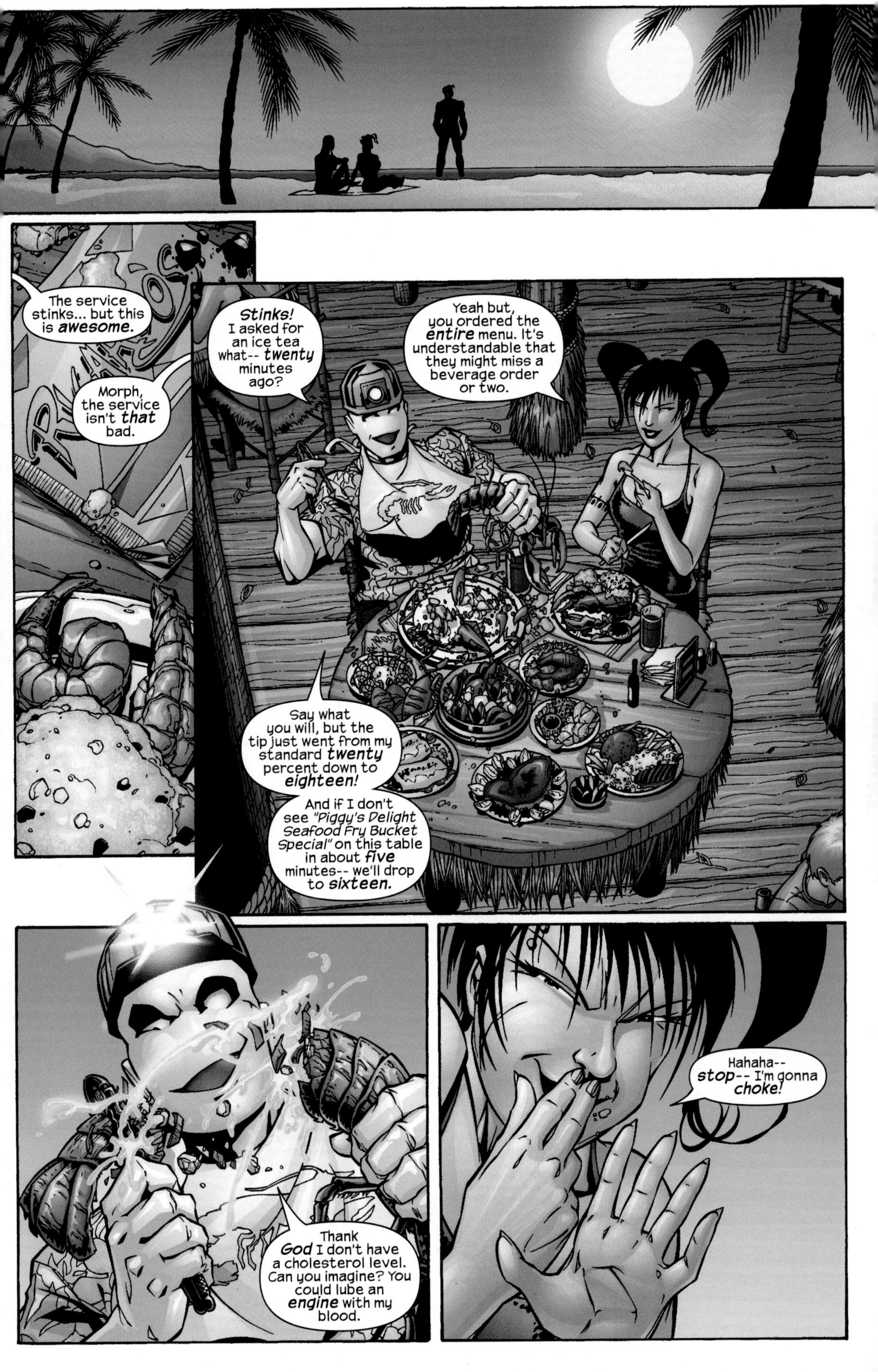
The service stinks... but this is awesome.
Morph, the service isn't that bad.
Stinks! I asked for an ice tea what-- twenty minutes ago?
Yeah but, you ordered the entire menu. It's understandable that they might miss a beverage order or two.
Say what you will, but the tip just went from my standard twenty percent down to eighteen!
And if I don't see "Piggy's Delight Seafood Fry Bucket Special" on this table in about five minutes-- we'll drop to sixteen.
Thank God I don't have a cholesterol level. Can you imagine? You could lube an engine with my blood.
Hahaha-- stop-- I'm gonna choke!

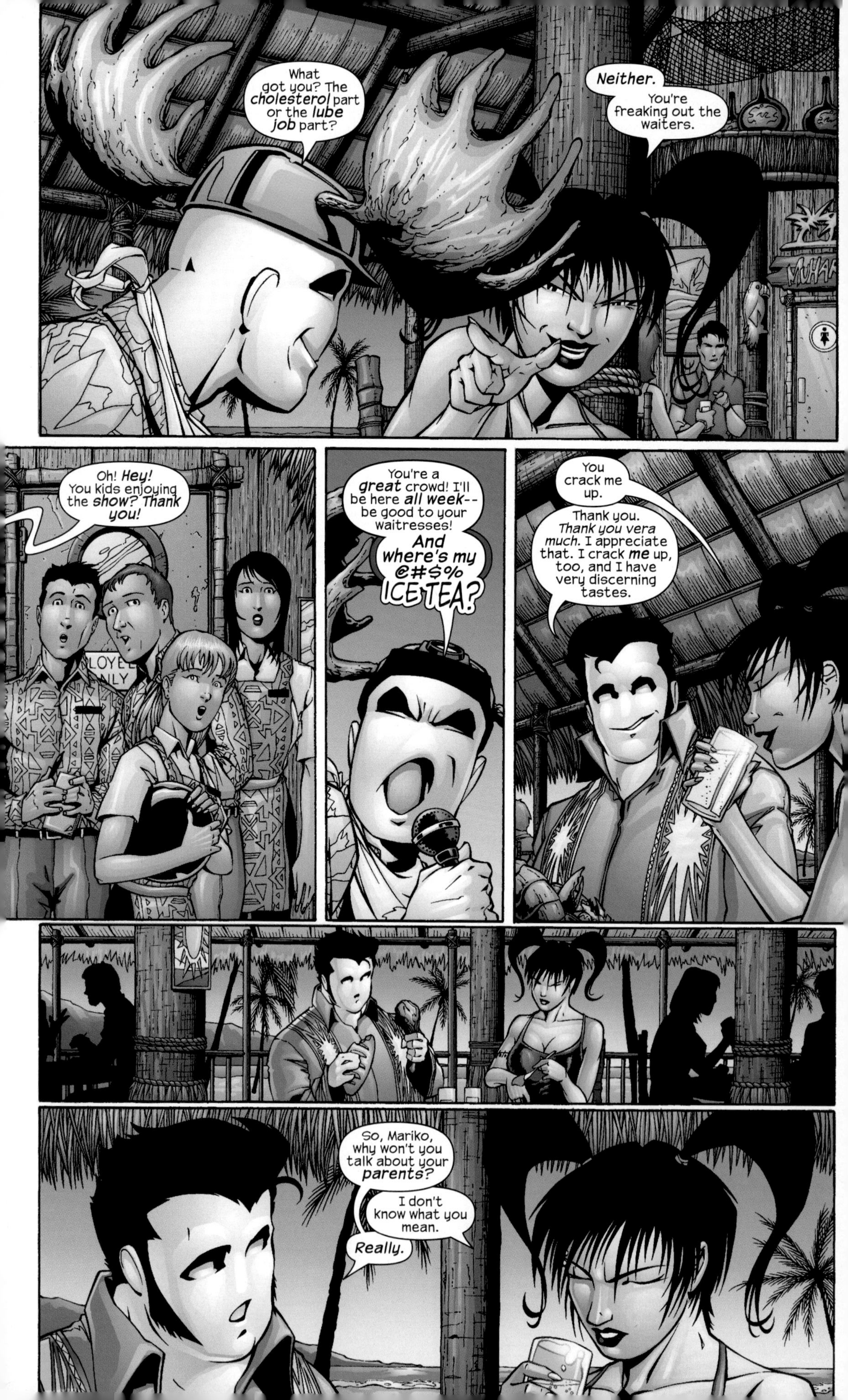
What got you? The cholesterol part or the lube job part?
Neither.
You're freaking out the waiters.
Oh! Hey! You kids enjoying the show? Thank you!
You're a great crowd! I'll be here all week-- be good to your waitresses!
And where's my @#$% ICE TEA?
You crack me up.
Thank you. Thank you vera much. I appreciate that. I crack me up, too, and I have very discerning tastes.
So, Mariko, why won't you talk about your parents?
I don't know what you mean.
Really.

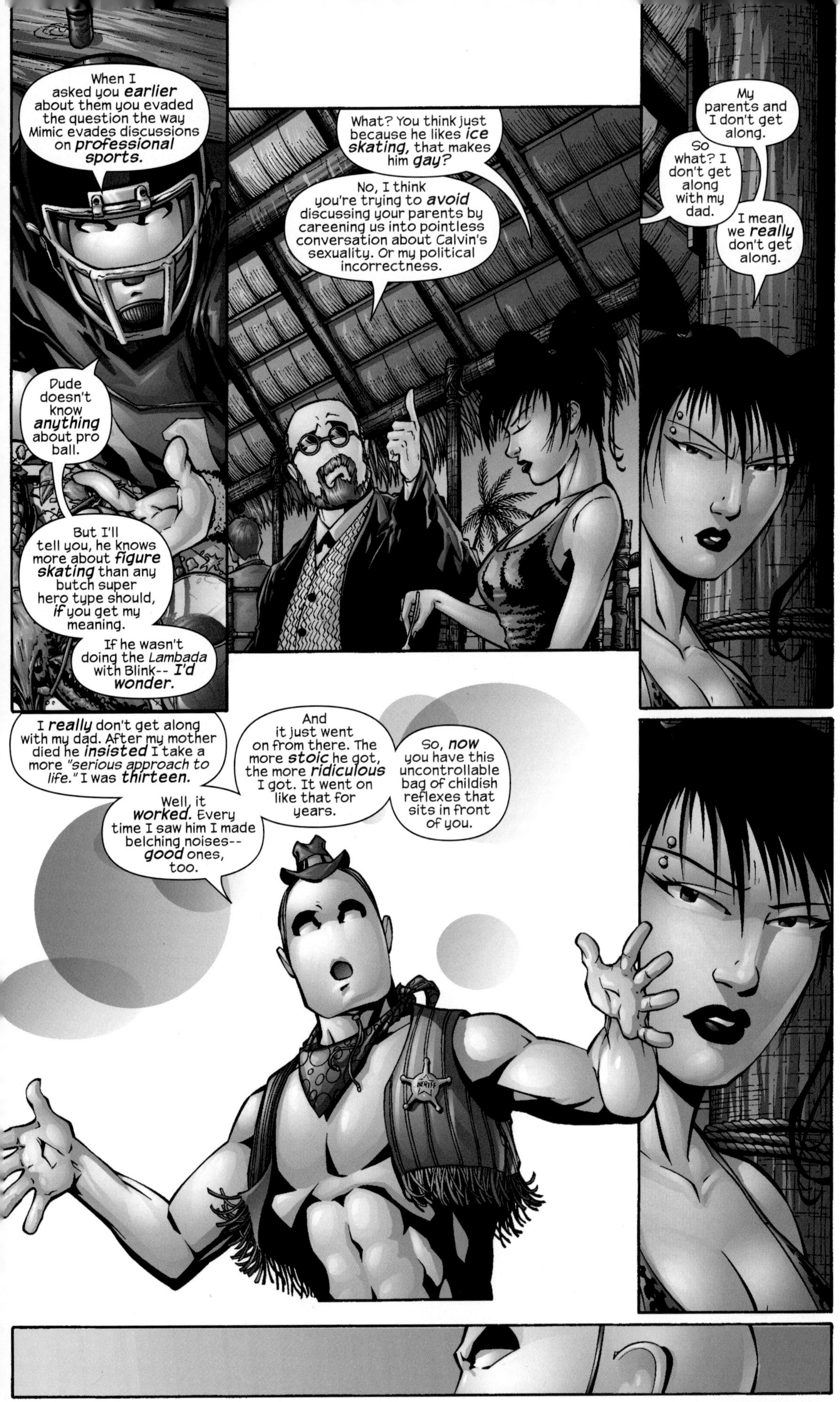

When I asked you earlier about them you evaded the question the way Mimic evades discussions on professional sports.
Dude doesn't know anything about pro ball.
But I'll tell you, he knows more about figure skating than any butch super hero type should, if you get my meaning.
If he wasn't doing the Lambada with Blink-- I'd wonder.
What? You think just because he likes ice skating, that makes him gay?
No, I think you're trying to avoid discussing your parents by careening us into pointless conversation about Calvin's sexuality. Or my political incorrectness.
My parents and I don't get along.
So what? I don't get along with my dad.
I mean we really don't get along.
I really don't get along with my dad. After my mother died he insisted I take a more "serious approach to life." I was thirteen.
Well, it worked. Every time I saw him I made belching noises-- good ones, too.
And it just went on from there. The more stoic he got, the more ridiculous I got. It went on like that for years.
So, now you have this uncontrollable bag of childish reflexes that sits in front of you.

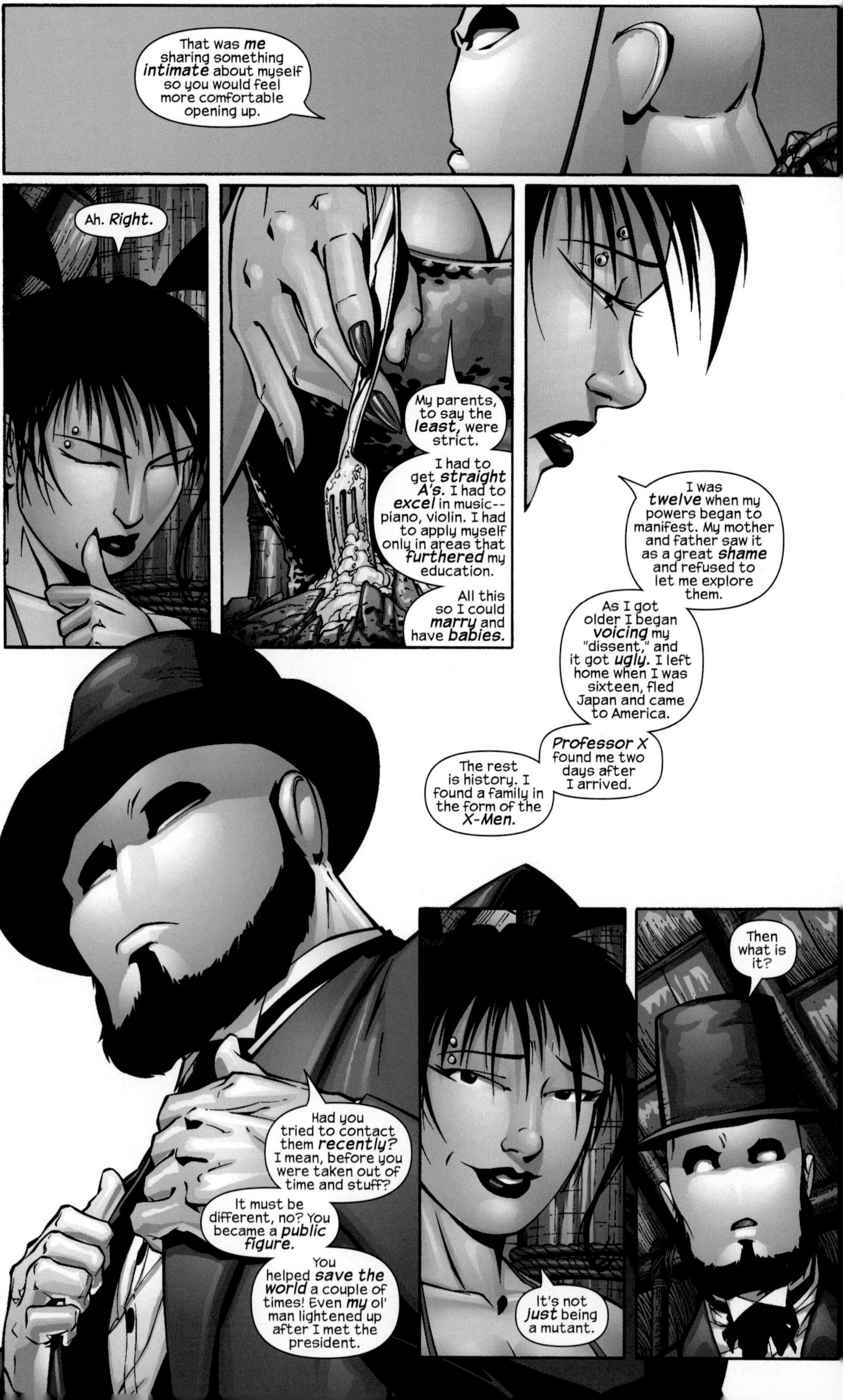
That was me sharing something intimate about myself so you would feel more comfortable opening up.
Ah. Right.
My parents, to say the least, were strict.
I had to get straight A's. I had to excel in music--piano, violin. I had to apply myself only in areas that furthered my education.
All this so I could marry and have babies.
I was twelve when my powers began to manifest. My mother and father saw it as a great shame and refused to let me explore them.
As I got older I began voicing my "dissent," and it got ugly. I left home when I was sixteen, fled Japan and came to America.
Professor X found me two days after I arrived.
The rest is history. I found a family in the form of the X-Men.
Had you tried to contact them recently? I mean, before you were taken out of time and stuff?
It must be different, no? You became a public figure.
You helped save the world a couple of times! Even my ol' man lightened up after I met the president.
It's not just being a mutant.
Then what is it?

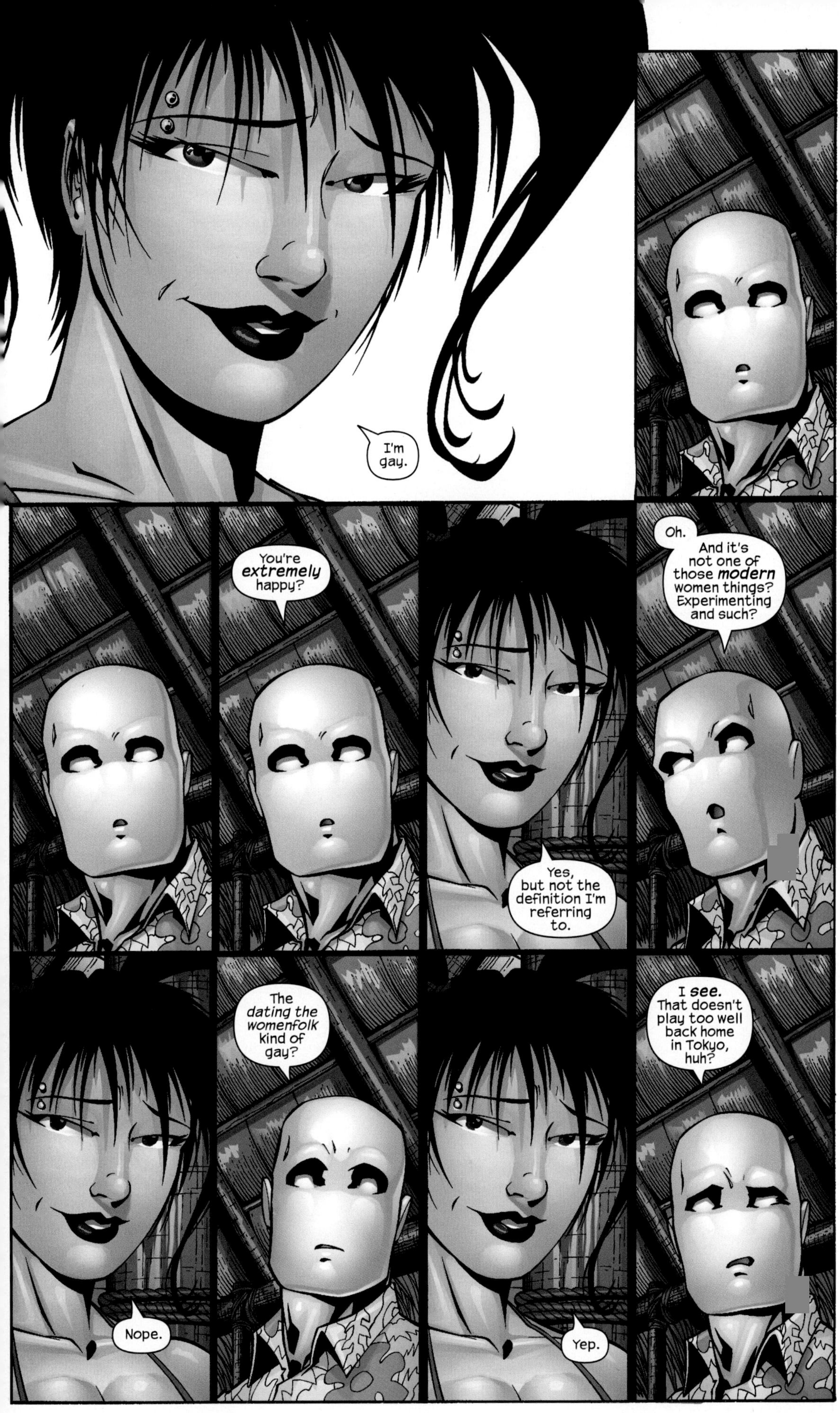
I'm gay.
You're *extremely* happy?
Yes, but not the definition I'm referring to.
Oh.
And it's not one of those *modern* women things? Experimenting and such?
Nope.
The *dating the womenfolk* kind of gay?
Yep.
I *see.* That doesn't play too well back home in Tokyo, huh?

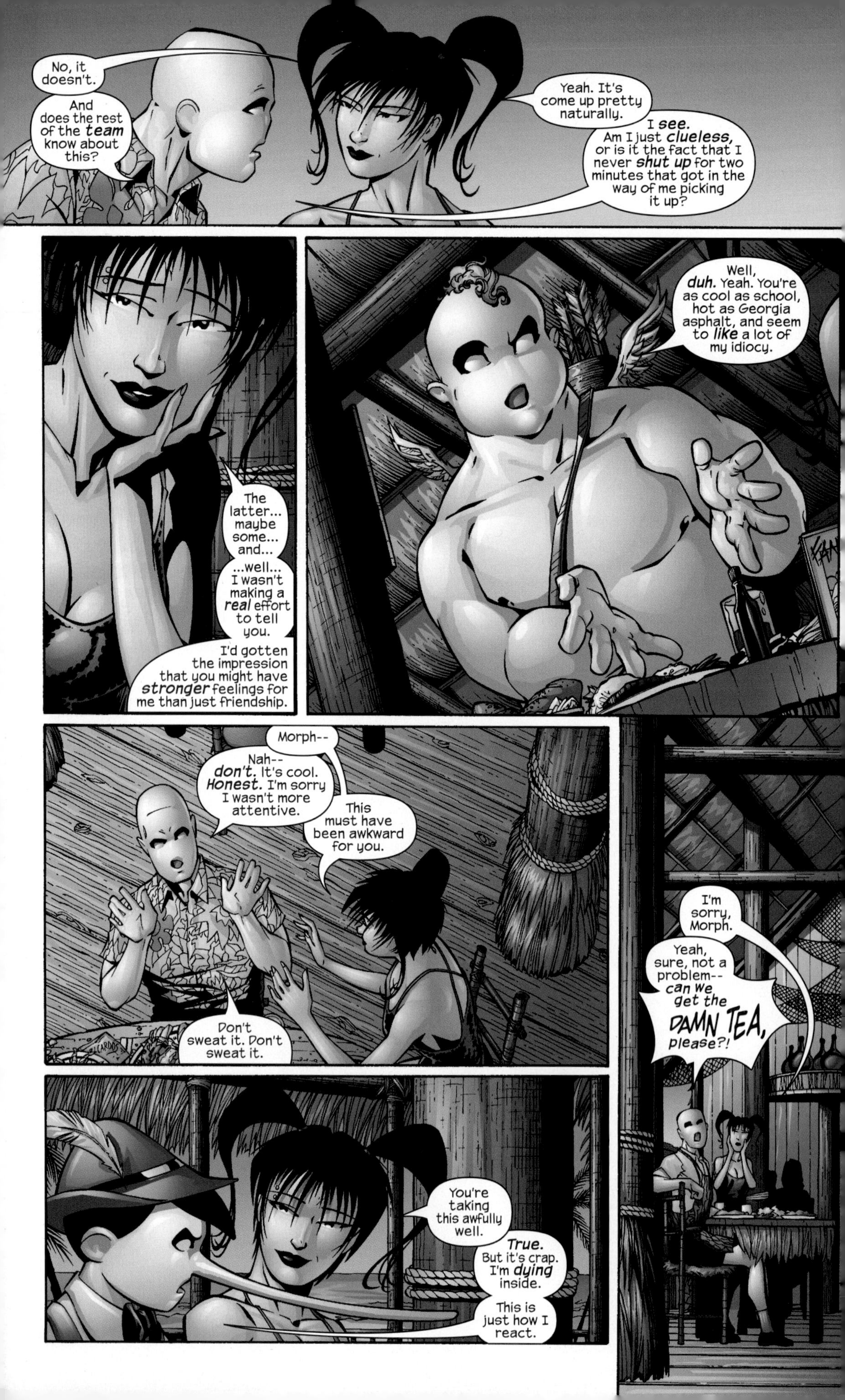

No, it doesn't.
And does the rest of the team know about this?
Yeah. It's come up pretty naturally.
I see. Am I just clueless, or is it the fact that I never shut up for two minutes that got in the way of me picking it up?
The latter... maybe some... and...
...well... I wasn't making a real effort to tell you.
I'd gotten the impression that you might have stronger feelings for me than just friendship.
Well, duh. Yeah. You're as cool as school, hot as Georgia asphalt, and seem to like a lot of my idiocy.
Morph--
Nah-- don't. It's cool. Honest. I'm sorry I wasn't more attentive.
This must have been awkward for you.
Don't sweat it. Don't sweat it.
I'm sorry, Morph.
Yeah, sure, not a problem-- can we get the DAMN TEA, please?!
You're taking this awfully well.
True. But it's crap. I'm dying inside.
This is just how I react.

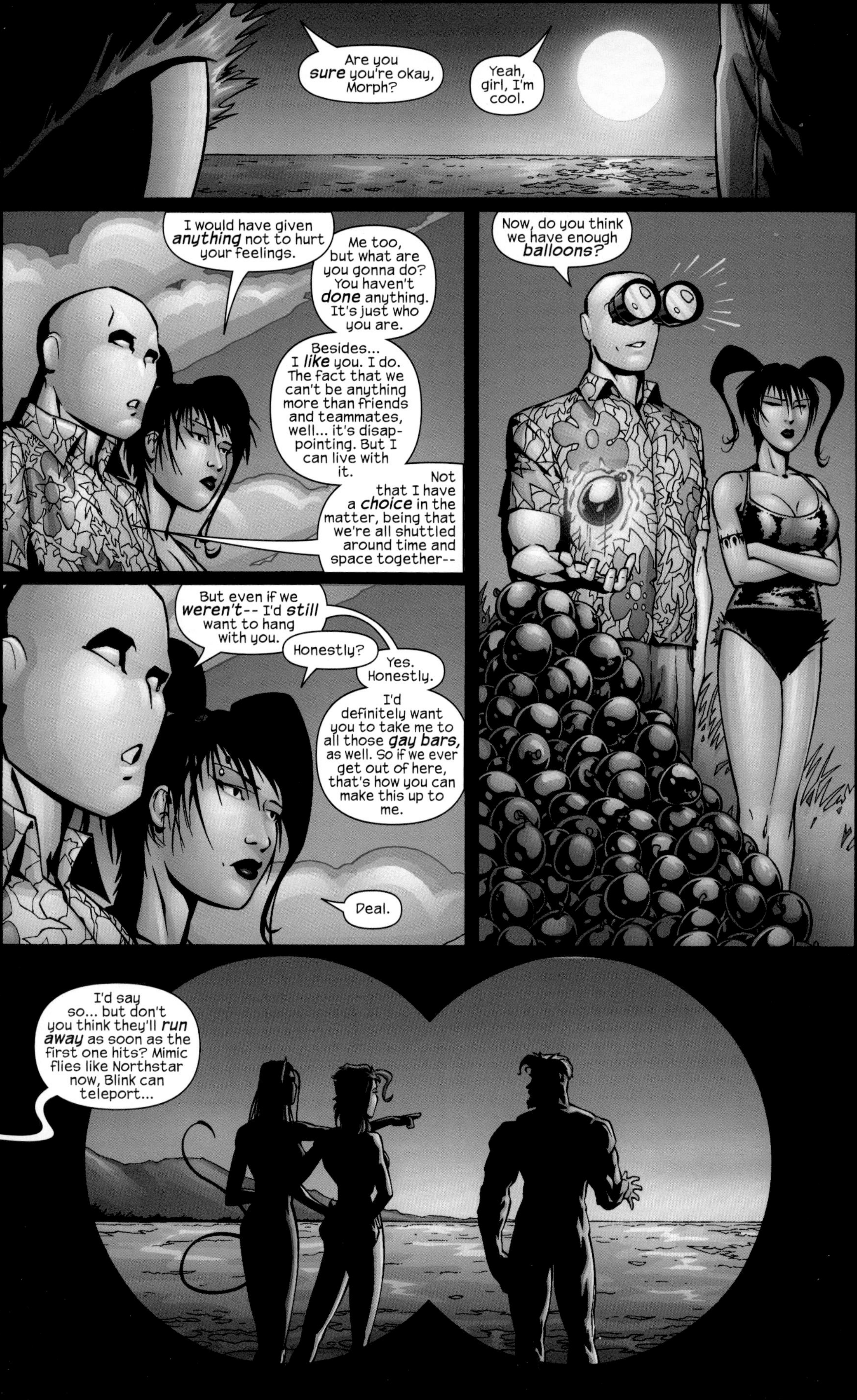

Are you sure you're okay, Morph?
Yeah, girl, I'm cool.
I would have given anything not to hurt your feelings.
Me too, but what are you gonna do? You haven't done anything. It's just who you are.
Besides... I like you. I do. The fact that we can't be anything more than friends and teammates, well... it's disappointing. But I can live with it.
Not that I have a choice in the matter, being that we're all shuttled around time and space together--
But even if we weren't-- I'd still want to hang with you.
Honestly?
Yes. Honestly.
I'd definitely want you to take me to all those gay bars, as well. So if we ever get out of here, that's how you can make this up to me.
Deal.
Now, do you think we have enough balloons?
I'd say so... but don't you think they'll run away as soon as the first one hits? Mimic flies like Northstar now, Blink can teleport...

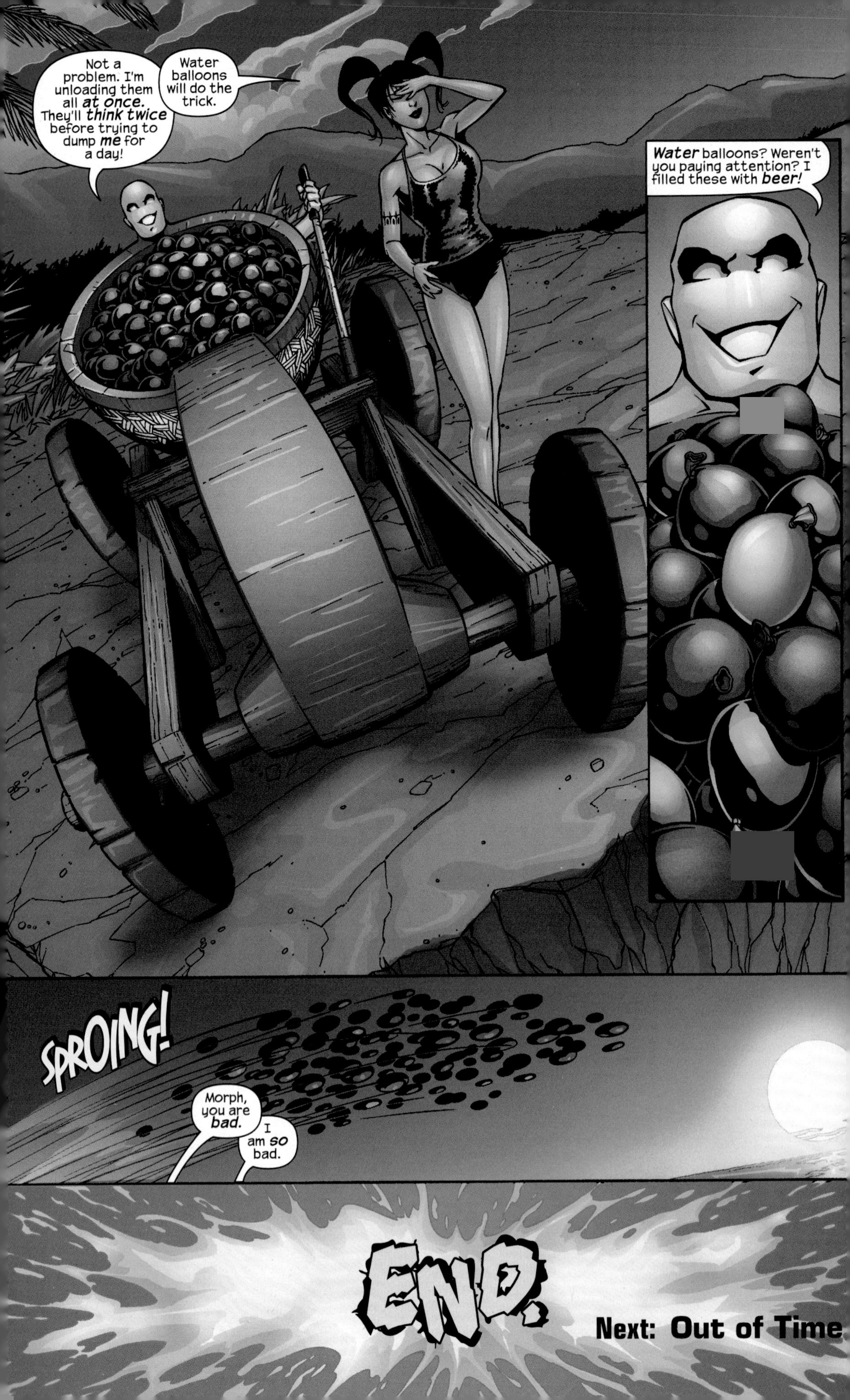

Not a problem. I'm unloading them all at once. They'll think twice before trying to dump me for a day!
Water balloons will do the trick.
Water balloons? Weren't you paying attention? I filled these with beer!
SPROING!
Morph, you are bad.
I am so bad.
END.
Next: Out of Time